Day-by-Day in NASCAR History

ALSO BY RONALD L. MEINSTEREIFEL
AND FROM MCFARLAND

This Day in Yankees History (2001)

Day-by-Day in NASCAR History

RONALD L. MEINSTEREIFEL

**Vincennes University
Shake Learning Resources Center
Vincennes, Indiana 47591-9986**

McFarland & Company, Inc., Publishers
Jefferson, North Carolina, and London

LIBRARY OF CONGRESS CATALOGUING-IN-PUBLICATION DATA

Meinstereifel, Ronald L., 1960–
    Day-by-day in NASCAR history / Ronald L. Meinstereifel.
        p.   cm.
    Includes index.

    ISBN 0-7864-1799-4 (softcover : 50# alkaline paper) ∞

    1. Stock car racing — United States — History — Chronology.
2. NASCAR (Association) — History — Chronology.   3. Automobile racing drivers — United States — Biography.   I. Title.
GV1029.9.S74M44   2004

                                                        2004014630

British Library cataloguing data are available

Cover photograph ©2004 Brand X Pictures

Manufactured in the United States of America

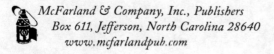
McFarland & Company, Inc., Publishers
   Box 611, Jefferson, North Carolina 28640
      www.mcfarlandpub.com

CONTENTS

PREFACE

I never dreamed I'd write a book about NASCAR, but here it is.

For most of my adult life, and prior to that as I pursued higher education, I have spent a great deal of time writing. I write evaluations, interventions, professional reports, smoking cessation programs and similar material for a living. As a hobby, and evolving into a second career, I enjoy researching and writing about sports. I have written books on the Pittsburgh Penguins, New York Yankees and Pittsburgh Pirates. Each successive exercise further refined my research strategies and developed my style. Although it is a bit dry and objective, it does lend itself to a scholarly review of the data. Being a psychologist by profession, I have always been interested in the personalities and quirks behind the performers as well as the statistics that define their existence in the history of their chosen sport.

As a kid, I was mostly a baseball fan. I regularly attended Pittsburgh Pirates games at Three Rivers Stadium in the 1970s and continue to make at least one yearly trek out of the wilderness of north-central Pennsylvania to attend a professional sporting event. In my life, I have been to three major league baseball stadiums that have been demolished, TRS, Veterans Stadium and Tiger Stadium.

I have always enjoyed a good live sporting event. Many years past, I spent several nights sleeping in my Datsun near the University of Louisville on Taylor Street with three college buddies in anticipation of the Kentucky Derby. I had never seen a horse race before that in my entire life, and never really did see a horse race then, until the 10th race, three removed from the main event, the "Derby race." By time, the crowd had significantly thinned and a spectator could actually see the track and the racing animals. In subsequent years, we did get to see the races through the help of giant television monitors strategically placed around Churchill Downs. This became a yearly event for a small core of friends until we gradually lost the tradition a decade ago. But I digress.

In the late 1980s, I relocated to upstate New York, first renting a home between Corning and Watkins Glen. When the weather conditions were right, you could hear the roar of racecar engines thundering across the rolling terrain from WGI, a few valleys to the north. Several years later I experienced my first Bud at the Glen. It was a spectacle, the atmosphere festival-like. Thousands of campers began setting up on the Thursday before the NASCAR event for a long weekend of racing and socialization. The area around the road course if spectacular and the fans were jovial and energetic.

One particular aspect that piqued my interest in racing was the non-traditional nature of the NASCAR driver. In the early days, the precursors of the current stock car racers were renowned for their cunning as well as their driving abilities, running moonshine in the rural areas of Alabama, Georgia, Tennessee, the Carolinas and Kentucky. While the traditional major league baseball player was honing his skills throwing fastballs with his father in the back yard, the aspiring moonshiner teamed up with a crack mechanic to soup up the engine and improve the suspension of a precious hot rod. They spent their late nights trying to outrun the revenuers and got together on weekends to compare their vehicles and compete in feats of speed and daring. The fast cars and moonshine were a long way from the traditional fastballs and hot dogs of the national pastime.

I was challenged and a little overwhelmed by approaching NASCAR as the theme of a "Day by Day..." type of book. Perhaps it was the idea of taking on an entire sport. Maybe it was my lack of historical knowledge of the sport or my comfortable familiarity with traditional baseball lore that caused some anxiety. Previously, I concentrated on mostly one franchise of a particular sport, not the entire sport itself. Taking on NASCAR as a whole meant a somewhat different approach.

I chose my data collection methods, which have greatly improved in indexing, tabulation and statistical functions over the years. I began compiling data — lots and lots of data. There are over 3200 entries in the book and in excess of 10,000 racing-related facts. The text covers the drivers, owners, locations and personalities of the sport as well as each sanctioned NASCAR race beginning in Charlotte in June 1949 and continuing, through Homestead, Florida, in November 2003.

Some notes on terminology may be helpful to the reader. NASCAR, upon incorporation, began running officially sanctioned races in 1949. The first top-level NASCAR class was known as Strictly Stock, a category that was used only during the inaugural season. The rules and limitations, as implied by the title, meant that only stock American automobiles were eligible for competition. As you will note, in the early days, such manufacturers and Studebaker, Nash and Hudson were top performers.

Following the 1949 season, NASCAR adopted the term Grand National for their top competition series. NASCAR remained under this moniker until corporate sponsorship renamed the series. The Winston Cup era began with the 1971 season. Winston maintained sponsorship until, as part of the tobacco settlement with the federal government, major limitations were placed on advertising. Thus, the cigarette manufacturer relinquished its association with NASCAR. At the conclusion of 2003, telecommunications giant Nextel assumed sponsorship and the 2004 season initiated the reign of the Nextel Cup as the pinnacle of the sport.

Several statistical notes during the 1950s and 1960s may be helpful. In those days, the NASCAR season began with races late the prior year. For instance, 1955 was the first season that began with a race the previous year. The November 1954 race at High Point, North Carolina, was the first official race of the 1955 season. This trend continued for several years until 1965 when the season began with a California race in January, but the next four seasons began the prior November with a Georgia race. Also, in the early seasons when sanctioned races were plentiful (the 1964 season held 62 official events, the largest season ever), as many as three events were held on one particular day. This usually resulted in a race being held on each coast, and possibly somewhere in the middle, at the same time. A number of drivers of that era competed only in races in specific venues, some quite successfully. Dan Gurney was one such driver. He predominantly competed at Riverside, California, and all five of his wins and three pole starts were on the road course. More recently, some drivers have chosen to concentrate on the road courses while others excel on the superspeedways.

NASCAR has grown substantially in popularity, especially in the past decade. The old stereotype of the stock car racing fan as a backward blue-collar Southern white male is disappearing. Although that formed the core of the early NASCAR fan base, popularity has spread nationwide and demographics have shifted significantly. Now races are regularly run in the Napa Valley, New Hampshire, Chicago, Texas and Phoenix. Exhibition events have been staged in Japan and Australia.

Another striking but rather pessimistic observation, in my review of the data, is that speed kills. Unfortunately, many good drivers died competing in events, testing tires, attempting to break speed records, or, ironically, in motor vehicle accidents between races. Major advances in technology have affected NASCAR more than many other typical "stick and ball" sports. The machines have become much faster and technology has forged ahead. These advances have saved lives as track and automotive technology has targeted driver safety. The traditional NASCAR owner, who might have filled his old pickup truck with spare parts and extra tires for a weekend race, has been replaced by multi-million dollar corporate sponsorships and a stable of cars, each designed specifically for a particular track type.

What had started with 50-mile races on short dirt tracks at fairgrounds at speeds similar to those I achieve on my way to work has evolved into marathon 500-mile events on paved 2.5 mile superspeedways with high banked turns where top speeds exceed 200 MPH. Crowds approaching 200,000 spectators are not uncommon.

In one respect, this project was more fun than my usual focus. The scope was broader and the material less familiar, which was more of a challenge. The process enabled me to gain a true appreciation for the heritage of the sport and the diversity of the participants and fans. I hope this book will be enjoyable and informative for all to delve into the colorful history of NASCAR.

Ron Meinstereifel

JANUARY

1

David "Dink" Widenhouse was born in 1932. Racing out of Concord, NC, Widenhouse ran 28 Grand National events 1954–56 and qualified on the pole once, in April 1955 in North Wilkesboro, NC. He finished in the top 10 eleven times.

Gary Fedewa was born in 1944. Fedewa, who raced out of Lansing, MI, made four Winston Cup starts in 1986 and one in 1987. His debut came at the Monster Mile in Dover in the 1986 Budweiser 500, won by Geoff Bodine.

Scott Riggs was born in 1971 in Durham, NC. Riggs debuted at the Nextel Cup level in 2004. He ran all 34 Busch Series races 2002–03 and all 24 Craftsman Truck races in 2001.

died as a result of injuries from a crash in the 1989 Atlanta Journal 500.

Donny Paul was born in 1961 in Berrien Springs, MI. Paul started three Winston Cup races in the 1980s, running one lap before engine trouble ended his debut in the 1984 Miller High Life 500 at Charlotte Motor Speedway.

Robby Gordon was born in 1969. Gordon has driven in a variety of events with limited success at the Winston Cup level. He took over for the Davey Allison team following Allison's death in a 1993 helicopter crash. In 2003, he ran both the Indianapolis 500 and the Pepsi 600 on the same day. Gordon won the 2003 Sirius at the Glen at Watkins Glen, NY.

2

Grant Adcox was born in 1950. Racing out of Chattanooga, TN, Adcox ran 60 career Winston Cup events with six top-10 finishes. He

3

Mickey McGreevey was born in 1926 in Hayward, CA. He started one Grand National race in 1955 and three in 1957. He finished 13th in his debut at the Bay Meadows Speedway in San Mateo, CA.

Dr. Wilbur Pickett was born in 1930. Racing out of Daytona Beach, FL, Pickett made his only Grand National start in 1969, a 20th-place finish in the Talladega 500.

Clifton "Coo Coo" Marlin was born in 1932. His son Sterling remained an active driver through 2004. Coo Coo ran 165 Grand National and Winston Cup races, with 51 top-10 finishes between 1966 and 1980, but never captured a checkered flag.

Clarence "Henley" Gray was born in 1933. Gray made 374 career starts 1964–77. He finished fourth in Grand National points in 1966. Gray raced out of Rome, GA.

Willy T. Ribbs was born in 1956. Ribbs, who raced out of San Jose, CA, ran three Winston Cup races in 1986 and was the inspiration for Richard Pryor's character in the movie *Greased Lightning*.

4

Bill Snowden died in January 1959, exact date unknown, at the age of 48. Snowden, a NASCAR pioneer, ran four races in the inaugural Strictly Stock season and recorded 20 other starts over the next three years. He finished with 15 top-10s.

Trent Owens was born in 1975. Owens raced out of Davidson, NC, in the Craftsman Truck Series, starting with six events in 2001. Owens is the nephew of racing patriarch Richard Petty.

5

Alfred "Doug" Yates was born in 1925. Racing out of Chapel Hill, NC, he ran 86 Grand National events 1952–65 and captured his first pole in 1960 in Columbia, SC, one of two on his career. He became a well-known Winston Cup team owner.

Troy Beebe was born in 1962. He made five Winston Cup starts 1989–90. Racing out of Modesto, CA, Beebe made his debut in the inaugural race at Sears Point, the 1989 Banquet Frozen Foods 300.

Billy Drew Wade died while testing tires at Daytona Beach, FL, in 1965 at the age of 34. In 1964, Wade finished fourth overall in points and won four straight races in June in New Jersey and upstate New York, the only victories of his career. He raced out of Houston, TX.

6

Early NASCAR driver Dick Rathmann was born in Los Angeles, CA, in 1924. Rathmann ran between 1951 and 1955 with 13 wins and 10 poles in 128 career races. He finished third in Grand National points in 1953. Dick Rathmann was actually born Jim Rathmann. Dick, born Jim, switched identities with his brother, Jim, born Dick, in the 1940s. Confused?

Pat Flaherty, who raced out of Chicago, IL in the 1950s, was born in 1926. Flaherty made one start at the Grand National level in 1951, earning $10 in his career as a top-level NASCAR driver.

George Althiede was born in 1933. Althiede raced out of Morristown, TN, and started 16 career Winston Cup races 1971–72. His career-best finish was 15th place in the 1972 Daytona 500, won by A.J. Foyt.

Jim Hurtubise died in 1989 at the age of 56. Hurtubise drove in 35 career races at NASCAR's highest level with one win and ten career top-10 finishes. His best year was 1966 with his only series win coming at Atlanta in March. He also recorded a second, a fifth, and two other top-10 finishes in six starts that year.

Carl Tyler died in 1993 at the age of 65. Tyler, who raced out of Bradford, PA, ran 12 Grand National events 1958–59. He earned nearly $900 at NASCAR's highest level. He finished 54th of 59 entrants in the 1959 Daytona 500 in his last top-level NASCAR race.

7

Marty Houston was born in 1968 in Hickory, NC. Houston ran consistently in the Busch and Craftsman Truck Series 1999–2001.

After 11 years of focus on NASCAR racing, Joe Gibbs signed a five-year contract to coach the Washington Redskins, a team he led to three Super Bowl championships (1982, 1987 and 1991). Gibbs replaced Steve Spurrier, who had earlier forfeited the final three years of his contract. Gibbs' son, J.D., is president of Joe Gibbs Racings.

8

Herbert Tillman was born in 1929. He ran 17 career Grand National races 1953, 1960–62. Tillman raced out of Miami, FL, and started a career-high nine races in 1960.

The Daytona Beach International Speedway Corporation held their first meeting in 1958, electing William H. G. France as president.

Bobby Hamilton Jr. was born in Nashville, TN, in 1977. Hamilton made 14 Winston Cup starts 2000–03, making his debut in Homestead, FL in the 2000 Pennzoil 400 presented by Discount Auto Parts.

9

Dick Johnson was born in 1928. He started 56 Grand National races 1967-69 with four top 10's in his final season at NASCAR's highest level.

Mark Martin was born in Batesville, AR, in 1959. Martin finished second in Winston Cup points in 1990 and 1994. He began his career in 1981 and remained active through 2003 with over 25 career victories.

10

Rodger Ward was born in 1921. He ran two Grand National events in 1963 and one in 1964. Racing out of Los Angeles, CA, Ward completed 450 career miles at NASCAR's highest level.

Harry Gant was born in Taylorsville, NC, in 1940. Gant ran 474 career races with 18 wins in his career. In 1991, when he was named NASCAR Driver of the Year, Gant won four straight races and finished second in a fifth.

Dublin, OH, native Bobby Rahal, born in 1953, is remembered for his 1986 Indianapolis 500 victory. Rahal ran his only Winston Cup race in 1984 at Riverside, CA. Rahal went on to operate successful car dealerships and co-own a CART race team with celebrity David Letterman.

Larry McReynolds was born in 1959 in Alabama. He became a NASCAR mechanic in the 1980s and advanced to become a successful crew chief for Ricky Rudd, Ernie Irvan and Dale Earnhardt, later venturing into broadcasting.

In the inaugural race of the 1971 Winston Cup season, Ray Elder won the Motor Trend 500 at Riverside, CA. It was the first of two career wins for Elder, both at Riverside.

Control of NASCAR was officially passed to Bill France, Jr. in 1972, from his father, Bill France, Sr.

11

Bill Wimble was born in 1932. He ran four Grand National races, two in 1958 and two in 1962. He drove out of Lisbon, NY, to log nearly 700 miles at NASCAR's top level.

Charles Allmond "Rex" Wickersham was born in 1934. Wickersham, racing out of Long Boat Key, FL, ran 41 Grand National events between 1960 and 1965. He finished in the top 10 four times.

Brett Bodine was born in 1959 in

Chemung, NY. The middle of the three racing Bodine brothers, Brett began Winston Cup racing in 1986. He won his only race at North Wilkesboro in 1990 yet remained active through 2003. He graduated from SUNY Alfred with an associate degree in mechanical engineering.

Stuart Joyce died in 1981 at the age of 64. Racing out of Wannamaker, IN, Joyce finished eighth in his only Grand National start in the 1952 Motor City 250 at the Michigan State Fairgrounds, winning $200.

Bobby Allison won the first NASCAR race of 1981 with a victory at Riverside International Raceway in the Winston Western 500. It was the 57th career first place finish for Allison.

In 1997, John Nemechek died from head injuries suffered during a NASCAR truck series accident in Homestead, FL. He was 27 years old. His older brother Joe continued to race in the Winston Cup series through 2003.

12

Lloyd Ruby was born in 1928. Ruby raced out of Wichita Falls, TX, to one Grand National start, a 22nd-place finish in the 1967 Motor Trend 500 at Riverside, CA.

Walter Ballard was born in 1933. Ballard, who raced out of Houston, TX, started 175 top-level NASCAR events between 1966 and 1978. He was the Winston Cup Rookie of the Year in 1971 and finished sixth in points in 1972, when he finished in the top 10 seven times.

Kerry Teague was born in 1961. He started five Winston Cup races 1991–95, racing out of Concord, NC. He crashed and finished 37th in his debut, the 1991 Mello Yello 500 at Charlotte Motor Speedway.

Clark Dwyer was born in 1964. Dwyer made 59 Winston Cup starts 1983–85 with one top-10 finish his rookie season at Dover Downs.

Al Bonnell died in 1980 at the age of 70. Bonnell started two races in the inaugural NASCAR season, 1949. He won the pole in his final top-level race, finishing 23rd in the seventh race of the season at Heidelberg Raceway in Pittsburgh, PA

Tim Williamson was killed in a Grand American race in Riverside, CA, in 1980, one day before his 24th birthday. He raced out of Seaside, CA, to compete in three Winston Cup events in California in 1979. His career highlight was a ninth-place finish in his debut at Riverside in the 1979 Winston Western 500.

Duane "Red" Duvall died in 1994 at the age of 70. Duvall started eight Grand National races between 1951 and 1954, finishing in third place in a 1951 race at Lakeview (AL) Speedway for his career-best.

13

Robert Barron was born in 1921. He made 32 Grand National starts 1960–61, racing out of Bradenton, FL, to record five top-10 finishes in 1961, including an 8th-place finish in the 1961 Richmond 200.

Aaron Ransom "Shorty" York was born in 1924. He ran 12 Grand National races between 1950 and 1960 and managed one second-place finish in 1951, but no other top 10's. He raced out of Mocksville, NC.

Ron Hornaday was born in 1931 and raced out of San Fernando, CA. He made 17 top-level NASCAR starts, mostly on the west coast, between 1955 and 1973, finishing in the top 10 four times. His career-best was a fourth place finish in a 1960 race event at the California State Fairgrounds in Sacramento.

William Leroy "Roy" Tyner, born in 1937, ran 311 Grand National races 1957–70. Racing out of Red Springs, NC, Tyner managed 71 top-10 finishes and ended the 1968 season 10th overall in series points.

Nicholas C. "Buddy" Young was born in 1943. He ran 23 Grand National races 1969-70 with seven top-10 finishes. Young raced out of Fairfax, VA.

Tim Williamson was born in 1956 and raced out of Seaside, CA. Williamson started three Winston Cup races in 1979 with a lone top-10 finish in his debut at the Winston Western 500 at Riverside, CA.

Ernie Irvan was born in 1959 in Salinas, CA. Irvan began his Winston Cup career in 1987 and was second to Ken Bouchard for 1988 Rookie of the Year. He won the 1991 Daytona 500. Irvan suffered serious injuries in a practice crash at Michigan in August 1994 but recovered to return to racing.

14

Darrell Waltrip won the first race of 1979 with a first-place finish in the Winston Western at Riverside, CA.

15

Lynwood "Sonny" Easley died in a crash at Riverside, CA, in 1978 at the age of 39. He ran 19 Winston Cup races 1972–77 with a career-best 5th place finish at Riverside in the 1977 Winston Western 500 his final year.

16

Lewis "Possum" Jones was born in 1932 in Florida. Jones started 47 races with one pole position (1958 at Columbia, SC) between 1952 and 1965. He earned 13 career top-10 finishes.

A.J. Foyt was born in 1935 in Houston, TX. Foyt won the Indianapolis 500 four times and ran Indy cars most of his career, with occasional forays into NASCAR. He ran his final Winston Cup race at the Brickyard 400 in 1994. He posted seven career wins in Winston Cup, including three races at Daytona.

Norm Benning was born in 1952 in Level Green, PA. He made four Winston Cup starts, three in 1989 and one in 1993. His debut came at Dover Downs, where he left after 226 miles due to steering problems.

In the first race of 1977, David Pearson captured the Winston Western 500 at Riverside International Raceway.

17

Lake Chambers Speed was born in 1948 in Kannapolis, NC. Speed ran 402 Winston Cup races 1980–98 with over 75 top-10 finishes, including his only top-level NASCAR victory in May 1988 at Darlington, SC. In 1985, Speed finished tenth in championship points.

In the 1965 Motor Trend 500, Dan Gurney captured his second straight road course win at Riverside International Raceway.

18

Allen Heth was born in 1918. He made four Grand National starts in 1951 and one in 1954, earning $100 in his career as a top-level NASCAR driver.

Ronnie Chumle was born in 1935. He started a total of seven Grand National/Winston Cup races between 1964 and 1972. In his second career race, he finished 34th in the Daytona 500, yielding to mechanical difficulties.

Mexico City, Mexico, native Pedro Rodriguez was born in 1940. Rodriguez ran six NASCAR races 1959–71. He died in the 1971 West German Grand Prix.

Bill Davis was born in 1951 in Arkansas. A success in the trucking industry, Davis went on to team with a young Jeff Gordon as an owner. Gordon later found success driving for Rick Hendrick.

Eddie Gray suffered a heart ailment in a 1969 Sportsman race at

Riverside, CA. He died in October of that year at the age of 49.

In the first race of the 1970 season, A.J. Foyt won the Motor Trend 500 at Riverside International Raceway.

Christian Fittipaldi was born in 1971 in São Paulo, Brazil. Fittipaldi ran his first Winston Cup race in the 2002 Checker Auto parts 500 at Phoenix and ran semi-regularly during 2003.

David Pearson won the 1976 Winston Western 500, the first race of the season, at Riverside, CA.

19

James Whitman, born in 1937, entered five Grand National events in 1960. Whitman raced out of Paramus, NJ, to complete over 1000 miles at NASCAR's top level.

Joe Weatherly was killed in a crash during the NASCAR race at Riverside, CA, in 1964; he was 41 years old. The race was won by Dan Gurney. Weatherly won 25 races in 230 events 1952–64. He was the Grand National Champion 1962–63. His final victory came in October 1963 in Hillsboro, NC, in the next to last race of the season.

Bobby Allison captured his 44th career win in the first race of 1975, the Winston Western at the Riverside International Raceway.

Darrell Waltrip won his second straight Winston Western 500 at Riverside, CA, in 1980.

20

Edward Glenn "Fireball" Roberts, who got his nickname because he was an outstanding baseball pitcher in his youth, was born in Daytona Beach, FL, in 1929. Roberts ran 15 years with 33 wins and 35 poles in 206 career starts. He finished second in points in 1950 and was voted the most popular driver in 1957. He died as a result of injuries suffered in a spectacular crash at Charlotte in 1964.

Ralph Jones was born in 1944. Racing out of Upton, KY, Jones started 20 Winston Cup races between 1977 and 1988. He finished 15th in the 1979 Daytona 500 and 26th in 1988.

Tim Flock captured both the pole and the checkered flag in the first NASCAR race of the 1952 season. Flock drove his Hudson to victory in the 100-mile event held at Palm Beach Speedway in West Palm Beach, FL, the first sanctioned Grand National race in Florida outside of Daytona. Flock went on to win the Grand National Championship that season and again in 1955.

In the 1963 Riverside 500, Dan Gurney won on the road course at Riverside, CA. It was the first of five career wins for Gurney, all at the Riverside track.

Canadian native Scott Maxwell was born in Toronto, Ontario, in 1964. Maxwell, a veteran of various sports car series, got his first NASCAR start at the 2003 Sirius @ the Glen at Watkins Glen. Prior to this race, Maxwell had never attended a Winston Cup race.

Billy Foster died in 1967 at the age of 29. Foster qualified ninth for the Riverside, CA, race, but died in practice. He finished seventh in his only other Grand National event, the 1966 Motor Trend 500.

Former NASCAR champion Tim Flock was posthumously inducted into the North Carolina Auto Racing Hall of Fame in 1999. A private ceremony was held at his home the previous February, a month before his death. Flock was the Grand National Champion in 1952 and 1955.

21

Pearley Jackson "Bud" Harless was born in 1924. Harless started 22 Grand National races 1953–55 and 1963–65, with two top-10 finishes. He raced out of Gilbert, WV.

Mike Kempton, racing out of Kansas, was born in 1947. He made two Winston Cup starts in each 1977 and 1979. His best finish was 18th in the 1979 Sun-Drop Music City USA 420 at Nashville, TN.

Dan Gurney won his fifth and final NASCAR race at Riverside with a first-place finish in the Motor Trend 500 in 1968.

Mark Donohue became the first driver to ride to victory in a Matador with a road race victory at Riverside, CA, in 1973 in the Winston Western 500. AMC fielded cars in NASCAR until 1975. It was Donohue's only career victory.

22

Bob Pronger was born in 1922. Pronger started nine career Grand National races 1951–61. Racing out of Blue Island, IL, his career highlight was winning the pole for the February 1953 beach-road race at Daytona Beach.

Buck Baker won the fifth race of the 1956 season with a first-place finish at the Arizona State Fairgrounds. Baker won the Grand National Championship consecutive seasons, 1956–57.

Parnelli Jones won the 1967 Motor Trend 500 at Riverside, CA, his fourth career victory.

Jeff McClure, born in 1967 and racing out of Harrisburg, NC, started one Winston Cup race. He finished 31st in the 1992 Champion Spark Plug 400 at Michigan International Speedway.

Cale Yarborough won the 1978 Winston Western 500 at Riverside, CA, in the first race of the NASCAR season. He went on to win nine more events on his way to his third straight Winston Cup Championship.

23

Emanuel "Manny" Zervakis was born in 1930. Zervakis raced out of Richmond, VA, to start 83 Grand National races 1956–63, ranking third in points in 1961. Zervakis won twice, both times in 1961, the first at Greenville, SC, in April. In the 1980s, he returned to Winston Cup as a team owner.

Jerry Grant was born in 1935. Grand started 19 races at NASCAR's top level 1965–74. He led two career laps and finished in the top-5 five times. Don Whittington, born in 1946, ran ten events 1980–81. Driving out of Lubbock, TX, Whittington finished in the top 10 once during his debut Winston Cup season, a 9th-place finish in the 1980 Winston Western 500 at Riverside, CA.

Terry Byers was born in 1950. Racing out of Wollongong, Australia, he made five Winston Cup starts 1989-90. He finished last in the 1990 Pepsi 400 after he was involved in a first-lap crash that knocked out A.J. Foyt and Richard Petty.

Dan Gurney continued his dominance at Riverside with his fourth win in five starts on the road course with a win in the 1966 Motor Trend 500.

Dick Joslin died in 1972 at the age of 45. Joslin started 10 Grand National Races between 1955 and 1960 with two top-10s. He finished seventh in his 1955 debut on the Beach & Road Course at Daytona Beach, FL, and 30th in the 1960 Daytona 500, his next-to-last NASCAR event.

Richard Petty won the 1972 Winston Western at Riverside International Raceway. It was his first of eight wins in 1972 when Petty captured his fourth of seven championships.

24

Robert Schacht was born in 1950. Schacht ran 23 Winston Cup races 1981–94, leading two career races. He raced out of Lombard, IL.

Mike Harmon was born in 1958 in Birmingport, AL. Harmon ran regularly in the Busch Series 2001–03, positioning himself for a potential Nextel Cup ride in 2004.

Gary Collins, born in 1960, made one start each in 1988, 1990, 1991, and 1994 at the Winston Cup level. Collins raced out of Bakersfield, CA.

25

Major Melton was born in 1930 in Laurinburg, NC. He started 20 races 1963–64 with one top-10 finish. Hs best finish was 9th in a September 1964 race at Orange Speedway in Hillsboro, NC.

Buddy Baker was born Elzie Wylie Baker Jr. in 1941, the son of Buck Baker. Baker finished 5th in points in 1977. He finished his NASCAR career with 19 wins at the Grand National/Winston Cup level. He was the first NASCAR driver to eclipse 200 MPH when he recorded a lap at 200.47 MPH in 1970 at Talladega.

Joel Davis, who made 30 career Grand National starts 1963–67, was born in 1941 and raced out of Tenneville, GA. His best finish was fourth in June 1966 at the Piedmont Fairgrounds in Spartanburg, SC.

T.W. Taylor was born in 1955. He ran four Winston Cup races 1992–93. Running out of Chester, VA, he managed to lead one lap and finish 40th in the 1993 AC Delco 500 at Rockingham, NC, in his brief career at NASCAR's highest level.

Larry Thomas died in an automobile accident in Tifton, GA, in 1965; he was 28 years old. Racing out of Thomasville, NC, Thomas was a rising Grand National star with 126 starts 1961–64. He was 8th overall in points in 1964, when he started 43 races and notched 27 top-10 finishes. He finished 16th in the 1964 Daytona 500.

1987 Budweiser at the Glen on the road course at Watkins Glen, NY.

Gary Bradberry was born in 1961. Racing out of Chelsea, AL, he started 16 Winston Cup races 1994–96. He made his debut with a 30th-place finish in the Hooters 500 at Atlanta and with a 43rd-place effort in the 2002 Sirius Satellite Radio 400 at Michigan.

26

Al Bonnell was born in 1909. He made two starts in NASCAR's inaugural season of 1949, capturing one pole and finishing in the top 10 once. He finished 9th in his debut in September at Langhorne, PA.

Dave Pletcher was born in 1952. Racing out of Clearwater, FL, Pletcher made three NASCAR starts 1987–88. He debuted in the 1987 Pepsi Firecracker 400 at Daytona, finishing 36th.

Cale Yarborough won the Winston Western in 1974 at Riverside.

27

George Follmer was born in 1934. He started 20 Winston Cup races 1972–87. Racing out of Arcadia, CA, Follmer captured one pole, in Riverside, CA, in the 1974 Tuborg 400 and finished fourth in the 1974 Atlanta 500.

Phil Good was born in 1955. He started eight Winston Cup races 1984–87, racing out of Williamsburg, VA. He finished 39th in his finale, the

28

Racing out of North Hollywood, CA, Jim Robinson was born in 1946. Robinson ran 21 Winston Cup races 1979–87 with two top-10 finishes.

David Green was born in 1958 in Owensboro, KY. Green was second in 1991 Rookie of the Year voting (behind Jeff Gordon) at the Busch Grand National level.

29

Frank Sessoms was born in 1933. Sessoms raced out of Darlington, SC, to start five top-level NASCAR races 1962–71 with two top-10 finishes.

Bob England, born in 1935, started seven Grand National and Winston Cup events 1969–71, all but one at Riverside or Ontario, CA. He raced out of Daly City, CA, to a career-best 13th-place finish in the 1971 Motor Trend 500.

Tommy Houston was born in 1945. He started 13 Winston Cup events between 1980 and 1985. Houston raced out of Hickory, NC. He finished 12th twice; in the 1981 Winston 500 at Talladega and the 1981 Old Dominion 500 at Martinsville, VA.

Jeff Davis was born in 1959. Racing out of Anaheim, CA, he started one race each in 1992, 1993 and 1997 in his brief Winston Cup career. He was 26th in his debut in the Pyroil 500K at Phoenix and ran his final two races at Sonoma, CA.

30

Ralph Zrimsek was born in 1918. Zrimsek ran one Strictly Stock race in 1949. Driving out of Canonsburg, PA, Zrimsek is, alphabetically, the last driver in a list of those with top-level NASCAR starts.

Norm Nelson was born in 1923. Racing out of Wisconsin, he won a 1955 race from the pole in Las Vegas in his second career Grand National start. Nelson ran five races in his career with a win, a third place finish and one additional top 10.

Al Smith was born in 1929. Racing out of Dayton, OH, Smith made one Grand National start and earned $25 in 1952 to conclude his NASCAR career.

31

Ed Samples was born in 1921. Racing out of Atlanta, GA, Samples ran 13 Grand National races in the 1950s with six top-10 finishes. His brother, Jesse Samples Sr., ran one race in 1965 while his son, Jess Samples Jr. (Ed's nephew), ran two races in 1987.

Herman "Brownie" King was born in 1934 in Tennessee. King started 97 races between 1956 and 1961. He finished 9th in points in 1957 when he finished in the top 10 16 times in 36 starts.

George T. Tallas was born in 1944. He ran two career Grand National and four Winston Cup races 1970–75, all at Riverside or Ontario, CA. He raced out of Sun Valley, CA. He finished 29th in the Winston Western 500 in his finale.

Richard "Rick" Wilson was born in 1953. He ran 203 career Winston Cup events 1980–93. Wilson qualified on the pole for the 1988 Valleydale Meats 500 at Bristol, TN. He raced out of Bartow, FL, and recorded 23 top-10 finishes.

Bobby Abel died in 1995 at the age of 64. Abel ran one Grand National race at Langhorne, PA, in September 1957.

FEBRUARY

1

Jimmy Thompson was born in 1924. He ran 46 career Strictly Stock and Grand National races 1949–62. Thompson, who raced out of Monroe, NC, managed nine top-10 finishes.

Max Berrier was born in 1936. He raced out of Wallburg, NC, and made seven career starts: two each in 1955, 1957 and 1959 and a final start in 1972, where he finished 18th in the Wilkes 400 at North Wilkesboro, NC.

Leonard "Doc" Faustina was born in 1939 in Las Vegas, NV. He started ten races 1971–76 at NASCAR's highest level. He finished 18th in his debut in the Winston 500 at Talladega, AL, and 24th in his final event, the 1976 Mason-Dixon 500 at Dover Downs.

Ed Sczech was born in 1944. Sczech raced out of San Antonio, TX, to four Winston Cup starts in 1973. His career-best came in his debut in the 1973 Alamo 500 at Texas World Speedway, a 20th-place finish.

Lee Petty gained a win in the first official race of NASCAR's fifth season, at West Palm Beach, FL, in 1953. Averaging 60.220 mph, Petty won the 100-mile race for the first manufacturer's win for automaker Dodge. Dick Rathmann won the pole in a Hudson.

Richard Petty won his first race at Riverside with a victory in the 1969 Motor Trend 500, his 93rd career checkered flag.

Gene Comstock died in 1980 at the age of 70. Comstock raced out of Chesapeake, OH, to start 29 Grand National races 1950–55 with six top-10 finishes and a career-best fourth-place finish at Weaverville, NC, in 1952.

2

Crew Chief Dave McCarty was born in Turbotville, PA, in 1956. He worked as a fabricator and general mechanic until he was named crew chief for Darrell Waltrip in December 1997.

3

Graham Taylor was born in 1939. He ran three career Winston Cup races 1992–93. He raced out of Port Royal, PA, to complete 20 total laps at NASCAR's highest level.

Marv Acton was born in 1944. He raced out of Porterville, CA, and made 14 career Winston Cup starts, 11 in 1971, one in 1974 and two in 1977. His best finish was in the 1971 Pickens 200 at Greenville, SC, an 11th-place effort.

Lennie Frank Waldo was born in 1944. He made four Grand National starts in 1968. Racing out of Columbus, OH, Waldo ran over 1000 miles at NASCAR's highest level.

William "Rocky" Moran was born in 1951. Moran ran three Winston Cup races in 1978, his only top-level NASCAR experience. His best event was his final one, a 20th place finish in the Los Angeles Times 500 at Ontario, CA.

4

Wilber "Bay" Darnell was born in 1931. He made three Grand National starts in his career, one each in 1954, 1964 and 1967. Driving out of Lake Bluff, IL, he finished 13th in his best start, the 1964 Atlanta 500.

Donald "Lee" Gordon was born in 1936. He made one Grand National start in 1969 and seven in 1970 to conclude his career. He raced out of Horseshoe, NC, and was the older brother of driver Cecil Gordon. His best finish was 14th in the 1970 Tidewater 300 at Hampton, VA.

Jimmy Insolo, who raced out of Mission Hills, CA, in the 1970s and '80s, was born in 1943. Insolo recorded 29 starts between 1970 and 1983, with no more than four (1975) in any one year. He had eight career top-10 finishes and led four races.

Bruce Jacobi died in 1987 at the age of 51. Jacobi suffered serious injuries at Daytona in 1983 and never recovered. His Winston Cup debut came in the 1975 Daytona 500, where he finished 12th.

Connie Saylor died in 1993 at the age of 52. Saylor, who raced out of Johnson City, TN, ran 58 career Winston Cup events with one top-10 finish and a lead in four events. He finished 12th in the 1982 Southern 500 at Darlington, SC.

5

Lee Schmidt was born in 1919. Schmidt, who raced out of Milwaukee, WI, ran one Strictly Stock race in NASCAR's inaugural season, 1949 and one Grand National race in 1950, winning $75 in his career at the top level.

Darrell Waltrip was born in 1947 in Owensboro, KY. Racing out of Franklin, TN, Waltrip began his Winston Cup career in 1972 with three top 10's in five starts. He captured his first victory at the 1975 Music City USA 420 in Nashville and won 84 career events, tied with Bobby Allison for third all-time. His career highlight was a win at the 1989 Daytona 500. He won the points championship three times; 1980–81 (winning 12 races each season) and 1985. Waltrip was voted Winston Cup's most popular driver 1989–90, breaking a five-year reign by Bill Elliott. He went on to become a popular color analyst on national NASCAR broadcasts. He is the older brother of Michael Waltrip, who also won the Daytona 500.

The 1950 NASCAR season began at Daytona Beach with a 200.16-mile event on the beach/road course. Harold Kite drove his Lincoln to the checkered flag with his 89.894 mph setting an average speed record, which remained until 1953. It was the longest course ever to host NASCAR competition at 4.17 miles long and the only career win for Kite.

Dorsey Schroeder was born in 1953. Racing out of Baldwin, MO, Schroeder started nine races 1991–2001, leading two career events. He finished 17th at the 1991 Budweiser at the Glen on the road course at Watkins Glen, NY in his Winston Cup debut. He finished 19th in the 1992 Daytona 500 by STP.

6

Lem Blankenship was born in 1945. He made one Winston Cup start, racing out of Keokuk, IA, to a 39th-place finish in the 1972 Atlanta 500.

Herb Thomas won the second race of the 1955 Grand National schedule at the Palm Beach Speedway in Florida.

7

Herb Thomas took the inaugural race of the 1954 Grand National season, a 100-mile contest on the half-mile dirt track in West Palm Beach, FL. Thomas, the Grand National Champion in 1951 and 1953, drove his Hudson to his 29th series victory. Dick Rathmann claimed his fifth career pole position.

8

John "Skimp" Hersey was born in 1913. He started one Strictly Stock race in NASCAR's inaugural season of 1949. He won a total of $25 at NASCAR's top level, racing out of St. Augustine, FL.

Mike Magill was born in New Jersey in 1920. Magill started two races in 1952 and three in 1953, his only Grand National appearances.

Dale Earnhardt Jr. won the first tune-up race of 2003 with a trip to victory lane in the Budweiser Shootout at Daytona Beach, FL. Geoffrey Bodine captured the pole.

9

Guy "Crash" Waller was born in 1919. Waller made one Grand National start in 1951, running 39 miles at NASCAR's top level and earning $25. He raced out of Atlanta, GA.

Tom Usry, born in 1937, ran one Grand National race in 1970. Usry, who drove out of Sanford, NC, managed 82 miles at NASCAR's highest level.

Jan Opperman raced out of Beaver Crossing, NE and was born in 1939. Opperman ran one Winston Cup race, finishing eighth in the rain-shortened 1974 Purolator 500 at Pocono, PA.

Todd Parrott was born in 1964. The son of legendary crew chief Buddy Parrott, Todd became a crew chief in 1996 for Dale Jarrett and promptly won the Daytona 500.

10

Perk Brown, whose real name was Jack B. Thomasson, was born in 1925. Brown won one pole in 1952, his rookie season in Grand National racing. He made 28 starts at NASCAR's highest level between 1952 and 1963.

Paul John Tyler II was born in 1942. He started 20 Winston Cup races 1971–73. Tyler raced out of Palo Alto, CA, to record one top-10 finish in 1972.

Marshall Teague won his first race of 1952 in NASCAR's second sanctioned event, on the 4.1-mile beach-road course at Daytona Beach, FL. Teague's win was the second straight to start the season for automaker Hudson. Pat Kirkwood became the first driver to post a pole qualifying time over 110 mph, shattering the old qualifying record by over 8 mph. It was the first pole ever for manufacturer Chrysler.

Richard Scribner was born in 1952.

Scribner ran two Winston Cup races in 1992, racing out of Orangevale, CA. His best was a 36th-place finish in the 1992 Save Mart 300K at Sonoma, CA.

In a pre-season tune up for the 2002 Daytona 500, Tony Stewart won the Budweiser Shootout at Daytona International Speedway. Kurt Busch captured the pole.

11

Marshall Teague won his first career NASCAR race in the inaugural race of 1951 at the beach/road course in Daytona Beach, FL. It marked the first manufacturer's win for Hudson. Tim Flock won the pole and became the first driver to qualify in excess of 100 mph (102.200) in his Lincoln.

Marshall Teague died in 1959 in a closed course speed record attempt at a new track, Daytona International Speedway, six days shy of his 37th birthday. Teague ran 23 Strictly Stock and Grand National starts 1949–52. He won two poles and seven races, including two at Daytona.

Pete Hamilton and David Pearson won NASCAR races at Daytona in 1971, tune-ups for the Daytona 500. It was the final of four career wins for Hamilton.

Neil Bonnett died in a practice crash in preparation for the 1994 Daytona 500. He was 47 years old. Bonnett's final of 18 career wins came in the 1988 Goodwrench 500 at Rockingham.

Dale Jarrett won a tune-up to the

1996 Daytona 500 with a victory in the Busch Clash.

Tony Stewart won the Budweiser Shootout at Daytona International Speedway in 2001, holding off Dale Earnhardt Sr. for the victory. Ken Schrader won the pole.

Earnhardt lost his life one week later in the 2001 Daytona 500.

12

Richard "Toby" Tobias was born in 1932. He started one Winston Cup race in 1973. Tobias raced out of Lebanon, PA, and died as the result of injuries in a 1978 race in Flemington, NJ.

John Kieper was born in Portland, OR, in 1932. He made 16 career starts between 1954 and 1977 with four poles and one win, all in eight races entered in 1956.

Fireball Roberts and Jack Smith won the third and fourth races of the 1960 NASCAR season at Daytona International Speedway. Smith won from the pole for the fourth of six times in his career, guiding his #47 Pontiac to his 13th career victory.

Darel Dieringer and Junior Johnson won qualifying races at Daytona in 1965 in preparation for the Daytona 500.

Veteran stock car driver Joe Booher died in 1993 of injuries suffered in a crash on the second lap of the Florida Dash 200 at Daytona International. A native of Montmorenci, IN, Booher was 51. He finished 38th in his final Winston Cup event, the 1988 Budweiser 500 at Dover Downs.

13

Bill Schmitt was born in 1936. Schmitt ran 44 career Winston Cup events 1975–93, finishing in the top 10 six times and leading one career lap.

Lee Petty won a 1955 race at the Jacksonville Speedway Park. He was a three-time Grand National Champion, 1954 and 1958–59.

In the 2000 Bud Shootout at Daytona, Dale Jarrett took the checkered flag. Mark Martin started from the pole.

Dale Earnhardt Jr. started from the pole and won the second of two Gatorade 125 races at Daytona International Speedway in 2003.

In the first of two Gatorade Shootout races held on this date in 2003, Jeff Green captured the pole but Robby Gordon recorded the victory at Daytona International Speedway in preparation for the Daytona 500.

14

Bill Chevalier was born in 1922. He started two Grand National races in 1954 and appeared once again in 1971 to conclude his driving career at NASCAR's highest level.

John Wright was born in 1923. He started one event in the inaugural

Strictly Stock season of 1949. Racing out of Ransomville, NY, Wright managed a top-10 finish in his only career race at NASCAR's highest level.

Edwin Keith "Banjo" Matthews was born in 1932 in North Carolina. Matthews started 51 races 1952–63 with three poles and 13 top-10 finishes. He was 10th in Grand National points in 1960.

Paul Feldner, who raced out of Richfield, WI, in the 1970s, was born in 1935. Feldner ran two Grand National races in 1970 with one top-10 finish. He concluded his NASCAR driving career with one more start in 1972.

Sam Ard was born in 1939. Racing out of Asheboro, NC, he made one Winston Cup start. He lasted one lap in the 1984 Goody's 500 at Martinsville to conclude one of the shortest NASCAR driving careers.

Bill Venturini was born in 1953. He made seven Winston Cup starts 1989–91, racing out of Chicago, IL, to run nearly 2000 career miles at NASCAR's top level.

Junior Johnson won the second annual Daytona 500 in 1960. Cotton Owens started on the pole.

Fred Lorenzen won a rain-shortened Daytona 500 in 1965. Lorenzen was the leader at the conclusion of 332 miles for the victory. Darel Dieringer held the pole position.

Scott Sharp was born in 1968 and raced out of East Norwalk, CT. Sharp, a driver in various divisions, started one Winston Cup race in 1992, finishing 19th in the Budweiser at the Glen at Watkins Glen, NY.

Richard Petty won his third Day-

tona 500 in 1971, his first win of the season. A.J. Foyt started on the pole but Petty prevailed to become the first three-time winner. Petty won his third career championship, the first under the Winston Cup sponsorship, with 21 wins that season.

Ricky Knotts died from injuries suffered in a crash at Daytona International Speedway in 1972.

Bobby Allison celebrated Valentine's Day 1982 with his second Daytona 500 win. It was the 66th victory of his career in the inaugural NASCAR race of the season. Benny Parsons was the pole-sitter.

Bobby Allison raced out in style. Allison's final career NASCAR win came in the 1988 Daytona 500 at the Daytona International Speedway. It was his 84th first place finish and third victory in the Great American Race.

Slick Johnson died at the age of 31, three days after a serious crash at the ARCA 200 at Daytona International Speedway in 1990. Johnson ran 68 career Winston Cup races 1979–87 and led a total of six races.

Kyle Petty won the pole but Dale Jarrett cruised to victory lane in the 1993 Daytona 500. It was the second career win for Jarrett.

Rookie driver Rodney Orr died in 1994 from serious injuries suffered in a practice crash at Daytona just three days after the death of Neil Bonnett at the same raceway. Orr was 31 years old.

Jeff Gordon captured the 1999 Daytona 500, winning the annual event from the pole. It was his second win in three years at the inaugural

NASCAR race of the season. It marked the first Winston Cup start for Tony Stewart, who finished 28th.

In the second of the two 2002 Gatorade 125s, Michael Waltrip won while Kevin Harvick qualified first.

In Race 1 of the twin Gatorade 125s at Daytona International Speedway in 2002, Jeff Gordon garnered the win while teammate Jimmie Johnson captured the pole.

15

Bud Kohler was born in 1921. Residing in Blue Island, IL, Kohler started one Grand National race in 1952, the Motor City 250 at Detroit, ran 140 career miles, and earned $25 for his 26th place finish in his Nash automobile.

Freddy Fryar was born in 1936. He made one start at the Grand National level in 1956, 1959, 1961 (a top-10 finish) and 1970. He made two starts in 1971 to end his NASCAR driving career. Fryar raced out of Baton Rouge, LA, to his only top-10 finish in the 1970 Alabama 500 at Talladega, AL.

Red Byron won on the combined beach/road course at Daytona in 1948, in what many consider the first official NASCAR race. However, this division, known as the Modified division, was not the official division that evolved into today's Winston Cup Series. In 1949 the Strictly Stock division was christened, which evolved into the Nextel Cup in 2004. Byron was the first points champion.

Bill Blair won at Daytona Beach, FL, for his third career Grand National victory in the second race of the 1953 NASCAR season. Blair averaged 89.789 mph in his Oldsmobile in the 159.9 mile-contest on the 4.1-mile beach-road course. Bob Pronger, also in an Olds, gained his first pole and became the first driver in history to qualify over 115 mph.

Jimmy Spencer was born in 1957. Spencer, racing out of Berwick, PA, began his Winston Cup career in 1989 and remained active in 2003. He captured his first win in the 1994 Firecracker 400 at Daytona Beach Florida in July and won his second race later that month at Talladega.

Buddy Baker won a tune-up to the 1973 Daytona 500 in a 1973 Dodge. While Coo Coo Marlin won a second race in a 1972 Chevrolet, a non-Winston Cup points event.

David Pearson won the 1976 Daytona 500, his only victory in the big race. Ramo Stott won the pole in the 18th running of the "Great American Race." Pearson edged Richard Petty, who crashed into the wall just short of the finish line.

Richard Petty won his seventh and final Daytona 500 in 1981. Bobby Allison won his first pole in the big race.

Bill Elliott won his second Daytona 500 in three years with a 1987 checkered flag finish. He also won the pole for the third consecutive time. His qualifying speed of 210.364 that year remains a Daytona 500 record.

Ernie Irvan and Dale Earnhardt each won a heat of the 1996 Gatorade Twin 125s at Daytona. Later that week, Dale Jarrett won the Daytona 500.

Dale Earnhardt Sr., who two years earlier won the pole, won his only Daytona 500 in 1998. Three years later, he died in a last-lap crash in the race. Bobby Labonte was the pole sitter and finished second.

16

Fireball Roberts won a qualifying race leading up to the 1962 Daytona 500, which he also won.

Joe Weatherly won his first race of 1962 with a win in the second tune-up race for the Daytona 500. Darel Dieringer captured the pole. Weatherly went on to win his first of two consecutive Grand National titles with nine wins in 1962.

Benny Parsons won the 1975 Daytona 500 for his only win in The Great American Race. Donnie Allison was the pole sitter.

Geoff Bodine won his only Daytona 500 in 1986. It was his fourth Winston Cup victory at the site of a horrendous Craftsman Truck Series crash that would nearly kill the popular driver in 2002. Bill Elliott won his second straight pole.

Davey Allison won the 1992 Daytona 500. Sterling Marlin was the pole sitter.

Michael Waltrip captured a rain shortened Daytona 500 in 2003 for his second win in three years at NASCAR's signature event. Jeff Green started from the pole position.

17

Marshall Teague was born in 1922. Racing out of Daytona Beach, FL, he won the first of seven career races in his hometown in a 1951 beach-road race. Teague ran 23 Winston Cup events with 11 top 10's and seven wins, including five of the first 15 races in 1951 driving a Hudson Hornet. He drove Indy Cars later in the 1950s and died attempting to set a speed record at Daytona.

Homer Newland was born in 1930. Racing out of Michigan, Newland ran one Grand National race in 1955 and two in 1969. He finished 27th due to engine trouble in his final event, the 1969 Talladega 500 won by Richard Brickhouse.

Cotton Owens won his first of nine career NASCAR races in 1957 at the Beach and Road Course, the precursor to the Daytona International Speedway. Banjo Matthews captured his first career pole.

Friday Hassler died in a crash in a 125-mile qualifying race at Daytona, FL, in 1972. He was 36. Hassler raced out of Chattanooga, TN, to start 135 races, qualifying on the pole and finishing third in the 1971 Maryville 200 at Smoky Mountain Raceway in Maryville, TN. His final race was the 1972 Winston Western 500 at Riverside, CA, where he finished 9th.

Richard Petty became the first driver to win two consecutive Daytona 500 races with his 1974 win. David Pearson started on the pole but Petty won the race for the fifth time in his career. The race was shortened to 450 miles due to the energy crisis of the mid–1970's. Petty began a string of five years when he was named the most popular Winston Cup driver. Petty won his fifth of seven driving championships in 1974 with 10 wins.

Buddy Baker won the 1980 Daytona 500. It was the fourth time he won the pole at the Great American Race and his first win. His average 177.602 MPH remains a race record by nearly 5 MPH over Dale Earnhardt Sr.'s 172.712 in 1998.

Bill Elliott captured his first Daytona 500 pole and win in 1985.

Ernie Irvan won the initial race of 1991, taking the checkered flag in the Daytona 500.

In the 2002 Daytona 500, Ward Burton surprisingly took the checkered flag, his first of two wins on the season. Jimmie Johnson qualified in the top starting slot.

18

Texas driver Jim McElreath was born in 1928. He ran three Grand National races in 1964 and one Winston Cup event in 1971.

In 1962, Fireball Roberts won the fourth Daytona 500. Roberts became the first person to take the pole and win the race.

Fireball Roberts dominated the 1962 Daytona 500 with a victory of over 30 seconds over the second-place finisher, Lee Petty.

Richard Petty won his fourth Daytona 500 race in 1973. Buddy Baker started on the pole. It was Petty's 149th career Grand National/Winston Cup victory.

Richard Petty won the 1973 Daytona 500. Averaging 157.205 mph, Petty defeated Bobby Isaac, who finished second.

The 1979 Daytona 500 on CBS was the first live telecast of a NASCAR race from start to finish. A raucous finish saw leader Davey Allison and runner-up Cale Yarborough crash on the last lap. Richard Petty profited for his sixth win at Daytona and his 186th career trip to victory lane.

Richard Petty won his sixth Daytona 500 in 1979. Buddy Baker won his third pole position start.

Derrike Cope won his first career NASCAR race in the 1990 Daytona 500 with a 1½ car length victory. Darrell Waltrip became the first Winston Cup driver to earn 10 million dollars in his career. Ken Schrader captured his third straight pole.

Dale Jarrett won the 1996 Daytona 500. Jarrett, the 1999 Winston Cup champion, finished third behind Terry Labonte in 1996.

Jeff Gordon won his first Daytona 500 in 1997. At just over 25½ years old, he became the youngest winner in the history of the big race. Mike Skinner, a rookie, was the pole sitter. The race finished under caution after an 11-car crash. Gordon went on to win his second points championship that season.

Michael Waltrip won his first NASCAR race in the 2001 Daytona 500. Waltrip's win was overshadowed by the death of his owner/teammate

Dale Earnhardt Sr., who died of injuries in a last lap crash into the wall. Earnhardt was the 27th fatality in the history of the track. Bill Elliott started from the pole position.

19

Jeff Purvis was born in 1959. Purvis, who raced out of Clarksville, TN, made 43 NASCAR starts 1990–96, leading briefly in three races. He finished a career-best 12th in the 1996 Daytona 500.

John Paul Jr. was born in Lawrenceville, GA in 1960. Paul ran two Winston Cup races in 1991, 411 miles at NASCAR's top level. His best finish was 16th in the 1991 Budweiser at the Glen at Watkins Glen, NY.

Mark Reed was born in 1969. Racing out of Bakersfield, CA, Reed started one Winston Cup race in 1990 and 1991.

Cale Yarborough and Charlie Glotzbach won the second and third races of the NASCAR season, in preparation for the 1970 Daytona 500. Talmadge "Tab" Prince died in qualifying. Prince, racing out of Dublin, GA, was making his Grand National debut at the time of his demise.

Bobby Allison's 47th career NASCAR win was his first Daytona 500 victory in 1978. Cale Yarborough, the winner in the last year's race, was the pole sitter.

Cale Yarborough won his fourth and final Daytona 500 in 1984. He also won his fourth and final pole at the trademark Florida track.

Darrell Waltrip won the 1989 Daytona 500 at Daytona International Speedway, his 73rd career Winston Cup win. Waltrip was voted the series's most popular driver that season and again in 1990.

Sterling Marlin won his second straight Daytona 500 in 1995. Dale Jarrett, a winner in 1993, was the pole sitter.

20

Bobby Unser was born in 1934. He ran four races at NASCAR's highest level 1969–72. Racing out of Albuquerque, NM, the brother of Al Sr. and uncle of Al Jr. managed two fourth place finishes. The Unsers are known mostly for their Indy Car racing.

Gary Myers finished in the top 10 in his only career Winston Cup race, a seventh-place in the 1971 West Virginia 500 at Ona, WV. Myers was born on this date in 1940 in Huntsville, AL.

In the first official NASCAR race at the new track at Daytona, in 1959, Bob Welborn won the qualifying event for the inaugural Daytona 500.

Scott Lagasse was born in 1959. Racing out of St. Augustine, FL, he started the annual Watkins Glen, NY, event in 1993 and 1994. He finished 13th in his debut in the 1993 Budweiser at the Glen.

David Pearson and Bobby Isaac won at Daytona, the fourth and fifth races of the NASCAR season, in preparation for the Daytona 500. Pearson won his first of 11 races that season, his third and final as the Grand National Champion.

A.J. Foyt won his only Daytona 500 in 1972. Foyt, who had started on the pole the previous year, saw Bobby Isaac win the pole in 1972.

Cale Yarborough won the 1977 Daytona 500. Donnie Allison won his second pole in three years. For Yarborough, the 1976 Winston Cup Champion, it was his first of nine wins in 1977, when he again won the points title.

Cale Yarborough won his third Daytona 500 in 1983. Ricky Rudd was the pole sitter at the Great American Race for the first time in his career.

Sterling Marlin won the 1994 Daytona 500, his first of two consecutive wins in the big race. Loy Allen was the pole sitter. It was Marlin's first career NASCAR victory. He was the 1983 Winston Cup Rookie of the Year.

Dale Jarrett rode from the pole position to a win in the 2000 Daytona 500. It was the first race of 2000 following Jarrett's Winston Cup championship of 1999.

21

Gene Comstock was born in 1909. He made 29 starts at the Grand National level in the 1950's. His best place was a fourth place finish in a 1952 race. Comstock raced out of Chesapeake, OH.

Jim Reed was born in 1926. Reed started 106 Grand National races 1951–63 with seven wins and five poles, racing out of Peekskill, NY. His first NASCAR victory came at Old Bridge, NJ, in 1958, when he won four races. Also that year, he won the shortest race in NASCAR history, a 25-mile event on a ¼-mile track in Buffalo, NY, in 1958. He later won a longer race, the 1959 Southern 500 at Darlington, his final career victory.

David Terrell was born in 1931. He ran 68 Grand National races 1952–58. Racing out of Newton, PA, Terrell recorded 23 top-10 finishes and ended up 12th in series points in both 1954 and 1955, when he led his one and only career race.

NASCAR was legally incorporated in 1948. There was some dispute over the official name; NSCRA (National Stock Car Racing Association) was one choice, but this was in use by a group in Georgia, so the National Association for Stock Car Auto Racing was chosen. The NASCAR name was suggested by driver Red Vogt. Bill France Sr. was named the first president.

Wayne Jacks was born in 1949. Racing out of Las Vegas, NV, he finished 41st in the 1993 Slick 50 500 at Phoenix, AZ, his only Winston Cup appearance.

Lee Petty dominated the 1954 beach-road course at Daytona Beach, FL. Petty won the pole, becoming the first driver to qualify over 120 mph. He then won the race in his Chrysler with an average speed of 89.108 mph in the 159.9-mile event. It was the 12th career win for Petty, his first at Daytona and first in a Chrysler. He went on to win the Grand National Championship for the first of three times that season.

Bobby Isaac's first career win came in a qualifying race for the 1964 Daytona 500.

Dave Marcis' fifth career win came in the 1982 Richmond 400. Darrell Waltrip started first for the 33rd time of his career and went on to win his second straight Winston Cup championship in 1982.

Neil Bonnett, in the #75 Pontiac, won his first race of 1988 with a first-place finish in the Pontiac Excitement 400 at Richmond, the second event of the Winston Cup season. Morgan Shepherd won his fifth career pole.

Mark Martin won the 1999 Dura Lube/Big K Mart 400 at Rockingham, NC. Ricky Rudd captured the pole, but finished a disappointing 30th.

22

Joe Booher was born in 1941. He made 21 Winston Cup starts 1978–88, finishing 16th in his debut at the 1978 Gwynn Staley 400 at North Wilkesboro, NC. Booher died in January 1993 after a crash at Daytona.

Lee Roy Carrigg was born in 1942. Racing out of Elloree, SC, he finished 17th at the 1970 Wilkes 400 in North Wilkesboro, NC, his career best. Carrigg made nine career Grand National starts, all in 1970.

Harold Morese died in 1953 in a non–NASCAR race at the Carrell Speedway in California. He ran one Grand National race in 1952, finishing 12th at the Wine Creek Race Track in Owego, NY.

Chuck Brown was born in 1954. Racing out of Portland, OR, Brown made 73 Winston Cup starts 1973–96, and won his only pole in 1994 at Bristol, TN, in a race won by Dale Earnhardt Sr.

In the first Daytona 500, Johnny Beauchamp and Lee Petty finished in an apparent dead heat. Beauchamp was originally declared the winner but photographic evidence gave the win to Petty three days later. Bob Welborn won the pole.

Junior Johnson and Johnny Rutherford won qualifying races at Daytona in 1963, the fifth and sixth points races of the NASCAR season. The victory was Rutherford's only career Grand National win.

Pete Hamilton won the 1970 Daytona 500, his only win in the big race. Former winner Cale Yarborough started from the pole. It was the first of four career wins for Hamilton, three coming in 1970. He was the 1968 Grand National Rookie of the Year.

Larry Foyt was born into a racing family in 1977 in Houston, TX. Foyt, who has attended every Indianapolis 500 since his birth, ran 20 Winston Cup events in 2003. He made his debut in the Subway 400 at Rockingham, finishing 36th.

The 1981 Richmond 400 was won by Darrell Waltrip in his #11 Buick, his 28th Winston Cup victory. Morgan Shepherd earned his first career pole and finished third. Waltrip had a great season with 12 wins and his first Winston Cup championship.

Jeff Gordon won his first race of

the season at Rockingham in the 1998 GM Goodwrench Service Plus 400. Rick Mast won the pole but finished 12th. Gordon went on to win his third Winston Cup points championship.

23

George Alsobrook was born in 1934. Racing out of Hiram, GA, Alsobrook ran 18 Grand National races 1958–62 with three career top-10 finishes.

Bill Elswick was born in 1948. He made 18 Winston Cup starts 1979–81, racing out of North Miami, FL. He finished 24th in the 1980 Daytona 500.

Julius "Slick" Johnson was born in 1948. Racing out of Florence, SC, he ran 68 Winston Cup races between 1979 and 1987 with seven top-10 finishes. He finished eighth and led four laps in the 1980 American 500 at Rockingham, NC.

Dean Combs was born in 1952. He made 24 Winston Cup starts in the early 1980's. Combs raced out of North Wilkesboro, NC, to record a career-best top-10 finish in a 1983 event.

In 1958, Paul Goldsmith won the 10th and final NASCAR race held on the Beach & Road Course at Daytona Beach, FL. The 1959 event at that site was held on the new Daytona International Speedway.

Richard Petty won the 1964 Daytona 500 to complete the first father-son duo to win the race. Lee Petty won the first one in 1959. Paul Gold-smith started on the pole in this one. It was the first of eight wins on the season for Richard, the year he captured his first of seven points championships.

LeeRoy Yarbrough won the 1969 Daytona 500, his only victory in the big race and the first trip to victory lane in his Grand National career. Buddy Baker started from the pole position.

Richard Petty won from the pole for the 57th of 61 times in his career in the 1975 Richmond 500. It was his 165th career win, 117th career pole and first of 13 wins that season. Petty won his third straight Winston Cup championship in 1975, outpacing #2 Dave Marcis.

Kyle Petty won the 1986 Miller High Life 400 at the Richmond International Speedway for his first career Winston Cup checkered flag. He became the third generation of Pettys to win a NASCAR event.

William "Roy" Tyner died in 1989 as a result of an apparent murder in Conover, NC, at the age of 52. Tyner ran 311 career Grand National races 1957–70, finishing the 1968 season a career-high 10th in series points.

Jeff Gordon won his second consecutive race to start the 1997 NASCAR Winston Cup season with a victory in the Goodwrench Service 400 at Rockingham. Dale Jarrett led most of the way.

Dale Jarrett captured the 2003 Subway 400 at the North Carolina Speedway in Rockingham, NC. Dave Blaney started on the pole for his first career top start at the Winston Cup level.

24

James "Harry" Gailey was born in 1936. Racing out of Clermont, GA, he made one Winston Cup start. He ran 141 career laps at NASCAR's highest level, finishing 31st in the 1971 Talladega 500.

Thomas Cox was born in 1936. He made 44 Grand National starts, 42 in 1962 and two the following season. He raced out of Asheboro, NC, to earn the 1962 Grand National Rookie of the Year title with ten top-10 finishes.

Fireball Roberts and Joe Weatherly won the third and fourth races of the 1961 season, qualifying for the Daytona 500. In the second event, Bobby Allison made his top-level NASCAR debut. Allison ran 717 more races in the following 25 years. Lee Petty was involved in a serious crash that limited his career to only six more races 1962–64.

Dewayne "Tiny" Lund won the 1963 Daytona 500. It was his first of five career Grand National victories. Fireball Roberts started in pole position for the third consecutive year at the superspeedway in Florida. Fred Lorenzen finished second.

LeeRoy Yarbrough and Fred Lorenzen won at Daytona, the third and fourth races of the NASCAR season. It was the 26th and final victory of Fred Lorenzen's career.

Michael Ritch was born in 1973. Ritch raced out of High Point, NC, to one start on the 1995 Winston Cup circuit.

Bobby Allison won the third event of 1974, his 42nd career NASCAR victory as well as his 42nd pole, at Richmond Fairgrounds Raceway in the Richmond 500. Allison snapped Richard Petty's string of seven straight wins at Richmond.

Darrell Waltrip won from the pole in the 1980 Richmond 400, the fifth time in his career he achieved the rare feat. It was his 24th career win and 18th pole start.

Dale Earnhardt Sr. earned his 12th Winston Cup victory at Richmond in 1985 in the Miller High Life 400. Darrell Waltrip won his 51st career pole and went on to win his third career Winston Cup championship.

Dale Earnhardt Sr. won his first race of 1991 in the second event of the Winston Cup season with a first-place finish in the Pontiac Excitement 400 at Richmond. Davey Allison won his 11th career pole. Earnhardt Sr. went on to win his second consecutive, and fifth overall, Winston Cup points championship over Ricky Rudd, the runner-up.

In the second race of the 2002 Winston Cup season, Matt Kenseth captured his first win of the season in the Subway 400 at the North Carolina Motor Speedway in Rockingham, NC. Ricky Craven started on the pole.

25

Butch Gilliland was born in 1958. He raced out of Anaheim, CA in the 1990's and made seven career Winston Cup starts 1990–95.

Davey Allison was born in Hueytown, AL, in 1961. Allison, the son of the legendary Bobby Allison, was the Rookie of the Year in 1987 and won 19 Winston Cup races. He was the 1987 Winston Cup Rookie of the Year and the 1992 Driver of the Year. Allison died in a helicopter accident at Talladega in July 1993.

Joe Weatherly won his 15th career race at the Concord Speedway (NC) in 1962.

In 1966, Paul Goldsmith and Earl Balmer won at Daytona, the third and fourth races of the NASCAR season. It was the only victory of Balmer's Grand National career.

Cale Yarborough became the third driver to win from the pole in the Daytona 500 with his 1968 triumph. He was the Grand National's most popular driver the previous season, 1967.

Richard Petty won the Richmond 500 at the Virginia State Fairgrounds in 1973. It was his sixth straight win at the track. Bobby Allison won his 36th career pole, his third straight at Richmond. It was the 150th career victory for Petty.

Mark Martin, driving the #6 Ford, won the 1990 Pontiac Excitement 400 at Richmond for his second career win. Ricky Rudd won his 17th career pole and finished third. Martin finished second to Dale Earnhardt Sr. in the 1990 Winston Cup points championship.

Dale Earnhardt Sr. won the 1996 Goodwrench Service 400 at the North Carolina Motor Speedway at Rockingham for his first win of the Winston Cup season.

26

The first beach speed record was set on the straightaway at Daytona Beach, FL, in 1903. A Winton automobile was clocked at 68.198 m.p.h.

Richard "Red" Cummings was born in 1924. Making his only Grand National start in 1950, Cummings raced out of Beverley, MA, to a 42nd-place finish at Langhorne (PA) Speedway in a Lincoln.

Don Puskarich was born in 1939. Puskarich ran 17 Winston Cup races in California 1975–82, racing out of Garden Grove, CA. His career-best came in his debut in the 1975 Winston Western 500 at Riverside, CA, where he finished 12th.

Tim Flock won for the second straight year at Daytona in 1956 on the Beach & Road Course.

Marvin Panch won the third Daytona 500 in 1961. Fireball Roberts qualified on the pole.

Mario Andretti won his only Daytona 500 in 1967 before his eventual transition to Indy-style race cars. Curtis Turner started on the pole.

The 1978 Richmond 400 was the tenth win of Benny Parsons' Winston Cup career. Neil Bonnet captured his eighth of 20 career pole starts.

In the 1984 Miller High Life 400 at Richmond, Ricky Rudd won his third career race while Darrell Waltrip earned his 47th career pole and finished second.

Jeff Gordon won the GM Goodwrench 500 at Rockingham, NC, for his third career win and first of seven checkered flag finishes in 1995. Gordon won his first points championship that year.

Steve Park won the Dura Lube 400 at Rockingham, NC, for his first career Winston Cup win in 2001. The victorious car was owned by Dale Earnhardt Sr., who had died the previous week in a crash at Daytona.

27

Tim Flock won a race at the Beach & Road Course at Daytona Beach, FL, and went on to capture his second Grand National Championship in 1955.

Todd Bodine was born in Chemung, NY, in 1964. The youngest of the three Bodine brothers, Todd began his Winston Cup career in 1992. His debut came at his home track of Watkins Glen, NY.

Ned Jarrett was victorious for the third time in the last four races at the Piedmont Interstate Fairgrounds (SC) in 1965. It was his 38th career win while Dick Hutcherson qualified for his third career pole.

Richard Petty became the first repeat winner of the Daytona 500 when he won the 1966 event. Petty started on the pole and became the first driver to average over 160 MPH in the race. The race was shortened five miles due to rain.

Richard Petty won for the fourth straight race at Richmond International Raceway with a victory in the 1972 Richmond 500. It was his 142nd career win. Bobby Allison qualified first and finished second. It was that way most of the 1972 season as Petty won his second straight, and fourth career, Winston Cup points championship with Allison finishing second.

Cale Yarborough won the 1977 Richmond 400 for his 42nd career win. Neil Bonnett started first for the second time in his Winston Cup career. Yarborough went on to win nine races in 1977 and earned his second straight Winston Cup championship.

Bobby Allison won his first race of 1983 in NASCAR's second event of the year at the Richmond Fairgrounds Raceway in the Richmond 400. It was his 74th career win and first of six on the season, when he won the Winston Cup Championship.

Rusty Wallace won his third straight race at the North Carolina Motor Speedway with a victory in the 1994 GM Goodwrench 500.

Bobby Labonte won the 2000 Dura-Lube/Big K 400 at the North Carolina Motor Speedway. Rusty Wallace started in the pole position. Labonte went on to win the Winston Cup Championship.

28

Billy Wade was born in 1930. He won four consecutive Grand National races in July 1964, his only victories in 70 starts, 1962–64. He also won five poles and finished in the top 10 in 37 other events. He was the 1963 Grand National Rookie of the Year.

Bill Shirey was born in 1932. Shirey raced out of Detroit, MI, to start 72 Grand National and Winston Cup races 1969–72. He finished in the top 10 three times.

Racing legend Mario Andretti was born in 1940. Andretti mostly raced Indy-cars, but did start 14 Winston Cup races with one win, in the 1967 Daytona 500. His nephew John went on to become a NASCAR regular in the 1990's.

John Kenney Jr. was born in 1943 in Poquoson, VA. Kenney made 13 Grand National starts 1969–70. He tied a career-best with a 12th-place finish in his last race, the 1970 Home State 200 at Raleigh, NC.

Jay Hedgecock was born in 1955. Racing out of High Point, NC, he made three Winston Cup starts in the early 1990's. His best finish was 25th in the 1994 Hanes 500 at Martinsville, VA.

Richard Petty won his first career NASCAR race in 1960 at the Charlotte Fairgrounds. He took home a purse of $800 in the sixth race of the season. Petty started 22 races in 1959 and was named Grand National Rookie of the Year.

Ned Jarrett won for the second straight time at the Asheville-Weaverville (NC) Speedway with a victory in 1965, the 39th of his career.

In the first NASCAR race held at the Ontario Motor Speedway in California, A.J. Foyt won the 1000th sanctioned NASCAR race in history in 1971 with a checkered-flag win in the Miller High Life 500.

Rusty Wallace won the 1993 Goodwrench 500 at Rockingham for his first victory of the Winston Cup season.

29

Ralph Earnhardt was born in Kannapolis, NC, in 1928. Ralph built his own cars and actually competed in 51 races at the top NASCAR level with five top-five finishes to his credit. In his debut in November 1956 at Hickory Speedway, he qualified first and finished second. He was the father of Dale Earnhardt Sr.

Richard Petty won his fifth Carolina 500 with a win at the North Carolina Motor Speedway at Rockingham, NC, in leap year 1976. Petty was named Winston Cup's most popular driver in 1976, the sixth of eight times in his career. It marked the first Winston Cup start for Bill Elliott, who finished 33rd.

MARCH

1

Bassett, VA, native Otis Martin was born in 1918. Martin started 23 races 1949–54 at NASCAR's highest level, with six top-10 finishes. He started fourth and finished 20th, due to heating problems, in the first Strictly Stock event held in June 1949 at Charlotte, NC. His best finish was also at Charlotte, a 6th-place in his #100 Mercury in April 1953.

Dave Marcis was born in 1941 in Wausau, WI. Marcis began his Winston Cup career in the 1968 Daytona 500. He finished second in points to Richard Petty in 1975, his most successful year. He ended his driving career in 2002 with five career wins and 14 poles.

Curtis Turner won at the Occoneechee Speedway in Hillsboro, NC, in 1959, his 15th career win.

Timothy Steele was born in 1968. Steele, who raced out of Coopersville, MI, started five Winston Cup events in 1994. He finished a career-best 33rd in a Bobby Allison-owned Ford in the Miller Genuine Draft 500 at Pocono, PA.

James Hylton won his first of two career NASCAR races with a 1970 win in the Richmond 500. Hylton was the 1966 Grand National Rookie of the Year.

Darryl Waltrip won the 1981 Carolina 500 at the North Carolina Motor Speedway in Rockingham, NC. It was the final year, after 15 straight runnings, of the Carolina 500; corporate sponsorship changed the race to the Warner W. Hodgdon Carolina 500 and eventually the Goodwrench 500.

Dale Earnhardt Sr. won the 1987 Goodwrench 500 at Rockingham. Earnhardt went on to win his second consecutive Winston Cup championship that season, driving to victory lane 11 times.

Bill Elliott won the 1992 GM Goodwrench 500 at Rockingham, NC. It was his first of four straight wins in March 1992.

T.C. Hunt died in 1995 at the age of 68. His best year in NASCAR was 1962 with two top-10 finishes in nine starts at the Grand National level. His best was a ninth-place at Augusta (GA) in September. Hunt raced out of Atlanta, GA.

Mark Martin won the 1998 Las Vegas 400 in Nevada. Dale Jarrett won the pole but finished a disappointing 40th. Martin went on to finish second to Jeff Gordon in the Winston Cup championship race, winning seven races on the season.

2

Lee Petty won his 31st career race at the Concord Speedway (NC) in 1958. Petty won his second of three Grand National driving championships in 1958.

Richard Petty's 15th Grand National win came in 1963 at Spartanburg, SC. Junior Johnson qualified for the 21st time in the pole position.

Cale Yarborough won the 1975 Carolina 500 at Rockingham, NC. Yarborough went on to finish ninth in points behind winner Richard Petty for the 1975 Winston Cup championship but went on to lead the pack in points the following three years.

Terry Labonte won the 1986 Goodwrench 500 at Rockingham. It was his second win at the North Carolina Motor Speedway.

Rusty Wallace won the 1997 Pontiac Excitement 400 at the Richmond International Raceway. His car was initially ruled too large after a post-race review but his victory was allowed to stand the next day. Geoff Bodine finished second.

Matt Kenseth, the 2003 Winston Cup champion, captured his only win of the season at the UAW-Daimler Chrysler 400 at Las Vegas Motor Speedway in Nevada. Bobby Labonte won the pole. Despite only one win, Kenseth finished in the top 10 24 other times in capturing his first championship.

3

Chuck Mahoney was born in Rome, NY, in 1920. Mahoney ran 16 early Strictly Stock and Grand National races with one pole and six top-10 finishes in 1950 to claim 7th in the points standings.

DeWayne Louis "Tiny" Lund was born in 1936 in Cross, SC. Lund ran 303 races between 1955 and his death at the 1975 Talladega 500, with five wins and six poles. He was 11th overall in points in 1957, when he entered a career-high 32 Grand National events. He won the 1963 Daytona 500 several days after pulling driver Marvin Panch from a wrecked car.

Clyde Lynn was born in 1936 in Virginia. He started 165 races 1965–76. Lynn was 4th in Grand National points in 1968, when he entered 49 events with 25 top-10 finishes.

Jack Smith won at the Concord Speedway (NC) in 1957. It was his second of 21 career wins.

Richard Petty captured his 16th career win in 1963 at the Asheville-Weaverville (NC) Speedway.

Richard Petty won his fourth Carolina 500 in 1974 at the North Carolina Motor Speedway in Rockingham, NC. It was his second of ten wins on the season when he won his fifth of seven driving championships.

Neil Bonnett won the 14th race of his career with a win in the 1985 Carolina 500 at Rockingham, NC.

Kyle Petty won the 1991 Goodwrench 500 at Rockingham, his only win of the Winston Cup season.

Jeff Gordon won the 1996 Pontiac Excitement 400 at Richmond International Speedway for his first win of the Winston Cup season. Terry Labonte earned his 23rd career pole and went on to capture the Winston Cup championship, edging Gordon.

At the UAW-Daimler Chrysler 400 at the Las Vegas Motor Speedway, Sterling Marlin captured his first of two wins of the 2002 season. Todd Bodine qualified first. Marlin won again in two weeks at Darlington.

4

NASCAR pioneer Buck Baker was born in 1919 in Charlotte, NC. Baker holds the distinction of being the only driver to race in the 1940s, '50s, '60s and '70s. He won 46 career races, including the first NASCAR race at Watkins Glen in 1957. He finished 11th in the first official NASCAR Strictly Stock race in 1949. Baker was first in Grand National points in 1956 and 1957.

Alex Tasnady was born in 1929. He raced out of Vineland, NJ and ran one Grand National race each in 1957, 1960 and 1967. He finished 24th in his finale, the 1967 Northern 300 at Trenton, NJ.

Ron Grana was born in 1940. Racing out of Farmington, MI, he started six Grand National/Winston Cup races between 1969 and 1972 with a lone top-10 finish in three starts in 1970.

One of two drivers named Gary Myers who raced in the 1970s was born in 1950. Racing out of Walnut Grove, NC, he ran 46 events 1974–78. He finished 11th in the 1977 Carolina 500 at Rockingham, NC, to tie a career-best.

In the final NASCAR race at the Palm Beach Speedway, Billy Myers captured his first of two career wins in 1956.

Rick Mast was born in 1957 in Lexington, VA. Mast began his Winston Cup career in 1988. He won the pole for the first Brickyard 400 in 1994.

For the second straight Spartanburg, SC, race, in 1961, Cotton Owens captured the checkered flag at the Piedmont Interstate Fairgrounds. It was his fifth career Grand National win. Ned Jarrett captured his sixth career pole.

Joe Weatherly won at Weaverville, NC, in 1962, the 16th victory of his Grand National career. It was his third of nine 1962 wins, his first of two consecutive championship season.

Bobby Allison won his 52nd career NASCAR race in 1979 at the North Carolina Motor Speedway in the third event of the season, the annual Carolina 500.

Bobby Allison won his first race of 1984, the 80th of his career, with a victory at the North Carolina Motor

Speedway in the 1984 Warner W. Hodgdon Carolina 500.

Kyle Petty won the 1990 Goodwrench 500 at Rockingham. Petty won from the top qualifying spot for the first time in his career in winning his third Winston Cup race.

Jeff Gordon won his first race of 2001 with a victory at Las Vegas in the UAW-DaimlerChrysler 400. Dale Jarrett won his first of five poles that season. Gordon went on to win six races and The Winston, capturing his fourth Winston Cup points championship.

5

Rex White won his second straight event at the Asheville-Weaverville Speedway in 1961. It was the 14th win of his career.

Richard Petty won his second straight Fireball 300, taking the checkered flag in 1967 at the Skyline Speedway in Weaverville, NC. It was the second of 27 wins on the season for Petty, who won his second of seven career points championships in 1967.

A.J. Foyt won his second straight race at the Ontario Motor Speedway with a win in the 1972 Miller High Life 500. It was the seventh and final Winston Cup win of his career.

David Pearson won the 1978 Carolina 500 at the North Carolina Motor Speedway in Rockingham, NC, for his 100th career win at NASCAR's top level.

Rusty Wallace won his first race of 1989 with a first-place finish in the

Goodwrench 500 at Rockingham. Wallace won six races that season on his way to the Winston Cup Championship.

Washington Redskins coach Joe Gibbs announced his retirement from football in 1993. Gibbs then pursued Winston Cup ownership on a full-time basis with solid success. He was elected to the Pro Football Hall of Fame and signed a five-year contract to return to the Redskins as head coach in 2004.

Terry Labonte won his second straight Richmond race in his #5 Chevrolet in the 1995 Pontiac Excitement 400. It was his 14th career win. Jeff Gordon won his fourth career pole. Gordon went on to win nine poles and seven races in 1995 to claim his first Winston Cup championship.

Jeff Burton drove a Ford to victory in the 2000 CarsDirect.com 400 at the Las Vegas Motor Speedway. Ricky Rudd started from the pole.

6

Bertrand G. "Bert" Robbins was born in 1931. Robbins, who raced out of Washington D.C., started seven Grand National races 1964–65 with three top-10 finishes.

Marshall Teague won his second straight race with a win in the 100-mile event at Jacksonville, FL. The 1952 race on the .5-mile dirt track was the third straight win to start the Grand National season for automaker Hudson. Teague also took the pole.

Lee Petty won the 1955 race at Oglethorpe Speedway in Savannah, GA, the final of two NASCAR-sanctioned events at the track.

Neil Bonnett won his second consecutive race of the Winston Cup season with a victory in the 1988 Goodwrench 500 at Rockingham. It was his final career victory.

Ernie Irvan won the 1994 Pontiac Excitement 400 at Richmond, his 10th career win.

Ted Musgrave qualified first for the first time in his Winston Cup career.

7

Janet Guthrie was born in 1938. Racing out of New York City, she started 33 Winston Cup races between 1976 and 1980. In 1977, she started a career best 19 races, finished in the top 10 four times and led one race for five laps.

Junior Johnson won from the pole to capture the 1965 Richmond 250. It was the ninth of 12 times in his career he both started and finished first. Johnson won 13 races in 1965 but finished 12th in championship points, won by Ned Jarrett.

Richard Petty won the 1971 Richmond 500 for his 121st career win. Dave Marcis earned his first career pole and finished fifth. Petty won 21 races in 1971 to claim his third Winston Cup points championship.

Dave Marcis won his second career event in the 1976 Richmond 400. Bobby Allison earned his 49th career pole start.

Duane Carter died of cancer in 1993 at the age of 79. Mostly an Indy car driver who competed in 11 Indianapolis 500 races, Carter was the father of Pancho Carter and cofounder of the United States Auto Club. He ran one Grand National race in 1950.

Davey Allison won for the only time in 1993 and the final time in his career, taking the checkered flag in the Pontiac 400 at Richmond. Allison died in a helicopter crash that July. Ken Schrader, who qualified first for the 12th time in his career, ended up a career-best ninth in Winston Cup points in 1993.

Jeff Burton won the 1999 Las Vegas 400 at Nevada's Las Vegas Motor Speedway. Bobby Labonte, who finished fifth, won the pole.

8

Mike Klapak was born in 1913. He ran 12 races at the Grand National level in the early 1950s. He had three career top–10 finishes, one in 1951 and two in 1953.

Ethel Mobley was born in Georgia in 1920. An early female competitor in Strictly Stock, Mobley ran two races in NASCAR's inaugural season of 1949.

Joe Dean Huss was born in 1939. He started three races in 1971 at NASCAR's top level. Huss raced out of Roanoke Rapids, NC, to a career-best 14th-place finish in his final, the 1971 Wilkes 400.

In 1953, the first and only sanctioned NASCAR Grand National event was held in Spring Lake, NC. Herb Thomas drove his Hudson to victory in the 100-mile dirt track race, averaging 48.789 mph. It was his 17th career Grand National victory with eight wins in 1952, seven in 1951 and one in 1950. He also captured his 15th career pole. Thomas won his second Grand National driving championship that season.

Ronnie Thomas was born in 1955. He started 197 Winston Cup races 1977–89. Racing out of Christiansburg, VA, Thomas recorded nine top-10 finishes and held the lead in three career events. He finished as high as 14th (1980) in the overall points standings. He was the 1978 Winston Cup Rookie of the Year.

Kirk Shelmerdine was born in 1958. Racing out of Philadelphia, PA, Shelmerdine ran one Winston Cup race each in 1981 and 1994, running two laps in the Budweiser NASCAR 400 in his debut. He returned to top-level NASCAR racing in 2002 with two starts and was a regular to start 2004.

Curtis Turner won at the Concord Speedway (NC) in 1959, his 16th of 17 career wins.

Richard Petty won the 1970 Carolina 500 at the North Carolina Motor Speedway in Rockingham, NC.

Dale Earnhardt Sr. won his second consecutive race of 1987 win with a first-place finish in the Miller High Life 400 at Rockingham. Alan Kulwicki won his first pole. Earnhardt won both Richmond races in 1987, 11 wins on the season, on his way to his second consecutive Winston Cup championship.

In the 1992 Pontiac Excitement 400 at Richmond, Bill Elliott won from the pole (the 14th time he both started and finished first) to capture his 26th career win. The 1988 Winston Cup champion finished 11th in points in 1992.

9

James Thirkettle was born in 1945. He ran nine Winston Cup races 1975–79. Racing out of Sylmar, CA, Thirkettle recorded three top-10 finishes and led one career lap in a 1978 race.

Danny Sullivan was born in 1950 in Louisville, KY. Sullivan was known for his IROC career but started one Winston Cup race, the 1994 Brickyard 400. Sullivan won the 1985 Indianapolis 500.

Jerry Bowman was born in 1962. He started 19 Winston Cup races in the 1980's. He raced out of Havre de Grace, MD, and ran all his events at Dover, Rockingham or Pocono.

David Pearson captured the 1969 Carolina 500 at the North Carolina Motor Speedway in Rockingham, NC. Pearson won his third Grand National Championship that season with 11 wins.

Cale Yarborough won the 1980 Carolina 500 at the North Carolina Motor Speedway in Rockingham, NC.

In the 1997 Primestar 500, Dale Jarrett led 242 of 328 laps for a victory at the Atlanta Motor Speedway. Ernie Irvan finished second.

Bobby Labonte won the 1999 Primestar 500 at Atlanta Motor

Speedway. John Andretti won the pole and finished 20th.

Bobby Labonte, the pole winner the previous week, won the 2003 Golden Corral 500 at the Atlanta Motor Speedway in Georgia. Ryan Newman started in the top spot.

10

Mike Wallace was born in 1959 in St. Louis, MO. The brother of drivers Kenny and Rusty, Mike debuted in Winston Cup in 1991 and ran 142 events through 2003 with 11 top–10 finishes.

Junior Johnson won at the Occoneechee Speedway in Hillsboro, NC, in 1963, his 30th of 51 career victories. Joe Weatherly, the 1963 Grand National champion, captured the pole.

David Pearson's fourth career win came in the 1964 Richmond 250. Ned Jarrett won his 19th pole. Both finished behind Richard Petty in the 1964 Grand National championship race, Jarrett finished second and Pearson fourth.

Matt Kenseth was born in 1972 in Cambridge, WI. He began his Winston Cup experience in 1998, progressing in the points standings each season and culminating with the Winston Cup championship in 2003. His first career win came in the 2000 Coca-Cola 600 at Lowe's Motor Speedway. He was the 2000 Winston Cup Rookie of the Year.

Dale Earnhardt Sr. won his second official race of the 1996 season with a victory in the Purolator 500 at the Atlanta Motor Speedway.

In the Golden Corral 400 at the Atlanta Motor Speedway, eventual 2002 Winston Cup points champion Tony Stewart captured his first of three victories of the season. Bill Elliott qualified first.

11

Troy Ruttman was born in 1930. Racing out of Mooreland, OK, he started seven Grand National races with five top–10 finishes 1962–64.

Harold "Frog" Fagan was born in 1940. He started 20 Grand National races 1967–71, notching his only top–10 finish in 1968. Frog raced out of Willowdale, Ontario, Canada.

Cale Yarborough's 60th career victory came in the 1979 Richmond 400. Bobby Allison qualified on the pole for the 52nd time and finished second. Yarborough slipped to fourth in Winston Cup points in 1979 after winning the past three championships.

Kevin Harvick, chosen to drive Dale Earnhardt's car after his death the previous month in the Daytona 500, captured his first career Winston Cup win at Atlanta Motor Speedway in the 2001 Cracker Barrel 500. Jeff Gordon finished second, inches off the lead. Dale Jarrett won the pole. Harvick won two races in 2001 and was named NASCAR Winston Cup Rookie of the Year.

12

Robert N. "Red" Byron Jr. was born in 1915 in Anniston, AL. Byron was the points champion in NASCAR's first season, 1949, when he ran six races, winning two. He raced nine other races 1950–51 and was the first driver to record two wins in NASCAR's top level.

Doug Easton was born in 1931. He started one career Grand National race, racing out of Horse Cave, NY, to a 35th-place finish in the 1969 Talladega 500.

Jimmy Lee Capps was born in 1938. He started 11 Grand National/Winston Cup races 1964–78. Running out of Jacksonville, FL, Capps had a career-best 10th-place finish in the 1976 Talladega 500.

John Sherman "Johnny" Rutherford III was born in 1938. Known primarily for Indy Car racing, Rutherford ran 35 top-level NASCAR races, 1963–88, with a surprising win in his rookie season at a qualifying race at Daytona in February. He won the 1976 and 1980 Indianapolis 500.

Robert "Bobby" Fox, who raced out of Bremerton, WA, in the 1980s, was born in 1948. Fox started one Winston Cup race in 1984.

Fireball Roberts became the first NASCAR driver to lead from the start and claim victory in a superspeedway race with a first place finish at Marchbanks Speedway in 1961 in the final NASCAR race held at the Hanford, CA, track. Bob Ross had his only career pole. Ross, who raced out of Lakewood, CA, made 17 Grand National starts 1956–63. He finished in the top 10 ten times.

John Andretti was born in 1963 in Bethlehem, PA. Andretti began Winston Cup racing in 1993 and won his first race at Daytona in the summer of 1997. His uncle, Mario Andretti, and cousin, Michael, race Indy cars. In 1994, Andretti finished 10th in the Indianapolis 500, then flew to Charlotte and finished 36th in the Coca-Cola 600 on the same day.

Bobby Isaac's final career NASCAR win came in the 1972 Carolina 500 at Rockingham, NC.

Jeff Gordon won the inaugural Purolator 500 at Atlanta Motor Speedway in 1995. Gordon was the 1995 Winston Cup Champion.

Dale Earnhardt Sr. won the 2000 Cracker Barrel 500 in his #3 Chevrolet at the Atlanta Motor Speedway. Dale Jarrett took the pole.

13

Charles "Duke" DeBrizzi was born in 1928. He started three Grand National races in 1957. DeBrizzi raced out of Jamesburg, NY, to finish a career-best 12th at Norfolk (VA) Speedway in his finale.

In the only Peach Blossom 500, held at the North Carolina Motor Speedway in Rockingham, NC, in 1965, Paul Goldsmith captured the checkered flag, the second and final time in his career he won from the pole.

Richard Petty won his sixth Carolina 500 in 1977 at the North Carolina Motor Speedway in Rockingham, NC.

Richard Petty won the second Warner W. Hodgdon Carolina 500 at the North Carolina Motor Speedway in 1983.

Ernie Irvan won the 1994 Motor-craft Quality Parts 500 at the Atlanta Motor Speedway.

14

Lee Petty was born in 1914 in Randleman, SC. The patriarch of the Petty clan, Lee won 54 Winston Cup races in 427 starts. He won the 1959 Daytona 500, where he was almost killed when his car sailed over the wall at Turn 4 in 1961. He was the Grand National Champion three times, 1954 and 1958–59. His son, Richard Petty, later surpassed his father's performance.

NASCAR pioneer Bill Rexford was born in 1927. Rexford, who raced out of Conowango Valley, NY, was the Grand National series champion in 1950, but ran just 16 more races at the highest level after that year. Altogether, Rexford drove 36 career races between 1949 and 1953 with only one win, at Canfield, OH, in 1950.

Jimmy Clark, born in 1936, made one Grand National start. Clark raced out of Dunn, Scotland, to a 30th-place finish in the 1967 American 500 at Rockingham, NC.

Ned Jarrett won at the Occoneechee Speedway in Hillsboro, NC for the second straight year in 1965. Jarrett won 13 races en route to his second Grand National Championship that season.

Richard Petty captured his second consecutive Carolina 500 with a victory at the North Carolina Motor Speedway in Rockingham, NC, in 1971.

Cale Yarborough began a two-year dominance at Bristol International Speedway with a win in the 1976 Southeastern 500, his 32nd career victory and first of the season. Buddy Baker qualified on the pole for the 22nd time of his career. Yarborough won his first of three consecutive Winston Cup Championships in 1976 with nine victories.

For the third straight Bristol race, Darrell Waltrip won from the pole in the 1982 Valleydale 500. It was the 15th of 24 times he achieved the feat in his career. It was his 40th career win and first of 12 in 1982, earning his second straight Winston Cup Championship.

Roy Hall died in 1991 at the age of 69. He made one Strictly Stock start in NASCAR's inaugural season, 1949, finishing sixth in the Wilkes 200. He made one Grand National start in 1952 and earned a total of $150 in his two-race career.

Jeff Gordon won his second race of 1999 with a victory in the Cracker Barrel 500 at the Atlanta Motor Speedway. Bobby Labonte qualified first but finished second.

15

Edwin Brown was born in 1920. He started nine races at the Grand National level between 1955 and 1968, racing out of Merridian, CA. His career-best was a second-place start and seventh-place finish in May 1955 at the Tucson Rodeo Grounds (AZ).

Walter Price, born in 1935 and racing out of San Fernando, CA, started five top-level NASCAR races 1964–74, all in California. His best finish was 17th in the 1966 Motor Trend 500 at Riverside, CA.

Tommy Andrews was born in 1936. Andrews notched only two career Winston Cup starts in 1971. He raced out of Huntsville, AL, to a 16th-place finish in his debut in the 1971 Myers Brothers 250 at Winston-Salem, NC.

Dennis DeVea was born in 1948. He led one lap in his only career Winston Cup start. DeVea raced out of Joliet, IL, to a 24th-place finish in the 1982 Gabriel 400.

Mickey Gibbs was born in 1958. He ran 36 Winston Cup races 1988–91, leading two races. Gibbs raced out of Glencoe, AL, to lead the 1988 Talladega DieHard 500 for two laps before retiring due to mechanical difficulties.

Curtis Turner won the fourth race of the 1958 points race with a victory at the Champion Speedway in Fayetteville, NC.

Glenn Dunnaway died in 1964 when he was killed at a train crossing in Camden, SC. Dunnaway, a NASCAR pioneer, started 19 races in the early years 1949–51.

Richard Petty won the final NASCAR-sanctioned race at the Savannah Speedway in Georgia in 1970. The track hosted ten races 1962–70.

Cale Yarborough won the Coca-Cola 500 in 1981 at Atlanta Motor Speedway, the first time the event was named after the popular soft drink.

Ricky Rudd won his first race of 1987 with a win in the Motorcraft Quality Parts 500 at Atlanta Motor Speedway.

Bill Elliott won the 1992 Motorcraft Quality Parts 500 at the Atlanta Motor Speedway.

16

Edward Ferree was born in 1952. Racing out of Saxonburg, PA, he started three Winston Cup events 1992–93. His best finish was 27th in the 1993 GM Goodwrench 500 at Rockingham, NC.

Lee Petty won the 100-mile event on the dirt track of Wilson (Legion) Speedway in 1958. It was his 32nd career Grand National victory.

David Pearson won the 1969 Cracker 200 at the Augusta International Speedway.

Richard Petty's 166th career win came in the 1975 Southeastern 500 at Bristol International Speedway. Buddy Baker started on the pole for the 20th time of his career.

Dale Earnhardt Sr. won for the first time in 1980, his second career win, at the Atlanta Motor Speedway with a checkered flag finish in the 1980 Atlanta 500. It was the final time the annual event was named the Atlanta 500 before corporate sponsorship changed the names of many events. Earnhardt Sr. went on to win his first of seven Winston Cup Championships in 1980, winning five times. Rusty Wallace, making his Winston Cup racing debut, finished second and went on to win the 1989 championship.

Morgan Shepherd won the inaugural Motorcraft Quality Parts 500 at Atlanta Motor Speedway in 1986.

At the Darlington Raceway, Ricky Craven captured the 2003 Carolina Dodge Dealers 400 for his only win of the season. Elliott Sadler started on the pole.

17

Tom Pistone was born in 1929 and raced out of Chicago, IL. "Tiger" made 131 NASCAR starts 1955–68, finishing in top 10 53 times. Pistone won his only two NASCAR races in a five-week span in 1959, at Trenton, NJ and Richmond, VA.

Ralph Moody's final of five Grand National wins came in 1957 at Wilson, NC.

The first race at the Savannah Speedway, a half-mile paved track in Georgia, was won by Jack Smith in the 1962 St. Patrick's Day 200.

Fred Lorenzen won the 1963 Atlanta 500 at the Atlanta Motor Speedway, his second straight victory in the annual event which began in 1960. Lorenzen was voted the most popular Grand National driver that season and again in 1965.

David Pearson won the 31st Grand National race of his career in the 1968 Southeastern 500 at Bristol, TN. Richard Petty was the top qualifier for the 69th time in his career. Pearson won the championship in 1968 over Petty, who won the previous season.

Cale Yarborough captured his second win in three races at Bristol in the 1974 Southeastern 500. Donnie Allison qualified for his 10th career pole start.

Bill Elliott won his first race at the Atlanta Motor Speedway in the 1985 Coca-Cola 500.

Sterling Marlin won for the second time in three weeks with a victory in the 2002 Carolina Dodge Dealers 400 at Darlington Raceway. Ricky Craven captured his second pole position start of the season.

18

William "Blackie" Pitt was born in 1925. Pitt raced out of Rocky Mount, NC, and made 81 Grand National starts in the 1950s. He ranked 11th overall in 1954, his rookie season. Blackie finished in the top 10 19 times in his career. His brother "Brownie" also made one series start in 1956.

Mark Donohue was born in 1937. started six Winston Cup races 1972–73 with a win in January 1973 at Riverside, CA. He hailed from Newtowne Square, PA, and won the 1973 Indianapolis 500.

Herb Thomas won in 1956 at the Wilson (NC) Speedway, his 45th career Grand National victory.

Rex White won at the Occoneechee Speedway in Hillsboro, NC, in 1962, his 22nd career win. White won the 1960 Grand National Championship.

David Pearson won the 1973 Carolina 500 at North Carolina Motor Speedway in Rockingham. Pearson, in a Mercury, took the checkered flag over second-place Cale Yarborough.

Buddy Baker won the 1979 Atlanta 500 at the Atlanta Motor Speedway, his second career win at the Hampton, GA track.

Benny Parsons won the 1984 Coca-Cola 500 at Atlanta Motor Speedway for his 21st and final Winston Cup victory. Parsons was the 1973 Winston Cup Champion and 1970 Rookie of the Year.

Dale Earnhardt Sr. won the 1990 Motorcraft Quality Parts 500 at Atlanta Motor Speedway. It was his first of nine wins during the 1990 Winston Cup season.

Ken Schrader won the Motorcraft Quality Parts 500 at Atlanta in 1991 for his first of two wins on the Winston Cup season.

Dale Jarrett won his first race of 2001 with a victory at Darlington in the Carolina Dodge Dealers 400. He won three more events that season. Season points champion Jeff Gordon captured his second pole start.

19

Frank James was born in 1938. He started seven races 1970–72 with one top–10 finish each in 1971 and 1972. He earned $8,000 for his career efforts.

Rick Newsom was born in 1950. He ran 82 career Winston Cup races 1972–86, never more than 12 (1973) in any one season. He died in a private plane crash in 1988.

Bill Sedgwick was born in 1955. Sedgwick raced out of Granada Hills, CA, to ten Winston Cup starts 1989–1993. His best finish was 15th in the 1991 Banquet Frozen Foods 300 at Sonoma, CA.

David Pearson came from two laps behind, aided by a competitor's mishap, to win the 1967 Southeastern 500 at Bristol. Cale Yarborough, who changed a late flat tire, finished second. Darel Dieringer won his sixth career pole.

Bobby Allison won his second race of the 1978 season with a victory at Atlanta International Raceway. The win was the 48th of his career and second win in the annual Atlanta 500 event.

Darrell Waltrip won his second race in three tries to start the 1989 Winston Cup season with a win in the Motorcraft Quality Parts 500 at Atlanta.

In the 2000 Mall.com 400 at Darlington Raceway, Ward Burton drove his Pontiac to the winner's circle. Jeff Gordon started from the pole position.

20

Bob Ashbrook was born in 1929. He started three Grand National races 1969–70, racing out of Akron, OH. His best race was a 17th-place finish at Michigan in June 1969 in the Motor State 500.

John Martin was born in 1939. Racing out of Irvine, CA, he started seven races at NASCAR's top level 1967–75. His best finish was 18th in his debut at Riverside, CA, in the 1967 Motor Trend 500.

Bobby Fleming was born in 1941. Racing out of Danville, VA, he started one Grand National race in 1969 and two Winston Cup races in 1974.

James Dotson "Jimmy" Vaughn was born in 1942. He ran five Grand National (1965–67) and three Winston Cup (1971) races in his career. He raced out of Greenville, SC.

Geoff Brabham was born in 1952. Racing out of Sydney, Australia, he started one Winston Cup race in 1994.

Dick Hutcherson won the 1966 Southeastern 500 at Bristol for his tenth career Grand National victory. David Pearson won his 19th career pole start.

Richard Petty won the 1977 Atlanta 500 at the Atlanta Motor Speedway, his second win at the Georgia track.

Dale Earnhardt Sr. won the 1988 Motorcraft Quality Parts 500 at Atlanta Motor Speedway.

Morgan Shepherd won his only race of 1993 with a first place finish in the Winston Cup Series fourth event, the Motorcraft Quality Parts 500 at Atlanta.

21

Truman Fontella "Fonty" Flock was born in Ft. Payne, AL, in 1921. He was one of four siblings to race from the 1940's to the 1960s. Fonty raced 1949–57 with 19 wins and 30 poles at NASCAR's highest level. He finished second in the first Winston Cup race held in 1949 at Charlotte, NC.

Bob Davis was born in 1925. Residing in Lighthouse Point, FL, he started one Winston Cup race. He finished 34th in the 1973 Talladega 500.

Herb Thomas and his Hudson were dominant at Atlanta, GA, in 1954. Thomas garnered his 26th pole

position and won his 31st race on the one-mile dirt track in a 100-mile event.

Richard Petty won the 1971 Hickory 276 at the Hickory Speedway in North Carolina. Petty won 21 races in 1971 on his way to his third Winston Cup championship.

Jeff Krogh was born in 1972 and raced out of Kamiah, ID. He started two Winston Cup races in 1996, finishing a career-best 35th at Sonoma, CA, in the Save Mart Supermarkets 300.

David Pearson won the 1976 Atlanta 500 at the Atlanta Motor Speedway, his second win in the annual event.

Darrell Waltrip won the 1982 Coca Cola 500 at the Atlanta Motor Speedway, his first victory in the annual event.

Jeff Burton won his second race of 1999 with a victory in the TranSouth Financial 400 at Darlington, SC. Jeff Gordon, who won the pole, finished third.

22

Billy Hagan was born in 1932. He started one race each at NASCAR's top level in 1969 (a top-10 finish), 1975 and 1979. Hagan raced out of Lafayette, LA.

Johnny Beauchamp won in 1959 at Lakewood Speedway in Atlanta, GA, for his first of two career NASCAR victories, one day shy of his 36th birthday.

Fred Lorenzen won at Bristol in the 1964 Southeastern 500, his second straight win at the Tennessee track. Marvin Panch captured his 12th career pole.

Wayne Niedecken died in 1993 at the age of 61. Niedecken started one Grand National race in 1953.

Dale Jarrett won his first race of 1998 in the TranSouth Financial 400 at Darlington, SC. Mark Martin qualified first and finished seventh.

23

Johnny Beauchamp was born in 1923. He recorded two career Grand National wins, in 1959 on a dirt track in Atlanta, GA, and in 1960 on a paved track in Nashville, TN. Beauchamp raced out of Harland, IA.

Buck Baker won for the second straight year at the Occoneechee Speedway in Hillsboro, NC, in 1958.

Gwyn Staley, who raced out of Burlington, NC, and entered 69 Grand National races 1951–58, died in a NASCAR convertible race at Richmond, VA, on this date in 1958. He won three races in 1957, all in a span of three weeks, for his only career victories. He finished in the top 10 38 other times.

Bobby Allison won at the Bristol International Speedway for the first time in the 1969 Southeastern 500. It was his 13th career win and his second driving a Dodge. Bobby Isaac qualified for his seventh of 50 career pole positions.

Dale Jarrett won his second straight race with a victory in the 1997 Transouth Financial 400 at Darlington

Raceway. Ted Musgrave finished second.

Kurt Busch captured the 2003 Food City 500 at the Bristol Motor Speedway in Tennessee. Ryan Newman started first.

24

Jack McCoy was born in 1938. He ran 20 events between 1963 and 1974 with five career top–10 finishes.

Jimmy Makar was born in New Jersey in 1956. Makar became a successful Winston Cup crew chief working with Dale Jarrett and Bobby Labonte.

Buck Baker won at the Occoneechee Speedway in Hillsboro, NC, in 1957. It was the first of ten wins for Baker in 1957, who captured his second straight Grand National Championship.

Scott Pruett was born in 1960 in Sacramento, CA. He was a 2000 NASCAR rookie when he ran 28 events. He managed just five more Winston Cup starts 2001–03 with a total of three top–10 finishes.

Junior Johnson won the second Hickory 250 at the Hickory (NC) Speedway in 1963.

David Pearson won his 32nd career Grand National race in the 1968 Richmond 300. Bobby Isaac earned his second career pole start. Pearson won 16 races in 1968 to capture his second Grand National championship.

Cale Yarborough won his fourth Atlanta 500 in 1974 at the Atlanta Motor Speedway.

Jeff Gordon captured his second win of the 1996 Winston Cup season with a first-place finish in the Transouth Financial 400 at Darlington.

Kurt Busch won the Food City 500 at Bristol (TN) Motor Speedway for his first of four Winston Cup victories on the season. Jeff Gordon qualified first for the first of three times in 2002.

25

Johnny Ray was born in 1937 and raced out of Eastaboga, AL. Ray ran eight Winston Cup races 1974–76 with a 28th-place finish in the 1976 Daytona 500.

Clyde "Butch" Lindley was born in South Carolina in 1948. Lindley ran 11 Winston Cup events 1979–85 with a career-best second-place finish in the 1982 Virginia National Bank 500 at Martinsville, VA.

Buck Baker won in 1956 at Lakewood Speedway in Atlanta, GA. Baker, who captured his first of two Grand National championships in 1956, won 14 races that season.

David Pearson won in Greenville, SC, in 1967. Dick Hutcherson qualified first for the 16th time of his career.

Cale Yarborough won at Bristol International in the 1973 Southeastern 500, his first victory of the Winston Cup season. Yarborough won from the pole for the fifth of 17 times in his career.

Richard Petty won the 1975 Atlanta 500 at the Atlanta Motor Speedway, his first win in the annual race and his second straight win at the Hampton, GA, track. Petty won 13 races in 1975 on his way to his sixth of seven points championships.

Bobby Allison won his second race of the 1979 season with a victory at North Wilkesboro Speedway in the inaugural Northwestern Bank 400, an annual event held until 1985. The win was Allison's 53rd career first place finish.

Elliott Sadler won the 2001 Food City 500 at Bristol for his first career NASCAR victory and only win of the season. Mark Martin qualified first.

26

Lella Lombardi was born in 1943 and raced out of Frugarolo, Italy. He started one Winston Cup race, finishing 31st in the 1977 Firecracker 400 at Daytona Beach, FL.

Tim Flock won the pole but brother Fonty captured the checkered flag in 1955 at Columbia, SC. Tim won the Grand National championship that season while Fonty finished tenth in points.

Bob Burdick won at the Atlanta Motor Speedway in the 1961 Atlanta 500, the first of three Grand National races held that year at the Georgia track. It was the only NASCAR victory of his career.

Bobby Allison won his 30th career race in 1972 at the Atlanta International Raceway (a.k.a. Atlanta Motor Speedway). It was his first win in the sixth NASCAR race of the season and his second win in three years at the annual Atlanta 500.

Rusty Wallace, driving the #27 Pontiac, won his second race of 1989 with a trip to victory lane in the Pontiac Excitement 400 at Richmond. It was his second win in three weeks. Geoff Bodine won his 23rd career pole. Wallace won six races in 1989 on his way to his first Winston Cup points championship.

Sterling Marlin's third career Winston Cup victory came in the 1995 TranSouth 500 at Darlington, SC. Jeff Gordon won his fifth career pole.

Rusty Wallace drove his Ford to victory in the 2000 Food City 500 at Bristol Motor Speedway. It was the first career win for Wallace. The pole-sitter was Steve Park.

27

Bill Jennings was born in 1926. Racing out of Syracuse, NY, he started one race in 1953, finishing ninth in his only Grand National start in May at the Columbia Speedway (SC).

William Caleb "Cale" Yarborough was born in 1939 in Sardis, SC. He won 83 career Grand National and Winston Cup events 1957–88 in 559 starts. His first career victory came in 1965 in a dirt-track race in Valdosta, GA. He raced out of Timmonsville, SC, and won the Winston Cup Championship 1976–78. He was the Grand National's most popular driver in 1967.

Bobby Mausgrover was born in 1940. Racing out of Keokuk, IA, he started 46 Grand National and Winston Cup races 1967–73 with one top-10 finish in his rookie season,

ninth-place in the 1967 Maryland 300 at Beltsville Speedway.

William "Bosco" Lowe was born in 1943. He ran seven Winston Cup races 1967–85 with his lone top–10 in his debut in the 1967 Buddy Shuman 250 at Hickory, NC.

Rodney Combs was born in 1950. He made 55 Winston Cup starts 1982–90 with one top–10 finish. Combs raced out of Cincinnati, OH to a career-best ninth-place finish in his debut in the Atlanta Journal 500.

Jim Paschal won in 1955 at Occoneechee Speedway in Hillsboro, NC.

Jeff Fuller was born in 1957 and raced out of Auburn, MA, to run eight races 1992–2000. He started his first Winston Cup race in 1992 and briefly led the 2000 Food City 500 at Bristol, TN.

Lee Petty won his third straight North Wilkesboro race in 1960.

Jim Hurtubise won the 1966 Atlanta 500 at the Atlanta Motor Speedway for the only win of his Grand National career. Hurtubise ran six events that season, winning once, came in second once, finished fifth once and had two other top 10s.

Bobby Allison won his first race of the season at Bowman-Gray Stadium in Winston-Salem, NC, in NASCAR's 9th event of the 1967 season. It was his fourth career victory.

Cale Yarborough won his third straight North Wilkesboro race with a victory in the 1977 Gwyn Staley 400. It was his third of nine wins on the season, when he won his second of three straight Winston Cup Championships.

Cale Yarborough won the Coca-Cola 500 in 1983 at Atlanta Motor Speedway.

Lake Speed won his first career race in 1988 with a victory in the TranSouth 500 at Darlington.

The 1994 TranSouth 500 at Darlington was the 60th career Winston Cup win for Dale Earnhardt Sr. Bill Elliott qualified first for the 46th time in his career. It was the first of four wins for Earnhardt Sr. in 1994, his final of seven seasons as the Winston Cup Champion.

The Haas-Carter Motorsports team ceased operations in 2002. Drivers Todd Bodine and Joe Nemechek both lost their Winston Cup cars in the process.

28

Herb Thomas won his second race of 1954, the series-leading 30th of his career. Thomas took the checkered flag in his Hudson on the half-mile dirt track in Jacksonville, FL, in the 100-mile event. Curtis Turner won his eighth career pole.

Al Keller gained his first career Grand National win in 1954 in a 100-mile event at the half-mile Oglethorpe Speedway in Savannah, GA, the first of two sanctioned events at the facility. Herb Thomas gained his 27th career pole position. Both drivers competed in Hudsons.

In the second sanctioned race scheduled for this date in 1954, and the second of three held at Oakland Stadium, Dick Rathmann won the 125-mile event on the half-mile dirt/paved track in Oakland, CA. It was the 11th career win and first of the season for Rathmann, driving a Hudson. Hershel McGriff won his first career pole.

Jerry O'Neil was born in 1956. Racing out of Auburn, NY, he made 16 Winston Cup starts 1989–94. His final event was a 34th-place finish in the 1994 Mello Yello 500 at Charlotte.

David Pearson captured his fifth career Grand National win in 1964 at Greenville-Pickens Speedway in South Carolina. Dick Hutcherson captured his first of 22 career pole starts.

David Pearson won from the pole at Bristol in the 1971 Southeastern 500. It was the 18th of 37 times in his career he both started and finished first. It was his 60th win and 55th pole.

Cale Yarborough won the inaugural Warner W. Hodgdon Carolina 500 at the North Carolina Motor Speedway in 1982. It was the first time that the annual race at the Rockingham, NC, track had corporate sponsorship.

Dale Earnhardt Sr. won his first race of 1993, taking the checkered flag in the TranSouth 500 at Darlington. Earnhardt Sr., who started from the pole by draw, established a track speed record for a 500 mile race with an average speed of 139.958 mph. He went on to win five more races in 1993 on his way to his sixth of seven Winston Cup Championships.

Terry Labonte won the 1999 Primestar 500 at the Texas Motor

Speedway in Fort Worth. Kenny Irwin Jr. won the pole but finished 15th.

29

Ben Lalomia was born in 1919. Racing out of Buffalo, NY, he made one start at the Grand National level in 1951 and earned $25.00 for his 39th-place effort in February 1951 on the Beach & Road Course at Daytona Beach, FL.

Allen Adkins was born in 1929. Racing out of Clovis, CA, Adkins started 14 Grand National races 1954–57 with eight top–10 finishes. His career highlight was a runner-up finish at Tucson, AZ in May 1955.

Oma Kimbrough was born in 1951 in Tyrone, PA. He ran the annual Winston Cup event at Watkins Glen, NY, three consecutive years 1989–91. He finished a career-best 24th in the 1991 Budweiser at the Glen.

Herb Thomas won his second straight race in 1953 in his Hudson. Thomas, who started from the pole, won on the .625-mile dirt track in North Wilkesboro, NC, averaging 71.907 mph over the 125-mile event. It was his 18th checkered flag. He was the Grand National driving champion for the second time in 1953.

Junior Johnson won the 1959 dirt-track event at the Wilson Speedway (NC). It was his 13th career checkered flag at the Grand National level. He was voted the most popular driver that season.

Doug Heveron was born in 1964. He started 31 career Winston Cup events in the mid–1980s. He led two races but failed to record a top–10 finish. Heveron raced out of Liverpool, NY. Hessert finished 15th in the 1986 Daytona 500.

Bobby Allison won his 17th career NASCAR race with a victory in 1970 at Atlanta Motor Speedway in the Atlanta 500. It was his first win of the season in the eighth race of the year. He was voted the most popular Grand National driver that season.

Darrell Waltrip won from the pole in the 1981 Valleydale 500 to begin a string of seven consecutive wins at the Bristol International Speedway. It was the seventh of 24 times he started and finished first in a top-level NASCAR event.

Dale Earnhardt Sr. won his third race in four starts with a trip to victory lane in the 1987 TranSouth 500 at Darlington. Earnhardt won 11 races in 1987, winning his third of seven Winston Cup Championships.

Bill Elliott captured his 38th career Winston Cup win in the 1992 TranSouth 500 at Darlington. Sterling Marlin captured his fifth career pole.

Jeff Gordon's second win of 1998 came in the Food City 500 at Bristol, TN. Rusty Wallace finished 33rd, but started on the pole.

30

Paul Dean Holt was born in 1936. He started 85 Grand National/Winston Cup races 1966–77. He finished with one top 10 in 1967 and was 18th in Grand National points during the

1968 season. He raced out of Sweet-water, TN.

Randy Tissot was born in 1944. He started 13 Winston Cup races 1973–75. Tissot, based in Holly-wood, FL, led eight laps in the 1974 Winston 500 at Talladega, finishing 32nd after engine problems. He finished 29th in the 1975 Daytona 500.

Herb Thomas won his first race of 1952 in the fourth race of the Grand National campaign at North Wilkes-boro, NC. It marked the first time an automaker, Hudson, started the sea-son with four straight wins. Thomas also qualified first for the 125-mile race on the .625-mile dirt track.

Jim Reed won his fifth career race in 1959 at Winston-Salem, NC's Bowman-Gray Stadium.

Marvin Panch won in 1964 at Bowman-Gray Stadium in Winston-Salem, NC, for his 10th career Grand National win.

Cale Yarborough won his third straight Atlanta 500 at the Atlanta Motor Speedway in 1969, his tenth career victory.

Dale Earnhardt Sr.'s third career Winston Cup win came at Bristol in the 1980 Valleydale Southeastern 500. Cale Yarborough captured his 46th career pole, but finished fifth.

Eddie Flemke died in 1984 at the age of 53. Flemke started one Grand National race, driving 58 miles at the Norwood Arena (MA) in the 1961 Yankee 500, finishing 12th.

Ryan Newman, who sat on the pole in two of the previous three races, finally won in 2003 at the Sam-sung/Radio Shack 500 at the Texas Motor Speedway. Bobby Labonte earned his second pole start of the season.

31

Jim Boyd was born in 1920. He started two Winston Cup races in California in 1975. He raced out of Cottonwood, CA, to a career-best 14th-place finish in his debut at Riverside, CA in the Tuborg 400.

Phillip "Pee Wee" Jones was born in 1928. Racing out of Clemmons, NC, he started seven Grand National races in the 1950s. His best finish was 13th at Asheville-Weaverville Speed-way in July 1955, his second career Grand National event.

Pat Fay was born in 1944. Racing out of Gustine, CA, he started four top-level NASCAR races in the early 1970s with one top–10 finish in a 1971 race.

Buck Baker's Chevrolet won the 100-mile Grand National race at the Asheville-Weaverville (NC) Speed-way in 1957.

Jeff McDuffie, the son of J.D. McDuffie, was born in 1962. Jeff started five Winston Cup races in the early 1980s, all at North Wilkesboro, NC, or Rockingham, NC. His best was a 16th-place in the 1982 Holly Farms 400.

Fireball Roberts won his 29th ca-reer Grand National race in the 1963 Southeastern 500 at Bristol, TN, in 1963. Fred Lorenzen captured his ninth career pole.

Cale Yarborough won the 1968 Atlanta 500 at the Atlanta Motor

Speedway, his second straight win in the annual event.

Jeff Gordon won his second consecutive race, and third of the 1996 Winston Cup season, taking the checkered flag in the Food City 500 at Bristol.

Racing legend Tim Flock died of cancer in 1998 at the age of 73 at his home in Charlotte, NC. Flock won the 1955 points championship with 18 wins. He also won the Grand National title in 1952.

APRIL

1

Tetsuo Fuchigami, better known as George Tet, was born in 1923. Racing out of Ozone Park, NY, Tet started three career Grand National races 1960–61.

Billy Carden was born in 1924. He started 73 Strictly Stock and Grand National races 1949–59. He won two career poles, both in 1951 in North Carolina, in Weaverville and Charlotte. He raced out of Mableton, GA.

Ray Hendrick was born in 1929. He started 17 Grand National/Winston Cup races 1956–74 with six career top–10 finishes. He raced out of Richmond, VA.

Bob Kauf was born in 1942. He ran five top-level NASCAR races at Riverside, CA, in the early 1970s. He finished a career-best 27th in the 1971 Motor Trend 500.

Ruben Garcia, who raced out of South El Monte, CA, in the 1980s, was born in 1946. Garcia started nine Winston Cup races 1984–88, all at Riverside, with a career-best 14th-place in the 1985 Winston Western 500.

Curtis Turner became the first driver with wins in the first three NASCAR seasons when he won the second event of 1951. Turner's win at Charlotte in the 112.5-mile event on the .75-mile dirt track was the first manufacturer's win for Nash.

Tom Hessert was born in 1951. He started his only Winston Cup race in 1982 and lasted 20 miles in the Mountain Dew 500 at Pocono, PA. He raced out of Trenton, NJ.

Emanuel Zervakis won his first of two career Grand National races in 1961 in Greenville, SC. Junior Johnson captured his 10th career pole.

Rex White won the inaugural Richmond 250 at Richmond International Raceway (VA). It was his 23rd of 28 career wins. White won eight races in 1962 and finished fifth in Grand National championship points, won that year by Joe Weatherly.

David Pearson won the 1973 Atlanta 500 at the Atlanta Motor

Speedway. Pearson averaged 139.351 mph to beat Bobby Isaac to the checkered flag in the annual event.

Dale Earnhardt Sr. won the first Winston Cup race of his career in 1979 at Bristol in the Southeastern 500. He was the 1979 Winston Cup Rookie of the Year.

Darrell Waltrip won the 1984 Valleydale 500, his seventh straight win at the Bristol International Speedway. Ricky Rudd captured his 10th career pole.

Dale Earnhardt Sr. won his second consecutive race of 1990 with a trip to victory lane in the TransSouth 500 at Darlington. Geoff Bodine captured his 26th career pole.

Defending Winston Cup Champion Alan Kulwicki was killed in a plane crash just five races into the 1993 season. The defending Winston Cup Champion was 38. His racing team was eventually sold to Geoff Bodine.

Dale Jarrett won for the second time in three weeks with a victory at the Texas Motor Speedway in 2001. The win gave Jarrett a 75-point lead over Jeff Gordon in the championship race. Dale Earnhardt Jr. won his first of two pole starts of the season.

2

Jimmy Ayers was born in 1917. Racing out of Gardendale, AL, Ayers ran 19 career Grand National races with eight top-10 finishes.

Cotton Owens won at the Occoneechee Speedway in Hillsboro, NC, in 1961.

Walt Hansgen suffered severe injuries practicing for the 24 Hours at LeMans in 1966. He died five days later. Hansgen ran three Grand National events 1964–65.

Cale Yarborough won the 1967 Atlanta 500 at the Atlanta Motor Speedway. He was the Grand National's most popular driver that season.

Driver Speedy Thompson died of a heart attack in 1972, one day shy of his 46th birthday. Thompson was racing at the Metrolina Speedway in Charlotte, NC, at the time. He ran in 14 Grand National/Winston Cup season, finishing second in points in 1956.

Darrell Waltrip won the 1978 Southeastern 500 at Bristol for his 10th career win. Neil Bonnett won the pole, the 10th of his career.

Harry Gant won his only race of 1989 with a first-place finish in the TranSouth 500 at Darlington.

Jeff Gordon won his fifth career race in 1995 in the Food City 500 at Bristol. Mark Martin won his 25th career first-place qualifying position.

Dale Earnhardt Jr. drove his Chevrolet to the winner's circle in the 2000 Direct TV 500 at the Texas Motor Speedway for his first career Winston Cup win. Terry Labonte was the pole-sitter. Adam Petty started the only Winston Cup race of his brief career. He became the fourth generation of Pettys to run a Winston Cup race. He blew an engine and finished in 40th place. He died in a practice crash just over one month later in New Hampshire. He was the son of Kyle, grandson of

Richard and great-grandson of Lee Petty.

3

Speedy Thompson was born in Monroe, NC, in 1926. Thompson ran 198 career races with 20 wins, his first coming in Macon, GA, in 1953 in a 100-mile event on a dirt track. He was third in points in three straight seasons 1957–59.

Lloyd George "Shorty" Rollins was born in 1929. Rollins, who raced out of Corpus Christi, TX, started 43 races 1958–60 with a win in a 50-mile race at Busti, NY, in July 1958 and 26 other top 10s. He was the 1958 Grand National Rookie of the Year.

John Dineen was born in 1946. He made one Winston Cup start each in 1976 and 1977 at Riverside, CA. Dineen raced out of El Cajon, CA to a 13th-place finish in his finale, the 1977 NAPA 400.

Tim Flock won his first career NASCAR Grand National race in the second event of the 1950 series at Charlotte Speedway, a .75-mile dirt track. Flock drove his Lincoln to the checkered flag in the 150-mile event. He went on to capture the Grand National Championship in both 1952 and 1955.

Buck Baker won at North Wilkesboro in 1955, his tenth career Grand National checkered flag.

In 1960, John Rostek won the final of four sanctioned races held at the Arizona State Fairgrounds. It was the only Grand National victory of his career.

Rex White won his 15th career Grand National race at Winston-Salem, NC, in 1961. It was his third career win at the quarter-mile Bowman-Gray Stadium, and the first of four straight wins at the track.

David Pearson won the 1966 Hickory 250 at Hickory, NC, his 14th career Grand National win. It was his first of 15 wins that season, his first of three as Grand National Champion.

Bobby Isaac won from the pole for the third time in his career in 1969 at Columbia (SC) Speedway. It was his sixth career Grand National win.

David Pearson won his fifth consecutive pole start at the Darlington Raceway, but Darrell Waltrip cruised to his fourth Winston Cup series win in the 1977 Rebel 500.

4

Ervin "Blackie" Wangerin was born in 1935. He ran 27 career Winston Cup events between 1971 and 1984. Racing out of Bloomington, MN, he competed in a career-high ten races in 1978. His career highlight was a 20th-place finish driving a Mercury in the 1979 Daytona 500.

Dick Rathmann won for the second straight week in 1954 with a checkered-flag finish in the 100-mile event at North Wilkesboro, NC, in 1954. Rathmann, driving a Hudson an average speed of 68.545 mph, won for the 12th time in his career. Gober Sosebee won the pole for the third time in his career.

Chet Fillip was born in 1957. Racing out of San Angelo, TX, he started

24 Winston Cup events in the mid–1980s. Fillip started a career-best 17 events in 1986.

Jack Smith won at the Columbia Speedway in 1959, his eighth career victory. It was the third of six times in his career that he won a race from the pole.

Ned Jarrett won at the Augusta International Speedway in 1962, his only win at the half-mile dirt track in Augusta, GA, that hosted 12 sanctioned NASCAR races in the 1960s.

A.J. Foyt won the 1971 Atlanta 500 at the Atlanta Motor Speedway.

Cale Yarborough won the 1976 Gwyn Staley 400. It was the first time in seven years that Richard Petty failed to win the spring race at North Wilkesboro. Petty finished second.

Dale Earnhardt Sr. captured his seventh career win, his first ever at Darlington, SC, with a win in the 1982 CRC Chemicals Rebel 500. Buddy Baker won his 38th career pole.

Rusty Wallace won his second race of the 1993 Winston Cup season with a first-place finish from the pole in the Food City 500 at Bristol. Wallace won from the pole for the fourth time in his career.

5

Dick Passwater gained his only Grand National win in 1953 on the .75-mile dirt track in Charlotte, NC. Passwater won the 112.5-mile event in an Oldsmobile. Tim Flock, driving a Hudson, started from the pole for the 12th time in his career.

Bob Welborn won his second career Grand National race in 1958 at the Champion Speedway. It was the first of four top-level NASCAR events hosted by the Fayetteville, NC, track between November 1957 and November 1958. Lee Petty won at North Wilkesboro in 1959, the first of three straight Grand National wins over two seasons at the track. Petty won his second of three points championships that season.

Rex White won at the Columbia Speedway in 1960, his eighth Grand National victory. White was 1960s most popular Grand National driver and points champion. It was his first of six wins on the season. Doug Yates captured the pole for the first of two times in his 86-race Grand National career.

Fred Lorenzen won his third straight Atlanta 500 at the Atlanta Motor Speedway in 1964.

Mike Bliss was born in 1965 in Milwaukee, OR. Bliss, a 2000 NASCAR rookie, ran 31 Winston Cup events 1998–2003 with one top–10 finish. Bliss has also raced in the Busch, Craftsman Truck and IROC Series.

Donnie Allison's third career victory came in the 1970 Southeastern 500 at Bristol, TN. David Pearson captured his 53rd career pole.

Richard Petty won the 1981 Northwestern Bank 400 at North Wilkesboro, his second straight win in the annual spring race. It was the first career start in the Winston Cup career of Mark Martin, who ran 566 races 1981–2003 and remained active in 2004.

Dale Earnhardt Sr. won his fourth

race in six events in the 1987 season with a first-place finish in the First Union 400 at North Wilkesboro.

Alan Kulwicki won his second straight Bristol race in the 1992 Food City 500. Kulwicki, who started first, won from the pole for the first and only time in his career. It was his first of two wins that season, when he won his only Winston Cup Championship. It was his 19th career top start and fourth of five career checkered flag finishes.

Mark Martin won at the Texas Motor Speedway in the 1998 Texas 500. Jeremy Mayfield qualified first but finished 23rd.

Lee Petty, the patriarch of the Petty family and 1954 Grand National Champion, died in 2000 at the age of 86. Petty raced in the first sanctioned Strictly Stock event at Charlotte in 1949 and won 54 career events

6

Dean Layfield was born in 1919. Racing out of Wellsville, NY, he made one Grand National start in 1957 and seven in 1958. He finished a career-best fourth-place in his debut in September 1957 at the New York State Fairgrounds in Syracuse, NY.

Herb Thomas was born in 1923 in Olivia, NC. He ran 230 career races with 48 victories. Thomas won 12 races each in 1953 and 1954. He led the most Grand National laps and races in three consecutive seasons, 1952–54 and was the points champion in 1951 and 1953. His first career win came in 1950 in a 100-mile dirt-

track race at Martinsville, VA. He won 48 races in less than six years, October 1950 through June 1956.

Pennsylvania native Dick Linder was born in 1923. Linder ran 28 races in NASCAR's early years 1949–56. He captured five poles and three wins in 1950 while finishing 8th overall in points.

Ramo Stott was born in 1934. Racing out of Keokuk, IA, Stott made 35 career Grand National and Winston Cup starts. He captured the pole, in surprising fashion, for the 1976 Daytona 500. Stott had 17 top–10 finishes.

Junior Miller was born in 1951 in Winston-Salem, NC. Miller ran 27 Winston Cup races 1976–81. His best finish was 13th in the 1980 Holly Farms 400 at North Wilkesboro, NC.

Dick Rathmann claimed his first-ever Grand National win with a first-place finish in the fifth race of 1952, a 100-mile event on the .5-mile dirt track in Martinsville, VA. It was the fifth straight win for Hudson.

Ken Bouchard was born in 1955. He made 33 Winston Cup starts 1987–94 racing out of Fitchburg, MA. He was named the 1988 Winston Cup Rookie of the Year, when he started 24 events and managed one top–10 finish.

Richard Petty won his 51st career Grand National race in 1967 at Columbia, SC. Dick Hutcherson won the 17th pole position of his career.

Bobby Isaac won the 1969 Hickory 250 at Hickory, NC. Isaac was voted the Grand National circuit's most popular driver in 1969.

Richard Petty won his sixth straight Gwyn Staley 400 in 1975. He was named the Winston Cup's most popular driver for the fifth of eighth times in his career that season.

Dale Earnhardt Sr.'s 13th career win came in the 1985 Valleydale 500 at Bristol. Harry Gant won his ninth of 17 career poles.

Rusty Wallace won the Valleydale 500 at Bristol in 1986. It was the first NASCAR Winston Cup win for Wallace, the 1984 Rookie of the Year.

Jeff Burton won the 1997 Interstate Batteries 500 at the Texas Motor Speedway for his first career NASCAR victory. Dale Jarrett, who had won the previous two races, finished second. It was the first sanctioned NASCAR race at the new speedway in Fort Worth. Burton was the 1994 Winston Cup Rookie of the Year.

Dale Earnhardt Jr. won the 2003 Aaron's 499 at the Talladega Superspeedway for his first victory of the season. Jeremy Mayfield started on the pole.

7

Theodore C. "T.C." Hunt was born in 1926. He made 24 Grand National starts 1960–69, with two top–10 finishes in 1962. His final event was a 28th-place finish in the 1969 Talladega 500.

Richard "Dick" Whalen was born in 1935. He ran one career Winston Cup race. He drove out of San Jose, CA, to a 19th-place finish in the 1979 NAPA Riverside 400 at Riverside, CA.

Fireball Roberts won at North Wilkesboro in 1957.

Joe Weatherly won for the second straight Richmond race, capturing the 1963 Richmond 250 for his 23rd career win. Weatherly won the 1963 Grand National driving championship despite winning just three races. Rex White won his 35th career pole and finished third.

David Pearson's 15th career Grand National win came in 1966 at Columbia, SC. Tom Pistone captured his second of five career poles.

Walt Hansgen died at the age of 46 from injuries suffered in a practice crash at LeMans five days prior in 1966. Hansgen made three Grand National starts 1964–65 with two third-place finishes and an additional top 10.

Loy Allen Jr. was born in 1966. Allen raced out of Raleigh, NC, to start 48 races 1993–99, winning three poles (all in 1994) and posting one top–10 finish.

Richard Petty won his third straight race at Hickory in the 1968 Hickory 250. Petty was voted the circuit's most popular driver for the third time in 1968.

Jimmy Clark was killed in a crash at the 1968 German Grand Prix at Hockenheim, Germany, at the age of 32. Clark had made his Grand National debut in 1967, running one event.

David Pearson won his 78th career race with a victory in the 1974 Rebel 450 at Darlington, SC. Donnie Allison captured his 11th career pole. It was the only time the annual race was run at 450 miles.

Ricky Rudd won his first race of 1991 with a trip to victory lane in the TransSouth 500 at Darlington.

8

Junie Dunleavy Jr. was born in 1924. Dunleavy became involved in racing mostly as an owner and car builder. His only Winston Cup series win as an owner came in 1981 in the Mason-Dixon 500 when Jody Ridley won at Dover.

Wayne Niedecken was born in 1931. Racing out of Pensacola, FL, Niedecken started one race and earned a total of $25 as a Grand National driver for his 12th place finish at Weaverville, NC, in 1953.

Also in 1951, a second series event was held in Gardena, CA. Marshall Teague won that 100-mile race, averaging 61.047 mph in his Hudson. Andy Pierce took the first career pole for himself and automaker Buick. The manufacturer didn't win a race until over four years later. It was the first official NASCAR race in the state of California, held at the Carrell Speedway.

Tim Flock won his second career NASCAR race with a checkered-flag finish at Mobile, AL, in 1951. It was the first win of the season for Flock, who averaged 50.26 mph in his Oldsmobile in the 112.5-mile event on a .75-mile dirt track. It was the first sanctioned NASCAR event held in the state of Alabama, the first of two races at the Lakeview Speedway.

Butch Mock was born in 1952. Mock drove in three Winston Cup races in the late 1970s and went on to field teams as an owner. Neil Bonnett later won four races driving for Butch Mock Motorsports.

Tim became the third Flock brother to capture a win at North Wilkesboro with his first victory at the North Carolina track in 1956.

Robert Pressley was born in 1959 in Washington, D.C. Pressley began his NASCAR career in 1994 with three starts, quickly progressing to 31 and 30 the following two years. He ran 205 events through 2002 with 11 top–10 finishes.

Bobby Isaac won the 1969 Greenville 200 at Greenville-Pickens Speedway (SC). David Pearson won his 42nd career pole and finished third in the race. It was the first time in 25 races that the event was given a name. The Greenville 200 was run twice in 1969 and once each in 1970 and 1971. It was the third consecutive win for Isaac.

Richard Petty's 124th career victory came in the 1971 Sandlapper 200 at Columbia Speedway in South Carolina. James Hylton qualified first for the fourth and final time in his top-level NASCAR career, but finished fourth.

Richard Petty won at North Wilkesboro Speedway in the 1973 Gwyn Staley 400. It was his 10th win at the North Carolina raceway and his fourth straight victory in the spring race at the track.

Darrell Waltrip's 17th career win came in 1979 at Darlington in the CRC Chemicals 500. Donnie Allison won his 17th pole. It was the first time a race at the South Carolina speedway featured a corporate sponsor.

Tim Richmond won the 1984 Northwestern Bank 400 at North Wilkesboro.

Davey Allison won his first of two races in 1990 with a first-place finish in the Valleydale Meats 500 at Bristol. Ernie Irvan captured his first career pole.

Dale Jarrett won his second consecutive race, his third victory in four weeks, in 2001 at Martinsville in the Virginia 500. Jarrett extended his points lead over Jeff Gordon, who started first for the third time on the season.

2003 Winston Cup champion Matt Kenseth won his second race of 2002 with a victory in the Samsung/Radio Shack 500 at the Texas Motor Speedway. Bill Elliott qualified first for the second time in four weeks.

9

Clarence "Hooker" Hood was born in 1926. An early NASCAR driver, Hood made five Grand National starts in the mid–1950s, earning $250, racing out of Memphis, TN.

Richard Brown was born in 1940. He started 50 Winston Cup races in the 1970s and finished in the top 10 three times. He raced out of Claremont, NC.

Amos Johnson was born in 1941. Racing out of Raleigh, NC, he finished 13th in his only Grand National race, the 1969 Talladega 500.

Fred Lorenzen's first career win came in 1961 at Martinsville, VA, in the Virginia 500. He would win 25 more events in his career. Rex White won the pole and finished second in the race.

David Pearson began a streak of three consecutive wins at the Greenville-Pickens Speedway (SC) with a 1966 win, his 16th career Grand National win. Pearson also won the June race that year and the March race in 1967 at the half-mile paved track. Tiny Lund qualified on the pole for the sixth and final time in his Grand National career.

In the final dirt-track race at the Hickory Speedway, which was paved later in 1967, Richard Petty won the 1967 Buddy Shuman Memorial. Petty also won the first paved race at the track in September.

Bobby Allison won his second straight race in the 1972 Southeastern 500 at the Bristol International Speedway. It was the 11th of 20 times in his career he started and finished first. It was his 31st career win and 27th pole.

Benny Parsons achieved Winston Cup win # 11 of his career with a victory at Darlington in 1978's Rebel 500. Bobby Allison won his 50th career pole.

Rusty Wallace continued his trend of winning every other week with his third win in six races in 1989. Wallace won the Valleydale Meats 500 at Bristol International Speedway. He was the 1989 Winston Cup Champion.

George Mantooth died in 1995 at the age of 69. Mantooth started the first official Strictly Stock race and finished 31st in his final event in 1956 at the Wilson Speedway (NC).

Dale Earnhardt Sr. won the 1995 First Union 400 at North Wilkesboro.

Mark Martin won the 2000 Goody's Body Pain 500 at the Martinsville

Speedway. Rusty Wallace started from the pole.

10

Donald Keith Ulrich was born in 1944. Ulrich raced out of Woodbury, NJ, to run 273 races between 1971 and 1992 with no wins and 16 top–10 finishes. His career-best was a fourth-place finish in the 1981 Mason-Dixon 500 at Dover, DE. He finished 13th in the 1979 Daytona 500.

Speedy Thompson's 15th career win came in 1958 at the Columbia Speedway (SC). Possum Jones captured the only pole start of his career.

Richard Petty's second career victory came in the 1960 Virginia 500. Glen Wood won his second straight pole at the track, but finished third.

Bobby Isaac became the only driver to win the Greenville 200, when he captured the race for the fourth straight time in 1971, the final running of the event, at Greenville-Pickens Speedway (SC). David Pearson won his 56th career pole but finished second in the race.

Kasey Kahne was born in Enumclaw, WA, in 1980. Kahne burst onto the Nextel Cup circuit in 2004, winning two pole starts in the first five races and finishing second in two of the first three races of the season.

Harry Gant's third career Winston Cup win came in the 1983 TranSouth 500 at Darlington, SC. Tim Richmond started first for the second time in his career.

Bill Elliott won his first race of 1988 with a victory in the Valleydale Meats 500 at Bristol. Rick Wilson won the only pole qualifying start of his career. Elliott won his only Winston Cup Championship that year.

Dale Earnhardt Sr. captured his 61st career victory at Bristol International Speedway with a win in the 1994 Food City 500. Chuck Brown won his only career pole start.

11

Al Keller was born in 1920. He started 29 races 1949–56. He had one pole and two wins in 1954, when he started 13 races and finished in the top 10 seven other times.

Marvin Panch won the 1964 Grand National race at the Skyline Speedway in Weaverville, NC, for his 11th career victory.

Marvin Panch won the 1965 Atlanta 500 at the Atlanta Motor Speedway.

David Pearson won in 1966 at Bowman-Gray Stadium. It was his 17th career Grand National victory and first at the Winston-Salem, NC, quarter-mile track.

David Pearson notched career victory #91 at the Darlington Raceway in the 1976 Rebel 500. Pearson won from the pole for the 31st time in his career, the third time he did it at Darlington.

Adam Petty made his professional debut as a driver at the Peach State Speedway in Jefferson, GA in 1998. It marked the first time an American family has had four generations of professional athletes.

Rusty Wallace won from the pole to capture the 1999 Food City 500 at Bristol Motor Speedway in Tennessee.

12

Curtis Morton "Pops" Turner was born in 1924. Turner was an early NASCAR star with 17 wins in 184 lifetime races between 1949 and 1968. He was the first president of the Charlotte Motor Speedway. He raced out of Roanoke, VA, to record his first win in NASCAR's debut campaign, driving to victory at Langhorne, PA, in September 1949. He was chosen as the most popular driver the first season the honor was awarded, 1956.

Howard Wayne Smith was born in 1939. Racing out of Advance, NC, Smith started 122 career top-level NASCAR events with nine top-10 finishes.

Buck Baker won his first Grand National race with a win at Columbia, SC, in a 100-mile race on the .5-mile dirt track in 1952. Baker notched the sixth straight victory to open the NASCAR season for automaker Hudson, averaging 53.460 mph. It was the second straight, and third career, pole position for Baker. He won 45 more NASCAR races in his career, competing until 1976.

Billy Myers suffered a heart attack and died in 1958 while racing at Winston-Salem, NC. Myers, who finished sixth in points in 1956, claimed two wins and 32 other top–10 finishes in 84 career starts 1951–58.

Speedy Thompson became the second consecutive driver to start first and finish first at the Piedmont Interstate Fairgrounds in Spartanburg, SC, in 1958. It was the fifth of seven times in his career he won from the pole, his 16th career victory and 13th top start.

David Pearson won the inaugural Joe Weatherly Memorial 150 at the Occoneechee Speedway in Hillsboro, NC, in 1964. Weatherly was a two-time winner at the one-mile dirt track in the early 1960s.

Pete Hamilton won the inaugural Alabama 500 at Talladega in 1970. It was his second career win and second of the season. Hamilton also won the 1970 Daytona 500.

Darrell Waltrip won the 1981 CRC Chemicals Rebel 500 at Darlington, SC. It was his 31st Winston Cup victory. Bill Elliott captured his first-ever pole position start.

Dale Earnhardt Sr. won his third consecutive race with a victory in the Valleydale Meats 500 in 1987 at Bristol.

Davey Allison won the 1992 First Union 400 at North Wilkesboro.

13

Bill Gazaway was born in 1905. Racing out of Atlanta, GA, he ran one career Winston Cup race, earning $200 for a lone 1960 lap at Atlanta before rear end difficulties ended his race. It was the 44th race of 1960, and Gazaway started 44th out of 45 cars and finished 45th driving a #45 Oldsmobile.

Dan Gurney was born in 1931. In 16 career starts from 1962 to 1980, Gurney won five races and qualified on the pole three times. Gurney captured all of his wins and poles at Riverside, CA (1963–66, 1968). He raced out of Costa Mesa, CA.

Larry Thomas was born in 1936. He ran 126 Grand National races 1961–64 with 56 top-10 finishes and an 8th place finish in the overall standings in 1964. His promising career was cut short by a tragic highway crash in January 1965.

Curtis Turner won at Lakewood Speedway in Atlanta, GA, in 1958. Turner won his second of three events that season and his 13th of 17 victories on his career.

Bill Meacham was born in 1960 in Pineville, NC. He managed one Winston Cup start in 1990 and two the following year. He finished 34th in his debut in the 1990 Pontiac Excitement 400 at Richmond, VA.

Ned Jarrett's 1962 win in the Arclite 200 at Columbia, SC, was his ninth career Grand National victory. The eventual points champion that season, Joe Weatherly, captured his third pole of the season and 11th of his career.

Buck Baker captured career win #44 at Greenville, SC, in 1963, his only win of the season. Jimmy Pardue captured his first of three career pole position starts.

Richard Petty garnered career victory #78 at Greenville, SC, in 1968.

David Pearson qualified first for the 28th time in his career.

David Pearson won the 1969 Richmond 500. It was Pearson's 50th career Grand National victory and the 14th time he both qualified and finished first. Pearson was the 1969 Grand National Champion.

Bobby Allison won his 45th career NASCAR race in 1975 at the Darlington Raceway in the Rebel 500. Trailing by as much as two laps late in the race, Allison was aided by several competitors' crashes to come from behind for his second win of the season. Darrell Waltrip finished second.

David Pearson won at Darlington for the second straight event. It was Pearson's tenth career win at the South Carolina track and the 105th and final victory of his career as a top-level NASCAR driver. Benny Parsons qualified first for the CRC Chemicals Rebel 500.

Dale Earnhardt Sr. won his first of five races in 1986 with a win in the Transouth 500 at Darlington. Earnhardt won his second of seven Winston Cup Championships that season.

Jeff Gordon won the 1997 Food City 500 at Bristol Speedway, edging pole sitter Rusty Wallace on the last lap. Gordon won his second points championship in 1997.

Jeff Gordon became the first driver of 2003 to win from the pole in NASCAR's regular season with a victory at Martinsville in the Advance Auto Parts 500.

14

Hully Bunn was born in 1920. He started his only career Grand National race in 1951. Bunn raced out of Bristol, CT, to an 11th-place finish in August at the Altamont-Schenectady Fairgrounds (NY) in his only Grand National start.

William "Whitey" Norman was born in 1926. He started 29 career races with eight top–10 finishes 1956–59 including a tenth-place in his debut in the Wilkes (NC) County 160.

Richard "Dick" Brooks was born in 1942. Brooks captured the 1973 Talladega 500 for his only Winston Cup win in 358 top-level NASCAR starts between 1969 and 1985. Brooks finished sixth in points in 1977 and eighth in 1978. He raced out of Porterville, CA, and finished in the top 10 in 149 additional events. He was the 1969 Grand National Rookie of the Year.

Fireball Roberts won at the Langhorne Speedway in Pennsylvania in 1957 for his 9th career victory.

Richard Petty began a string of four straight wins at South Boston, VA, with a victory in the 1963 South Boston 400. Ned Jarrett qualified first and finished third in the 100-mile event on the paved ¼-mile track.

Tony Raines was born in 1964 in LaPorte, IN. Raines started 42 races 2002–03, with a career-best 6th-place finish in the Pop-Secret Microwave Popcorn 400 at Rockingham in November 2003.

For the second straight Spartanburg, SC, race, Ned Jarrett captured the checkered flag in a 1964 event. It was the first of 14 wins for Jarrett that season. Dick Hutcherson won his second career top start.

Rusty Wallace won his first of two races on the 1991 Winston Cup circuit with a victory in the Valleydale Meats 500 at Bristol. It was his 19th career win and 10th career pole, the third time in his career he started and finished first.

Terry Labonte won his first of two races of the 1996 season with a first-place finish in the First Union 400 at North Wilkesboro. Labonte won the Winston Cup Championship that season, 12 years after his first championship in 1984.

Bobby Labonte's only win of 2002 came at Martinsville Speedway in the Advance Auto Parts 500. Jeff Gordon qualified first for the second time in three weeks.

15

Ray Erickson was born in 1918. A competitor in the early NASCAR years, Erickson finished seventh in points in the inaugural Strictly Stock season. Erickson started 12 events 1949–53 with one second place and one third place finish in four events his rookie season. He raced out of Chicago, IL, and debuted at Hamburg, NY, in September 1949 with a second-place finish.

Raymond Williams was born in 1939. He ran 93 Grand National and Winston Cup events 1970–78. He raced out of Chapel Hill, NC, to record eight top–10 finishes.

Hugh Pearson was born in 1947. Pearson ran nine Winston Cup races in the 1970s with one top 10 in his final career event in 1977.

Donald Waterman was born in 1950. He ran nine Winston Cup races in the early 1980s with one top–10 finish in 1981. He led two career events, one each in 1981 and 1982.

Fonty Flock became the first driver of 1951 to claim the pole and win the race with a first-place finish in the 95-mile contest on a one-mile dirt track in Hillsboro, NC. It was the second career win for Flock but his fourth pole in his last six chances.

Richard Petty won the Gwyn Staley 400 at North Wilkesboro in 1962, the first of three straight Grand National wins over two seasons at the track. Petty was named the most popular Grand National driver for the first of eight times that season.

Jimmy Pardue won at Bowman-Gray Stadium in Winston-Salem, NC, in 1963 for his 17th career Grand National win. Richard Petty started on the pole, and Fred Harb finished second.

Richard Petty won his 125th career event in 1971 in the final race at the Smoky Mountain Raceway in Maryville, TN. The track hosted 12 top-level NASCAR events 1965–71. Friday Hassler qualified first for the first of two career poles, both in 1971, and finished third.

David Pearson took the checkered flag at the 1973 Rebel 500 at Darling-ton, SC. Benny Parsons finished second. It was Pearson's 69th career win.

Darrell Waltrip's 59th career win came in the 1984 TranSouth 500 at Darlington. Benny Parsons qualified on the pole for the 18th time in his career.

Bill Elliott won from the pole for the third time in his career as he gained a win in the 1985 TranSouth 500 at Darlington, SC.

Gene White died in 1986 at the age of 54. Racing out of Marietta, GA, White ran 23 Grand National races 1956–61 with four top–10 finishes. His career-best was fifth place in September 1958 at the Fairgrounds Raceway in Birmingham, AL.

Buck Baker died at the age of 83 in 2002. Born Elzie Wylie Baker, Buck ran 636 career Grand National and Winston Cup races with 46 career wins and 44 poles. He was the Grand National Champion in 1956 and 1957.

16

Bob Flock was born in Georgia in 1918. The oldest of three racing brothers, and one sister, Bob won four races in seven years and competed with his two brothers in the first official NASCAR race in 1949 at Charlotte.

Tommy Moon was born in 1925. He started ten Grand National races in the 1950s with five top–10 finishes. He won the pole for the June race in Augusta, GA in 1952.

Curtis Turner became the first driver to win a race in each of the first two official NASCAR seasons with a victory on the one-mile dirt track at Langhorne, PA, in 1950. Turner averaged 69.399 mph in the 150-mile event, the third of the season.

Joe Weatherly won at the Hickory Speedway in 1960, his second career win and first of four in 1960.

Rex White won his second consecutive North Wilkesboro race with a 1961 victory. White won the 1960 Grand National Championship.

Ned Jarrett captured the 1964 Columbia 200 in South Carolina, his 25th career Grand National win. David Pearson won the pole for the seventh time in his career.

Darel Dieringer won the 1967 Gwyn Staley 400 at North Wilkesboro. It was the final of seven career Grand National wins for Dieringer, Grand National's most popular driver in 1966.

David Pearson won from the pole in the 1972 Rebel 400 at Darlington. It was the 19th time in his career that Pearson won a race after qualifying first.

Darrell Waltrip won the 17th and final Gwyn Staley 400 in 1978, an annual event replaced by bank sponsorship on the circuit in 1978.

Dale Earnhardt Sr. won his first race of 1989 with a first-place finish in the First Union 400 at North Wilkesboro.

Jeff Gordon drove his #24 Dupont Chevrolet to victory in the 2000 Die Hard 500 at Talladega. Jeremy Mayfield was the pole-sitter.

17

Jack Reynolds, who raced out of Hawthorne, NJ, was born in 1928. Reynolds ran 14 Grand National races 1950–52 with eight top–10 finishes.

Pete Torres was born in 1944. He started one Winston Cup race in 1971 and two in 1975, all at Riverside, CA. He raced out of Alhambra, CA, to finish 16th in the 1975 Tuborg 400, his final top-level NASCAR event.

Mike Chase was born in 1952. He started 13 Winston Cup events 1990–94, racing out of Bakersfield, CA, to a career-best 24th-place finish in the 1990 Champion Spark Plug 400.

In the first NASCAR race ever held at the Montgomery Motor Speedway in Alabama, eventual Grand National Champion Tim Flock took the win and $1000 first-prize in 1955. The track hosted six Grand National events between 1955 and 1969.

Tony Glover was born in 1957. Glover began as a crew chief in 1983 and gained success in Ernie Irvan's pits in the early 1990s, highlighted by a win in the 1991 Daytona 500.

In the final sanctioned Grand National race at Wilson, NC, in 1960, Joe Weatherly drove his #12 Ford to victory. It was the third of 25 top-level NASCAR wins for Weatherly. The Wilson Fairgrounds, also known as the Wilson County and Legion Speedway, hosted 12 races between 1951 and 1960. It was the second consecutive day that Weatherly captured the checkered flag.

Dick Hutcherson's first of 14 career Grand National wins came in

Greenville, SC, in 1965. Hutcherson started 52 events that year, winning nine and finishing second in Grand National championship points to Ned Jarrett. Bud Moore captured the only pole position of his career.

Jim Paschal won the 1966 Gwyn Staley 400 at North Wilkesboro, his 19th career victory.

Cale Yarborough continued his dominance at Bristol with his third straight win at the Tennessee track, a victory in the 1977 Southeastern 500. Yarborough started and won from the pole for the ninth time in his career.

Johnny Beauchamp died in 1981 at the age of 58. Beauchamp started 23 races between 1953 and 1961 with his final of two Grand National victories in August 1960 at the Nashville Speedway.

Darrell Waltrip won his second straight Northwestern Bank 400 in 1983.

Terry Labonte won his first race of 1988 with a first-place finish in the First Union 400 at North Wilkesboro.

Ray Kelly, who started one Winston Cup race, died at the age of 45 in 1992. Kelly finished 36th in the 1986 Budweiser 400 at Riverside, CA.

Terry Labonte won the 1994 First Union 400 at North Wilkesboro.

Tommy Ingram died in 1995. He had started two races in 1967, his only experience at the Grand National level, finishing 35th in his debut in the Virginia 500 at Martinsville, VA.

H.B. Bailey, who raced out of Houston, TX, 1962–93, died in 2003 at the age of 66. Bailey ran 85 career Grand National and Winston Cup races with five top–10 finishes. He finished sixth in the 1965 Southern 500.

18

Hap Jones was born in 1927. Racing out of Jackson Center, PA, he made one start in 1951 and one in 1954, with a sixth-place finish in his first race at Pine Grove Speedway in Shippenville, PA.

Geoffrey Bodine was born in Chemung, NY, in 1949. The oldest of three racing Bodine brothers, Geoff was the 1982 Winston Cup Rookie of the Year. In 1986 he won the Daytona 500. After Alan Kulwicki's death in 1993, Bodine purchased and operated the existing racing team. Bodine helped design and produce bobsleds for the U.S. Olympic Team. He was the 1982 Winston Cup Rookie of the Year.

Herb Thomas won his fourth race of the 1954 season, the fifth straight for automaker Hudson, with a win in the 100-mile dirt track event at Hillsboro, NC, in 1954. Thomas, in his Hudson Hornet, averaged 77.386 mph on the one-mile track. It was his 32nd career win. Buck Baker won his eighth career pole.

Curtis Turner won in 1958 at the Southern States Fairgrounds in Charlotte, NC. He won 17 races 1949–68 with a ninth-place finish in the first sanctioned race and a first-place finish in the fourth Strictly Stock event at Langhorne, PA, in 1949.

Glen Wood won his first career Grand National race in 1960 at Bowman-Gray Stadium, a ¼-mile paved oval in Winston-Salem, NC. Wood went on to win the next two events held at the track, capturing all three scheduled 1960 races. He won again in 1963 to account for all four of his career wins at the same track. Between Wood and Rex White, they accounted for nine consecutive victories there 1959–62. Wood's final Grand National win came in 1963. He was the most popular Grand National driver in 1958.

Junior Johnson won the 1965 Gwyn Staley 400 at North Wilkesboro, his 41st career checkered flag.

Bobby Isaac's second career win came at the Columbia Speedway in 1968. Richard Petty captured the pole for the 70th time in his career.

Richard Petty won the 1970 Gwyn Staley 400 at North Wilkesboro.

Richard Petty won his second straight Gwyn Staley 400 in 1971. It was the seventh win of the season for Petty, who won 21 races in 1971 on his way to his third Winston Cup Championship.

Darrell Waltrip won the 1982 Northwestern Bank 400 at North Wilkesboro. Waltrip won his second of three Winston Cup Championships that season.

Rusty Wallace won his second straight race, and third event of the 1993 Winston Cup season, taking the checkered flag in the First Union 400 at North Wilkesboro.

Pioneer Bill Rexford died in 1994 at the age of 67. Rexford became Winston Cup's youngest champion in 1950, when he ran 17 races with 11 top–10s He ran three races in NASCAR's inaugural season and a total of 36 career races 1949–53 with his only win at Canton, OH, in May 1950. He raced frequently in Indy cars.

John Andretti won his first career Winston Cup race in the 1999 Goody's Body Pain 500 at Martinsville, VA. Andretti started 21st while Tony Steward won the pole but finished a disappointing 20th.

19

Junie Gough was born in 1925. He earned $50 as a Grand National driver with one 1955 start, a 19th-place finish at Lincoln Speedway (PA). Gough raced out of Rising Sun, MD.

Jack Roush was born in 1942 in Kentucky. He first fielded a Winston Cup team in 1988, sponsoring Mark Martin. His team finished second in points in both the 1990 and 1994 seasons.

Robert Yates was born in 1943. Yates has owned and operated several teams and is regarded as a mechanical innovator. He started in NASCAR as an engine builder in 1968 and went on to successful leadership positions.

John Borneman Jr. was born in 1949. He started eight Winston Cup races 1977–81, all at Riverside or Ontario, CA. He raced out of El Cajon, CA, to a 12th-place finish in his finale, the 1981 Winston Western 500 at Riverside.

Lee Petty, in a Dodge, gained his

second win of 1953 and the eighth of his career with a first-place finish in the 100-mile race on the half-mile dirt track in Richmond, VA. Buck Baker took the pole. Petty finished second overall in Grand National points that season to Herb Thomas. It was the first appearance of Grand National cars at the Richmond International Raceway. The track, initially a dirt oval, was paved in 1968 and re-measured at .542 miles in 1971. It was reconfigured to a .75 mile "D" shape in 1988. With a one-year hiatus in 1954, NASCAR ran one race per year 1955–58 and least twice per year since 1959.

Fireball Roberts won in 1957 at the Southern States Fairgrounds in Charlotte, NC.

Robert Tartaglia was born in 1959. He ran one Winston Cup race at Riverside in 1979 and one in 1981. He raced out of Reedley, CA, to a 24th place finish in his debut in the 1979 NAPA Riverside 400.

Dick Linder died in an Indy Car race at Trenton, NJ, in 1959. He was 36. Linder ran 28 Strictly Stock and Grand National events 1949–56 will all five career poles and three wins during the 1950 season.

Alfred Unser Jr., known as "Little Al," ran one career Winston Cup race in 1993. Racing out of Albuquerque, NM, Unser was known mostly for his Indy Car racing.

Ned Jarrett won from the pole for the second of eleven times in his career, cruising to both his tenth win and tenth top start with a 1962 checkered flag at the Greenville-Pickens Speedway, a half-mile paved track in Greenville, SC.

Fred Lorenzen won the 1964 Gwyn Staley 400 at North Wilkesboro.

Jack Roush was seriously injured in a plane crash on his 60th birthday in 2002.

20

Bobby Abel was born in 1930. He raced out of Wrightsville, PA, to one Grand National start in 1957 at Langhorne, a 46th place finish due to engine problems.

Richard "Reds" Kagle was born in 1932. He made 25 Grand National starts 1954–61 with nine top-10 finishes. His career best was fourth place in the 1959 Capital City 200 at Richmond, VA.

John Anderson was born in 1944. Racing out of Massillon, OH, Anderson started 32 Winston Cup races 1979–83 with three career top-10 finishes, his best a fifth-place in the 1979 Champion Spark Plug 400 at Michigan.

Phil Finney was born in 1950 and raced out of Merritt Island, FL. He started seven Winston Cup races 1971–80, his best a 16th-place finish in the 1972 Richmond 500.

Bill Blair won his second career Grand National race in the seventh event of 1952 at Atlanta, GA. Blair drove his Oldsmobile to victory in the 100-mile race on a one-mile dirt track at an average speed of 66.877 mph. It was the first race won by a manufacturer other than Hudson on the NASCAR season, although Tim Flock, driving a Hudson, won his ninth career pole.

Bob Welborn won his second straight Martinsville race, the third Grand National win of his career, in the 1958 Virginia 500. Buck Baker won his 35th career pole.

Cotton Owens won for the seventh time on the Grand National circuit in 1961 at Columbia Speedway. It was the eighth career pole, third of 1961 for Ned Jarrett.

Bobby Allison's 14th career victory came in 1969 at the North Wilkesboro Speedway in the annual Gwyn Staley 400.

Richard Petty won the 1980 Northwestern Bank 400 at North Wilkesboro.

Dale Earnhardt Sr. won his second consecutive race of the 1986 season with a win at North Wilkesboro in the First Union 400.

At the Martinsville Speedway in 1997, Jeff Gordon won his second straight race with a victory in the Goody's 500, holding the lead most of the race.

Bobby Hamilton won from the pole in the #4 Kodak Ford for his third career win and fifth career pole in the 1998 Goody's Headache Powder 500 at Martinsville, VA.

21

John McVitty died at the age of 40 qualifying for a race at Langhorne, PA, in 1956. McVitty, who raced out of Mamaroneck, NY, made his debut with an eighth-place finish at Fonda Speedway (NY) in 1955 and managed two other top–10 finishes in ten more races 1955–56.

In 1962 at the Rambi Race Track in Myrtle Beach, SC, Jack Smith captured his 19th career win. Ned Jarrett won his 11th career pole.

Richard Petty won the 1963 Virginia 500 for his 18th career Grand National victory. Rex White started on the pole position for the 36th and final time in his career.

David Pearson won the 1968 Gwyn Staley 400 at North Wilkesboro. It was his third of 16 wins in 1968, his second of three seasons as Grand National Champion.

Richard Petty won his fifth straight Gwyn Staley 400 in 1974. Petty began a string of five years when he was named the most popular Winston Cup driver. He won his fifth points championship and won ten races in 1974.

Neil Bonnett won the seventh and final Northwestern Bank 400 at North Wilkesboro in 1985. The race was replaced in 1986 by the First Union 400.

Darrell Waltrip won his first of two races of the 1991 Winston Cup series with a victory in the First Union 400 at North Wilkesboro.

Rusty Wallace won his first race of 1996, taking the checkered flag in the Goody's Headache Powder 500 at Martinsville for his 42nd career victory. Ricky Craven qualified on the pole for the first time in his career.

Dale Earnhardt Jr. won his first of two races of the 2002 Winston Cup season with a checkered flag finish in the Aaron's 499 at Talladega. Jimmie Johnson, who won the pole at Daytona, qualified first for the second of five times of the season.

22

Howard W. "Tommy" Thompson was born in 1922. He made 22 Grand National starts 1950–59. Racing out of Louisville, KY, Thompson was a surprise winner in a 250-mile event, driving his Chrysler to victory in 1951 at Detroit, MI.

James Ronald "Bunkie" Blackburn was born in 1936. He started 71 Grand National races 1960–70. He raced out of Fayetteville, NC, to a fourth-place finish in the 1966 Rebel 400 at Darlington, SC.

Robert Lee "Bobby" Watson was born in 1936. Racing out of Prestonburg, KY, he ran one Grand National race, running 11 laps and finishing 28th in the 1970 Southeastern 500 at Bristol, TN.

George Behlman, born in 1944, started one Winston Cup race each in 1973 and 1974 at Riverside, CA. Racing out of Grove, CA, Behlman finished 16th in his debut, the Tuborg 400.

Marshall Teague won his third race of 1951, his second victory in his last two starts, with a first-place finish in the 150-mile event in Phoenix, AZ. Hudson took over the season manufacturer's lead with three wins as Teague averaged 60.153 mph on the one-mile dirt track. Fonty Flock won his second straight pole. It was the first sanctioned NASCAR race in the state of Arizona.

Steve Perry was born in 1955 in Dallas, TX. He made one NASCAR start in 1991, driving 244 career miles on the circuit.

For the fourth straight race at the Langhorne Speedway, the driver that started on the pole won the race. In this 1956 race, Buck Baker captured his 15th career win on the one-mile dirt track in Pennsylvania, his 18th top start.

Junior Johnson won for the second consecutive time at the Hickory Speedway in 1961.

Richard Petty won the 1962 Virginia 500 for his seventh career victory. Fred Lorenzen won his second straight pole at the track but finished fourth in the race. Richard's dad, Lee, finished fifth.

Richard Petty's 187th career win came in 1979 in the Virginia 500 at Martinsville. Petty went on to the 1979 Winston Cup championship, breaking Cale Yarborough's three-year reign at the top of NASCAR. Darrell Waltrip captured his 12th career pole and finished third. On the season, Waltrip was the runner-up to Petty in the championship race.

Brett Bodine won his only Winston Cup race in 1990 at the First Union 400 at North Wilkesboro.

Bobby Hamilton edged Tony Stewart in 2001 to take the checkered flag at the Talladega 500. It was his only win of the Winston Cup season. Stacey Compton won his first ever pole position start.

23

Johnny Grubb was born in 1914. Racing out of Beckley, WV, he started four Grand National races in 1950 with one top–10 finish. He started one additional race the following season.

John "Jack" Harden was born in 1934. Racing out of Huntsville, AL, he started ten Grand National races in 1967 for his only top-level NASCAR experience.

Skip Manning was born in Louisiana in 1945. He started 79 Winston Cup races 1975–79 and was 14th overall in points in 1977 when he recorded eight of his 16 career top 10s. He was the 1976 Winston Cup Rookie of the Year.

Ned Jarrett's fourth career win came in 1960 at the Greenville-Pickens Speedway in South Carolina. Curtis Turner won his 13th career pole.

For the second time in his career, Richard Petty both qualified first and finished first in a 1961 race at Richmond. It was the fourth career win for Petty and his third pole. Petty cracked the top 10 in Grand National points for the second straight season in 1961.

Rex White's 24th career Grand National win in 1962 was his fourth straight at Bowman-Gray Stadium in Winston-Salem, NC.

Chad Little was born in 1963 in Spokane, WA. Little began his Winston Cup career in 1986. Little ran 217 events 1986–2002 with 16 top–10 finishes. He was 15th in points in 1998, a career best. He holds a law degree from Gonzaga University.

Richard Petty won his 53rd career Grand National event at Martinsville in the 1966 Virginia 500. Darel Dieringer won his eighth career pole. Petty went on to win 27 races and the Grand National championship that season.

P.J. Jones was born in 1969. Jones made six Winston Cup starts in 1993 with one top–10. He also made two starts the following season.

Richard Petty continued to dominate the spring race at North Wilkesboro with his third straight win in the Gwyn Staley 400 in 1972. Petty won eight 1972 races en route to his fourth Winston Cup Championship.

Darrell Waltrip's 12th Winston Cup victory came in the 1978 Virginia 500 at Martinsville. Lennie Pond earned his first career top qualifying position.

Darrell Waltrip won his third race of 1989 at Martinsville in the Pannill Sweatshirts 500, his 76th career checkered flag. Waltrip started his season with a win in the Daytona 500. Geoff Bodine won his 24th pole position.

Rusty Wallace's third straight win at Martinsville, VA came in the 1995 Hanes 500. It was his 40th career win. Bobby Labonte earned his second career pole start.

24

Jack Etheridge was born in 1916. A competitor in NASCAR's inaugural season, he finished in the top 10 in his only event. He also started one Grand National race each in 1967 and 1969. He raced out of Jacksonville, FL.

James Cushman was born in 1929. He started seven Grand National races 1956–63, racing out of Lansing, MI. His career-best was a ninth-place finish in March 1962 at Asheville-Weaverville (NC) Speedway.

Johnny Dodson was born in 1931 in King, NC. He started 15 Grand National races in the mid–1950s. He debuted in the 1956 Raleigh 250 with a 29th-place finish and had his best race later that year, a seventh-place in October at Shelby, NC.

Johnny Benson Sr. was born in 1937 and started one career Winston Cup event, in 1973. His son, Johnny Benson Jr., was the 1996 Winston Cup Rookie of the Year.

Johnny Barnes was born in 1942. He started 13 races in the 1970s, racing out of Port Charlotte, FL. His best finish was a 15th-place in the 1973 National 500 at Charlotte Motor Speedway.

Carl Adams was born in 1942. Adams raced out of National City, CA, and made 28 Winston Cup starts 1971–75 with five top–10 finishes. His best race was a 6th place finish in the 1975 Purolator 500 at Pocono.

Ron Hutcherson, born in 1943, started ten Winston Cup races 1972–79 with two top–10 finishes. He raced out of Keokuk, IA, and is the son of Dick Hutcherson, who won 14 career Grand National races.

Warren Tope, born in 1947, ran two Winston Cup races in 1975. Tope raced out of Troy, MI, and died practicing for a street race during his rookie season at NASCAR's highest level.

Tim Flock won his 20th career Grand National win in 1955 at Langhorne, PA. It was the 19th time in his career that he started from the pole. Flock won his second and final Grand National Championship that season.

Lee Petty won his 50th career race, his second straight win at the Skyline Speedway in Weaverville, NC, with a Grand National win in 1960 over Joe Lee Johnson.

Jim Paschal won from the pole at Martinsville in the 1966 Virginia 500. It was the fourth and final time of his career that he both qualified and finished first.

Hermie Sadler was born in 1969 in Emporia, VA. He started 24 races at the Winston Cup level 1996–2003. Sadler also raced extensively in the Busch Series and briefly drove Craftsman Trucks.

Cale Yarborough's 45th career win came in the 1977 Virginia 500 at Martinsville. Neil Bonnett earned his fourth career pole start.

Rolf-Johann Stommelen died in 1983 at Riverside, CA. Stommelen raced out of Siegen, Germany, and made one Winston Cup start in 1971.

At the 1983 Virginia National Bank 500, Darrell Waltrip won his 53rd career Winston Cup race. Ricky Rudd, who won his ninth career pole, finished fifth. After winning the Winston Cup championship 1981–82, Waltrip finished second in 1983.

Dale Earnhardt Sr. won his second race of the Winston Cup season with a victory in the 1988 Pannill Sweatshirts 500 at Martinsville. Ricky Rudd captured his 15th career pole. After consecutive Winston Cup championships, Earnhardt won just three races in 1988 and finished third overall behind circuit winner Bill Elliott.

Rusty Wallace's 1994 win in the Hanes 500 at Martinsville was the 33rd of his career. Wallace finished third to Dale Earnhardt Sr. in Winston Cup points in 1994. It was the sixth time in his career he both qualified and finished first.

25

Gober Sosebee won for the first time in over two years, his second and final career victory, with a checkered flag finish at Macon, GA, in 1954. Sosebee garnered his second Grand National career win in the 100-mile event on the half-mile dirt track, averaging 55.410 mph in his Oldsmobile.

Frank Schneider's only Grand National victory came in 1958 at the Old Dominion Speedway in Manassas, VA. Eddie Pagan won his fifth career pole. The .375-mile paved track hosted nine Grand National events 1958–66. Schneider ran 27 Grand National races 1949–58 with one win and one pole.

Fred Lorenzen continued his mastery at Martinsville with his fourth straight win at the Virginia track in the 1965 Virginia 500. Junior Johnson won his 40th career pole.

Richard Petty won for the seventh time in the past nine events at Martinsville, winning the first Winston Cup race held at the track. Petty's win in the 1971 Virginia 500 was the 127th of his career. Donnie Allison

qualified first for the fifth time in his career and finished fifth. Brother Bobby finished second. Petty won the first Winston Cup championship that season, winning 21 races.

The 1976 Virginia 500 was won by Darrell Waltrip for his third career Winston Cup victory. Dave Marcis captured his 10th career pole.

Harry Gant's first of 18 Winston Cup wins came in the 1982 Virginia National Bank 500 at Martinsville. Terry Labonte qualified first for the third time in his career.

Rusty Wallace won his third consecutive NASCAR start with a victory in the Hanes 500 at Martinsville. It was his fourth Winston Cup win of the season and 25th of his career. Geoff Bodine earned his 30th career pole start.

Dale Earnhardt Sr. captured the checkered flag at Talladega in the 1999 Die Hard 500. Ken Schrader qualified on the pole and finished sixth.

26

John DuBoise was born in 1919. Racing out of Paterson, NJ, he started seven races 1950–52, with a fourth place finish in a Plymouth as his Grand National career best in 1951 at Morristown Speedway (NJ).

Dick Rathmann won the 100-mile event held on the half-mile dirt track in Macon, GA, in 1953. It was the sixth career win for Rathmann, his first in seven sanctioned Grand National races that season.

Reading, PA, hosted their second

and final top-level NASCAR race, a 1959 Grand National event won by Junior Johnson. The half-mile dirt track was originally built in 1924.

Fred Lorenzen won the 1964 Virginia 500, his second straight win at Martinsville. Lorenzen also started first, winning from the pole for the sixth of eleven times in his career.

Morgan Shepherd won his first NASCAR race in the 1981 Virginia 500 with a 15-second margin of victory at Martinsville Speedway. Ricky Rudd won his first career pole and managed a third-place finish.

Dale Earnhardt Sr. won his 26th career event in the 1987 Sovran Bank 500 at Martinsville. Morgan Shepherd won his fourth pole. Earnhardt won 11 races on his way to his second consecutive Winston Cup championship in 1987. It was his fourth straight race of 1987.

Mark Martin, who won the three previous poles at Martinsville, finally made it to victory lane in the 1992 Hanes 500. Darrell Waltrip qualified first for the 58th time in his career and finished third.

Bobby Labonte won the 1998 Die Hard 500 at Talladega from the pole for his second win of the season. Jimmy Spencer's #23 Winston car was the runner-up.

27

Robert Bondurant was born in 1933. He started one Grand National race each in 1963 and 1965 and made two Winston Cup starts in 1981, all at Riverside, CA. His best finish was his finale, 18th in the 1981 Winston Western 500.

Herb Thomas won his 10th career Grand National race, his second straight at the Central City Speedway, driving his Hudson to victory lane at an average speed of 53.853 mph on the .5-mile dirt track in Macon, GA, in 1952. Jack Smith won the first pole position of his career in a Studebaker for the 99-mile event.

Marvin Panch won a 1957 race at Spartanburg, SC, his fourth of 17 career Grand National wins. Speedy Thompson qualified first, his eighth career pole.

Jim Reed won his first of seven career Grand National races in 1958 at Old Bridge, NJ, starting from the pole. He won three more races that season and three more the following season.

Kirk Bryant was born in 1962. He started five Winston Cup races in the mid–1980's. He raced out of Thomasville, NC, to his debut in the 1986 Daytona 500, where he crashed on the 24th lap and finished 41st.

Richard Petty won the 1969 Virginia 500 at Martinsville. Bobby Allison qualified first for the ninth time in his career and finished third in the race. It was Petty's 94th career Grand National victory.

The 1975 Virginia 500 was won by Richard Petty for his 169th career victory on the top-level NASCAR circuit. Benny Parsons captured his second of 21 career top qualifying positions. Petty won 13 races that season and cruised to his second consecutive Winston Cup points championship.

Darrell Waltrip won from the pole for his 25th career win in the 1980 Virginia 500 at Martinsville. It was the sixth of 24 times in his career he both qualified and finished first. Waltrip won five races that season and finished fifth, behind Winston Cup champion Dale Earnhardt, in the points race.

Leon Sales died in 1981 at the age of 57. Sales, who raced out of Winston-Salem, NC, won at North Wilkesboro in 1950, his rookie season. He ran eight Grand National races 1950–52 with two other top–10 finishes.

Ricky Rudd won his first race of 1986 with a trip to victory lane in the Sovran Bank 500 at Martinsville. Tim Richmond captured his sixth career pole.

Kurt Busch became the first two-time winner of 2003 with a victory in the Auto Club 500 at California Speedway in Fontana. Steve Park captured the pole.

28

Steve McGrath was born in 1924. Racing out of New Canaan, CT, McGrath started three races in 1953 and one in 1960. He finished 29th in a Pontiac in the 1960 Southern 500 at Darlington, SC, his finale.

Driving a Ford, Art Watts won his only career Grand National race in 1957 in Portland, OR, his home base for racing operations. Watts also captured his first pole.

The Greensboro Agricultural Fairgrounds held three Grand National races between 1957 and 1958. The inaugural race was won on this date in 1957 by Paul Goldsmith in a Ford.

Richard Petty won his third straight North Wilkesboro race in 1963 with a checkered flag finish in the Gwyn Staley 400. He became the third consecutive driver to win three straight events at the track, preceded by Rex White and his father Lee to victory lane.

Tiny Lund's second of five career Grand National wins came in 1965 at Columbia, SC, in the second Columbia 200.

Bobby Allison won the 15th event of the 1967 NASCAR season at Savannah Speedway. It was his fifth career victory.

Cale Yarborough claimed his sixth career checkered flag in the 1968 Virginia 500 at Martinsville. David Pearson captured his 30th career pole start and finished second.

Cale Yarborough cruised his Chevrolet to victory at Martinsville in the 1974 Virginia 500 for his 22nd career win. It was the seventh of 17 times he both qualified first and won the race. Yarborough finished second to Richard Petty for the 1974 Winston Cup championship.

Harry Gant won the 1985 Sovran Bank 500 for his seventh career Winston Cup victory. Darrell Waltrip earned his 53rd career top start. On the season, Waltrip won the Winston Cup championship while Gant finished third overall.

Dale Earnhardt Sr. captured his second win of the 1991 Winston Cup series with a trip to victory lane in the Hanes 500 at Martinsville. Earnhardt Sr. won four times in 1991 on his way to his second consecutive Winston Cup championship. Mark Martin qualified first for his 13th career pole.

Sterling Marlin won his first of two races of 1996 with a first-place finish in the Winston Select 500 at Talladega.

Jimmie Johnson, who won the pole the previous week at Talladega, cruised to victory lane in the 2002 Auto Club 500 at the California Speedway. Ryan Newman qualified first.

29

Larry Frank, who raced out of Indianapolis, IN, was born in 1931. Frank started 102 events 1956–66. He finished 14th in Grand National points in 1962, when he captured his only top-level NASCAR victory in the Darlington 500.

Dale Earnhardt Sr. was born in 1951 in Kannapolis, NC. Earnhardt was a seven-time Winston Cup champion and considered by many as the greatest stock car driver ever. He was the 1979 Winston Cup Rookie of the Year. He died in a crash on the last lap of the 2001 Daytona 500.

Fonty Flock won the shortest race of 1951, a 93.75-mile event at North Wilkesboro, NC, on a .625-mile dirt track. Flock also won his third straight pole, his fourth in his last five attempts. It was his second win of the season.

Buck Baker won at the Virginia State Fairgrounds (aka Richmond Fairgrounds, Strawberry Hill Speedway and Atlantic Rural Exposition Fairgrounds) in 1956 for his second straight win, fourth of the season and 16th of his career. Baker captured the pole to win for the fifth time from the top starting position. Baker went on to capture the 1956 Grand National driving championship, moving up steadily from fourth in '53, third in '54 and second in '55.

Bobby Johns' second of two career Grand National wins came in the 1962 Volunteer 500 at Bristol. Johns had won the pole for the fall 1961 race. Fireball Roberts qualified first for this event, his 26th top start in Grand National racing.

David Pearson won his second straight race in 1973 at Martinsville, driving his 1971 #21 Mercury to victory lane for his 70th career victory at NASCAR's top level. It was the 22nd of 37 times in his career that he qualified first and won the event.

Geoff Bodine won the 1984 Sovran Bank 500 at Martinsville Speedway for his first career NASCAR victory, driving a Rick Hendrick Chevrolet. Joe Ruttman won his third and final Winston Cup pole. Bodine was the 1982 Winston Cup Rookie of the Year.

Geoff Bodine won his first of three races in 1990 with a trip to victory lane in the Hanes Active wear 500 at Martinsville. It was the second consecutive week that a Bodine won; brother Brett won the previous race week. Bodine won from the pole for the first of three times in his career.

Rusty Wallace won his only race of

2001 at the California Speedway in the NAPA Auto Parts 500. Bobby Labonte won his only pole position start of the Winston Cup season.

30

Bill Lutz was born in Kentucky in 1929. He started four Grand National races 1956-60 and recorded his lone career top 10 in his only race of 1957.

Racing out of Randleman, NC, Joe Millikan was born in 1950. He finished sixth in points in 1979, when he captured the pole position for a Nashville race. In 80 starts between 1974 and 1986, Millikan posted 38 top–10 finishes.

Junior Johnson won the 1961 Virginia 500 Sweepstakes at Martinsville for his 22nd career Grand National win. Rex White captured his 20th career pole start.

Michael Waltrip was born in 1963 in Owensboro, KY. He began in the Winston Cup Series in 1985 with five starts, following his older brother Darrell into the upper echelon of racing. His breakout win at the 2001 Daytona 500 was overshadowed by the death of car owner Dale Earnhardt Sr.

Andy Hillenburg was born in 1963. He started four Winston Cup races in the mid–1990s. Hillenburg raced out of Indianapolis, IN.

Richard Petty won from the pole for the 15th time in his career in the 1966 Rebel 400 at Darlington. It was the first time the annual 300 mile event was increased to a length of 400 miles.

Richard Petty won from the pole for the 21st of 62 times in his career in the 1967 Richmond 250. It was his 54th career win and 51st pole. Petty dominated the season with 27 wins in 48 starts to capture his second Grand National driving championship.

Richard Petty won at Columbia Speedway in South Carolina in 1970 for his 105th career Grand National victory. Larry Baumel qualified first for the only time in his career.

Richard Petty won the 1972 Virginia 500 at Martinsville in his #43 Plymouth for his 144th career win. Bobby Allison qualified first and finished second. The Winston Cup championship race ended much the same way with Petty finishing first and Allison second.

Elliott Sadler was born in 1975 in Emporia, VA. Sadler debuted at the Winston Cup level in 1998 and has started 177 events through 2003 with his lone win in 2001 at Bristol in the Food City 500. He was the runner-up to 1999 Rookie of the Year Tony Stewart.

Mark Martin won the 1995 Winston Select 500 at Talladega, AL, his 16th career Winston Cup victory and first of four in 1995.

Jeremy Mayfield, who won the pole the previous week, won the NAPA Auto Parts 500 at the California Speedway in 2000 for his first career Winston Cup victory. Mike Skinner won the pole.

MAY

1

Buck Baker won his second straight event at the Charlotte Speedway in 1955, winning $1000 in his Buick.

The grandstands of the Greensboro Agricultural Fairgrounds burned in 1955. The seats were rebuilt and the track eventually hosted three Grand National events 1957–58.

LeeRoy Yarborough won the 1964 Savannah 200 in a Plymouth at Savannah Speedway in Georgia.

Darrell Waltrip won the 1977 Winston 500 at Talladega.

Richard Petty won the Winston 500 for the first time in his career in 1983.

Phil Parsons won the 1988 Winston 500 at Talladega, his only career win.

Dale Earnhardt Sr. won his second straight race at Talladega in the 1994 Winston 500.

Eddie Anderson died in 1995 at the age of 68. Anderson raced out of Blue Island, IL, to start five Grand National races in 1951. Driving a Nash, Anderson finished a career-best 11th in his finale at Speedway Park in Jacksonville, FL.

2

Herb Thomas won his fourth race of 1954, piloting his Hudson Hornet to victory at the 150-mile race at Langhorne, PA, in 1954. It was his 33rd career Grand National victory. Lee Petty claimed the pole position.

Junior Johnson won at the Hickory Speedway in 1959, when he was named the most popular Grand National driver of the season.

Richard Petty's first win at Columbia, SC, came in 1963, his 20th career Grand National win. Petty won from the pole for the fifth time in his career.

Junior Johnson won his 42nd career race at Bristol in the 1965 Southeastern 500. Marvin Panch started at the pole position for the 18th time of 24 in his career.

Buddy Baker won his second straight Darlington event in the 1971 Rebel 400. Donnie Allison won his sixth career pole.

Buddy Baker's third straight win at Talladega came in a Ford in the 1976 Winston 500.

Darrell Waltrip won the Winston 500 for the second time in his career in 1982.

Ernie Irvan won his first race of the 1993 Winston Cup series with a trip to victory lane in the Winston 500 at Talladega. It was his second straight win at the track.

Jeff Gordon won his third race of the season in the 1999 California 500 Presented by NAPA. Jeff Burton won the pole and finished second.

3

Larry Hess was born in 1935. He started 27 Grand National events in the 1960s with three top–10 finishes his rookie season of 1965. He raced out of Salisbury, NC.

Buck Baker won his second career NASCAR race with a first-place finish in the 150-mile contest at Langhorne, PA, in 1953. Baker drove his Oldsmobile to an average speed of 72.743 for the win on the one-mile dirt track.

Born in 1956, Ed Pimm made five NASCAR starts 1987–88. He raced out of Newburg, NY, to briefly lead one lap in his debut in the 1987 Winston 500 at Talladega, AL, before retiring due to engine problems.

Jack Smith won from the pole for the first of six times in his career with a 1958 win at Greenville-Pickens Speedway in South Carolina. It was his sixth career win and fifth career pole.

Lee Petty, the 1959 Grand National champion, won the 1959 Virginia 500 at Martinsville for his 40th career win. Petty won 11 races that season in capturing his third and final Grand National Championship. Bobby Johns captured his first of two career top qualifying positions.

Bobby Isaac won the 1968 Dixie 250 at the Augusta International Speedway, driving a Dodge.

Bobby Allison won his 62nd career NASCAR race in 1981. The victory came at the Alabama International Motor Speedway for his second win of the season. It was his first career victory in a Buick.

Davey Allison won his first career race in 1987 with a first-place finish in the Winston 500 at Talladega, AL, in a race that was shortened to 473.48 miles due to darkness. Allison went on to become the 1987 Winston Cup Rookie of the Year.

Davey Allison won the 1992 Winston 500 at Talladega, a two-car-length victory over Bill Elliott.

Mark Martin cruised to victory in the 1998 California 500 Presented by NAPA at the California Speedway in Fontana. Jeff Gordon captured the top starting spot and finished fourth.

Joe Nemechek won his first career Winston Cup race with a victory in the 2003 Pontiac Performance 400 at Richmond International Raceway. Terry Labonte won the pole.

4

Dr. Donald Tarr was born in 1929. He ran 48 races at NASCAR's highest level 1967–71 with nine top–10 finishes. He raced out of Miami Beach, FL.

Peter Holden Gregg was born in 1940. Racing out of Jacksonville, FL, he made one career Winston Cup start in 1973, logging 51 miles as a driver at NASCAR's top level.

Dick Rathmann captured his second career victory, and second of 1952, with a first-place finish in the 150-mile contest at Langhorne, PA. After nine races in the NASCAR season, manufacturer Hudson had won all but one race and had taken the pole seven times. Herb Thomas claimed his sixth career pole for this race, also in a Hudson.

Fireball Roberts won the first of two 1957 races held at the Cleveland County Fairgrounds in Shelby, NC.

Jimmy Perdue's first of three Grand National wins came in 1962 at the Southside Speedway in Richmond, VA. Rex White captured the pole position, his 28th. The track hosted four Grand National events, one in 1961, two in 1962 and one in 1963.

Bobby Isaac won the final Fireball 300 at the Asheville-Weaverville Speedway in 1969. Isaac won the final two races run at the speedway, also known as the Skyline Speedway, in western NC.

Buddy Baker won the 1975 Winston 500 at Talladega.

Buddy Baker won the Winston 500 for the third time in his career in 1980.

Bobby Allison won his 82nd career race after almost two years away from the winner's circle in 1986 at Alabama Motor Speedway. It was his only win of the season.

Driving a Buick, Bobby Allison won the 1986 Winston 500 at Talladega over runner-up Dale Earnhardt Sr.

On the road course at Sears Point, Mark Martin ended a 42-race winless streak with a win in the 1997 Save Mart Supermarkets 300. Jeff Gordon finished second. It was the 20th career win for Martin.

Tony Stewart, the 2002 Winston Cup champion, won for the second time of the Winston Cup season with a trip to victory lane in the Pontiac Performance 400 at Richmond. Reigning Daytona 500 champion Ward Burton qualified first

5

Duane Carter was born in 1913. He made one Grand National start in 1950, racing out of Fresno, CA. He finished seventh in the seventh race of the season at Dayton, OH, in his only start at NASCAR's top level.

Bob Welborn was born in 1928 in Denton, NC. He started 183 career Grand National races and won nine events 1952–64. He was fourth in Grand National points in 1955. His first victory came in October 1957 at Martinsville, VA. A short-track specialist, Welborn is credited with the first NASCAR win at the Daytona International Speedway in 1959, an event that qualified him for the pole in the first Daytona 500.

Les Covey was born in 1939. He started seven career Winston Cup races, all in 1972. Covey raced out of Paris, Ontario, Canada, to a 21st place finish in his finale, the 1972 Delaware 500.

Larry Pollard was born in 1954. Pollard, who raced out of Victoria, British Columbia, Canada, made four NASCAR starts in 1987.

Speedy Thompson captured his fifth career Grand National checkered flag at Columbia, SC, in 1956 driving a Dodge.

Paul Goldsmith won his third career race in 1957 at Richmond. Russ Hepler captured his only career pole. Hepler raced out of Clarion, PA, in the 1950s, running 13 career Grand National events, finishing in the top 10 twice.

Jack Smith won the inaugural Hickory 250 at the Hickory Speedway in 1962 in a Pontiac. It was his 20th career Grand National win.

Jim Paschal won in 1963 at the Tar Heel Speedway, a quarter-mile dirt track that hosted three events 1962–63. Paschal won the first two sanctioned events at the arena.

David Pearson captured the 1968 Fireball 300 at Weaverville, NC, for his 34th career Grand National victory.

David Pearson, driving a Mercury, won his third straight Winston 500 with a 1974 win at Talladega.

Bill Elliott won the 1985 Winston 500 at Talladega, his first win at the famed Alabama track.

Marion "Rod" Perry died in 1992 at the age of 67. Racing out of Miami, FL, Perry made his only NASCAR start in a 1957 race on the Beach & Road Course at Daytona Beach, FL, and earned a total of $100 for his 15th-place effort.

Rusty Wallace captured his second win in three weeks in the 1996 Save Mart Supermarkets 300 on the road course at Sears Point.

Tony Stewart won his first race of 2001 at Richmond in the Pontiac Excitement 400. It marked the first time in his career that he won a Winston Cup race prior to June. Mark Martin won his second pole position start of the season.

6

Bill Snowden was born in 1910. Snowden raced out of St. Augustine, FL, to start 24 Strictly Stock and Grand National races 1949–52, finishing ninth in series points in 1951. Snowden finished in the top 10 15 times.

Julius Franklin "Jackie" Rogers III was born in 1943. Racing out of Wilmington, NC, Rogers ran 41 races 1974–76 with 10 top–10 finishes.

Curtis Turner captured his second race of 1951 with a first-place finish in the 100-mile contest at Martinsville, VA. It was his seventh career NASCAR win to lead all drivers at the time.

At the first sanctioned race at the Concord Speedway in 1956, Speedy Thompson captured the checkered flag driving a Chrysler. The half-mile dirt track hosted 12 events between 1956 and 1964.

Fred Lorenzen won from the pole for the second time in his career. It was the second win and first pole of Lorenzen's Grand National racing career, coming in the 1961 Rebel 300.

Joe Weatherly won at the Concord Speedway in 1962, his second straight win at the North Carolina track. Weatherly's 17th career win was his fourth of the season, when he earned his first of two championships.

David Pearson won the 1973 Winston 500 at Talladega, his fourth major win of the Grand National season. The race was marked by a spectacular 10th-lap crash involving pole-sitter Buddy Baker and Cale Yarborough that subsequently collected a second wave of cars. Wendell Scott, Lennie Pond, Bobby Allison and at least ten others were involved. Luckily, although there were serious injuries, no one was killed. It was often regarded as the worst accident in NASCAR history. Only 17 of the 60 cars that started the race were running at the finish.

Driving a Ford, Bobby Allison won his 54th career NASCAR race in 1979 at the Alabama International Motor Speedway. It was his third win of the season.

Cale Yarborough won the 1984 Winston 500 at Talladega, AL, in a Chevrolet.

Dale Earnhardt Sr. won the 1990 Winston 500 at Talladega. It was his third of nine wins that season, his fourth as Winston Cup Champion.

Harry Gant, driving an Oldsmobile, won his first of five races in 1991 with a checkered-flag finish at Talladega in the Winston 500.

Dale Earnhardt Jr. won the Pontiac Excitement 400 in a Chevrolet, his second win of the 2000 Winston Cup season. Rusty Wallace won the pole.

7

Emile "Buzzy" Reutimann was born in 1941. He qualified and started in one Grand National race in 1963, finishing tenth in the second event of 1963 at the Golden Gate Speedway in Tampa, FL. Reutimann raced out of Harrisburg, PA.

Junior Johnson won his first NASCAR race in 1955 at the Hickory Speedway in North Carolina. It was his first of five wins that season, when he finished sixth in Grand National points.

Richard Petty won the 1966 Tidewater 250 at Langley Field Speedway (VA). Petty started first and finished first for the 17th of 62 times in his career. It was the 44th career Grand National win for Petty.

David Pearson won the 1972 Winston 500 at Talladega, his 62nd career victory. It was the first Winston Cup event for 21-year old Darrell Waltrip, who finished 38th and ran 808 more NASCAR races over 29 years.

Benny Parsons won at Nashville for the second straight event in the 1977 Music City USA 420. It was the sixth career win for Parsons. Darrell Waltrip, who earned his seventh pole start, finished third.

Samuel Hollis Smith, one of two "Sam Smiths" to start a Grand National race, died in 1982 at the age of 46. This Sam Smith raced out of Union, SC, to start one event in 1965.

Darrell Waltrip won from the pole for the 18th time in his career in the 1983 Marty Robbins 420 at Nashville, TN. It was his 54th career victory at NASCAR's top level.

Davey Allison won the 1989 Winston 500 at Talladega International. It was his only win of the season.

Dale Earnhardt Sr. won the Save Mart Supermarkets 300K in 1993 at Sonoma, CA.

8

Don Hume was born in 1933. He started 15 total Grand National/Winston Cup races 1964–65 and 1981–85. Hume raced out of Belvedere, NJ.

Larry Esau was born in 1947. He started four Winston Cup races in the mid–1970s. Esau raced out of San Diego, CA, and is the brother of Ron Esau.

Tim Flock, in a Chrysler, won the first NASCAR-sanctioned race at the Arizona State Fairgrounds in over four years. It was the second of four events held at the one-mile dirt track.

Bobby Labonte was born in 1964 in Corpus Christi, TX. The younger brother of Terry, Bobby began his Winston Cup experience in 1991, running 366 events through 2003. He was the 2000 points champion, when he won four events and had 20 other top–10 finishes. He has 21 career wins through 2003.

Junior Johnson won the 1965 Rebel 300 for his 43rd career Grand National win. Fred Lorenzen won his fourth pole in the last past five races at the South Carolina track.

Darryl Sage was born in 1965 and raced out of Murfreesboro, TN. He started eight races 1982–83 at the Winston Cup level. As a 17-year old rookie, Sage finished 16th in his debut in the 1982 Busch Nashville 420 at Nashville Speedway (TN).

For the second straight Nashville race, Cale Yarborough won and Benny Parsons captured the pole. Yarborough's 34th career win came in the 1976 Music City USA 420. Parsons finished third.

In the 1982 Cracker Barrel Country Store 420, Darrell Waltrip, driving a Buick, won his third straight Nashville race, winning from the pole for the 17th time in his career for his 44th top-level NASCAR win. Waltrip went on to the 1982 Winston Cup points championship.

9

John Sears was born in 1936. Sears, who raced out of Ellerbe, NC, ran 318 races 1964–73. He finished fifth in points two consecutive years, 1967–68. He qualified on the pole two times and had 127 top–10 finishes.

Tim Flock won his first race of 1953, his 17th career Grand National victory, with a first-place finish on the .5-mile dirt track of the Hickory Speedway (NC) in the second sanctioned NASCAR race of the day. Flock took the checkered flag in the 100-mile event driving a Hudson. It was the first of 35 races held at the track between 1953 and 1971.

Buck Baker won his second straight

Grand National race in 1953 at Columbia, SC, in the 100-mile feature event. Baker captured his third career win on the half-mile dirt track, averaging 53.707 mph in his Oldsmobile. Herb Thomas, driving a Hudson, captured his 17th career pole position.

Buck Baker earned his first win of 1954 with a checkered-flag finish in the 100-mile event at Wilson, NC, on the half-mile dirt track. It was his sixth career NASCAR win. Jim Paschal captured the pole position. It was the 150th sanctioned race since NASCAR officially started in 1949.

Fred Lorenzen won his fifth pole in the past seven events at Darlington in 1964. Lorenzen also captured the checkered flag, winning from the pole for the seventh time in his career in the Rebel 300.

Tim Fedewa, who raced out of Holt, MI, was born in 1967. Fedewa ran his only Winston Cup event in 1994, finishing 23rd in the SplitFire Spark Plug 500 at Dover, DE.

Grand National win #58 for David Pearson came in the 1970 Rebel 400 at Darlington, SC. Charlie Glotzbach earned his fifth career pole start.

Benny Parsons won his first NASCAR race in the 1971 Halifax County 100 at the South Boston Speedway in Virginia. It was the only Winston Cup race, and the final top-level NASCAR event, held at the track, which hosted nine Grand National events between 1960 and 1970. Bobby Isaac qualified first for the 40th of 50 times in his career.

Benny Parsons won his 18th career Winston Cup race in the 1981 Melling Tool 420 at Nashville Speedway. Ricky Rudd qualified on the pole for the second time in his career and finished fifth.

Weldon Adams died in 1995 at the age of 56. Adams raced out of Augusta, GA, to 25 career Grand National starts and seven top–10 finishes 1950–64. His best finish was a third-place at Martinsville, VA, in October 1950.

Henry "Smokey" Yunick died in 2001 at the age of 77 of leukemia in Daytona Beach, FL. Yunick was involved in racing at many levels, serving as a mechanic, an Indianapolis 500 winning crew chief and a winning NASCAR team owner. His trademark "Best Damn Garage in Town" was a popular racing garage in Daytona Beach.

10

George Wiltshire was born in 1947. He started two Winston Cup events, one each in 1971 and 1975. He raced out of Corona, NY, to a 28th-place finish in his debut in the 1971 Islip 250 at Islip, NY.

Dick Rathmann won his third career race, and second straight, with a trip to victory lane at Darlington, SC, in 1952. Rathmann drove his Hudson an average speed of 83.818 mph to win the 100-mile event on the 1.25-mile paved track. There were no time trials.

Buck Baker won his 17th Grand National race at the Greenville-Pickens Speedway (SC) in 1956. Rex White captured his first of 36 career pole starts.

In 1966, in the first sanctioned race at the Middle Georgia Raceway, a half-mile paved track on the site of the former Central City Speedway in Macon, GA, Richard Petty drove his Plymouth to victory lane in the Speedy Morelock 200. The track hosted nine Grand National events 1966–71.

LeeRoy Yarbrough won his eighth career Grand National event in the spring race at Darlington in the 1969 Rebel 400. Cale Yarborough qualified on the pole for the tenth time of his career.

Darrell Waltrip cruised to his first NASCAR Winston Cup victory in 1975 in the Music City USA 420 at Nashville. It was the first of 24 times in his Winston Cup career that he won a race from the pole.

Richard Petty recorded win #192 in the 1980 Music City USA 420. Cale Yarborough won the 47th pole of his career and finished third.

Mark Martin won the 1997 Winston 500 at the Talladega Superspeedway. Dale Earnhardt finished second.

11

Tim Flock was born in 1924 in Fort Payne, AL. The youngest of the three racing brothers (joining Bob and Fonty), Tim won 39 races in 187 starts between 1949 and 1961. He won 18 races and 18 poles in 1955 to capture the Grand National championship, which he also won in 1952. He drove eight career races with his pet monkey, Jocko Flocko, as a passenger.

Bugs Stevens was born Carl S. Berghman in 1934. Stevens raced out of Rehoboth, MA, to make three Grand National starts in 1970 with one top–10 finish.

Gene Felton was born in 1936. He ran 469 laps in his only Winston Cup start, a 16th-place finish in the 1976 Dixie 500 at Atlanta, GA. Felton raced out of Marietta, GA.

Ervin Pruitt was born in 1940. Pruitt, who raced out of Spartanburg, SC, started nine Grand National races 1968–69 with one top–10 finish each year. His best was a seventh-place finish in the 1968 Western North Carolina 500 at Weaverville, NC.

Larry "Butch" Hartman was born in 1940. He started 20 Grand National/Winston Cup races 1966–79 with five top–10 finishes. His career-best was a fifth-place finish in the 1972 National 500 at Charlotte, NC.

Bob Welborn won at the Greensboro Agricultural Fairgrounds in 1958, the final of three Grand National races held at the .333-mile dirt track in North Carolina.

Joe Weatherly won the 1963 Rebel 300 at Darlington, SC, his 24th career Grand National victory. Fred Lorenzen captured his third pole in the past five events at the track, the 11th of his Grand National career.

David Pearson won his 35th career Grand National event at Darlington in the 1968 Rebel 400.

Clarence Lovell died in a highway crash in 1973 at the age of 26. Lovell had finished in the top 10 in two of four Winston Cup races he had entered that season, prior to his death.

Richard Petty's 158th career win came in Nashville, TN, in the 1974 Music City USA 420. Bobby Allison won his 44th career pole while brother Donnie finished second.

12

Racing out of Oregon, Carl Joiner was born in 1924. He made 16 NASCAR starts, no more than three in any one season, between 1957 and 1977. He had one top 10 in 1971 and 1972.

James "Cotton" Hodges was born in 1926. He started one race each in 1953, 1954 and 1963, earning $100 as a driver at the Grand National level. Hodges raced out of Hollywood, FL.

Cerry Ezra "Jabe" Thomas was born in 1930. He ran 322 career Grand National and Winston Cup races 1965–78. Thomas, who raced out of Christiansburg, VA, managed 77 top–10 finishes and finished as high as 6th in series points in 1971.

Gene White was born in 1931. He ran 23 Grand National races 1956–61. Racing out of Marietta, GA, White managed four career top-10 finishes.

Charles "Hoss" Ellington was born in 1935. He started 21 Grand National races 1968–70 and recorded four top–10 finishes in 1969, racing out of Wilmington, NC.

Gary Johnson was born in 1940. Racing out of Modesto, CA, he had four Winston Cup starts 1976–78, all at Riverside, CA. He finished a career-best 20th in the 1977 Winston Western 500.

Speedy Thompson won at the Hickory Speedway in 1956 in a Chrysler.

Nelson Stacy's second career win was his second in a row at Darlington. Fred Lorenzen won his sixth career pole in the 1962 Rebel 300.

Cale Yarborough won the 1973 Music City 400 at Nashville Fairgrounds Speedway in a 1971 Chevrolet.

Cale Yarborough won the 1979 Music City USA 420 at Nashville Speedway. Joe Millikan won his only career pole in 80 career Winston Cup starts.

Darrell Waltrip won from the pole for the 21st of 24 times in his career in the 1984 Coors 420 at Nashville Speedway. It was his 60th career win.

Adam Petty died in a crash at the New Hampshire International Speedway, practicing for a 2000 Busch race. Adam, the fourth generation of Petty race car drivers, was 19 years old.

13

Robert Kennedy was born in 1936. Racing out of Thousand Oaks, CA, he started one career Winston Cup race. He finished 19th in the 1983 Budweiser 400 at Riverside, CA.

Theodore "Ted" Fritz, born in 1936, ran ten laps, and earned $620 as a Winston Cup driver. Fritz raced out of Modesto, CA, to a 33rd-place finish in the 1975 Tuborg 400 at Riverside, CA.

Terry Ryan was born in 1938. Racing out of Davenport, IA, Ryan started 12 races 1976–77 with four top–10 finishes.

Buck Baker won at the Occoneechee Speedway in Hillsboro, NC, in 1956. Baker won 14 events that season en route to his first Grand National Championship.

Rich Bickle was born in 1961. Racing out of Edgerton, WI, Bickle made 85 career Winston Cup starts 1989–2001 with three top–10 finishes. He ran 24 of 34 events in 1999, his busiest season at NASCAR's highest level. His best finish was fourth place at Martinsville in 1998.

The Starlite Speedway in Monroe, NC, was a half-mile dirt track that hosted one Grand National event, won by Darel Dieringer on this date in 1962 in a Ford. Dieringer was voted the circuit's most popular driver in 1966. The Starlite Speedway was the site of a fatal crash by James Sears on August 3, 1973. Sears made six NASCAR starts 1967–71.

Richard Petty's 55th career win came in the 1967 Rebel 300, the spring race at Darlington, SC. It was the seventh of 27 wins on the season for Petty, who won his second of seven career points championships in 1967.

Gene Coyle died in 1991. He started two Winston Cup races in 1984 racing out of Piscataway, NJ, finishing 18th in the Like Cola 400 at Pocono, PA, in his debut.

He started 23 Grand National races 1954–62 with nine finishes in the top 10. Driving out of Baltimore, MD, Dodd Jr. finished a career-high fifth at Forsyth County Fairgrounds (NC) in 1955.

Darlington International Speedway ran a spring event for the second time in their history in 1960, the Rebel 300. The race was won by Joe Weatherly, his fourth career Grand National victory.

Ned Jarrett won his second straight Tidewater 250 at the Langley Field Speedway in Hampton, VA. Dick Hutcherson captured his fourth career pole and finished second. It was Jarrett's 41st career Grand National victory as he went on to the points championship in 1965 with Hutcherson finishing second.

Cale Yarborough won the 1978 Winston 500 at Talladega. It was his second of ten wins in 1978, his third straight Winston Cup Championship year.

Nelson Stacy died in 1986 at the age of 64. Stacy ran 45 career Grand National races 1952–65 with four victories, which included back-to-back wins at Darlington in the 1961 Southern 500 (fall) and the 1962 Rebel 300 (spring). He finished in the top 10 twenty other times. Nelson won the 1962 World 600 and left competitive racing after the 1965 season.

14

John Dodd Jr. was born in 1933.

15

Ted Chamberlain, a NASCAR pioneer, was born in 1906. Chamberlain started 63 races between 1949 and 1959 at the Strictly Stock and Grand National level. He raced out of St. Petersburg, FL.

Travis Branton Tiller, born in 1937, ran 51 career Winston Cup races 1974–83. Tiller raced out of Triangle, VA, to log over 9500 NASCAR miles.

Danny Letner won the only NASCAR-sanctioned race held in Tucson, AZ in 1955 at the Tucson Rodeo Grounds. It was his second and final Grand National victory.

Tim Flock won his 22nd career Grand National race in 1955 with a victory at Martinsville. Jim Paschal won the pole. Flock won 18 races in 1955 on his way to his second of two Grand National Championships.

Four Grand National events were run at the Starkey Speedway in Roanoke, VA, between 1958 and 1964. Jim Reed won the first race held at the ¼-mile paved track, the second and final time of his career, both within 20 days in his #7 Ford. Reed finished tenth in Grand National points in 1958 and a career-best ninth the following year.

The Langley Field Speedway hosted nine Grand National events 1964–70. Originally a .4-mile dirt oval, the track was paved in 1968 and re-measured at .395 miles. The first event at the Hampton, VA, track was the 1964 Tidewater 250, won by Ned Jarrett for his 26th career win.

Junior Johnson won his 44th career Grand National race in 1965 at Bowman-Gray Stadium, his second straight victory at the Winston-Salem, NC, track.

David Pearson went from 40th in Grand National points in 1965 to #1 in 1966. His 18th career win came in the 1966 Richmond 250. Tom Pistone captured his third of five career poles, four of which came in 1966. Pearson won 15 events that season and outdistanced James Hylton, who was the runner-up.

Bobby Isaac won his second straight Beltsville 300 in 1970, the final of ten NASCAR races held at the Maryland raceway, and his first of 11 wins of the season. Isaac won his only Grand National Championship in 1970.

Cal Yarborough won the 1977 Mason-Dixon 500 at Dover Downs International Speedway. It was his sixth of nine wins on the season, his second of three straight Winston Cup Championships.

Driving a Buick, Bobby Allison won his 75th career race in 1983 at Dover Downs International Speedway. It was his second of six wins of the season, when he won his only Winston Cup Championship.

Dale Earnhardt Sr. won his third race of 1986 with a first-place finish in the Coca-Cola 600 at Charlotte Motor Speedway.

Ernie Irvan won for the second time in his career at Sears Point, with a first-place finish in the Save Mart Supermarkets 300K in 1994.

Dale Jarrett won his first race of 1999 at Richmond, VA, in the Pontiac Excitement 400. Jeff Gordon won the pole but finished 31st. Jarrett won three more races that season on his way to the Winston Cup Championship.

16

Roy Mayne was born in 1935. Racing out of Sumter, SC, he started 139 races 1963–74 with 22 top–10 finishes. His career-best was a fourth-place finish in the 1965 Southern 500 at Darlington, SC.

Jim Paschal won at Martinsville, VA, in 1954 on a half-mile dirt track for his second career Grand National victory. Paschal drove his Oldsmobile to the win in the 100-mile feature race with an average speed of 46.153 mph. It was his second career win and second straight at Martinsville.

Doug French was born in 1959. Racing out of Howell, NJ, he started one Winston Cup race in 1987. He ran 75 career laps at NASCAR's highest level.

Ned Jarrett won the 1964 Hickory 250 at Hickory, NC, driving a Ford.

Bob Flock, the oldest of the three Flock brothers, died in 1964 at the age of 46. Flock achieved four wins at the top NASCAR level in seven seasons of competition.

Junior Johnson won the 1965 Hickory 250 at Hickory, NC, his 45th career checkered flag.

Bobby Isaac won the 1969 Beltsville 300 in Maryland. Isaac was voted the Grand National circuit's most popular driver that season.

The first Winston 500 was run at Talladega in 1971. Prior to that date, the track was known as the Alabama International Motor Speedway. Donnie Allison edged his brother Bobby after leader Dave Marcis had late mechanical problems.

Benny Parsons won the 1976 Mason-Dixon 500 at Dover Downs International Speedway.

Bobby Allison won his 67th career NASCAR race with a first place showing at Dover Downs International Speedway in 1982. It was his second win of the season.

Geoff Bodine won his only race of 1993 with a trip to victory lane in the Save Mart 300 on the road course at Sears Point.

17

Ben Cannaziaro was born in 1910. He started one Strictly Stock race in NASCAR's inaugural season of 1949, racing out of Trenton, NJ.

Ernest Lloyd "Sonny" Hutchins, born in 1929, started 88 races at the Grand National/Winston Cup level 1955–74 with seven top–10 finishes. Hutchins raced out of Richmond, VA.

Lee Petty won for the third time in the 1953 Grand National season with a first-place finish in the 100-mile race on the .5-mile dirt track at Martinsville, VA. Petty, driving a Dodge, captured his ninth career NASCAR win.

Tom Pistone's first of two career Grand National wins came in 1959 at Trenton, NJ, in a Thunderbird.

Richard Petty won the 1964 race at South Boston (VA) Speedway for his 30th career win. The ¼-mile paved oval took a three year hiatus before Grand National cars took to the track again in 1968 with Petty winning again. Marvin Panch captured his 15th career pole and finished second in the race and tenth in Grand National points behind Petty, who won eight races on the season and earned his first points championship.

David Pearson won the 1968 Beltsville 300 in Maryland. It was his sixth of 16 wins that season, his second of three as Grand National Champion.

For the second straight race at Langley Speedway in Hampton, VA, David Pearson won from the pole in the 1969 Tidewater 375. It was the 15th of 37 times he both started and finished first in a Grand National race. Pearson won his second consecutive points championship, and third overall, in 1969.

At the 1981 Mason-Dixon 500 at Dover Downs, team-owner Junie Dunleavy earned his only career victory after 50 years of competition. Driver Jody Ridley got the win over Bobby Allison for the only Winston Cup victory of his career. Ridley was the 1980 Winston Cup Rookie of the Year.

Scott Brayton won the pole position for the 1996 Indianapolis 500 but was killed when a tire deflated and he crashing into a wall during a practice run.

Jeff Burton won the second event on this date in 2003, the All-Star Open at Lowe's Motor Speedway in Concord, NC. Steve Park qualified first.

Jimmie Johnson won the 2003 NASCAR Nextel All-Star Challenge at the Lowe's Motor Speedway in Concord, NC. Bill Elliott started first. After sponsoring NASCAR's top series since 1971, Winston was replaced by Nextel to start the 2004 season.

18

John Soares Jr. was born in 1942. Soares raced out of Hayward, CA, to start 13 races 1970–75, 1985. He finished with two career top–10 finishes.

Dick Rathmann and his Hudson remained dominant in 1952, with his third straight win of the season. This race, a 100-mile event on a .5-mile paved track at Dayton, OH, was his fourth career win, all in the current Grand National campaign. It marked the first time that NASCAR ran two consecutive races on paved tracks.

Junior Johnson won at North Wilkesboro in 1958 in a Ford. It was the 50th points race of the season and Johnson's fifth of six wins that year.

Richard Petty won at the Old Dominion Speedway in Manassas, VA, in 1963. It was the sixth time in his career he both qualified and finished first.

David Pearson won the 1968 Tidewater 250 at Langley Speedway. Pearson's win was the 37th of his career while Richard Petty qualified first for the 72nd time.

Bobby Isaac won the 1970 Tidewater 300 at Langley Speedway from the pole for his 23rd career win. Isaac went on to win 11 races and the Grand National championship that season. It was the 13th of 20 times in his career that he both started and finished a race first.

James Malloy, who ran one Grand National race in 1966, died one week before his 40th birthday in 1972 after crashing in practice for the Indianapolis 500.

Bobby Allison won his first race of the season in the 1980 Mason-Dixon 500 at Dover Downs International Speedway. It was his 57th career first-place finish.

Geoffrey Bodine won his second race of 1986 with a victory in the Budweiser 500 at Dover Downs.

Michael Waltrip won the Winston Select at Charlotte Motor Speedway in 1996.

Ryan Newman won the 2002 NASCAR Nextel All-Star Challenge at the Lowe's Motor Speedway in Concord, NC. Matt Kenseth captured the pole. The annual competition was one of three all-star events on the day. Jeremy Mayfield won from the pole in the All-Star Open while Ryan Newman captured the No Bull Sprint. Ken Schrader had started first. Newman was named 2002 Winston Cup Rookie of the Year.

19

Jody Ridley was born in 1942. Ridley raced out of Chatsworth, GA, to 140 Winston Cup starts 1973–89. His only win was at Dover in the May 1981 Mason-Dixon 500, but he finished in the top 10 in 55 other races. He was the 1980 Winston Cup Rookie of the Year.

In the 1957 Virginia 500 at Martinsville, Billy Myers and Tom Pistone made contact, sending Myers' car off the course and into spectators causing several severe injuries and killing one boy. Buck Baker captured his 29th career win and went on to win the 1957 Grand National championship. Paul Goldsmith won his third of nine career pole starts.

Ned Jarrett won for the 11th time on the Grand National circuit in 1962 at Spartanburg, SC. Cotton Owens qualified first for the 11th pole of his career.

The final sanctioned Grand National race at the Southside Speedway was won in 1963, from the pole, by Ned Jarrett. It was the fifth of 11 times in his career he both started and finished first. It was the 16th win and 16th pole of his career. Jarrett won eight races and finished fourth in championship points that season. The track hosted four Grand National events 1961–63, each with a different winner.

Jim Paschal won the 1967 Beltsville 200 in Maryland, driving a Plymouth, his 21st career checkered flag.

Cale Yarborough won the 1974 Mason-Dixon 500 at Dover Downs International Speedway.

David Pearson won his fourth career Dover Downs race with a checkered flag finish in the 1975 Mason-Dixon 500.

Bill Holland died at the age of 76 in 1984. He ran eight career races in the early days of Grand National,

1951–52, with two top–10s in 1951. His career-best was fourth-place in the 1951 Wilkes County 150.

Bill Elliott won the Budweiser 500 in 1985 at Dover Downs.

Using a backup car, Jeff Gordon won the 2001 Winston, a non-points competition at the Lowe's Motor Speedway. Rusty Wallace started first. Gordon went on to win his fourth Winston Cup Championship.

20

Buck Baker, on his way to the Grand National championship, won from the pole at Martinsville in 1956 in the inaugural Virginia 500 for his 19th career victory. It was the fourth of 15 times in his career that he both started and finished first.

Richard Petty won from the pole to capture his second straight Tidewater 250 in 1967 at Hampton, VA. It was the 23rd time in his career that he qualified first and won the race. Petty won 27 races in 1967 on his way to his second Grand National Championship.

Tony Stewart was born in 1971 in Columbus, IN. Stewart debuted at the Winston Cup level in 1999 and was named Rookie of the Year. He started 176 events through 2003. Stewart won three races in 2002 and was the points champion after finishing second in points the previous season. Stewart has also driven Busch, Craftsman Truck and IROC Series cars.

Neil Bonnett won the 1979 Mason-Dixon 500 at Dover Downs.

Richard Petty won for the seventh time at Dover Downs International Speedway with a victory in the 1984 Budweiser 500.

Dale Earnhardt Jr. rode his #8 Ford to victory in the 2000 Winston at the Lowe's Motor Speedway. Bill Elliott started from the pole.

21

Cotton Owens was born in South Carolina in 1924. Owens ran 160 career Grand National races 1950–64 with nine wins and 84 additional top–10 finishes. He finished second in points to Lee Petty during the 1959 season. He preferred dirt tracks and retired from active NASCAR racing as the series ran on mostly paved surfaces. He went on to successful car ownership. In 1966 David Pearson led his team to the series championship.

George Poulos was born in 1932. Racing out of Charlotte, NC, Poulos started 23 races in 1967, his only season on the NASCAR circuit.

Curtis Turner became the first NASCAR driver to win consecutive races with his second straight win in 1950. He also became the first driver with three wins when he took the checkered flag in his Olds in the fourth event of the season, a 75-mile short-track race at Martinsville, VA. Turner won four races in 1950 to lead all drivers, but finished sixth in championship points. Buck Baker claimed his first of 43 career pole starts.

Joe Weatherly won the second race

in preparation for the second annual World 600, scheduled for the following week. It was his second of eight wins that season.

Richard Petty won the first of two races held in 1961 at the Charlotte Motor Speedway.

Lloyd Dane won on the road course at Riverside, CA, in 1961 for his final of four career Grand National checkered flags.

Richard Petty won the final of eight sanctioned races held at the New Asheville Speedway in 1971 with a victory in the Asheville 300.

David Pearson won at Dover Downs in the 1978 Mason-Dixon 500.

Darrell Waltrip won the 1983 Valleydale 500 at Bristol, his fifth straight win at the Tennessee track. Neil Bonnett captured his 17th of 20 career top starts, but finished fourth.

Rusty Wallace spun out Darrell Waltrip late in the race to take the victory in 1989 at the Charlotte Motor Speedway. Ken Schrader finished second in the fifth edition of The Winston. Wallace went on to capture the Winston Cup Championship.

22

Bobby Johns was born in 1934. He started 141 races at NASCAR's top level between 1956 and 1969. Johns finished 3rd in points in 1960; recorded two career wins; had 34 other top–10s and earned two poles.

Glenn Francis was born in 1942. Racing out of Bakersfield, CA, he started 16 Grand National and Winston Cup races 1970–85, no more than two in any one year.

John Alexander was born in 1954. Alexander raced out of Elmira, NY, to make one Winston Cup start. He retired from the 1990 Budweiser at the Glen at Watkins Glen, NY, due to an oil leak on lap 35.

Tim Flock won at Richmond in 1955, his 23rd career victory. Flock went on to win 18 races in 1955, capturing his second Grand National points championship over runner-up Buck Baker.

Lee Petty won in 1959 at the Southern States Fairgrounds in Charlotte, NC. Petty won his final of three Grand National Championships that season.

Marvin Panch won the 1966 World 600 at Charlotte Motor Speedway. It was Panch's final career win.

Dale Earnhardt Sr. won The Winston, a non-points all-star-type race held at the Charlotte Motor Speedway, in 1993.

23

Joe Jernigan was born in 1915. He started four races 1950-51 but died in a race at Royall Speedway in Richmond, VA, in 1951. He debuted on the Beach & Road Course at Daytona with a 22nd-place finish in February 1950.

James Malloy was born in Colorado in 1932. Malloy ran one Grand National event in 1966 and died in 1972 while practicing for the Indianapolis 500.

Lee Petty drove his Chrysler to victory in the only sanctioned race ever run at the Sharon (PA) Speedway, which was just over the state line in Trumball County, OH. Dick Rathmann won the pole. It was Petty's 13th career win and Rathmann's eight career pole position. The track remains in operation and is partially owned by Sharon native, NASCAR driver Dave Blaney.

Wally Dallenbach Jr. was born in 1963 in Basalt, CO. He ran 226 Winston Cup events 1991–2001 with no wins and 23 top–10 finishes. In 1999, Dallenbach ran every race on the circuit and finished 19th in championship points. Dallenbach finished second in the 1993 Bud at the Glen, his best performance. His father, Wally Sr., was an Indy car driver while Wally Jr. specialized in road courses.

Fred Lorenzen won the 1965 World 600 at Charlotte Motor Speedway, his second win in the annual event.

Bobby Isaac won from the pole in the 1971 Kingsport 300, the final top-level Winston Cup event hosted by the Kingsport International Speedway in Kingsport, TN. It was the 19th of 20 career victories from the pole position for Isaac, his 34th career victory.

Allen "Rags" Carter died in 1993 at the age of 64. Carter started his only Grand National race in 1952 in West Palm Beach, FL, finishing sixth.

24

Sandy Lynch was born in 1922.

Racing out of Jacksonville, FL, he ran two races in 1951 and earned $25 in career NACAR winnings. In his debut, he finished 66th of 82 cars in the 1951 Southern 500 at Darlington, SC.

Jack Thomas Smith was born in 1924. Smith, the most successful of over 35 NASCAR drivers with the same last name, raced out of Sandy Springs, GA. He started 263 career Grand National races with 21 wins, his first coming at Martinsville, VA, in October 1956. He was fourth in series points in 1962 and finished fifth two other times.

Herb Thomas won his third race of the Grand National season, taking the checkered flag on the half-mile dirt track of the Powell Motor Speedway in Columbus, OH, in 1953. Thomas, driving a Hudson, averaged 56.127 mph to capture his 19th career win. It marked the final NASCAR event run in the state of Ohio to date. Thomas went on to capture his second Grand National driving championship in 1953.

Charles Dyer died of a heart attack at the age of 39 in 1957 during a race in Fredericksburg, VA. He started three Grand National races in 1955.

NASCAR Grand National racing returned to Winston-Salem, NC, in 1958, after a nearly three-year absence, with the debut race at Bowman-Gray Stadium, a ¼-mile paved oval. Bob Welborn captured the checkered flag for his fifth career win and his fourth victory of the season.

Rex White won from the pole at Nashville, TN, in 1959, the second of seven times in his Grand National career that he started and finished first. It was his third career win and first of five in 1959.

Terry Fisher was born in 1962. Racing out of Sandy, OR, he started four Winston Cup races 1989–95. He debuted in the 1989 Banquet Frozen Foods 300 on the road course at Sonoma, finishing 25th. He ran three of four career races at that track, with a career high 15th-place finish in 1990.

A terrible crash on the backstretch of the 1964 World 600 at Charlotte Motor Speedway caused severe burns to Fireball Roberts, who died over a month later from his injuries. Jim Paschal captured the bittersweet victory in his Plymouth.

Ricky Craven was born in 1966 in Newburgh, ME. Craven began his Winston Cup career in 1991 in one race but returned in 1995 as the Rookie of the Year in regular appearances. He finished third in the 1997 Daytona 500.

The 1970 World 600 at Charlotte Motor Speedway was won by Donnie Allison, his second straight win at the North Carolina track.

Bobby Allison won his third race of 1981 with a victory in the World 600 at the Charlotte Motor Speedway. It was the 63rd first place finish of his career.

Kyle Petty won the 1987 Coca-Cola 600 at Charlotte Motor Speedway.

Dale Earnhardt Sr. won the 1992 Coca-Cola 600 at Charlotte Motor Speedway.

Jeff Gordon won from the pole for a victory in the 1998 Coca-Cola 500 at the Charlotte Motor Speedway. Rusty Wallace's #2 Miller Lite car finished second.

25

Bud Moore was born in 1927. Moore has entered cars in NASCAR's top division since 1961. His cars boast 63 career wins, with three points championship teams and a victory in the 1978 Daytona 500.

Henry "Smokey" Yunick was born in 1933. Yunick, a successful mechanic in Daytona Beach, fielded cars in the early days of NASCAR with eight career victories. Yunic ran four miles at NASCAR's highest level in a 1952 Grand National event.

Pat Mintey, born in 1947 and racing out of Arleta, CA, ran three Winston Cup races at Riverside, CA, in the 1980s. He finished a career-best 34th in the 1981 Winston Western 500.

Buck Baker's 20th career victory came in 1956 at the Lincoln Speedway in New Oxford, PA. Baker won 14 races in 1956.

Paul Andrews was born in 1957. Andrews was the crew chief for Alan Kulwicki when he won the 1992 Winston Cup Championship.

LeeRoy Yarbrough won the 1969 World 600 at Charlotte Motor Speedway.

Richard Petty won the 1975 World 600 at Charlotte Motor Speedway. He was named the Winston Cup's most popular driver for the sixth of eight times in his career that season.

The race was the first of Dale Earnhardt Sr.'s career, a 22nd place finish.

Benny Parsons won the 1980 World 600 at Charlotte Motor Speedway for his 15th career Winston Cup victory.

Jeff Gordon won the 1997 Coca-Cola 600 at the Charlotte Motor Speedway. The race was eventually shortened to 500 laps when it was stopped at 12:59 A.M. Rusty Wallace finished second.

Jimmy Johnson captured his first checkered flag of the 2003 Winston Cup season (he won an all-star race the prior week) with a victory in the Coca-Cola 500 at Lowe's Motor Speedway in Concord, NC. Ryan Newman qualified first.

26

William "Whitey" Gerkin was born in 1930. He started five Grand National races in the 1960s, leading one 1967 race. Gerkin raced out of Melrose Park, IL.

James Elmo "Pee Wee" Wentz was born in 1941. He ran six Winston Cup races 1971–74. Wentz raced out of Danville, VA, and managed one top–10 finish his final season at NASCAR's top level.

Larry Baumel was born in 1944. He started 45 Grand National races 1969–71. Baumel raced out of Wisconsin and recorded two career top–10 finishes, his best being 9th in the 1970 Mason-Dixon 500 at Dover.

Sam Posey was born in 1944 and raced out of Sharon, CT. Posey started one Grand National race, a 28th-place finish in the 1970 Motor Trend 500 at Riverside, CA.

Eddie Pagan won his second career Grand National race in 1957. Art Watts won his second pole, both at the Portland Speedway in Portland, OR. Watts also won the previous race at the facility.

Stacy Compton was born in 1967 in Lynchburg, VA. Although he started two races in 1996 and three in 1999, he was a 2000 NASCAR rookie. Compton ran 88 Winston Cup races with one top–10 and two poles 1996–2003.

Buddy Baker won his second straight race in Charlotte with a victory in the 1968 World 600 at Charlotte Motor Speedway.

David Pearson won the 1974 World 600 at Charlotte Motor Speedway.

Darrell Waltrip won his third "Spring race" at Charlotte Motor Speedway in 1985 in the first Coca-Cola 600. The corporate sponsorship replaced the former "World 600." Waltrip went on to his third and final Winston Cup Championship in 1985.

Davey Allison won his first of five 1991 Winston Cup races with a trip to victory lane in the Coca-Cola 600 at Charlotte.

Dale Jarrett won for the second time on the 1996 Winston Cup circuit with a victory in the Coca-Cola 600 at Charlotte Motor Speedway.

In the 2002 Coca-Cola 600, Mark Martin won his only race of the Winston Cup season at the Lowe's Motor

Speedway. Jimmie Johnson qualified first for the third time of the season.

27

Neil Cole was born in 1926. He made 19 Grand National Starts 1950–53. He won the 1951 Thompson, CT, race from the pole, his best performance. Cole raced out of Oakland, NJ.

Announcer Dick Berggren was born in 1942. Berggren, nationally known as a writer and television personality, has a doctorate in psychology from Tufts University and began working in stock car racing circles after teaching for eight years at Emanuel College.

The first Grand National race held in the state of Oregon was held in 1956 at the Portland Speedway, a half-mile paved track. Herb Thomas captured his 46th career victory. The track hosted seven top-level NASCAR races 1956–57.

Speedy Thompson won at the Charlotte Speedway in 1956.

Eddie Gray helped close Ascot Stadium to Grand National drivers in 1961, winning the final NASCAR-sanctioned event held at the .4-mile dirt track in Los Angeles.

Nelson Stacy won the 1962 World 600 at Charlotte Motor Speedway. It was the third career win for Stacy, and second of three in 1962.

Ned Jarrett won at the Cleveland County (NC) Fairgrounds in the final season of Grand National competition at the dirt track in Shelby. It was his 42nd career win.

Jeremy Mayfield was born in 1969 in Owensboro, KY. Mayfield began his Winston Cup experience in 1993, starting 309 events through 2003, with three wins and seven top qualifying starts. His first victory came in the 1998 Pocono 500.

Buddy Baker drove his Dodge to a first-place finish in the 1973 World 600 at Charlotte, NC. David Pearson finished second.

Darrell Waltrip won the 1979 World 600 at Charlotte Motor Speedway, his second straight win in the annual event.

Bobby Allison won his 82nd career NASCAR race in 1984 at the Charlotte Motor Speedway in the final World 600. The World 600 was run from 1960 to 1984 and was replaced by the Coca-Cola 600 beginning in 1985.

Rusty Wallace, in a Pontiac, won the 1990 Coca-Cola 600 at Charlotte Motor Speedway for his first of two Winston Cup wins of the season.

Jeff Burton, who started the day 25th in Winston Cup points, won in 2001 at Lowe's Motor Speedway in the Coca-Cola 600. Ryan Newman started first for the only time in 2001.

28

Ray Fox Sr. was born in 1917 in Pelham, NH. Fox was a renowned mechanic and engine builder who later settled in Daytona Beach, FL, and worked with many of the top drivers of the 1950s and 1960s.

Marvin Panch was born in 1926 in Oakland, CA. Panch ran 216 races 1951–66 with 17 wins and 109 other top–10 finishes. He was second in Grand National points during the 1957 season, when he won a career-high six events. He won the pole position 21 times in his career.

Ronnie Kohler was born in 1927 and raced out of Paterson, NJ. Kohler recorded 13 starts in the 1950s with six top–10 finishes, including a third-place in a Plymouth at Monroe County (NY) Fairgrounds in his debut in July 1951.

Gary Baker was born in 1946. Racing out of Nashville, TN, he ran one career Winston Cup event. He finished 22nd in the 1980 Winston 500 at Talladega, AL.

Richie Panch, son of Marvin Panch, was born on his father's 26th birthday in 1954. Panch ran 47 Winston Cup races 1973–76 with 11 top–10 finishes.

Junior Johnson in 1955 won the first of three Grand National events hosted by the North Carolina State Fairgrounds in Raleigh (1955, 1969, 1970) on a half-mile dirt track. Johnson drove an Oldsmobile.

Ned Jarrett's fifth career Grand National win came at the Piedmont Interstate Fairgrounds in Spartanburg, SC, in 1960. Jack Smith quali-fied first for his 12th career pole.

David Pearson won his first career race in 1961 at Charlotte in the second annual World 600. Pearson was the 1960 Grand National Rookie of the Year.

Dick Dixon was killed in a modified race at Thompson, CT, in 1967. He started 11 Grand National events 1960–65, finishing third in back-to-

back races at Asheville, NC, and Harris, NC, in May 1965.

Jim Paschal won the 1967 World 600 at Charlotte Motor Speedway, his 23rd of 25 career Grand National victories over 23 years Cale Yarborough qualified first but finished 41st due to a steering problem.

Bobby Isaac won the 1970 Maryville 300 for his third of 11 wins on the season. Bobby Allison won the top starting spot for the 11th time. Isaac was the Grand National champion that season while Allison finished second.

Buddy Baker won the 1972 World 600 at Charlotte Motor Speedway.

Darrell Waltrip won the 1978 World 600 at Charlotte Motor Speedway.

Darrell Waltrip won his fourth race of the season with a first-place finish in the Coca-Cola 600 at Charlotte.

Bobby Labonte won the 1995 Coca-Cola 600 at Charlotte, NC. It was his first career NASCAR win as he cruised to victory over his brother Terry, who finished second.

Matt Kenseth drove his Ford to victory lane at the 2000 Coca-Cola 600 at the Lowe's Motor Speedway. It was his first career Winston Cup win and he went on to become the 2000 Rookie of the Year. Dale Earnhardt Jr., after consecutive wins, took the pole.

29

Joe Weatherly was born in Norfolk, VA, in 1922. Originally a motorcycle racer, Weatherly shifted to Grand National racing in the mid–1950s. Know as "The Clown Prince," he finished first in championship points in 1962 and 1963. He ran 230 events with 25 trips to Victory Lane. He was voted the most popular Grand National driver of 1961 but died as a result of injuries in a 1964 crash at Riverside.

George Davis was born in 1938. He started 28 career Grand National races in the late 1960s, 21 in 1967. He raced out of Adelphi, MD, to career-best fifth-place at Savannah Speedway (GA) in August 1967.

Alfred "Al" Unser Sr. was born in 1939. He is most famous for his Indianapolis 500 victories. Unser made five starts at NASCAR's highest level. He ran three Grand National races 1968–69, finishing in the top–10 in each event. He also started two 1986 Winston Cup races, with less success.

Born in 1950 and racing out of Huntsville, AL, James Means ran 455 Winston Cup races 1976–93 with 17 top–10 finishes. He was 11th in points in 1982.

Herb Thomas won from the pole position for the 14th time in his Grand National career with a first-place finish in the 1954 Raleigh 250, run on a one-mile paved track at Raleigh, NC. Thomas, driving a Hudson, averaged 73.909 mph in the 150-mile event.

The Forsyth County Fairgrounds in Winston-Salem, NC, hosted two career Grand National races, both won by Lee Petty in 1955. The inaugural event at the half-mile dirt track was Petty's 22nd career win. The track was also known as the Winston-Salem Fairgrounds or the Dixie Classic Fairgrounds.

Ken Schrader was born in 1955 in St. Louis, MO. Schrader began his Winston Cup career in 1984 and was the 1985 Rookie of the Year. He won his first race in the 1988 DieHard 500 at Talladega and won the pole for the Daytona 500 1988–90.

Bobby Hamilton was born in 1957 in Nashville, TN. Hamilton was the 1991 Winston Cup Rookie of the Year and won his first race in 1996 at Phoenix. He drove a car in the movie *Days of Thunder*, starring Tom Cruise.

Lee Petty won at the Occoneechee Speedway in Hillsboro, NC, in 1960 for Grand National win #51 of his career.

Junior Johnson won at the New Asheville Speedway in North Carolina in 1965.

In the final of seven events hosted by the Dog Track Speedway in Moyock, NC, a quarter-mile dirt track, David Person captured the checkered flag for his 19th career Grand National victory and sixth of the 1966 season.

Driving a Dodge, Richard Petty won the 1977 World 600 at Charlotte Motor Speedway.

Neil Bonnett won his second straight World 600 in 1983 at Charlotte.

Darrell Waltrip won his first race of 1988 with a first-place finish in the Coca-Cola 600 at Charlotte Motor Speedway.

Jeff Gordon, 22 years old, won his first Winston Cup race in 1994 in only his 42nd NASCAR start. Gordon also won the pole for the 1994 Coca-Cola 600 at Lowe's Motor Speedway in Charlotte.

30

Bill "Red" Hammersley was born in 1908. He started one Grand National race each in 1952 and 1953, earning a total of $50 driving at NASCAR's top level. Hammersley raced out of Mariners Harbor, NY.

Gene Cline, born in 1930, started 13 career Grand National races, all in 1966. Cline raced out of Rome, GA, to record two top–10 finishes in his only season at NASCAR's top level.

Norm Palmer was born in 1940. Palmer ran seven Winston Cup races 1977–85 with two top–10 finishes. He died in the 1980s following a private vehicle accident.

Bill Rexford won the 100-mile event on a .5-mile dirt track in Canfield, OH, in an Oldsmobile in the fifth NASCAR Series event of the season. It was the only Grand National win of his career. It was the first-ever NASCAR race held in Ohio. Rexford went on to capture the Grand National driving championship that season.

Marshall Teague won the 100-mile event at Canfield, OH, in 1951 for his fourth checkered flag of the season. Teague averaged 49.308 mph on the .5-mile dirt track in his Hudson.

Herb Thomas won his third race of 1952 as Hudson remained dominant with victories in all but one of the first 12 Grand National races of the season. Thomas took the check-

ered flag at an average speed of 48.057 at the .5-mile dirt track in Canfield, OH, in a 100-mile event. Dick Rathmann, who won the previous three races, won the pole.

Fonty Flock won his first race of the Grand National season in the first race held on the new one-mile paved Raleigh Speedway in Raleigh, NC. Flock drove his Hudson at an average speed of 70.629 for his 12th career NASCAR checkered flag. The track hosted seven Grand National races 1953–58. Ebenezer "Slick" Smith qualified for his only career pole Start. Smith raced out of Atlanta, GA, starting 50 career Grand National races 1949–55. He recorded 18 career top–10 finishes.

Buck Baker won the first of two NASCAR races held on this date in 1954. Baker cruised his Oldsmobile to his seventh career Grand National victory, his second of the season, in the 99.75-mile event at Charlotte's .75-mile dirt track. Al Keller took the pole position for the first time in his career.

A pair of newcomers qualified on the pole and won the race at Gardena, CA, in 1954, the second sanctioned event of the day. John Soares gained his first Grand National win while Danny Letner won the pole in the 248-mile event on the half-mile dirt track. It was the first win for Dodge on the season and the final NASCAR race of four held at the Carrell Speedway, the first track in California to host a NASCAR Grand National event.

Buck Baker won from the pole for a victory at the New York State Fairgrounds in Syracuse in 1956. In each of the three races held at the track, the pole sitter captured the checkered flag.

In 1956, Herb Thomas won the first of two sanctioned NASCAR events at the Redwood Speedway, a .625-mile dirt oval in Eureka, CA.

In 1957, Lloyd Dane won the final of two NASCAR events of the day, and the final of two sanctioned races at the Eureka Speedway in Eureka, CA. The event was shortened to 153 laps due to a crash by George Seeger. It was the third of four career wins for Dane.

Buck Baker won on the half-mile dirt track of the Lincoln Speedway in New Oxford, PA, in 1957 for his 30th career Grand National checkered flag. Marvin Panch won his sixth career pole, but finished fourth.

Fireball Roberts won his 15th career Grand National race in 1958 in the inaugural Northern 500 at Trenton Speedway on the New Jersey State Fairgrounds. The one-mile paved track hosted eight top-level NASCAR events between 1958 and 1972.

Parnelli Jones won at Ascot Stadium in Los Angeles in 1959. It was his third and final career victory, all on the west coast.

Carl Daniel "Smokey" Purser died in 1964, age unknown. Purser raced out of Lumber City, GA, to make one career Grand National start in 1952.

David Pearson won the 1962 World 600 at Charlotte Motor Speedway, his second win in the last three annual World 600 races.

A crash at the 1964 Indianapolis 500 claimed the life of David Mac-Donald, age 26. MacDonald had entered seven NASCAR races 1963–64 with four top–10s.

LeeRoy Yarbrough won for the third time in his Grand National career in Greenville, SC, in 1964. Marvin Panch qualified first for the 16th of 21 times in his career.

In 1965, Ned Jarrett captured the second of two Grand National races held at the Harris Speedway in North Carolina.

Bobby Allison won his 20th career race, his first driving a Mercury, with a win in 1971 at the Charlotte Motor Speedway in the World 600.

Neil Bonnett won the 1982 World 600 at Charlotte Motor Speedway.

Dale Earnhardt Sr. won the 1993 Coca-Cola 600 at Charlotte. It was his second Winston Cup series win of the season in addition to a victory the previous week in The Winston. Jeff Gordon was the runner-up.

Jeff Burton won his third race of the season in 1999's Coca-Cola 600 at Lowe's Motor Speedway outside Charlotte. Bobby Labonte won the pole and finished second.

31

Johnny Roberts was born in 1924. Roberts, who raced out of Brooklyn, MD, ran 13 Grand National races 1953–61 with one top–10 finish in 1955.

William Claren, born in 1925, started his only Grand National race in 1954. He raced out of Montclair, NJ, to drive a Jaguar to a fourth-place finish at Linden Airport (NJ).

John Callis, born in 1949, started seven Winston Cup events in the early 1980s. He raced out of Orlando, FL, to a 20th-place finish in the 1983 Mason-Dixon 500 at Dover, DE.

Ned Jarrett won at the New Asheville Speedway in 1964, his second straight win at the .4-mile paved track in North Carolina.

Richard Petty won the Asheville 300 in 1968, winning from the pole for the 36th time in his career and earning his 79th career win. Petty was voted the circuit's most popular driver for the third time in 1968.

Bobby Isaac's 25th career win came in the 1970 Virginia 500 at Martinsville. Isaac won 11 races that season on his way to the Grand National driving championship.

Donnie Allison won his fourth career pole while his brother Bobby finished second in the race.

Davey Allison won the 1987 Budweiser 500 at Dover Downs. It was his second win in three races on the season.

Harry Gant won his second straight race at Dover with a win in the 1992 Budweiser 500.

Dale Jarrett won his second race of the season in the MBNA Platinum 400 at Dover, DE. Rusty Wallace qualified first but finished 18th.

JUNE

1

Bob Moore was born in 1921. Racing out of Kent, OH, he ran nine races 1950–52 with three top–10 finishes. He finished tenth in his final event at Monroe Speedway (MI).

Darel Dieringer was born in 1926 in Indianapolis, IN. He started 181 Grand National and Winston Cup events between 1957 and 1975, including seven wins and 11 pole-position starts. He finished third in points in 1965 and won the 1966 Southern 500, when he was named the Grand National's most popular driver in voting by fans.

Robert "Bob" Williams was born in 1937. He ran two Winston Cup events in 1971. He raced out of Jackson, MS, to a career-best 20th-place finish in the 1971 Wilkes 400 at North Wilkesboro, NC.

Jim Sauter was born in 1943. Racing out of Necedah, WI, Sauter started 76 races 1980–96 with four top–10 finishes, holding the lead in four career events.

Charles "Chuck" Little was born in 1944 and raced out of Spokane, WA. He started one Winston Cup race, a 28th place finish at Riverside, CA, in the 1975 Winston Western 500.

Tom Sneva was born in 1948. Known mostly as an open-wheel racer, Sneva did start eight career Winston Cup races with one top–10 finish. He raced out of Spokane, WA.

Gober Sosebee won his first of two career Grand National races with a first-place finish at the .5-mile dirt track of the Hayloft Speedway in Augusta, GA, in 1952. It was the only top-level NASCAR event ever held at the track. Sosebee, who had won two poles in prior seasons, cruised his Chrysler to only the manufacturer's second victory. Tommy Moon won his first career pole position, in a Hudson, for the 100-mile contest, which was shortened to 77 miles due to rain. On the season, through 13 races, 11 had been won by Hudson with one win each for Oldsmobile and Chrysler.

Tim Flock and his Hudson won the second of two sanctioned races held on this date in 1952. Flock, whose brother Fonty won the pole, won the 100-mile contest at Toledo, OH, at an average speed of 47.175 mph. It was the 10th career win for Tim and the 16th pole for Fonty.

Paul Goldsmith won his third of four races during the 1957 Grand National Season at Lancaster, SC, his fourth of nine career checkered flags.

Eddie Gray won the first NASCAR-sanctioned race at Riverside International Raceway in California in 1958's Crown America 500. It was the first of four career wins for Gray, all in the state of California.

Davy Jones was born in 1964. Racing out of Chicago, IL, Jones made seven Winston Cup starts in 1995, his only season of racing at NASCAR's top level. His best finish was 20th at the TranSouth Financial 400 at Darlington, SC.

Lance Hooper was born in 1967. Racing out of Palmdale, CA, Hooper debuted at the Winston Cup level with a start in 1996 and ran nine races through 2002. He finished 24th twice, the first time in the 1997 Bud at the Glen at Watkins Glen, NY.

Bobby Isaac won the 1969 Macon 300 at Middle Georgia Raceway in Macon, GA. Isaac was voted the Grand National circuit's most popular driver that year and won the driving championship in 1970.

Cale Yarborough won from the pole in the 1980 NASCAR 400 at the Texas World Speedway It was his 65th win and 50th top start, the 13th of 17 times he started and finished first.

Darrell Waltrip won the 1986 Budweiser 400 at the California Speedway in Riverside, CA.

Ricky Rudd won for the first time in 1997 in the Miller 500 at Dover Downs International Speedway. It was the 15th consecutive season with a Winston Cup win for Rudd. Mark Martin finished second.

The #99 Ford of Jeff Burton won the 2000 Pepsi 400 at Daytona. It was Burton's third win of the season. Dale Jarrett captured the pole.

Ryan Newman won his second straight pole qualifying start, but this time went on to win in the 2003 MBNA Armed Forces Family 400 at Dover International Speedway for his second win of the Winston Cup season.

2

Donald "Satch" Worley was born in 1948. Worley ran five Winston Cup races in the 1970s with a top–10 finish in his first career event.

Tighe Scott was born in 1949. Racing out of Pen Argyle, PA, Scott ran 89 Winston Cup races 1976–82 with 18 top–10 finishes and a lead in two races. He debuted in the 1976 Daytona 500 and finished 35th after a crash.

Kyle Petty was born in 1960 in Randleman, NC. Kyle, whose grandfather Lee and father Richard where NASCAR legends, began in the Winston Cup Series in 1980. His son Adam was a promising driver who died in 2001 in a practice crash.

Jim Paschal won in 1961 at Spartanburg, SC, his eighth career win.

Fred Lorenzen won the 1963 World 600 at Charlotte Motor Speedway. It was his 16th career Grand National victory.

David Pearson won at the New Asheville (NC) Speedway in 1966, capturing the inaugural Asheville 300 for his 20th career victory just four days after winning at Moyock, NC.

Jim Paschal won the second annual Asheville 300 at New Asheville Speedway in 1967.

David Pearson won the 1968 Macon 300 at Middle Georgia Raceway. It was his eighth of 16 wins that season, his second of three as Grand National Champion.

Terry Labonte won his second straight Budweiser 400 in 1985 at Riverside, CA.

Ken Schrader won his second race of 1991 with a first-place finish in the Budweiser 500 at the Monster Mile in Dover, DE.

Jeff Gordon won the Miller 500 at the Monster Mile in Dover for his fourth win of 1996.

Jimmie Johnson, who captured the pole the previous week, cruised to victory lane in the 2002 MBNA Armed Forces Family 400 at Dover International Speedway. Matt Kenseth won his first pole of the season.

3

Art Malone entered one NASCAR event each in 1961 and 1962, with a top–10 in each race and a career-best eighth in his debut in the Old Dominion 500 at Martinsville. Malone was born this date in 1936 and raced out of Lutz, FL.

Connie Saylor was born in 1940. Saylor ran 58 Winston Cup events 1978–89 with one top–10 finish, an eighth-place in his debut in the 1978 Atlanta 500. He led four races in his career, including three laps at the 1982 Southern 500, where he finished 12th.

Glenn Steurer was born in 1955. Steurer, who raced out of Canoga Park, CA, made five Winston Cup starts in the mid–1980s with one top–10 finish in 1986.

Herb Thomas won at the Merced Fairgrounds Speedway in Merced, CA, in 1956 in the only NASCAR event held at the track.

Dick Hutcherson captured his second career win in 1965 at Nashville Speedway (TN). Tom Pistone won his first of five career poles.

David Pearson won at Dover Downs in 1973 in the Mason-Dixon 500.

Cale Yarborough won both 1978 races at Nashville, his first in the Music City USA 420. It was his 52nd career win. Yarborough won ten races that season and captured the Winston Cup championship. Lennie Pond won his second career pole and finished in the runner-up position in his #54 Chevrolet.

Jamie McMurray was born in Joplin, MO, in 1979. The 2003 Winston Cup Rookie of the Year, Mc-Murray won his first race in 2002 at the Lowe's Motor Speedway in the UAW-GM Quality 500.

Darrell Waltrip's 19th career win

came in the 1979 Texas 400. Buddy Baker won his second straight pole at the track.

Terry Labonte won the 1984 Budweiser 400 at Riverside, CA, his first of two seasons. Labonte went on to record his first of two Winston Cup Championships that season.

Derrike Cope won the 1990 Budweiser 500 at Dover Downs. It was the second win of the season for Cope, who took the Daytona 500 in the initial race of the Winston Cup campaign. Dick Trickle, the 1989 Rookie of the Year, won his only career pole.

Jeff Gordon won his second Winston Cup race of the season in 2001 at Dover Downs in the MBNA Platinum 400. Gordon, who two weeks earlier won the Winston, remained in second place in the points race behind Dale Jarrett. Gordon won his fourth Winston Cup Championship that season.

4

Max King, born in 1913 and racing out of Cartersville, GA, started one race in 1953. King came away with $25 in his only NASCAR experience, a 16th-place finish at Lakewood Speedway in Atlanta, GA, in July 1953.

Gayther "Runt" Harris, born in 1927, started eight Grand National races 1950–62 with one top-five finish in 1957. He raced out of Fredericksburg, VA.

Jerry Hufflin, born in 1944, started three career Winston Cup events,

two in 1974 and one in 1990. Hufflin ran out of Greenville, SC, to a 25th-place finish in his debut in the 1974 Richmond 500.

Edward "Hank" Lee died of a heart attack in 1952. Lee started one race each in 1951 and 1952, winning a total of $75 in Grand National money.

Ned Jarrett won in Birmingham, AL, in 1961. Jarrett's win was his only checkered flag finish during his first of two Grand National Championship seasons.

Elmo Langley won his first NASCAR race in 1966 at Spartanburg, SC. Langley went on to drive periodically for ten more seasons with one more win, ironically in July 1966. It was the final Grand National race of 22 hosted at the Piedmont Interstate Fairgrounds in Spartanburg, SC, between 1953 and 1966. The track was also known as the Hub City Speedway.

Bobby Allison won his 32nd career NASCAR race in 1972 at Dover Downs International Speedway. It was his third win of the season as he captured the Mason-Dixon 500.

Dale Earnhardt Sr. won his second race of the season with a trip to victory lane in the 1989 Budweiser 500 at Dover Downs.

Kyle Petty won the 1995 Miller Genuine Draft 500 at Dover Downs, DE.

Tony Stewart in his #20 Pontiac won the MBNA Platinum 400 in 2000. Rusty Wallace started from the pole. It was the first win of Stewart's career.

5

Lynwood "Sonny" Easley was born in 1939. He started 19 Winston Cup races 1972–77 but was killed in a crash at Riverside, CA, in 1978. His best finish was fifth place at Riverside in the 1977 Winston Western 500.

Henry "Butch" Miller was born in 1952. Racing out of Michigan, Miller ran 41 Winston Cup races 1986–94 with one lone top–10 finish. He came in eighth in the 1990 AC Spark Plug 500 at Pocono, PA.

Steve Kinser was born in 1954. Racing out of Bloomington, IN, he managed five starts in 1995 at the Winston Cup level. He finished 40th in his debut, crashing on the 27th lap of the 1995 Daytona 500.

Junior Johnson won in 1958 in Columbia, SC, for his eighth career checkered flag.

Jack Smith won at Spartanburg, SC, in 1959, his ninth Grand National win. Cotton Owens captured his fourth of 11 career pole starts.

Lee Petty won at Richmond International Raceway in 1960. Petty had six wins in 1960 after winning the championship the prior year with 11 wins. Ned Jarrett qualified on the pole for the first of 35 times in his Grand National career, and finished third. Jarrett developed quickly and won the 1961 championship.

Bobby Hillin was born in 1964 in Texas. Hillin started his first Winston Cup race when he was a 17-year-old high school student. He captured his first win in the 1986 Talladega 500.

Bobby Isaac won the 1969 Maryville 300 at the Smoky Mountain Raceway. David Pearson, who won the pole, finished second.

Ricky Rudd won his first career NASCAR race in the 1983 Budweiser 400 at Riverside, CA. He was the 1977 Winston Cup Rookie of the Year.

Bill Elliott won his second race of 1988 with a win in the Budweiser 500 at Dover Downs. Elliott won his only Winston Cup Championship that year.

Rusty Wallace won his second straight race at Dover Downs with a win in the 1994 Budweiser 500.

6

Wilbur Rakestraw was born in 1928 in Georgia. Rakestraw ran 30 Grand National races 1956–61. He was one of four Rakestraws that ran in the 1950s including Ansel, Benny and Tyre. Wilbur recorded six top–10 finishes.

E. J. Trivette was born in 1936. He started 177 career Grand National and Winston Cup races 1959–71. Racing out of Deep Gap, NC, Trivette managed 29 top–10 finishes, including 15 in 1969 when he finished a career-high 11th in series points. He finished 26th in the 1969 Daytona 500.

Curtis Turner won his first race of 1954 in the 17th event of the Grand National circuit at the half-mile dirt track in Columbia, SC. Driving an Oldsmobile an average speed of 56.719 mph, Turner gained the 10th victory of his career while Buck Baker won his ninth career pole position.

Ned Jarrett won in Birmingham, AL, in 1965, his 44th career victory and 29th pole position start.

Richard Petty won his second straight race at the Middle Georgia Raceway with a victory in the Macon 300 in 1967.

Richard Petty notched his 80th career Grand National win in a 1968 race at the Smoky Mountain Raceway in Maryville, TN. It was his ninth of 16 victories that season.

David Pearson won the pole, his seventh top start of 16 that season. Petty finished third to Pearson in the season championship.

Bobby Allison won his second consecutive NASCAR race, the 21st win of his career, with a 1971 victory at Dover Downs International Speedway in the Mason-Dixon 500. It was the third race ever at the Dover, DE, track.

David Pearson won the 1976 Riverside 400 at Riverside International Raceway in California.

Bobby Allison won his 64th NASCAR race in 1982 with a victory at Pocono International Raceway in the Van Scoy Diamond Mine 500. It was his third win of the season. There were no time trials.

Clyde Lindley died in 1990 at the age of 52 from injuries suffered in an All Pro race in Bradenton, FL. Lindley ran 11 races 1979–85 with a career-best second-place finish in the 1982 Virginia National Bank 500 at Martinsville, VA.

Dale Earnhardt Sr. earned his third points race win of 1993 with a victory at the Monster Mile of Dover in the Budweiser 500. It was also his third consecutive win, including a first-place finish in the non-points The Winston.

Terry Labonte won his first race of the season with a victory at Richmond in the 1998 Pontiac Excitement 400, his 20th career Winston Cup win. Jeff Gordon, who qualified on the pole, finished 37th due to his involvement in an accident but won his third championship that season.

Bobby Labonte won from the pole in the 1999 MBNA Platinum 400 at Dover, DE. Jeff Gordon was the runner-up.

7

George Mantooth was born in 1925. He raced once in 1949 and once in 1956 at NASCAR's highest level but failed to earn any prize money. He was a competitor in the first Strictly Stock event in June 1949 at Charlotte, finishing 26th.

In the only sanctioned race held in the state of Louisiana, Lee Petty claimed his fourth victory of the 1953 season with a win on the half-mile dirt track at Shreveport. Petty averaged 53.199 mph in his Dodge while Herb Thomas claimed the pole for the 100-mile race. It was the 10th career win for Petty.

Tim Richmond was born in Ashland, OH, in 1955. Richmond ran 185 career races with 13 wins and 78 top–10 finishes. He was third in points in 1986. Controversy surrounded his later years when he refused a physical for medical clearance and was not allowed to race. He died of AIDS in 1989.

Ned Jarrett won the 1964 Dixie 400 at Atlanta Motor Speedway.

Cale Yarborough won the 1970 Motor State 400 at Michigan International Speedway.

The Texas World Speedway in College Station hosted eight top-level NASCAR events 1969–81. The final event was won by Benny Parsons, the 18th of his 21 career Winston Cup wins. Terry Labonte won his second-ever pole position.

Ernie Irvan won the Save Mart Supermarkets 300K at Sonoma, CA, in 1992.

8

Lloyd Moore was born in 1912. Racing out of upstate New York, Moore ran 49 races in the Strictly Stock and Grand National series 1949–54. He finished fourth in points in 1950 and won a race in Winchester, IN, his only career victory at NASCAR's top level.

Tim and Fonty Flock pulled a repeat of the previous Grand National race with the former gaining the win and the latter capturing the pole position for the second straight week. Tim guided his Hudson to an average speed of 81.008 mph on the one-mile dirt track in Hillsboro, NC, for his third win of 1952. Fonty's qualifying time was the first to eclipse 90 mph on a dirt track.

Eddie Pagan won the first race held at Ascot Stadium in Los Angeles, CA, in 1957.

Jack Smith won his 15th career race in 1961 at Greenville, SC. Ned Jarrett won his ninth career pole.

Bryan Baker, born in 1961 and racing out of Charlotte, NC, started one Winston Cup race. He finished 29th after crashing just over halfway through the 1986 Delaware 500 at Dover Downs.

Richard Petty won at the Smoky Mountain Raceway in the 1967 East Tennessee 200 for his 58th career victory. Jim Hunter captured the only pole of his career in five Grand National events 1965–67, but finished out of the top 10.

In 1968, Richard Petty, driving a Plymouth, won the final NASCAR race run at the Birmingham International Raceway in Alabama on the half-mile dirt track. Bobby Isaac finished second.

Richard Petty won the 1975 Tuborg 400 at Riverside. It was the seventh win of the season for Petty, who won 13 races in 1975 on his way to his sixth of seven points championships.

Darrell Waltrip won his second straight race at Riverside in 1980 in the Warner W. Hodgdon 400.

Tim Richmond won the Miller High Life 500 at Pocono International Raceway in 1986, his 6th Winston Cup victory. Geoff Bodine captured his 24th career pole.

Jeff Gordon won the 1997 Pocono 500. Jeff Burton finished second. Gordon went on to his second points championship that season.

Tony Stewart, the 2002 Winston Cup champion, won his first race of 2003 at Long Pond, PA, with a checkered flag finish in the Pocono 500. Jimmy Johnson qualified first.

Pocono 500 at Long Pond, PA. Sterling Marlin qualified first.

9

David Wishart Hobbs, who raced out of Upper Buddington, England, in the 1970s, was born in 1939. Hobbs made two Winston Cup starts in 1976, leading one race for two laps.

Clay Young was born in 1947. He raced out of Smyrna, GA, to start five Winston Cup events between 1980 and 1993. He finished a career-best 19th in the 1980 Atlanta Journal 500.

Richard Petty won in Birmingham, AL, in 1963, his 22nd career Grand National victory.

David Pearson won at the Smoky Mountain Raceway in the 1966 East Tennessee 200 for his 21st career win. Pearson won 15 races that season on his way to the Grand National championship. Tom Pistone qualified on the pole for the fourth of five times in his career.

Cale Yarborough swept both races held at Riverside International Raceway in 1974 with a win in the Tuborg 400.

Bill Elliott won from the pole in the 1985 Summer 500 at Pocono International Raceway in Pennsylvania. It was Elliott's 10th win and 11th pole of his Winston Cup career.

Davey Allison won for the second time in three weeks with a victory on the road course at Sears Point, CA, in the 1991 Banquet Frozen Foods 300.

Dale Jarrett's first of two 2002 Winston Cup victories came in the

10

Vic Elford, who raced out of South London, England, in the 1960s and '70s, was born in 1935. Elford started four Grand National and Winston Cup races 1969–72 with a top–10 finish in his final NASCAR appearance.

Tim Flock won the 100-mile race at the Columbus Speedway in 1951, the only NASCAR-sanctioned race at the Georgia city. It was his second win of the season and third of his career. Gober Sosebee, who held the pole for the first NASCAR Daytona race, won his second career pole. It was the first pole position for a Cadillac automobile and the first official NASCAR race in the state of Georgia.

Junior Johnson won from the pole for his 4th career victory in 1955 at the Lincoln Speedway. It was the first of seven Grand National events staged at the Abbottstown (New Oxford), PA, half-mile dirt track between 1955 and 1965.

Thomas "Cotton" Priddy, age 27, died as a result of injuries suffered 57 miles into the Grand National race in LeHi, AR, on this date in 1956. Priddy, who raced out of Louisville, KY, had started just two NASCAR races in 1953 before his fatal mishap in his third career series start. Also killed in the race was Clint McHugh. Ralph Moody won his first of five career NASCAR races in the event at the Memphis-Arkansas Speedway. It was the fourth of five sanctioned races held at the dangerous track.

Rex White's 17th Grand National win came in 1961 at the Myers Brothers Memorial at Bowman-Gray Stadium in Winston-Salem, NC.

Fred Lorenzen won at the Atlanta Motor Speedway in the 1962 Atlanta 500.

Bobby Allison won his sixth career race with a victory at the Birmingham International Speedway in NASCAR's 24th race of the 1967 season. It was his third victory of the season and the first time he won in a Dodge after winning his first five in a Chevrolet.

Richard Petty won at the Texas World Speedway in the 1973 Alamo 500, his fourth victory of the Winston Cup campaign. Buddy Baker won his 15th career pole.

Bobby Allison won his fourth race of the 1979 NASCAR season in the Riverside 400 at Riverside International Raceway. It was his 55th career first place finish.

Cale Yarborough won his 81st career race at the Pocono International Raceway in 1964 with a victory in the Van Scoy Diamond Mine 500. Benny Parsons won his 19th career pole.

Rusty Wallace, driving a Pontiac, won his second race in three weeks with a trip to victory lane in the 1990 Banquet Frozen Foods 300 on the road course at Sears Point.

Ed Samples died in 1991 at the age of 70. Samples, who raced out of Atlanta, GA, ran 13 Grand National races 1951–52, 1954 with six top–10 finishes.

Jeff Gordon won his second consecutive Winston Cup race with a 2001 victory in the K-Mart 400 at Michigan International Speedway. Gordon took over the points lead from Dale Jarrett. Gordon also captured his fourth pole position start of the season and went on to the Winston Cup Championship.

11

Truceson Burgess "Tru" Cheek, who raced out of Sylmar, CA, was born in 1937. He made one Winston Cup start each in 1971 and 1972 at Riverside, finishing 24th in his debut in the Winston Golden State 400.

Duane "Pancho" Carter Jr. was born in 1950. Carter started 14 career Winston Cup races 1985–95. His father, Duane Carter Sr., ran one Grand National race in 1950.

Richard Petty won at the Concord Speedway (NC) in 1964, the final Grand National event at the track which hosted 12 races between 1956 and 1964.

David Pearson won the 1972 Motor State 400 at Michigan International Speedway.

Benny Parsons won the 1978 NAPA 400 at Riverside International Raceway.

Ricky Rudd, in a Buick, won his only race of 1989 with a first-place finish in the inaugural Banquet Frozen Foods 300 at Sears Point International Raceway. It was the first sanctioned NASCAR race at the 2.52-mile road course.

Terry Labonte captured the 1995

UAW-GM Teamwork 500 at Pocono. It was the 15th Winston Cup victory of Labonte's career.

Tony Stewart captured his second straight race with a win in the 2000 K-Mart 400 at Michigan International Speedway. Bobby Labonte started from the pole.

12

Richard Clayton "Dick" Eagan, who raced out of Springdale, CT, in the early 1950s, was born in 1919. Eagan ran six Grand National events 1950–52 with a career-best third place finish in a 1951 race.

Robert "Bobby" Greene, who raced out of Siler City, NC, in Strictly Stock's inaugural 1949 season, was born in 1925. Greene started two races at first season, earning a total of $50 as a top-level NASCAR driver.

Bill Cheesbourg was born in 1927. Cheesbourg raced out of Tucson, AZ, to run two Grand National events in 1951 and earned $50 at NASCAR's top level.

Innes Ireland, who raced out of Prestiegne Rads, United Kingdom, was born in 1930. Ireland started two NASCAR races in 1967 with one top–10 finish.

Skimp Hersey died in 1950 at the age of 37 from burns suffered in a crash the previous day at Lakewood Speedway, Florida. Hersey ran one race in NASCAR's inaugural season of 1949.

The only sanctioned race held in Bradford, PA, was won by Junior Johnson in 1958, his 9th career victory. Bob Duell, from nearby Warren, PA, won his only series pole position and finished third on the .333-mile dirt track of the New Bradford Speedway.

Marvin Porter won the second NASCAR race run at Marchbanks Speedway in Hanford, CA, in 1960. It was the final of his two career Grand National wins. Porter raced out of Lakewood, CA, and made 34 career Grand National starts 1957–67. He burst onto the scene with a win at San Jose in a 58-mile race, one of two held on 9/15/57. Frank Secrist captured his only career pole start.

Richard Petty won at the Asheville-Weaverville (NC) Speedway in the inaugural Fireball 300 in 1966 for his 46th career checkered flag.

Richard Petty, driving a Dodge, won the 1977 NAPA 400 at Riverside, CA.

Bobby Allison won his third of six races of 1983 with a first place finish at Pocono International Speedway in the Van Scoy Diamond Mine 500. It was his 72nd career win. Allison won his only Winston Cup Championship that season.

Rusty Wallace won his first race of 1988 with a victory in the Budweiser 400 at Riverside, CA. It was the final NASCAR race at the track, which opened in 1958.

Rusty Wallace won the 1994 UAW-GM Teamwork 500. It was the seventh time in his career that he won from the pole and marked his 35th career Winston Cup victory.

13

Automaker Jaguar captured its first and only NASCAR checkered flag in the first sanctioned race at Linden, NJ, in 1954. Al Keller won his second and final career race, both in the 1954 season, with an average speed of 77.469. Buck Baker captured his second consecutive, and 10th career, pole position.

Junior Johnson's 16th career Grand National win came in 1959 at Greenville-Pickens Speedway (SC). Jack Smith qualified first for the ninth time in his career.

Dirk Stephens was born in 1963. Stephens ran two Winston Cup events in 1993. He raced out of Tumwater, WA, to a 30th place finish in his debut at the Save Mart Supermarkets 300k at Sonoma, CA.

Marvin Panch won the 1965 Dixie 400 at Atlanta Motor Speedway, his second straight win at the Hampton, GA, track.

Bobby Allison won his third straight NASCAR race, and the 22nd of his career, with a 1971 win at Michigan International Speedway.

David Pearson won his sixth race in the last eight starts at the Michigan International Speedway with a win in the 1976 Cam 2 Motor Oil 400.

Tim Richmond won his first of 13 career NASCAR races in 1982 at the Riverside International Speedway in the Budweiser 400.

Kyle Petty won his only Winston Cup race of 1993, taking the checkered flag in the Champion 500 at Pocono.

Dale Jarrett won for the second time of the season in the 1999 K Mart 400 Presented by Castrol Super Clean. Jeff Gordon, who won the pole, finished second. Jarrett won the Winston Cup Championship, ending Gordon's two year reign as top driver.

14

Fareed Joseph "Fred" Harb, who raced out of High Point, NC, in the 1950s and '60s, was born in 1930. Harb ran 144 career Grand National events with 42 top–10s.

Herb Thomas kept pace with Lee Petty by capturing his fourth victory of the 1953 Grand National campaign, winning the shortest race of the season in Pensacola, FL (70 miles). Thomas, driving his trademark Hudson, averaged 63.316 mph on the half-mile dirt track. Dick Rathmann qualified first, also in a Hudson, his fourth career pole. It was the 20th career win for Thomas who went on to his second Grand National driving championship that season.

Lee Petty won the final NASCAR event held at Lakewood Speedway in Atlanta, GA, in 1959. It was the 11th event sanctioned at the one-mile dirt track, which was replaced by the Atlanta Motor Speedway on the Grand National circuit in 1960. This race was apparently won by Richard Petty (and would have been his first career win), but his father won after a successful protest.

Richard Petty won his 32nd career

race in 1964 at Nashville Speedway. David Pearson, who finished second, qualified for his ninth career pole start.

Richard Petty won the Falstaff 400 at Riverside International Raceway in 1970.

Darrell Waltrip won for the fourth time in six races at Riverside, CA, in the 1981 Warner W. Hodgdon 400.

Tim Richmond won the Miller High Life 500 in 1987 at Pocono International Raceway, his third straight victory at the Pennsylvania superspeedway. Terry Labonte captured his 15th career pole.

Alan Kulwicki's 5th career Winston Cup checkered flag came in 1992 in the Champion Spark Plug 500 at Pocono International Raceway in Pennsylvania. It was his final of two wins that season, when he was the Winston Cup Champion.

Mark Martin won the 1998 Miller Lite 400, his fourth win of the season, at Michigan Speedway. Ward Burton qualified for the pole and finished eighth.

15

Herb Thomas gained his 12th career win with a checkered-flag finish on the .75-mile dirt track at Charlotte, NC, as automaker Hudson won for the 14th time in 16 races on the 1952 season. Fonty Flock, winless on the season, won his third straight pole for the 112.5-mile event.

William "Bill" Ingram, who raced out of Acworth, GA, in the 1980s,

was born in 1954. Ingram managed one Winston Cup start in 1989, running 481 miles at NASCAR's top level.

Speedy Thompson won in 1956 at the Southern States Fairgrounds in Charlotte, NC.

Fireball Roberts won the final of two sanctioned Grand National events held at the Tennessee-Carolina Speedway, which was also known as the Newport or Cocke County Fairgrounds. His 1957 win at the Newport, TN, track was the 12th of his career. Speedy Thompson won the pole, his ninth.

Junior Johnson won the Grand National race in Reading, PA, in 1958, his 10th career victory. He would also win the second and final running of this event.

Tiny Lund won the 1966 Beltsville 200 in Maryland, his third career victory.

In the 1969 Motor State 500, the first NASCAR race at the Michigan International Speedway, Cale Yarborough captured the win.

David Pearson won the 1975 Motor State 400, his second straight win at the Michigan International Speedway.

Benny Parsons won the 1980 Gabriel 400 at Michigan International Speedway, his second win of 1980 and 16th career Winston Cup win.

Bill Elliott won his second straight "June race" at Michigan with a win in the 1985 Miller 400.

Bill Elliott won his first race of 1986 with a victory in the Miller American 400. It was his third straight win at Michigan International Speedway and his fourth victory in the last five races at the track.

Ernie Irvan won the Miller 400 in 1997 at the Michigan International Speedway. Irvan had suffered serious injuries in a practice crash at the raceway three years earlier. Bill Elliott finished second.

Kurt Busch became the first three-time winner of the 2003 Winston Cup season with a victory in the Sirius 400 at Michigan International Speedway. Bobby Labonte won his third pole of the season.

16

Larry Grayson Smith was born in 1942. Smith ran 38 top-level NASCAR races, driving out of Lenoir, NC. He finished in the top 10 nine times, but was killed in the 1973 Talladega 500. Smith was the 1972 Winston Cup Rookie of the Year.

Frank Mundy won his first of three career NASCAR races (and his first pole) with a first-place finish at the 100-mile event at Columbia, SC, in 1951. It was the first-ever sanctioned NASCAR dirt-track race in the state of South Carolina and the first win for manufacturer Studebaker. The track hosted Grand National racing 1951–71.

Johnny Allen won his only career race in 1962 in the Myers Brothers Memorial at Winston-Salem, NC, in a 50-mile paved short-track event at Bowman-Gray Stadium. Alphabetically, he is the first driver listed of all the NASCAR race winners in history.

Either Rex White or Glen Wood had won the nine previous races at the track.

Donnie Allison won his first career NASCAR race at Rockingham, NC, in the 1968 Carolina 500. Allison was the 1967 Grand National Rookie of the Year.

Richard Petty won the 1974 Motor State 400 at Michigan International Speedway. Petty won his fifth of seven driving championships in 1974 with 10 wins.

Darrell Waltrip won the 1991 Champion Spark Plug 500 at Pocono. It was the second Winston Cup win of the season for Waltrip and the 80th of his Winston Cup career. Dale Earnhardt finished second.

Jeff Gordon won his second consecutive race in 1996, his fifth win of the Winston Cup season, taking the checkered flag in the UAW-GM Teamwork 500 at Pocono. Gordon started on the pole to capture his 14th career win.

Matt Kenseth's third victory of 2002 came at the Michigan International Speedway in the Sirius 400. The previous week's winner, Dale Jarrett, qualified first.

17

Bill Widenhouse was born in 1929. He ran 31 Grand National events 1950–64. Racing out of Midland, NC, Widenhouse managed five top–10 finishes.

Tim Flock won his 24th career Grand National race in 1955 at the

Monroe County Fairgrounds in Rochester, NY. Flock won the points championship that season.

Emanuel Zervakis captured the final of two career Grand National wins, both in 1961. This one came at the Norwood Arena in the only NASCAR race ever run in the state of Massachusetts.

Bob Pronger was presumed dead on this date in 1971. The circumstances surrounding his demise remain uncertain. It was reported that he disappeared due to "underworld connections." Pronger started nine Grand National races 1951–61, winning the pole for the February 1953 beach-road race at Daytona Beach.

Bobby Allison won his 40th career race with a victory at the Riverside International Raceway in the 1973 Tuborg 400. He was voted the most popular Winston Cup driver for the fourth consecutive time that season.

Buddy Baker won the 1979 Gabriel 400 at Michigan International Speedway.

Bill Elliott won the inaugural Miller High Life 400 at Michigan International Speedway in 1984. It was his first win of 1984 and the second of his career. He was named 1984's most popular Winston Cup driver, the first of five consecutive seasons.

Harry Gant won the 1990 Miller Genuine Draft 500 at Pocono for his only win of the Winston Cup season, the 12th of his career.

Pappy Hough died at age 93. Hough ran 21 races in the 1950s, with nine starts and four top–10 finishes in 1951. His best race was a fifth-place finish at the Monroe (NY) County Fairgrounds in 1951.

Ricky Rudd won for the only time in the Winston Cup season with a checkered flag finish at Pocono International Raceway in the 2001 Pocono 500. Rudd won from the pole, his only top start of the season as well.

18

Frank Mundy was born Francisco Melendez in 1918. Mundy, a NASCAR pioneer, ran 53 races 1949–56. He captured four poles and won three races in 1951, when he finished fifth overall in points.

Dean Dalton, who raced out of Asheville, NC, in the 1970s, was born in 1945. Dalton started 118 races with ten top–10 Winston Cup finishes 1971–77.

Bill Blair won his first race, and a Mercury took the checkered flag in a NASCAR race for the first time in 1950. Blair won the sixth event of the season, a 100-mile race on a .5-mile dirt track in Vernon, NY. Chuck Mahoney also registered the first pole position start for Mercury.

The Fonda Speedway at the Montgomery County (NY) Fairgrounds hosted four Grand National races between 1955 and 1968. Junior Johnson won the first race at the half-mile paved track in 1955, his 5th career win.

Lee Petty won at Columbia Speedway in 1959 for his 43rd career Grand National victory. Bob Burdick won his second and final pole of his career, both in 1959.

Richard Petty won his first-ever race at the North Carolina Motor Speedway in Rockingham, NC, in 1967 with a win in the inaugural Carolina 500.

Ray Elder captured his second win at Riverside in two years with a first-place finish in the 1972 Golden State 400, his final career Winston Cup win.

Cale Yarborough won his second straight "June race" at the Michigan International Speedway with a victory in the first annual Gabriel 400 in 1978.

Thomas D. "Tommie" Elliott died in 1989 at the age of 53. Elliott started seven Grand National events 1951–58 with four top–10 finishes.

Terry Labonte won the 1989 Miller High Life 500 at Pocono. It was his first win of the season and ninth of his Winston Cup career. Rusty Wallace won his 7th career pole.

Bobby Labonte won the 1995 Miller Genuine Draft 400 at Michigan.

The #12 Ford of Jeremy Mayfield won the 2000 Pocono 500 for his second career checkered flag. Rusty Wallace won the pole for the second time in three races.

19

Ray Johnstone, who raced out of San Bernardino, CA, was born in 1928. He made six starts at the Grand National/Winston Cup level 1969–72, all at either Riverside or Ontario, CA. He finished 11th in his debut in the 1969 Motor Trend 500 at Riverside.

David Ezell, who raced out of Jacksonville, FL, in the 1950s and '60s, was born in 1928. Ezell competed in three career Grand National races with a third place finish in his first-ever event in 1952. He also ran once each in 1956 and 1961.

Bill Baker was born in 1931. He made three Winston Cup starts at Riverside, racing out of Pismo Beach, CA. His career-best was a 16th-place finish in the 1977 NAPA 400 on the road course.

Charlie Glotzbach was born in 1938 and raced out of Edwardsville, IN. Glotzbach, nicknamed Chargin' Charlie, raced at NASCAR's highest level in four decades with four victories and 12 poles in 124 career starts 1960–92. His first Grand National victory was recorded at Charlotte in October 1968.

Clarence Lovell was born in 1946. He started 16 career Winston Cup races, 12 in 1972 and four the following season. He recorded two top–10 finishes in 1973.

The first official NASCAR Strictly Stock division race was held at Charlotte Speedway in 1949. The 150-mile race was apparently won by Glenn Dunnaway in a Ford until it was discovered that an illegal stabilizer spring was utilized and the win was given to Jim Roper and his Lincoln, his only career first-place finish at NASCAR's highest level.

Herb Thomas won a race from the pole for the 15th time in his career, and became the first driver to record 35 wins at NASCAR's top level in the 100-mile event at Hickory, NC, in 1954. Thomas' race average speed of

82.872 mph eclipsed his qualifying speed by nearly 1 mph. It was the second time in his career that he won the race with a faster time than his qualifying speed. It was the fastest race average ever recorded at the Hickory Speedway.

The Airborne Speedway in Plattsburg, NY, hosted one Grand National event. Lee Petty won his 23rd career race in the 1955 race on the half-mile dirt track.

The Charlotte Motor Speedway opened in 1960 with a 600-mile race. The 1½ mile track represented growth for NASCAR and the third recognizable superspeedway. The win was the second and final Grand National victory for Joe Lee Johnson.

In the first NASCAR-sanctioned race ever held at the Augusta International Speedway in 1962, Joe Weatherly took the checkered flag in a Pontiac for his 19th career win.

David Pearson won the second and final Grand National race hosted by the Boyd Speedway in Chattanooga, TN, actually south of the Georgia-Tennessee state line, in the 1964 Confederate 300. Richard Petty captured his 20th career pole and finished second.

Dick Hutcherson won at the Greenville-Pickens Speedway in South Carolina in 1965, his third career win and second in a row at Greenville. Ned Jarrett qualified for his 30th career pole start.

Richard Petty's 95th career Grand National win came in the 1969 Kingsport 250, the first of three top-level NASCAR events hosted by the Kingsport Speedway in Tennessee.

Cale Yarborough took the checkered flag in his Oldsmobile at the Michigan International Speedway in the 1977 Cam 2 Motor Oil 400.

Cale Yarborough won in 1983 at Michigan International Speedway. It was the sixth and final running of the annual Gabriel 400. Yarborough won it three times, including the first (1978) and last (1983) running and 1982.

Geoff Bodine won the 1988 Miller High Life 500 at Pocono, his first win of the Winston Cup season and sixth of his career. Alan Kulwicki qualified first for the 5th time in his career. A severe crash effectively ended the driving career of Bobby Allison. He sustained head injuries which relegated him to car owner status and he never drove another Winston Cup event.

Rusty Wallace won the 1994 Miller Genuine Draft 400 at Michigan.

20

Frank Arford died in a crash at Langhorne, PA, in 1955 in qualifying for the Grand National race. Arford had started four Grand National races that season, his only NASCAR experience.

Jack Smith won his third career Grand National race in 1957 at Columbia Speedway, a half-mile paved track in South Carolina.

Ronald Lee "Ron" Hornaday Jr., who raced out of Palmdale, CA, was born in 1958. Hornaday started six Winston Cup races 1992–95, managing to lead one career lap in 1994.

Junior Johnson won for the second

straight time in Wilson, NC, in 1959, with a 100-mile dirt track win at the Wilson Fairgrounds. It was his 15th career win.

Richie Petty, from Randleman, NC, was born in 1968. He made four NASCAR starts in the 1990s, but never achieved the fame of his namesakes.

Bobby Isaac won the 1970 Hickory 276 at Hickory, his third straight victory at the North Carolina track. It was his fifth of 11 wins in 1970, when he was the Grand National Champion.

Bobby Allison won his fourth straight race, his 23rd career NASCAR win, with a 1971 victory in the Golden State 400 at the Riverside International Raceway.

Cale Yarborough won the 1982 Gabriel 400 at Michigan International Speedway, his second win in the annual event.

Ricky Rudd captured his only victory of the 1993 Winston Cup series with a trip to victory lane in the Miller 400 at Michigan International Speedway.

Bobby Labonte won the 1999 Pocono 500 in Pennsylvania. Sterling Marlin won the pole and finished fourth while Jeff Gordon was the runner-up.

21

Cecil Owen Gordon was born in Asheville, NC, in 1941. Gordon, who raced out of Horse Shoe, NC, 1968–85, ran 450 Grand National and Winston Cup races 1968–85.

Gordon finished third overall in points in both 1971 and 1973, despite never having won a top-level NASCAR event. He did finish a career-best second in the 1975 Mason-Dixon 500 at Dover, DE. He went on to success as a shop foreman for Dale Earnhardt Sr.

Al Loquasto was born in 1943. A Pennsylvania native who raced out of Easton, Loquasto ran one Winston Cup race in 1981 and five in 1982. His best finish was 16th in the 1982 Van Scoy Diamond Mine 500 at Pocono, PA.

James Raptis was born in 1947. Raptis, who raced out of Woodstock, GA, made three Winston Cup starts in 1977. His best finish was 30th in his debut at the Talladega 500.

Dick Rathmann, who won the pole the previous week in Florida, took the checkered flag in the 200-mile event on the one-mile dirt track in Langhorne, PA. Driving his Hudson a race-average of 64.434 mph, Rathmann won his second race of the 1953 Grand National campaign, the seventh win of his NASCAR career. Automaker Jaguar captured their first pole position in a car driven by Lloyd Shaw. It was the only career Grand National race for Shaw, who raced out of Toronto, Ontario, Canada.

Phil Parsons was born in 1957. Parsons, who finished ninth in series points in 1988, ran 201 career Winston Cup races with one win (1988 Winston 500) and 39 additional top–10 finishes.

Tom Pistone drove his #59 Ford to the final of two career Grand

National wins in 1959 at Richmond, VA, just one month following his first win. Buck Baker secured his 39th career pole and finished third. Baker finished fifth and Pistone sixth in the Grand National championship race.

Ned Jarrett won at Birmingham, AL, in 1964, his 30th career win. Richard Petty finished second.

Bobby Isaac won for the second straight Greenville 200 race at Greenville-Pickens Speedway (SC). It was the seventh of 20 times in his career he qualified first and won the race. It was his 13th Grand National win and his 14th career pole. The named race was actually run twice that season, once in April and once in June, both won by Isaac.

Joseph F. Eubanks died in 1971 at the age of 45. Eubanks raced out of Spartanburg, SC, in the 1950s and early '60s to capture three poles and a checkered flag in 159 career Grand National races 1950–61. He finished a career-best fifth overall in points in 1954, his final of three consecutive seasons in NASCAR's top 10 in series points.

Bobby Allison captured his fourth win of 1981 with a first place finish at the Michigan International Speedway in the Gabriel 400. It was the 64th career victory for Allison.

Tim Richmond won his second consecutive Winston Cup race with a trip to victory lane in the 1987 Budweiser 400 at California Speedway. It was his 13th and final win.

Davey Allison won the 1992 Miller Genuine Draft 400 at Michigan International Speedway.

Jeremy Mayfield's first career win came in 1998 in the Pocono 500. Jeff Gordon, the eventual Winston Cup season champion, captured the pole and finished second.

22

Buck Clardy, who raced out of Greenville, SC, was born in 1925. He made one career Grand National start in 1951, a 30th-place finish on the Beach & Road Course at Daytona Beach, FL, driving a Nash.

Speedy Thompson won at the Monroe County Fairgrounds in Rochester, NY, in 1956 for his 10th career Grand National Victory.

Bill Amick won the first and only Grand National race ever held on the half-mile dirt track at the Capital Speedway in Sacramento, CA, in 1957. It was his only career victory.

Jim Paschal won his 10th career Grand National race in 1962 at the Southside Speedway in Richmond, VA. Rex Smith won his 30th career pole and was the runner-up. White finished fifth and Paschal sixth in the point race that season.

Richard Petty won his 82nd career Grand National race in 1968 at Greenville-Pickens Speedway in South Carolina. David Pearson won his 35th career pole and finished second in the main event.

Jeff Gordon won the California 500 by NAPA at the California Speedway in 1997. It was his seventh win in 15 races on the season. Terry Labonte finished second. It was the first Winston Cup race in Southern

California since 1988 and the inaugural race at the California Speedway.

In the 2003 Save Mart 350 on the road course at the newly named Infineon Raceway in Sonoma, CA, road racing specialist Boris Said captured his first career pole. However, Robby Gordon cruised to the win, taking both road course races in 2003 with a victory in August at Watkins Glen, NY.

23

Bruce Jacobi was born in 1935. Jacobi ran 20 Winston Cup races between 1975 and 1981. He recorded his only three top–10 finishes in his rookie season in 15 starts. He died at Daytona in 1983.

Joe Jernigan was killed at the age of 36 in a race at the Royall Speedway in Richmond, VA, in 1951. Jernigan made four Grand National starts 1950–51. Driving the Lambert's Auto Ford, Jernigan finished a career-best 13th place in April 1950 at Langhorne Speedway (PA).

Herb Thomas captured his circuit-leading fifth win of 1953, the 21st of his Grand National career, with a win in the half-mile dirt track race in High Point, NC. Thomas, who also won the pole, drove his Hudson to the checkered flag with an average speed of 58.186 mph. It was the first of two races hosted at the Tri-City Speedway.

Harstville Speedway, a ⅓-mile dirt track in Hartsville, SC, hosted one Grand National race. The 1961 event was won by Buck Baker for his 43rd career win, his only victory of 1961. Emanuel Zervakis won his second and final Grand National pole start.

Rex White's 25th career win came in 1962 at the South Boston Speedway in Virginia. White won three more races in 1962 to finish his career with 28. Jack Smith won his 16th career pole, one of seven on the season. In the 1962 points championship, Smith finished fourth and White fifth behind champion Joe Weatherly.

Buck Baker won at the I-75 (Valdosta) Speedway in Georgia in 1964 for his 45th Grand National checkered flag. Ned Jarrett started on the pole.

Bobby Allison won his second race in four days, his fifth straight NASCAR win, with a victory at Meyer Speedway in 1971. It was the only Winston Cup event hosted by the ½-mile paved track in Houston, TX. Allison started first and finished first for the seventh of 20 times in his career. It was his 24th career win.

Richard "Toby" Tobias died in 1978 at the age of 56 as a result of an accident at a race in Flemington, NJ. Tobias made one Winston Cup start in 1973, running 50 miles.

Davey Allison won for the third time in four weeks with a victory in the 1991 Miller Genuine Draft 400 at Michigan.

Rusty Wallace won for the third time in 1996 with a trip to victory lane in the Miller 400 at Michigan.

Ricky Rudd's only 2002 victory came on the road course of the Infineon Raceway at Sonoma, CA, in the Dodge/Save Mart 350. The eventual Winston Cup champion, Tony Stewart, qualified first. In the season's only other road course race, at Watkins Glen in August, Stewart won while Rudd started first.

24

Donald White was born in 1926. He ran 23 Grand National and one Winston Cup event between 1954 and 1972. Racing out of Keokuk, IA, White finished in the top 10 in half of his starts and led one race in 1966.

Curtis Turner won for the third time in 1951 with a checkered-flag finish on a paved .5-mile track in Dayton, OH. It was the second official NASCAR race on a paved raceway and the first such race in the state of Ohio.

Joe Rogers died in a crash at the Arlington Downs Speedway in 1951. Rogers had made his Grand National debut earlier that season, running one career race at NASCAR's top level.

Tim Flock won in 1955 at the Southern States Fairgrounds in Charlotte, NC, driving a Chrysler.

John Kieper won his only career Grand National race in 1956 at Portland, OR. Kieper had captured the pole in a race at the speedway in May, only to lose to Herb Thomas. Thomas captured his 38th career pole in the June race.

James Brown (not *that* James Brown) was born in 1960 and raced out of Portland, OR. Brown ran 23 Winston Cup events 1981–90. Brown led 4 laps in one race in 1984 and managed one top–10 finish in 1982.

Waymond Lane "Hut" Stricklin was born in 1961 in Birmingham, AL. Stricklin raced out of Calera, AL, starting his Winston Cup career in 1987. He married the daughter of NASCAR driver Donnie Allison.

Junior Johnson won the second of four Grand National events held at the Starkey Speedway in 1961. Johnson captured his 23rd career win in his #27 Pontiac at the Roanoke, VA, ¼-mile paved track while Rex White captured his 22nd career pole and finished second. White was the 1960 Grand National champion but finished second to Ned Jarrett in 1961.

The Rambi Race Track in Myrtle Beach, SC, hosted 11 Grand National races 1956–65. The final event was won in 1965 by Dick Hutcherson. It was the first of four times in his career that Hutcherson won a race from the pole. It was his fourth series win and sixth career pole.

Richard Petty began a string of three straight wins at Greenville, SC, with a 1967 win. He also won both races held there in 1968. The 1967 win was his 60th Winston Cup victory and the 24th time in his career won from the top starting position.

David Pearson, driving a Mercury, won the 1973 Yankee 400 at Cambridge Junction, MI. Pearson drove his Mercury to victory lane with an average speed of 153.485 mph.

Dale Earnhardt Sr. won the 1990 Miller Genuine Draft 400 at Michigan International Speedway for his fourth win of the Winston Cup season.

In the first road course race of 2001, Tony Stewart captured his second win of the season in the Dodge/Save Mart 350K at Sears Point Raceway (CA). Robby Gordon was involved in a costly conflict with Kevin Harvick. Points leader Jeff Gordon won his fifth pole of the season.

25

Dr. Edmond C. "Ed" Hessert, who raced out of Trenton, NJ, in the 1960s and '70s, was born in 1932. Hessert ran 22 career Grand National and Winston Cup events, starting 16 races with four top-10's rookie year, when he briefly led one race.

Jimmy Florian won his first and only NASCAR race in a 100-mile dirt track event in Dayton, OH, in 1950. It was the first official win for Ford, averaging 63.354 mph on the .5-mile oval.

Lee Petty won his 14th career race and third of the season in 1954 at the half-mile dirt track in Hickory, NC. Petty captured the 100-mile event in a Chrysler. Herb Thomas won his second straight pole position, the 30th of his career.

Lee Petty captured his 33rd career Grand National win in 1958 at the Lincoln Speedway in New Oxford, PA. Ken Rush captured his second, and final, career pole.

David Pearson won his 22nd career Grand National race in 1966 at Greenville, SC. It was also the 22nd time he started from the pole. It was the sixth time in his career he won from the top starting position.

Richard Petty won the 1972 Lone Star 500 at the Texas World Speedway for his 145th career victory and 105th pole position start. It was the 56th time he started and finished first.

Bill Elliott won his first race of 1989 with a trip to victory lane in the Miller High Life 400 at Michigan International Speedway.

The Dupont Chevrolet of Jeff Gordon finished first in the first road race of the 2000 Winston Cup season, the Save Mart/Kragen 350K at Sears Point, CA. Rusty Wallace won his third pole position in four weeks, but again failed to win.

26

John C. "Pap" White was born in 1922. He ran one Grand National race each in 1950 and 1951. Driving out of High Point, NC, White finished in the top 10 in his final event.

David Sisco was born in 1937. Sisco raced out of Nashville, TN, to start 133 NASCAR races in the 1970s, finishing in the top–10 31 times. In 1974, he finished tenth overall in the points standings.

Stan Barrett was born in 1943. Barrett raced out of Bishop, CA, and made 19 starts 1980–90 with two top–10 finishes. He came in 9th in the 1981 Talladega 500, his career best.

Joe Fields, born J.E. Liesfeld Jr. in 1948, raced out of Montpelier, VT, in the 1980s. Fields started six Winston Cup races in 1981 and nine more 1982–86.

Glen Wood won his second straight race at Bowman-Gray Stadium. Wood, who won all four of his career Grand National races at the Winston-Salem, NC, track, won all three 1960 races staged there.

Kevin Lapage was born in 1962 in Shelburne, VT. Lepage debuted at the Winston Cup level in October 1997, finishing 40th after a crash at the 1997 UAW-GM Quality 500 at Charlotte. He started 139 events 1997–2003 with seven top-10 finishes.

Steve Grissom was born in Gadsden, AL, in 1963. He was the runner-up to Jeff Burton for Rookie of the Year in 1994. Grissom appeared in one Winston Cup race in 1990 and 1993 before garnering a regular spot in 1994.

Richard Petty won his 33rd career Grand National race in 1964 at Spartanburg, SC. David Pearson won his 11th career pole.

David Pearson won the North State 200 at the North Carolina State Fairgrounds in Raleigh in 1969, marking the first Grand National race at the arena since 1955. The track hosted one more race in 1970.

The Kingsport Speedway, also known as the MARCA Motorsports Community Speedway among other names, hosted two Grand National events and one Winston Cup race, one each 1969–71. Richard Petty won the 1970 Kingsport 100 from the pole, his 107th career victory and his 45th win from the pole.

Richard Petty closed the Greenville-Pickens Speedway to top-level NASCAR racing with his 129th win in the final event held at the South Carolina track, the 1971 Pickens 200. Bobby Allison qualified in the top spot for the 19th time of his career.

Ethel Mobley died at the age of 64 in 1984. Mobley, who raced out of Atlanta, GA, was one of the women who competed in NASCAR's first season. She ran two races in 1949, finishing 11th driving a Cadillac in the second event on the Beach & Road Course at Daytona Beach, FL.

Rusty Wallace won his second race of 1988 with a first-place finish in the Miller High Life 400 at Michigan International Speedway.

27

Bobby Myers was born in Winston-Salem, NC, in 1927. Myers ran 15 career Grand National races in the 1950s with three top–10 finishes. He died in a crash at Darlington, SC, in September 1957.

Hudson dominated the 100-mile event held at Williams Grove Speedway in 1954. Herb Thomas captured his 36th career victory with an average speed of 51.085 on the half-mile dirt track. Dick Rathmann qualified first, his eighth career pole, also in a Hudson. It was the only Grand National race held at the Mechanicsburg, PA, track.

Rex White won at Bowman-Gray Stadium at Winston-Salem, NC, in 1959. It was his first of six wins over three seasons (three events were staged yearly) at the track, including four in a row 1961–62.

Johnny Benson was born in 1963

in Grand Rapids, MI. He was the 1996 Winston Cup Rookie of the Year and has run 264 events through 2003 with his only win in 2002 at Rockingham. He has finished in the top–10 57 other times.

Cale Yarborough's first career NASCAR win was in 1965 at the Valdosta 75 Speedway, the final of three events stated at the Georgia track 1962–65.

In 1967 Jim Paschal won the first NASCAR race in almost 11 years held at the Montgomery Motor Speedway in Alabama. It was the fourth of six sanctioned events held at the track.

Bobby Isaac qualified first and won the 1970 Greenville 200, his third of four straight wins at the Greenville-Pickens Speedway (SC). It was his 27th career win, 30th career pole, and the 15th of 20 times in his career he won from the top spot.

Jeff Gordon won from the pole on the road course at Sonoma to capture the checkered flag in the 1999 Save Mart/Kragen 350 at the Sears Point Raceway.

28

Junior Johnson was born in Ronda, NC, in 1931. Johnson ran 313 races between 1953 and 1966 with 50 top-level NASCAR wins and 47 poles. He later went on to success as an owner. He was 6th overall in points in 1955 and 1961, when he won ten races. He debuted with a 38th-place finish in the 1953 Southern 500 at Darlington, SC, and was the most popular Grand National driver of 1959.

Terry Petris was born in 1951. Racing out of Bakersfield, CA, Petris made three NASCAR starts at Riverside, CA, in the 1980s. He finished 24th in his debut in the 1986 Budweiser 400, crashing on the 88th lap.

Fonty Flock captured the feature event, a 100-mile contest on a half-mile dirt track in Wilson, NC, in 1953. Flock took the checkered flag, the fourth consecutive win for automaker Hudson, averaging 53.803 mph. It was his second win of the season and the 13th Grand National win of his career.

Mike Skinner was born in 1957 in Ontario, CA. Skinner made his Winston Cup debut with three races in 1986, but did not race regularly at that level until 1997, when he was named Rookie of the Year driving for Richard Childress. He was the first NASCAR Craftsman Truck Series champion.

Lee Petty won at the Hickory Speedway in 1958. Petty won seven races that year en route to his second of three Grand National Championships.

Rex White won at Skyline (Asheville-Weaverville) Speedway in 1959, his sixth career win and third of the season.

Dale Earnhardt Sr. won the 1987 Miller American 400 at Michigan International Speedway for his seventh win of the season.

Jeff Gordon won from the pole for the second time in 1998 with a road course win at Sears Point Raceway in the Save Mart/Kragen 350. Gordon won his third Winston Cup Championship that season.

29

Leonard "Pee Wee" Martin was born in 1922. Pee Wee started one race in 1949 and two in 1950, earning a total of $150 in NASCAR competition.

Don Noel, born in 1929 and racing out of California, started 24 races 1960–79, no more than four (1961) in any one season. He managed four top–10 finishes.

Raymond "Friday" Hassler, who raced out of Chattanooga, TN, in the 1960s and '70s, was born in 1935. Hassler ran 135 career Grand National and Winston Cup events, winning two poles and finishing 16th in championship points in 1971. He managed 48 career top–10 finishes. He was killed in a qualifying race for the 1972 Daytona 500.

Larry Caudill was born in 1948 and raced out of North Wilkesboro, NC, to record one Winston Cup start in 1987.

Tim Flock won his third race in the last four events, and his fourth of 1952, with a first-place finish in a 250-mile contest at Detroit, MI. Hudson remained dominant in the manufacturer's race. Dick Rathmann took the pole, also driving a Hudson. It was the final of two sanctioned races held at the Michigan State Fairgrounds.

Lee Petty won from the pole at Spartanburg, SC, in 1957. It was the fourth of six times Petty achieved the feat of starting and finishing first. It was his 27th win and sixth career pole on the Grand National circuit.

Rex White won the 1958 Grand National event at Asheville-Weaverville Speedway for his second career win.

Eddie Bierschwale was born in 1959. Bierschwale raced out of San Antonio, TX to 117 Winston Cup starts 1983–92 with one top–10 finish in 1989.

Jeff Burton was born in 1967 in South Boston, VA. Burton debuted in the Winston Cup Series in 1993 and was the 1994 Rookie of the Year. His older brother Ward also races in NASCAR. Jeff won his first Winston Cup race in the first race at the Texas Motor Speedway in 1997.

30

Lou Figaro captured his first-ever NASCAR pole position and his only Grand National win in a 100-mile event on a .5-mile dirt track at the Carrell Speedway in Gardena, CA, in 1951, the second of four events at the track. He became the second driver to win in a Hudson that season.

Dave Mader III was born in 1955 in Maylene, AL. He ran ten career Winston Cup races 1988–92, four more than his father who raced in 1961. Mader III led seven laps in the 1992 Hanes 500 at Martinsville, VA, finishing 21st.

Sterling Marlin, son of Coo Coo, was born in Tennessee in 1957. Sterling led the Winston Cup Series in laps and miles in 1995 on his way to a 3rd place finish in points. Marlin began his Winston Cup career in 1976, substituting for his injured father "Coo Coo." He won the 1983

Rookie of the Year honors. In 1994 and 1995, he won the Daytona 500.

In 1957 Grand National Champion Buck Baker in a Chevrolet won the first of two Grand National races held at the Jacksonville (or Onslow) Speedway in North Carolina. It was his fifth of ten wins that season.

Junior Johnson won the 1963 Dixie 400 at Atlanta Motor Speedway, his 32nd career checkered flag.

Roy Mulligan died of electrocution in 1975 at the age of 35. Mulligan started one Winston Cup race in 1971.

Gayther Wallace "Runt" Harris died in 1990 at the age of 63. Harris ran eight Grand National races between 1950 and 1962 with a fifth place finish, a career-best, in his only 1959 event.

JULY

1

Leonard Fanelli, who raced out of New Rochelle, NY, in the 1950s, was born in 1912. Fanelli made one start in 1951, earning a total of $50 at NASCAR's top level.

It was a great week in 1951 for automaker Hudson. For the second straight day, the manufacturer won a sanctioned race, this time taking both the pole and checkered flag at the 100-mile event at the Grand River Speedrome in Grand Rapids, MI. Marshall Teague won his fifth race of the season on a .5-mile dirt track while Tim Flock won his fourth pole position. It was the first Grand National race sponsored in the state of Michigan.

Buddy Shuman won his first Grand National race in 1952 with a first-place finish on the .5-mile dirt track in Niagara Falls, Ontario, Canada. The 100-mile event was the first sanctioned NASCAR race held outside the United States and continued the success of automaker Hudson as they won their 16th of 18 races on the season. Another Hudson driver, Herb Thomas, took the pole, the seventh of his career.

Lee Petty won the 100-mile Grand National event at Skyline Speedway (aka Asheville-Weaverville Speedway) in 1956 for his 25th career victory.

Davey Allison won the 1989 Pepsi 400 at Daytona International Speedway. It was his second win of the season.

Jeff Gordon won the 1995 Pepsi 400 at Daytona. Gordon went on to win his first Winston Cup Championship.

2

Richard Petty was born in Randleman, NC, in 1937. "The King" went on to become the most successful Winston Cup driver in history with 200 wins in 1184 career starts. He won the points total seven times; 1964, 1967, 1971–72, 1974–75 and

133

1979. He won 27 races, and ten straight, during the 1967 season. He was voted the most popular driver eight times, including five straight years 1974–78.

Bill Seifert was born in 1939. Racing out of Skyland, NC, Seifert started 235 Grand National and Winston Cup races 1966–79 with 49 top–10 finishes. He was 13th overall in points in 1969.

Roger Hamby, who raced out of Ferguson, NC, was born in 1943. Hamby started 66 Winston Cup events 1977–81 with two top–10s in 26 starts in 1978, when he finished 21st in championship points.

Curtis Turner became the first driver to win from the pole in NASCAR's top series. Turner won the 100-mile event on a .5-mile dirt track in Rochester, NY, in 1950 to establish the mark, averaging 50.614 mph in his Oldsmobile. It was his fourth career win.

Edward "Fireball" Roberts suffered severe injuries in a crash at Charlotte, NC, in 1964. Roberts, who captured his first career win in Hillsboro, NC, in 1950, earned 35 career wins in 206 starts 1950–64.

David "Swede" Savage died in 1973 from injuries suffered in the Indianapolis 500 that year. Savage ran nine top-level NASCAR races in the 1960s with five top–10 finishes.

Bill Elliott won his third Winston Cup race of the season with a victory in the 1988 Pepsi Firecracker 400 at Daytona.

Jimmy Spencer won his first career NASCAR race in 1994 with a win at Daytona International Speedway.

3

Larry Phillips was born in 1942. Racing out of Springfield, MO, he made his only NASCAR Winston Cup start in 1976, a 13th-place finish in a Ford at the Los Angeles Times 500 at Ontario, CA.

Herb Thomas' sixth win of the 1953 Grand National campaign came in the 100-mile event at Rochester, NY, on the half-mile dirt track. It was the 21st win of his career, the fifth straight win for manufacturer Hudson.

For the second time during the 1954 season, Herb Thomas won a race with an average speed that exceeded the top qualifying speed. Thomas gained his 37th career victory in Spartanburg, SC, in his Hudson in the 100-mile event on a half-mile dirt track. Hershel McGriff won the pole, the second of his career.

James "Jimmy" Horton, who raced out of Folsom, NJ, in the 1980s and '90s, was born in 1956. Horton ran 48 Winston Cup events 1987–95.

Gene Lovelace died of a heart attack during a 1970 race at Southside Speedway in Richmond, VA. Lovelace started one Grand National race in 1964.

Dale Earnhardt Sr. won the 1993 Pepsi 400 at Daytona. It was his fourth win of the season.

Dare Jarrett won the 1999 Pepsi 400 from Daytona International Speedway in Florida. Joe Nemechek started on the pole and finished 16th. It was the third of four wins for Jarrett during his 1999 Winston Cup Championship season.

4

Robert Sydney "Bob" Brown was born in 1943. Racing out of Milan, TN, he made nine career Winston Cup starts 1971–73 with a career-best 18th-place finish in the 1971 Southeastern 500 at Bristol, TN.

Mike Potter was born on the 4th of July in 1949. Potter, who raced out of Johnson City, TN, started 60 NASCAR races 1979–93, qualifying for at least one race each year except 1991.

Tim Flock won the first sanctioned NASCAR race in Owego, NY, his 13th career Grand National win and his fifth of the 1952 season. The 100-mile race on a .5-mile dirt track was the 17th win in 19 tries for automaker Hudson. Flock also took his third pole of the season.

Lee Petty won his fifth race of 1953, the 11th of his NASCAR career, on the half-mile dirt track in Spartanburg, SC. Petty drove his Dodge to victory lane in the 100-mile event, averaging 56.934 mph. Buck Baker captured the pole in an Oldsmobile, the fifth of his Grand National career. It was the first Grand National race held at the Piedmont Interstate Fairgrounds, which hosted 22 events 1953–66.

Herb Thomas won the race from the pole at Weaverville, NC, in 1954. It was his second win in two days and the 16th time he sat on the pole and took the checkered flag. Thomas won this 100-mile event on a half-mile dirt track in his Hudson Hornet.

In the second Raleigh 250, Fireball Roberts took the checkered flag at the Raleigh Speedway in 1956. The event was held for three consecutive years on July 4th, won in 1957 by Paul Goldsmith and in 1958 by Roberts again. The 1958 race was the final of seven Grand National events hosted at the one-mile paved track 1953–58.

In the 1957 Raleigh 250, Paul Goldsmith drove to victory in his #3 Ford. It was his final of four wins that season, when he finished 13th in Grand National points.

In the final Raleigh 250, in 1958, at the Raleigh (NC) Speedway, Fireball Roberts won in his #22 Chevrolet.

Fireball Roberts won the Firecracker 250 at Daytona International Speedway in 1959, the second event at the superspeedway.

Jack Smith won for the second time in 1960 at Daytona in the Firecracker 250.

David Pearson won the 1961 Firecracker 250 at Daytona for his second career Grand National win.

Fireball Roberts won for the third time at Daytona in 1962 with a victory in the Firecracker 250.

Fireball Roberts won his second straight summer race at Daytona with a win in the 1963 Firecracker 400, the first year the race length was increased from 250 miles.

A.J. Foyt earned his first career NASCAR win at Daytona with a victory in the 1964 Firecracker 400 at Daytona Beach, FL.

A.J. Foyt earned his second straight Firecracker 400 win in 1965. The victory was also the second of his career.

Sam McQuagg won the 1966 Firecracker 400 at Daytona, the only win of his Grand National career. Mc-Quagg was the 1965 Grand National Rookie of the Year.

Cale Yarborough won the 1967 Firecracker 400. He was voted the Grand National's most popular driver that season.

Cale Yarborough won the 1968 Firecracker 400, his second straight win in the July 4th race at Daytona.

LeeRoy Yarbrough won his second straight race with a checkered flag finish in the 1969 Firecracker 400 at Daytona Beach, FL.

Donnie Allison won the 1970 Firecracker 400 at Daytona. He was voted the most popular Grand National driver that season.

Bobby Isaac won the 1971 Firecracker 400 at Daytona.

David Pearson won the 1972 Firecracker 400 at Daytona.

David Pearson kept on winning in 1973 with a first-place finish in the Firecracker 400 at Daytona in a 1971 Mercury. Richard Petty finished second.

David Pearson won his third straight Firecracker 400 in 1974 at Daytona.

Richard Petty won the 1975 Firecracker 400 at Daytona Beach, FL. Petty won 13 races in 1975 on his way to his sixth of seven points championships.

Cale Yarborough won the 1976 Firecracker 400 at Daytona Beach, FL. Yarborough went on to win a total of nine races on his way to the Winston Cup Championship.

Richard Petty won the 1977 Firecracker 400 for his 185th career Win-

ston Cup victory. Neil Bonnett, who later died at the track, qualified on the pole.

David Pearson won the 1978 Firecracker 400 at Daytona Beach, FL.

Neil Bonnett won the 1979 Firecracker 400 at Daytona Beach, FL.

Bobby Allison won for the second time in his career at Daytona in the 1980 Firecracker 400. It was his 58th career win.

Cale Yarborough won the 1981 Firecracker 400 at Daytona Beach, FL.

Bobby Allison won for the second time at Daytona in 1982. It was his fourth win of the year and his 69th career NASCAR victory.

Buddy Baker won the 1983 Firecracker 400 at Daytona Beach, FL.

Richard Petty captured his 200th, and final, career NASCAR win, at Daytona in 1984 in the annual Firecracker 400. President Ronald Reagan watched the race from the private suite of Bill France. Petty reportedly talked politics with Reagan after the race.

Greg Sacks won the 1985 Pepsi Firecracker 400, his only career victory.

Tim Richmond won for the second time in three weeks with a victory in the 1986 Pepsi Firecracker 400 at Daytona.

Bobby Allison won his 83rd career NASCAR race in 1987 at Daytona International Speedway in the Pepsi Firecracker 400. It was his only win of the season and the next-to-last of his career. It was the third time in his career that he prevailed on the Fourth of July.

Bobby Allison won the 1987 Pepsi Firecracker 400 at Daytona, taking the late lead and holding off Buddy Baker for the checkered flag.

Preston "Hop" Holmes died in 1989 at the age of 56. Hop ran 71 laps in a 1965 Grand National event, his only appearance at NASCAR's top level.

Ernie Irvan won the 1992 Pepsi 400 at Daytona.

5

Roscoe A. Thompson was born in 1922. Racing out of Forrest Park, GA, Thompson ran 29 Grand National events 1950–62, led one career race and finished in the top 10 twice.

Dave Harry Hirschfield, who raced out of Midlothian, IL, in the 1950s and '60s, was born in 1930. Hirschfield ran two Grand National aces in 1960, earning a total of $100 as a top-level Grand National driver.

Bob Scott died in an Indy Car race at Darlington, SC, in 1954. Scott ran one Grand National race in 1950.

Tony Bonadies died in a crash in an ARDC Midget race at Williams Grove, PA, in 1964 at the age of 47. Bonadies started two Grand National races in 1952.

John Patterson died in 1969. The driver out of Huntington, WV, ran 25 career Grand National races 1952–59 with six top–10 finishes.

Warren Tope died as a result of injuries suffered practicing for a street race in 1975 at the age of 28. Tope, running out of Troy, MI, had

started two Winston Cup races that season.

John Andretti won the 1997 Pepsi 400 at Daytona International Speedway. It was the first career NASCAR win for Andretti, the nephew of Indy Car legend Mario Andretti. In 1994, he became the first driver to compete in the Indianapolis 500 and the Coca-Cola 600 on the same day. He edged Terry Labonte by less than .03 seconds for the win.

Greg Biffle won his first career Winston Cup race with a first-place finish in the 2003 Pepsi 400 at Daytona International Speedway in Florida. Steve Park captured the pole.

6

Gwyn Edward Staley was born in 1927. Staley ran 30 Grand National races in the 1950s, finishing fourth in series points in 1955. Staley captured his three career wins within the space of a month in August–September 1957 at Myrtle Beach, SC, Syracuse, NY, and Langhorne, PA.

Rolland "Ron" Gautsche, who raced out of Truckee, CA, in the 1970s, was born in 1935. Gautsche started five Winston Cup races 1971–72.

Clinton "Delma" Cowart was born in 1941 and raced out of Savannah, GA. Cowart ran 21 career Winston Cup events 1981–92.

Tim Flock took his second straight pole and won a race again, just two days after accomplishing the feat. Flock averaged 44.499 mph on the .5-mile dirt track in Monroe, MI, to cruise to victory in his Hudson in the 100-mile event, the 20th official race of the 1952 NASCAR season. It was the seventh consecutive win for manufacturer Hudson and the only Grand National race ever staged in Monroe, MI.

Tim Flock won from the pole at Spartanburg, SC, in 1955 for his 16th career Grand National victory. It was the ninth of 16 times in his career that he both qualified and finished first.

Randy Porter was born in 1964 and raced out of Greenville, SC. He started two Winston Cup races in 1992, finishing 24th in his debut in the 1992 Coca-Cola 600.

In the first NASCAR race ever held at the one-mile paved track at Dover Downs International Speedway in Delaware, Richard Petty captured the checkered flag in the 1969 Mason-Dixon 300.

Tom Cherry, who raced out of Muncie, IN, died at the age of 79 in 1990. He started one Grand National race in 1953 and finished in the top–10.

Bill Elliott won the 1991 Pepsi 400 at Daytona for his only victory of the Winston Cup season.

Sterling Marlin won his second and final race of 1996 with a first-place finish in the Pepsi 400 at Daytona.

Michael Waltrip won at the Daytona International Speedway in the 2002 Pepsi 400, his only points-race victory of the season. Kevin Harvick qualified first for his only pole start of the season.

7

Eddie Yarboro was born in 1938. He ran 33 races at NASCAR's top level between 1966 and 1973. Racing out of Elkin, NC, Yarboro recorded five top 10 Grand National finishes.

Michael "Mike" Hiss, who raced out of Norwalk, CT, in the 1970's, was born in 1941. Hiss ran one Winston Cup race, finishing 22nd in the 1976 Los Angeles Times 500.

Stan Fox was born (as Stanley Cole Fuchs) in 1952. He raced out of Janesville, WI, and made two Winston Cup starts in 1992, finishing a career-best 36th in the Die Hard 500 at Talladega, AL.

Lee Petty won at Spartanburg, SC, in 1956, his 26th career Grand National win. Fireball Roberts qualified first for the fifth of 35 times in his career.

Rex White's 1962 victory at Columbia, SC, was his 26th career Grand National win. White won the 1960 Grand National Championship.

Ned Jarrett won for the second straight time at Myrtle Beach, SC. Jarrett's 17th career Grand National win came in 1963. Richard Petty qualified on the pole for the 12th time in his career.

Fireball Roberts died of injuries suffered in a May crash at the Charlotte Motor Speedway in 1964. He was 35. On the season, Roberts had finished in the top 10 in six of nine races.

Elmo Langley's second and final NASCAR win came just over one month after his first win. Langley captured the checkered flag in 1966 at Manassas, VA. Bobby Allison earned his first of 59 career pole starts.

Joseph Schlesser died in 1968 as a result of an accident in the French Grand Prix. Schlesser, who ran out of Neuilly-sur-Seine, France, ran two Grand National races in 1964 with one top–10 finish.

Bobby Allison won his 11th career NASCAR race in 1968 in the Islip 300 at the Islip (NY) Speedway. It was his only win of the year.

Richard Petty won the first of two top-level NASCAR races held at the Albany-Saratoga Speedway in Malta, NY, with a victory in the 1970 Albany-Saratoga 250.

Dale Earnhardt Sr. won his second consecutive race, his fifth win of the season, in the 1990 Pepsi 400 at Daytona International Speedway.

Kenny Irwin died of multiple injuries suffered in a crash into the wall during practice laps for the 2000 thatlook.com 300 at New Hampshire International Speedway. He was 30 years old and was the 1998 Winston Cup Rookie of the Year.

Dale Earnhardt Jr. returned to Daytona in 2001 and won the first Winston Cup race held at the track since his father's death in February, taking the checkered flag in the Pepsi 400. Sterling Marlin captured his only pole start of the season.

8

Leo Jackson was born in 1933. Jackson was a NASCAR team owner who began entering cars in 1985. He ran Harry Gant in September 1994,

when he won four straight Winston Cup races.

J. Graham Shaw was born in 1937. Shaw, who raced out of Columbia, SC, ran two Grand National events in the 1964 season. His best finish was 11th in November 1963 at Augusta, GA.

Fonty Flock won the first sanctioned NASCAR race held at Bainbridge, OH, in 1951. Flock captured his third checkered flag of the season and his fifth pole in the 100-mile event on a .5 mile dirt-track in his Oldsmobile.

Rick Knoop was born in 1953. Racing out of Atherton, CA, he started five Winston Cup races in the 1980s, one each in 1981 and 1986 and three in 1987. He finished 20th in the 1987 Delaware 500 at Dover, DE, his final event.

Lloyd Dane won the first Grand National race ever held at the California State Fairgrounds in Sacramento, CA, in 1956. It was his first of four career wins.

Ned Jarrett won from the pole at the 1964 Old Dominion 400 at Manassas, VA. It was his 31st win and 21st pole of his career.

Junior Johnson won his 47th career race in 1965 at the Old Dominion Speedway in Manassas, VA. Ned Jarrett captured his 31st career pole and finished third. Jarrett won 13 races and finished second 13 times on his way to the Grand National championship in 1965.

Benny Parsons won the 1973 Volunteer 500 at Bristol for his second career victory. Cale Yarborough, who won the spring race from the pole, won his 23rd career pole in the July event. Parsons won just one event in 1973 en route to his only career Winston Cup Championship.

9

G.C. Spencer was born in 1925. Spencer raced out of Jonesboro, TN, to 415 Grand National and Winston Cup starts 1958–77 with 138 top–10 finishes and a lead in 12 career events. He qualified on the pole for the May 1955 race in Hickory, NC.

Bruce Hill, who raced out of Topeka, KS, in the 1970s and '80s, was born in 1949. Hill ran 100 career Winston Cup events with 21 top–10 finishes. In 1975, Hill finished 16th in championship points and was named Winston Cup Rookie of the Year.

Mark Thompson was born in 1951. He made one Winston Cup start in 1992. He raced out of Jacksonville, FL.

Scott Autrey was born in 1953. Autrey raced out of San Angelo, TX, to start one Winston Cup event. Finishing 34th in the 1985 Winston Western 500 at Riverside, CA.

Jim Paschal won his fourth career race in 1955 at Columbia Speedway in South Carolina. Jimmie Lewallen, who won the pole, finished second.

Fred Lorenzen won his first race at the Atlanta Motor Speedway in 1961 with a victory in the Festival 250.

Junior Johnson won the final of six Grand National events hosted at Old Bridge Stadium, NJ, between 1956 and 1965. Johnson's 1965 win in the Old Bridge 200 was his 48th career checkered flag.

Richard Petty won the Northern 300 at Trenton Speedway (NJ) in 1967 for his 61st career Grand National victory.

Richard Petty won the final NASCAR-sanctioned event held at the Oxford Plains Speedway, the .333-mile paved track in Maine that hosted three races 1966–68. His win came in the 1968 Maine 300, the final top-level NASCAR race hosted in the state to date.

In the final of three career NASCAR races held at the Thompson International Speedway in Connecticut, Bobby Isaac captured the checkered flag in 1970. He was the Grand National Champion with 11 wins that season.

Bobby Allison won his 33rd career NASCAR race in 1972 at Bristol International Speedway in the annual Volunteer 500. It was his second Bristol win of the season and his fourth overall. It was the 12th time he won from the pole in his career.

Dale Earnhardt Sr. captured his eighth race of the season in the Summer 500 at Pocono in 1987. Tim Richmond won the pole for the 14th time of his career.

Jeff Gordon won for the first time at the New Hampshire International Speedway, his 7th career Winston Cup win, taking the checkered flag in the 1995 Slick 50 300.

Tony Stewart won his third race of the year as his Pontiac took the Thatlook.com 300 at Loudon, NH. Rusty Wallace won his fourth pole in six races. The win was bittersweet as fellow competitor Kenny Irwin Jr. had died earlier in the week in a practice crash.

10

Donald Thomas was born in 1932. He started 79 Grand National races 1950–56 and won from the pole in Atlanta in November 1952 for his only career victory. He placed 9th in series points in both 1952 and 1953, when his brother Herb was the champion.

Red Byron won the second-ever sanctioned NASCAR race, the first ever held at Daytona in 1949 on the Beach & Road Course. Byron went on to become the first series points champion.

Dick Rathmann won his third race of 1953, the eighth of his Grand National career, with a checkered flag finish in the 100-mile event at Morristown, NJ. Rathmann, driving a Hudson on the half-mile dirt track, became the first driver with an average race speed (69.417mph) that was faster than the qualifying time (61.016 mph).

Dick Rathmann's 13th career Grand National win came in 1954 at the Santa Fe Speedway at Willow Springs, IL, the first race ever sanctioned in the state of Illinois. Rathmann drove his Hudson to victory in the 100-mile event on a half-mile dirt track. Buck Baker sat on the pole, the 11th of his career, in the only race ever run at NASCAR's top level at the track.

Tim Flock won at the Asheville-Weaverville Speedway in 1955, a half-mile dirt track that was paved in 1958. It was the 27th career win for Flock, who won the points championship in 1952 and 1955.

In the final of four sanctioned Grand National races at the Heidelberg Speedway in Pittsburgh, PA, Lee Petty rode his 17th pole to his 53rd series victory.

Ned Jarrett won in 1963 at the Savannah Speedway. Jarrett was the Grand National Champion in 1961 and 1965.

Billy Wade won four career Grand National races within one month in 1964. The first victory came from the pole at Old Bridge, NJ, in the Fireball Roberts 200. The race was run in Roberts' honor. He had died earlier in the week from injuries in a crash at Charlotte.

Over 17 years after hosting their first NASCAR race, the Thompson International Speedway in Connecticut saw David Pearson capture the 1969 Thompson Speedway 200.

Brendan Gaughan was born in 1975 in Las Vegas, NV. Gaughan made his Winston Cup debut in 2004 after running the Craftsman Truck Series 1997–2003.

Adam Petty was born in 1980. In 1998, Petty became the first four-generation athlete in United States history. He died at the age of 19 in a practice crash in 2000 at Loudon, NH.

Darrell Waltrip won his 45th career race in the 1982 Busch Nashville 420. Morgan Shepherd won his second of seven career pole position starts. Waltrip went on to the 1982 Winston Cup points championship.

Ricky Rudd won the 1994 Slick 50 300 at Loudon, NH, for his 15th career NASCAR win.

11

Johnny Sudderth was born in 1929. Sudderth ran eight Grand National races 1960–63 running out of Atlanta, GA. He spun out in his final event, the 1963 Atlanta 500, and finished 45th.

Rolf Stommelen was born in 1943 in Germany. Racing out of Siegen, Stommelen made one Winston Cup start in 1971. He died in 1983 racing at Riverside, CA.

Lee Petty became the first driver to cruise to a win in each of NASCAR's first four seasons with a win in 1952 at Morristown, NJ. Petty, who gave Plymouth their first win since his last victory in July 1951, averaged 59.661 mph in the 100-mile event, just over 1 mph slower that Herb Thomas' qualifying speed.

Lee Petty won his fourth race of 1954 with a victory in the 100-mile race at Grand Rapids, MI. It was the second consecutive day that a NASCAR race was sanctioned that season. Petty gained his 15th career win while Herb Thomas was the pole-sitter for the 32nd time in his Grand National career. It was the final of two Grand National events held at the Grand River Speedrome.

Jimmy Perdue's final of three career Grand National wins came in 1963 at Moyock, NC, at the Dog Track Speedway.

In NASCAR's 30th event of the 1967 season, Bobby Allison won his 7th career race. The victory came in the Maine 300 at the Oxford Plains Speedway, where Allison had won his first race in July 1966.

Richard Petty's 84th career win came in 1968 in the final of four Grand National events staged at the Fonda Speedway a Montgomery County, NY, track that first saw Grand National racing in 1955.

Pedro Rodriguez died in 1971 of injuries suffered in the West German Grand Prix. Rodriquez had run three Winston Cup races that season and six overall with a top–10 finish in his debut in 1959.

Charlie Glotzbach's final of four wins at NASCAR's top level came in 1971 at Bristol in the Volunteer 500. Richard Petty qualified on the pole for the 98th time.

Darrell Waltrip won for the fourth straight time at the Nashville Speedway with a 1981 victory in the Busch Nashville 420. Mark Martin won his first pole position. Waltrip went on to win the 1981 Winston Cup points championship.

Rusty Wallace started 33rd but finished first in the 1993 Slick 50 300 at Loudon, NH. It was his fifth win of the Winston Cup season and his 26th career victory in the inaugural race of at the New Hampshire International paved superspeedway. Davey Allison finished third, his final race prior to his death in a helicopter crash. Mark Martin finished second.

Jeff Burton came from a 38th place start to win the 1999 Jiffy Lube 300 at the New Hampshire International Speedway in Loudon, NH. Jeff Gordon won the pole and finished third.

12

Benny Parsons was born in Ellerbe, NC, in 1941. Parsons was the Winston Cup Champion during the 1973 season, winning just one race but recording 20 other top–10 finishes in 28 starts. Parsons ran 526 career races 1964–88 with 21 wins and 20 poles. He was the 1970 Winston Cup Rookie of the Year.

Jimmy Crawford, who raced out of East Point, GA, was born in 1944. Crawford started 15 career Grand National and Winston Cup races 1970–74.

Joseph R. "Rick" Hendrick III was born in North Carolina in 1949. Racing out of Charlotte, NC, Hendrick started one Winston Cup race each in 1987 and 1988. He became an influential owner. Hendrick debuted in 1984 with Geoff Bodine behind the wheel. Jeff Gordon won the title for Hendrick in 1995 and Terry Labonte did the same in 1996.

Herb Thomas won the pole and the race, his eighth win of the season and 22nd of his career, with a first-place finish in the 100-mile event on the one-mile dirt track at Atlanta in 1953. Thomas averaged 70.685 mph in his dominant Hudson. Thomas won his second Grand National driving championship that season.

Marvin Panch won in 1957 at the Southern States Fairgrounds in Charlotte, NC. It was his fifth of 17 career Grand National victories. Tiny Lund won the pole but finished last due to a gas line problem.

Jim Paschal won the only Grand National race held at McCormick Field, a quarter-mile paved track in Asheville, NC, in 1958. The track was in a baseball stadium, designed around the diamond. Lee Petty crashed into a dugout in a warm-up race. It was the first NASCAR race in the city of Asheville.

Billy Wade won his second of four races within the month in 1964 on the road course in Bridgehampton, NY.

Bobby Allison won his first NASCAR race in 1966 at the Oxford Plains Speedway in a Chevrolet. It was the first race ever sanctioned in the state of Maine.

Richard Petty won the 1970 Schaefer 300 at Trenton Speedway in New Jersey. It was his 109th career win.

Dale Earnhardt Sr.'s fourth career win came in the 1980 Busch Nashville 420. Cale Yarborough, who qualified for his 53rd career pole start, finished second.

Jeff Burton won the 1998 Jiffy Lube 300 at New Hampshire International Speedway in his #99 Exide Ford. Ricky Craven won his third career pole, but finished 29th. It was his first of two wins on the season.

13

Donald Porter died in 1958 in a non-series race in Portland, OR. Porter had started nine Grand National races 1956–57 with four top–10 finishes his final year.

The first sanctioned race at the New Asheville (NC) Speedway, a .4-mile paved track, was held in 1962 and won by Jack Smith. It was the 21st and final win of Smith's Grand National career. The track hosted eight top-level NASCAR races between 1962 and 1971.

Glen Wood won his final of four career Grand National races in 1963. All of his wins came at Winston-Salem, NC.

Richard Petty won from the pole for his 62nd career Grand National win at the Fonda Speedway in Fonda, NY, in 1967.

David Pearson won the 1969 Northern 300 at Trenton Speedway (NJ) for his 54th career Grand National checkered flag.

Davey Allison died in 1993 following injuries suffered when the helicopter he was flying crashed while attempting to land in the infield of the Talladega International Speedway the previous day. He was 32 years old. He was the 1992 Driver of the Year.

Jeff Burton won his second race of the 1997 Winston Cup season with a victory in the Jiffy Lube 300 at Loudon, NH. Dale Earnhardt finished second.

Ryan Newman's third Winston Cup win of 2003 came at the Chicagoland Speedway in Joliet, IL, in the Tropicana 400. Tony Stewart captured his first pole qualifying start of the season.

14

Bill Blair was born in 1911. He started 123 top-level NASCAR races 1949–58, racing out of High Point, NC. Blair finished 4th in Strictly Stock points in the inaugural season of 1949. He won three career races, the first coming in 1950 in a 100-mile dirt track race in Vernon, NY, and the final win at Daytona Beach, FL, on the beach-road course in 1953.

Eddie Pagan's final of four career Grand National wins came in 1957 in Portland, OR, where he also won in May of the same year. Art Watts captured his fourth career pole, three of which came at the Portland Speedway. It was the final of seven top-level NASCAR races hosted in the state of Oregon.

In 1957, in the final race held at the Memphis-Arkansas Speedway in LeHi, AR, Marvin Panch took the checkered flag. It was also the last time that NASCAR ran a sanctioned race in the state of Arkansas.

Richard Petty captured career win number eight in 1962 at Greenville-Pickens Speedway (SC). Rex White captured his 32nd of 36 career pole starts, but finished fourth in the race.

Ned Jarrett won at the New Asheville Speedway in 1963.

Marvin Panch won from the pole at the Islip (NY) Speedway in 1965 for his 15th career checkered flag.

David Pearson won his 23rd Grand National race, beating Richard Petty who had won his 45th pole, in 1966 at the Fonda Speedway in NY.

LeeRoy Yarbrough won from the pole in the Northern 300 at Trenton Speedway in 1968 for his 6th career victory.

The Albany-Saratoga Speedway hosted one Grand National race and one Winston Cup race. Richard Petty won the 1971 Albany-Saratoga 250 for his 130th win and 99th pole, the final race held at the .362-mile paved oval. He matched the feat, winning from the pole, the next day at Islip.

Cale Yarborough won both 1974 races at Bristol International Speedway with a victory in the 1974 Volunteer 500. It was his 25th career victory while Richard Petty notched his 110th career pole start.

Darrell Waltrip won from the pole for the third time in his career in the 1979 Busch Nashville 420. It was the 20th win and 15th pole start of his Winston Cup career.

Geoff Bodine won the final race held at the Nashville Speedway, which hosted 42 Grand National and Winston Cup races between 1958 and 1984. His win in the 1984 Pepsi 420 was the second of his career. Ricky Rudd captured his 13th career pole.

Ernie Irvan won the 1996 Jiffy Lube 300 at New Hampshire International, his first of two wins of the Winston Cup season and his 13th career checkered flag.

Kevin Harvick won one Winston Cup race in 2002, the Tropicana 400 at Chicagoland Speedway in Joliet, IL, one week after capturing his only pole start of the season. Ryan Newman captured the top spot for this event.

15

Herb Thomas won his second career race with a first-place finish at the Heidelberg Speedway in Pittsburgh, PA, in 1951. Fonty Flock captured his second straight pole in the 100-mile event on a .5-mile dirt track. Thomas won his first of two Grand National championships that season.

Tim Flock won from the pole in 1955 at Morristown Raceway. It was his 28th win and the final of five sanctioned NASCAR events staged at the half-mile dirt speedway in New Jersey between 1951 and 1955.

Billy Wade's third of four victories in July 1964 came in the first Grand National race held at the Islip Speedway, a .2-mile paved track in Islip, NY. Wade also captured the pole.

Richard Petty won from the pole, his 63rd career victory, at Islip, NY, in the inaugural Islip 300 in 1967. It was the 15th of 27 wins on the season for Petty, who won his second of seven career points championships in 1967.

Richard Petty won the 1969 Maryland 300 at the Maryland's Beltsville Speedway.

Richard Petty won at Islip, NY, in 1971. The race was the final of six held on the shortest track to host a Grand National event, at .2 miles. This race was the shortest ever held on that track at 46 miles. It was Petty's 131st career victory and the 100th time he started from the pole.

Truman Fontell "Fonty" Flock died in 1972 at the age of 51. Flock, a NASCAR pioneer along with brothers Bob and Tim, ran 154 Grand National races 1959–57 with 33 poles and 19 wins. In 1951, he finished second to Herb Thomas in Grand National points and won a career-best eight races and qualified first 12 times. A career highlight was his win in the 1952 Southern 500.

Cale Yarborough, driving an Oldsmobile, won the 1978 Nashville 420 for his 54th career win. Lennie Pond started on the pole for the third time in his career and for the second straight race at the Nashville Speedway.

Kevin Harvick, driving Dale Earnhardt's car, won his second race of 2001 at Chicagoland Speedway in the Tropicana 400. Robert Pressley came in second while Todd Bodine captured his first of three pole starts of the season.

16

Wally Campbell, who raced out of Trenton, NJ, was born in 1926. Campbell started 11 Strictly Stock and Grand National races 1949–53. His only pole came in 1950 at Langhorne, PA, in a race won by Fonty Flock. He died in 1954 in a sprint car practice session in Salem, IN.

James Rathmann was born Dick Rathmann in 1928. Jim switched identities with his brother, Dick, born Jim in the 1940s. Jim ran three races at NASCAR's highest level, one each in 1949, 1950 and 1951. He raced out of Alhambra, CA, and captured the checkered flag in the 1960 Indianapolis 500.

Ed Negre, born in 1929 and racing out of the state of Washington, ran 338 career Grand National and Winston Cup races 1955–79. He finished 12th in points in 1971, his best ranking. He finished in the top–10 26 times.

Shorty Rollins gained his only Grand National win in Busti, NY, in 1958. It was the only sanctioned event ever held at the State Line Speedway, a .333-mile dirt track, and the only win of Rollins career. He finished fourth in points that season, his first at NASCAR's top level, and was named the Grand National Rookie of the Year.

Just four days after his first victory, Bobby Allison won his second NASCAR race with a first-place finish for Chevrolet at Islip Speedway in 1966.

Bobby Allison won his second consecutive NASCAR race in 1972 at the Trenton Speedway. It was his 34th career NASCAR win and fifth of the season. The race marked the final NASCAR event at the New Jersey track, which hosted eight Grand National/Winston Cup races between 1958 and 1972. A ninth event scheduled for 1973 was rained out and never rescheduled.

Benny Parsons won the 1976 Nashville 420, after starting the prior two races at the track on the pole. It was his fifth career victory. Neil Bonnett captured his first career pole start.

Darrell Waltrip won his sixth career race in the 1977 Nashville 420. Benny Parsons won the top qualifying slot for the seventh time in his career.

Dale Earnhardt Sr. won his eighth career Winston Cup race at Nashville Speedway in the 1983 Busch Nashville 420. Ron Bouchard won his third and final pole, one each 1981–83.

Bill Elliot captured his second win of the season in the 1987 Talladega 500. Elliott started the season with a win in the Daytona 500 to take two-thirds of the Winston Million races.

Dale Jarrett's fourth career Winston Cup victory came in the 1995 Miller Genuine Draft 500 at Pocono.

17

Elias Wayne Gillette, who raced out of Atlanta, GA, was born in 1938. Gillette competed at the Grand National level in 1969, starting his only 16 races at NASCAR's top level.

Wally Campbell died in 1954, one day after his 28th birthday, in sprint car practice in Salem, IN. His career highlight was capturing the pole for a 1950 Grand National race at Langhorne, PA. He started 11 career top-level NASCAR events.

Eddie Dickerson, who raced out of Milford, DE, in 1980, was born in 1955. Dickerson managed two starts in his only Winston Cup season.

The Cleveland County Fairgrounds in Shelby, NC, hosted six Grand National races 1956–65. The inaugural event on the half-mile dirt oval was won by Speedy Thompson in 1956.

The only Grand National race ever run in Montgomery, NY, was staged at Stewart Air Force Base in 1960. Rex White captured the checkered flag in the one and only Empire State 200 for his ninth career win. John Rostek captured the only pole position of his career (five total starts).

In 1962, Joe Weatherly won his second straight event at the Augusta International Speedway, a half-mile dirt track in Augusta, GA. It was his 19th career victory and sixth of 1962, when Weatherly was the Grand National Champion.

Ernie Cope, who raced out of Tacoma, WA, was born in 1969. Cope started one Winston Cup race, managing just 19 laps before engine trouble forced him from the 1995 Dura Lube 500 at Phoenix.

Geoff Bodine won from the pole for his 15th career Winston Cup victory in the 1994 Miller Genuine Draft 500 at Pocono.

18

Glen Wood was born in Stuart, VA, in 1925. He ran 62 Winston Cup races between 1953 and 1964 with four wins. His first victory came in April 1960 at Winston-Salem, NC, where he won all of his career races.

He started on the pole 14 times. The patriarch of the Wood family, he went on to become director of racing after his retirement from driving. He was the most popular Grand National driver of 1958.

Only two sanctioned NASCAR races have been held in Canada. The final one was won by Lee Petty in 1958 at the Canadian National Exposition Speedway, a .333-mile paved track in Toronto. Lee's son, Richard, made his first career Grand National start.

Marvin Panch won at Watkins Glen in 1965, his 16th career Grand National victory. Top-level NASCAR racing was absent from the track until 1986, when Winston Cup began a yearly event at the 2.3 mile road course.

Richard Petty won his 132nd career Grand National event, taking the checkered flag in the 1971 Northern 300 at Trenton Speedway.

Dale Earnhardt Sr. came in first for the fifth time in the 1993 points race with a victory in the 1993 Miller 500 at Pocono. It was the 58th first-place finish of his career.

Buffalo Civic Stadium, also known as War Memorial Stadium. It was his third career win, all in 1958 when he finished tenth in Grand National points.

Fireball Roberts captured his 31st career win in 1963 at Old Bridge, NJ. The race was run in his honor the following year, just one week after his death from a crash at Charlotte.

Billy Wade's final of four career Grand National wins came at Watkins Glen in the 1964 The Glen 151.8. All four of his wins came in a span of nine days. It was the second sanctioned Grand National event run at the track. Lee Petty made his final of 427 Grand National starts and finished 22nd, one slot behind his son Richard.

Bobby Allison won his 18th career NASCAR race at the Bristol International Speedway in the 1970 Volunteer 500. It was his first victory as a driver-owner, piloting a Dodge. Cale Yarborough captured his 20th top qualifying position.

Darrell Waltrip's 81st career victory came in the 1992 Miller Genuine Draft 500 at Pocono International Raceway in Pennsylvania.

19

Armond Holley, who raced out of Columbus, MS, in the 1960s, was born in 1934. He made five career Grand National starts in 1967.

In the shortest race distance ever in a sanctioned NASCAR race, Jim reed won the 25-mile event on the ¼-mile track in Buffalo, NY, in 1958. It was the only race ever run at the

20

Pete Hamilton was born in 1942. Hamilton drove for the Richard Petty team in the early 1970s and won the 1970 Daytona 500 and both races at Talladega that season. He made 64 starts 1968–73 with three poles and four wins. He was the 1968 NASCAR Rookie of the Year.

Tim Flock won for the third time in four races with a first-place finish on the .5-mile dirt track in South Bend, IN. Flock drove his Hudson to victory in the 100-mile event while Herb Thomas claimed his second consecutive pole. It was the only sanctioned race held at the Playland Park Speedway, the second NASCAR race in the state of Indiana.

Jack Smith won at the Hickory Speedway in the 1957 Buddy Shuman 250. It was his fourth of 21 career victories.

Cotton Owens won both 1961 races at Columbia, SC. The second event of the season saw Owens win from the pole for the third and final time of his career.

Joe Weatherly won at the Savannah Speedway in 1962, the second of ten career events staged at the Georgia track. Weatherly's 20th career win was his seventh of 1962.

David Pearson's 55th career Grand National win came in the 1969 Volunteer 500 at Bristol International Speedway. Cale Yarborough won his 12th of 71 career pole starts.

Jerry Titus was seriously injured in a race at Elkhart Lake, WI, in 1970. He died less than a month later from his injuries at age 41. Titus raced out of Tarzana, CA, to a 39th-place finish in his only Grand National event, the 1968 Motor Trend 500 at Riverside, CA.

Cale Yarborough won the 1974 Nashville 420. The race was the first pole start for Darrell Waltrip, who would manage 58 more top starts in his career. Yarborough went on to finish second in Winston Cup points to Richard Petty that season.

Cale Yarborough's 30th career win came in the 1975 Nashville 420. Benny Parsons captured his third career pole but finished fourth.

Tim Richmond won the 1986 Summer 500 with a victory at Pocono International Raceway. It was Richmond's second straight win and third in four events. It was also his second straight win at Pocono.

Dale Jarrett won the Pennsylvania 500 at Pocono Raceway in 1997. Jeff Gordon finished second.

Jimmie Johnson's second win of the 2003 Winston Cup campaign came at the New Hampshire International Speedway in the New England 300. The eventual season champion, Matt Kenseth, captured his first pole start of the season.

21

Axel Anderson was born in 1921. Anderson raced out of Patchogue, NY, to five Grand National starts, two in 1955 and three in 1958.

Samuel Eugene Colvin, who raced out of Greenville, SC, was born in 1934. He started one Grand National race, finishing 11th in a September 1958 event at Fairgrounds Raceway in Birmingham, AL.

The only Grand National race held in Chicago was won by Fireball Roberts at Soldier Field in 1956 on a half-mile paved track inside the famed football stadium.

Jack Ely, who raced out of Bethel, CT, 1986–89, was born in 1957. Ely ran three Winston Cup events, two in 1986 and one in 1989.

Robert "Bobby" Gerhart, who raced out of Lebanon, PA, was born in 1958. Gerhard started 24 Winston Cup events 1983–92, entering no more than five races in any one season.

Jim Reed won at the Heidelberg Speedway in Pennsylvania in 1959 for his sixth career Grand National win. Dick Bailey qualified for the top spot for the only time in his career.

Ned Jarrett won from the pole for the third of eleven times in his career with a 1962 victory at Myrtle Beach, SC.

Ray Platte died in 1963 from injuries he suffered in a modified race in South Boston, VA. Platte raced in many series in his lifetime and made one Grand National start in 1955.

Richard Petty captured his first career road-course win, his 23rd career victory, in 1963 at Bridgehampton, NY.

David Pearson won from the pole at the Lincoln Speedway in New Oxford, PA, in 1964 for his 8th win and 12th career top start. It was the inaugural running of the Pennsylvania 200 Classic.

David Pearson swept both Bristol races in 1968, winning the Volunteer 500 on this date for his 39th career Grand National victory. LeeRoy Yarbrough captured his eight of nine career pole starts.

For the second consecutive Pocono race, Bill Elliott won from the pole. His 12th career win came in the 1985 Summer 500 at the Pennsylvania super speedway.

Rusty Wallace won the 1991 Miller Genuine Draft 500 at Pocono. It was the second and final win of the Winston Cup season for Wallace, who captured the 20th checkered flag of his career.

Rusty Wallace won for the fourth time in 1996 with a trip to victory lane in the Miller 500 at Pocono. It was his 45th career Winston Cup victory.

Ward Burton, the reigning Daytona 500 champion, captured his second and final win of the 2002 season with a first-place finish in the New England 300 at New Hampshire International Speedway. Bill Elliott earned his third top qualifying spot of the year.

22

Herb Thomas won his second straight Grand National race in 1953, the 23rd win of his career. Thomas also won his 22nd pole position, driving a Hudson to victory in the 100-mile race on the half-mile dirt track in Rapid City, SD. It was the first and only sanctioned NASCAR race held in the state of South Dakota. For the second time in series history, a driver ran a race with an average speed (57.720 mph) that exceeded the qualifying time (55.727 mph).

Joe Weatherly won from the pole for the second of six times in his Grand National career in 1961 at Myrtle Beach, SC. It was the eighth win and fifth pole of his career.

David Pearson won the 1973 Dixie 500 at Atlanta International Raceway, his second straight win at the Georgia track, driving his Mercury to victory over Cale Yarborough.

Harry Gant won his 4th career Winston Cup race in the 1984 Like Cola 500 at Pocono International Raceway. Bill Elliott captured his 4th career pole position.

Geoff Bodine won his second race of 1990 with a first-place finish at the AC Spark Plug 500 at Pocono. It was his 9th career Winston Cup win.

Dale Jarrett won the 19th Winston Cup race of 2001 at Loudon, NH, in the New England 300. Jarrett moved into the points lead for the final time of the season, eventually losing out to Jeff Gordon, who sat on the pole for this event for his sixth top qualifying start of the year.

23

Johnny Gouveia, a driver with every vowel in his last name, was born in 1927. Gouveia raced out of New Bedford, MA, to start five Grand National races, one in 1952 and four in 1955, with his lone top–10 finish.

David MacDonald was born in 1937. Racing out of El Monte, CA, he ran two NASCAR Grand National races in 1963 and five the following year. He died in a crash at the 1964 Indianapolis 500.

At Charlotte in 1950, Curtis Turner won the pole and the race for the second consecutive event, the first time the feat was achieved in NASCAR history. It was his fifth win

in only the 17th series event and the second time on the season that he had won two races in a row.

Buck Baker's 41st career Grand National win came in 1960 at Myrtle Beach, SC, in 1960. Ned Jarrett, the previous year's winner at the track, qualified for his second career pole. Jarrett won 35 poles in his career.

Richard Petty won from the pole at Bristol in the 1967 Volunteer 500, the 28th time he both started and finished on top. It was his 64th career win and 61st pole start.

Buckshot Jones was born in 1970 in Monticello, GA. Jones ran 56 Winston Cup events 1997–2003 with one top–10 finish in 1998. He also ran regularly in the Busch Series 1995–2001.

Bobby Allison won his 35th NASCAR career race, his third consecutive win in 1972. The win came at the Atlanta International Raceway in the annual Dixie 500.

Bill Elliott won his second race in three weeks with a win in the 1989 AC Spark Plug 500 at Pocono.

Sterling Marlin won the 1995 DieHard Talladega 500 for his fourth career win and third victory of the season.

After four pole positions in the previous six races, Rusty Wallace finally won with a trip to victory lane in the 2000 Pennsylvania 500 at Pocono International Raceway. The previous week's winner, Tony Stewart, started from the pole.

24

Johnny Anderson was born in 1942. He ran nine Winston Cup races 1971–74, all but one at either Riverside or Ontario, CA. He raced out of Palmdale, CA, to a career-best 17th-place finish in the 1972 Miller High Life 500 at Ontario.

Buck Baker won the final of two Grand National races held at the Norfolk Speedway, a .4-mile dirt track in Virginia. It was the 32nd career win for Baker while Bill Amick claimed his third of five career poles.

Paul Goldsmith's final of nine career Grand National wins came in the 1966 Volunteer 500 at Bristol.

Richard Petty won from the pole for the 46th time in his career in the 1970 East Tennessee 200. It was his 110th career victory.

Richard Petty won the pole for the Nashville 420 and cruised to his 133rd career victory at NASCAR's top level. It was the 54th time he started and finished first.

Tim Richmond's third career pole position start resulted in his third Winston Cup victory in 1983 at the Like Cola 500 at Pocono International Raceway.

Bill Elliott won his second consecutive race, his fourth of 1988 and the 27th of his career, with a trip to victory lane in the AC Spark Plug 500 at Pocono. Morgan Shepherd qualified first. Elliott won his only Winston Cup Championship that year.

Jimmy Spencer won the Die Hard Talladega 500 in 1994.

25

Joey Arrington was born in 1956. Racing out of Rocky Mount, VA, Arrington made nine career Winston Cup starts. His best finish came in his final top-level NASCAR event, 13th place in the 1980 Richmond 400.

Cotton Owens closed the Monroe County Fairgrounds in Rochester, NY, to Grand National racing with a victory in 1958. Owens' second career win came in the final of eight events hosted between 1950 and 1958.

Jerry Hill, who raced out of Brandywine, MD, in the 1990s, was born in 1961. Hill ran eight Winston Cup events 1991–93 and ran regularly in the Craftsman Truck Series 2001–04.

Ned Jarrett won at Bristol, TN, in the 1965 Volunteer 500, his 45th career Grand National win. Fred Lorenzen captured the pole, his 27th of 33 of his career.

Johnny Roberts died in 1965 at the age of 31 as a result of injuries suffered in a modified race in New Oxford, PA. Roberts ran 13 career Grand National races 1953–61.

Richard Petty won his 80th career race in the Smoky 200 at Smoky Mountain Raceway. Bobby Isaac won his fourth career pole.

Bobby Isaac's 29th of 37 career NASCAR wins came in the 1970 Nashville 420. LeeRoy Yarbrough won the ninth and final pole position of his Grand National career.

Bobby Allison won for the second time in 1982 at Pocono International Raceway in the Mountain Dew 500.

It was Allison's 66th career first place finish and his fifth win of the year. Cale Yarborough started first for the 62nd time.

At Talladega in 1993, a spectacular crash between Ted Musgrave and Neil Bonnett damaged a catch fence designed to protect fans. Luckily no spectators were injured. Darrell Waltrip began a skein of 40 consecutive races in which he finished running.

Dale Earnhardt Sr. won his sixth race of the 1993 Winston Cup season with a victory at Talladega in the DieHard 500. It was his final win of the season, his sixth as the Winston Cup Champion.

Bobby Labonte cruised to victory in the 1999 Pennsylvania 500 at Pocono Raceway in Long Pond, PA. Mike Skinner won his third career pole, but finished 10th. Skinner finished 10th in Winston Cup points in 1999.

26

Jack Anderson was born in 1936. Racing out of Pearisburg, VA, Anderson started 36 races in the mid–1960s, 31 in 1964 when he finished in the top 10 four times.

Buddy Rogers Arrington was born in 1938. Arrington raced out of Martinsville, VA, to finish 7th overall in Winston Cup points in 1982 and 9th in 1978. He made 560 career starts with 103 top–10 finishes.

In the first and only sanctioned race held in the state of Nebraska, Dick Rathmann captured the checkered flag in a 100-mile event on the half-mile dirt track at the Lincoln City Fairgrounds in North Platte. Rathmann, driving a Hudson, won his fourth race of 1953 and the ninth of his Grand National career. Herb Thomas held the pole position, his 23rd pole to match his 23 series wins.

Jim Reed won the only Grand National event ever held at Wall Stadium in Belmar, NJ, in 1958 on the .333-mile paved track. It was the fourth win of his career, all in 1958.

Jack Smith won in 1959 at the Southern States Fairgrounds in Charlotte, NC, his tenth career Grand National win.

Racing out of Oshawa, Ontario, Canada, Randy MacDonald was born in 1962. He started four Winston Cup races 1994–96, debuting with a 24th-place finish in the 1994 AC-Delco 500 at Rockingham, NC.

For the third straight Bristol race, Fred Lorenzen cruised to victory lane with his 17th Grand National victory in the 1964 Volunteer 500. Richard Petty captured his 22nd top qualifying position.

Richard Petty won from the pole for the 42nd time in his career in the 1969 Nashville 400. It was his 98th career Grand National victory.

Darrell Waltrip dominated the inaugural Mountain Dew 500 at Pocono International Raceway in 1981. Waltrip won his 26th career pole and captured his 34th career checkered flag.

Ernie Irvan won the 1992 Talladega 500 for his sixth career victory.

Jeff Gordon won the 1998 Pennsylvania 500 at Pocono. Ward Burton captured the pole but finished 34th due to an accident. It was Gordon's fifth of 13 wins in his third Winston Cup championship season.

27

Gene "Stick" Elliott, who raced out of Shelby, NC, in the 1960s and '70s, was born in 1934. Elliott ran 91 Grand National and two Winston Cup races 1962–71 with 15 top–10 finishes and one 2nd in 65.

Frank Graham, who raced out of Charleston Heights, SC, in the 1960s, was born in 1940. Graham started a total of eight Grand National races 1961–64 with his lone top–10 finish occurring in 1962.

Jack Sellers was born in 1944. Sellers raced out of Sacramento, CA, to start one Winston Cup race each in 1990 and 1992. He finished 40th in both of his starts at Sonoma, CA.

Dick Hutcherson won from the pole in the 1967 Smoky 200 at Maryville, TN. It was the fourth and final time Hutcherson started and finished first. It was his 13th career Grand National win. Richard Petty finished second.

David Pearson won the 1968 Nashville 400 for his 40th career Grand National win. Richard Petty finished second and started in the top qualifying position for the 74th time of his career.

Richard Petty won his 99th career Grand National race in the 1969 Smoky 200. David Pearson again won the pole and finished second.

Petty finished second to Pearson for the Grand National championship that season.

In the 1980 Coca-Cola 500, Neil Bonnett cruised to his 6th career Winston Cup victory. Cale Yarborough, who sat on the pole for the 54th time in his career, finished third at Pocono International Raceway event.

Bobby Hillin, just 22 years old, won the 1986 Talladega 500, his first and only Winston Cup win.

Bobby Hillin Jr. won the 1986 Talladega 500 at Talladega International Speedway.

Ryan Newman's fourth victory of the 2003 Winston Cup season came from the top qualifying spot in the Pennsylvania 500 at Pocono Raceway.

28

Earl Moss was born in 1925 in North Carolina. Racing out of Creedmoor, Moss ran 11 Grand National races in the 1950s with two top–10 finishes. His best finish was 6th in April 1951 at Occoneechee Speedway in Hillsboro, NC, in the #110 Ford.

For the second of eleven times in his career, Fred Lorenzen won from the pole. His win at Bristol, TN, in the 1963 Volunteer 500 was his eighth career win and 12th top qualifying start.

Paul Lewis' only Grand National win came in the 1966 Smoky 200 at Smoky Mountain Raceway in Maryville, TN. Buddy Baker captured the first pole of his career. He would qualify first another 39 times.

Richard Petty won the 1974 Dixie 500 at Atlanta Motor Speedway, his fourth career win in the annual event. It was the 160th career checkered flag for Petty, who won his fifth of seven driving championships in 1974 with 10 wins.

Cale Yarborough won the 17th Annual Talladega 500 in 1985, over Neil Bonnett. Bill Elliott captured the pole but finished fourth.

Dale Earnhardt Sr. won the Die Hard 500 at Talladega. It was his third of four wins on the 1991 Winston Cup series.

Jeff Gordon won the Diehard 500 at Talladega, his sixth victory of the 1996 Winston Cup season.

Bill Elliott dominated the week at Pocono Raceway in 2002, starting from the pole and winning the Pennsylvania 500. It was his fourth pole and first of two consecutive wins of the season. They were his only wins of the Winston Cup campaign.

29

Otis A. "Rock" Harn, who raced out of North Augusta, SC, in the 1960s, was born in 1924. Harn ran four Grand National events 1962–66.

In the first-ever sanctioned Grand National event on the .5-mile dirt track at Weaverville, NC, Fonty Flock claimed his fourth win of 1951. Billy Carden claimed his first pole position in the 100-mile event.

The Altamont-Schenectady Fairgrounds hosted two Grand National events in the 1950s. The final race was won by Junior Johnson on this date in 1955 on the half-mile dirt track. It was his 6th career win.

Marvin Panch won at the Montgomery Motor Speedway in Alabama in 1956. It was almost 11 years before Grand National cars returned to the track. It was Panch's first career NASCAR victory.

Harry Goularte, who raced out of Morgan Hill, CA, was born in 1956. Goularte started eight Winston Cup races 1977–87, with no more than two appearances in any one season.

Bristol, TN, began a tradition of stock car racing in 1961, hosting their first Grand National race, The Volunteer 500. Jack Smith captured his 16th career win while Fred Lorenzen sat on the pole for the third time in his career.

Jim Paschal won the Southeastern 500 at Bristol, TN, in 1962. It was his 11th of 24 career Grand National wins. Fireball Roberts captured his 29th top qualifying spot.

Richard Petty won his third straight Nashville 400 in 1967. Dick Hutcherson won his 20th of 22 career poles. It was the 17th of 27 wins on the season for Petty, who won his second of seven career points championships in 1967.

Ned Setzer died on this date in 1977. Setzer raced out of Claremont, NC, to start 10 Grand National races 1965–66 with three top–10 finishes.

Dale Earnhardt Sr. won his second straight Talladega 500 in 1984.

Joe Littlejohn died in 1989 at the age of 81. A South Carolina native, Littlejohn started one race in each of

NASCAR's first two seasons. He won the pole at Daytona in 1950's first race, his final Grand National appearance.

Dale Earnhardt Sr. won his third race in four weeks, his sixth win of 1990, with a trip to victory lane in the Die Hard 500 at Talladega.

Bobby Labonte, the 2000 Winston Cup champion, won for the first time in 2001 in the 20th race of the season at Pocono, the Pennsylvania 500. Todd Bodine earned his second pole start in three weeks.

30

Ben Arnold was born in 1936. Arnold ran 132 races between 1968 and 1973 with 21 top–10 finishes. He finished 10th overall in Winston Cup points in 1972. He raced out of Fairfield, AL.

Neil Bonnett was born in Bessemer, AL, in 1946. Bonnett began his Winston Cup career in 1974 and was practicing for the 1994 Daytona 500 when he died in a crash.

Buck Baker won from the pole at Morristown, NJ, in 1954 for his eighth career victory.

Baker drove his Oldsmobile to the checkered flag in the 100-mile event held on a half-mile dirt track. It was the 12th time he was the top qualifier.

The New York State Fairgrounds in Syracuse, NY, was the sight of three Grand National races in the 1950s. Tim Flock captured the first race on the one-mile dirt track, originally a horse track dating back to the 19th century.

The second of two Grand National events held in Lancaster, SC, was Speedy Thompson's 13th career Grand National victory. Thompson qualified first for the 1957 event, winning from the pole for the fourth of seven times in his career.

Richard Petty won at the Greenville-Pickens Speedway in 1963 for his 24th career victory. Ned Jarrett qualified on the pole for the 17th time in his career and was the runner-up in the race.

For the second straight Nashville 400 race, Richard Petty won from the pole. It was the 19th of 61 times in his career he both started and finished first. It was the 47th win and 46th pole of his career.

Darrell Waltrip won the 1978 Coca-Cola 500 at Pocono in 1978 for his 14th career victory. Benny Parsons won his 11th career pole.

Cale Yarborough won the 1979 Coca-Cola 500 at the Pocono International Raceway for his 62nd career victory. Harry Gant won his first Winston Cup pole.

Terry Labonte won his second race of 1989 with a first-place finish in the Die Hard 500 at Talladega.

31

Louise Smith was born in 1916. Smith was a pioneering woman on the Grand National circuit. She raced out of Greenville, SC, to start 11 Grand National races 1949–52.

Billy Rafter was born in 1929. Rafter, who raced out of Clarence Center, NY, ran 35 early Grand

National races 1949–58. He finished in the top–10 11 times.

Buck Simmons was born in 1946. Racing out of Baldwin, GA, Simmons ran eight Winston Cup events 1979–80. His best finish came in his debut, 14th-place in the 1979 Dixie 500 at Atlanta, GA.

Lee Petty claimed his first win of 1951 on the .5-mile dirt track in Rochester, NY. It was his third career win, one in each of NASCAR's first three campaigns. It was the 11th straight 100-mile race. Fonty Flock claimed his seventh pole position.

Tim Flock, the eventual Grand National Champion, won at the Bay Meadows Race Track in San Mateo, CA, in 1955.

Mike Alexander was born in 1957. Racing out of Franklin, TN, Alexander started 74 career Winston Cup races with 11 top–10 finishes 1980–90.

Fireball Roberts won the inaugural NASCAR event at the Atlanta Motor Speedway, taking the checkered flag in the 1960 Dixie 300.

Richard Petty won for the third time in four races at the Nashville Speedway with a victory in the 1965 Nashville 400.

Penny Parsons won the 1977 Coca-Cola 500 at Pocono International Speedway for his 7th career Winston Cup victory. Darrell Waltrip won his 8th career pole, but finished third.

Dale Earnhardt Sr. won his first race at Talladega with a win in the 1982 Talladega 500.

John Anderson died in 1986 in a highway crash in Charlotte, NC, at the age of 42. Anderson ran 32 Winston Cup events 1979–83.

Ken Schrader won his first career race in 1988 with a one-car-length victory in the Die Hard 500 at Talladega. Schrader was the 1985 Rookie of the Year.

AUGUST

1

Eddie Pagan was born in 1918. Pagan, who raced out of Lynwood, CA, managed four wins and 38 other top–10 finishes in 62 career starts 1954–63. His most consistent season was 1958 when he finished ninth in Grand National Series points. His first victory came in April 1960 at Winston-Salem, NC, where he won all of his career races. He died on his birthday in 1984 at the age of 66.

Bobby Isaac was born in 1932 in Catawba, NC. Isaac drove a Dodge to 13 poles and 11 wins en route to capturing the 1970 Grand National championship. The previous season he had 20 poles and 17 wins and was voted the Grand National's most popular driver. He last raced in NASCAR in 1976 and died in 1977.

Jerry Sisco was born in 1941. He raced out of Nashville, TN, to start four Winston Cup races; 1974 (1) and 1976 (3). His best finish was 11th in the Southeastern 400 at Bristol, TN.

His brother David ran 133 career races in the 1970s.

Bob Keselowski started one Winston Cup race, running 17 laps and finishing 41st in the 1994 UAW-GM Teamwork 500 at Pocono, PA. He was born in 1951 and raced out of Rochester Hills, CA.

In the third sanctioned NASCAR race in a span of four days, including two in a row in New York State, Fonty Flock captured the checkered flag in the 12th consecutive 100-mile event on the 1951 schedule. It was the first Grand National race held on the .5-mile dirt track at Altamont, NY. It was Flock's second win in four days and his fifth of the season.

Danny Letner gained his first Grand National win with a checkered-flag finish at the paved-dirt track in Oakland, CA, in 1954. Letner drove his Hudson at an average speed of 53.045 mph for the victory on the half-mile track. Marvin Panch won his first pole position, the first of the season for manufacturer Dodge.

It was the final of three sanctioned NASCAR race staged at Oakland Stadium, all in the 1950s.

Chuck Stevenson died in 1995, at the age of 75. Stevenson raced out of Montana to start one race each in the 1955 and 1956 season. His only win was his final Grand National appearance in November 1955 at Willow Springs International Raceway in Lancaster, GA.

Ned Jarrett won his first NASCAR race at Myrtle Beach, SC, in 1959. It was the first of 50 Winston Cup victories for Jarrett. Bob Welborn, the winner of the 1958 race at the track, qualified for his sixth of seven career poles.

Richard Petty won the 1971 Dixie 500 at Atlanta Motor Speedway, his second straight win in the annual event. It was the 15th win of the season for Petty, who won 21 races in 1971 on his way to his third Winston Cup championship.

Richard Petty won his 179th career top-level NASCAR race in the 1976 Purolator 500 at Pocono International Raceway in Pennsylvania. Cale Yarborough won his 32nd career pole.

Darrell Waltrip won the 1982 Talladega 500, his second straight win at the Alabama track.

Jeff Gordon became the first two-time winner of the Brickyard 400 in 1998, the fifth running of the annual event. Ernie Irvan took the pole for the second straight year.

2

Michael P. Eagan, who raced out of Dunkirk, NY, was born in 1926. Eagan finished fourth in his only career Strictly Stock race in 1949, NASCAR's inaugural season.

Herb Thomas won his 24th career NASCAR start with a victory in the 100-mile dirt-track event, the 25th official race of 1953. For the third straight race, Grand National cars made their debut in a state; this time the location was Davenport, IA. Also, for the third time in five races, the winner had an average speed faster than the qualifying time (62.500 vs. 54.397 mph). Buck Baker held the poll. It remains the only top-level NASCAR race run in Iowa.

Ned Jarrett won his second NASCAR race one day after his first, with a first-place finish at Charlotte in 1959. Jarrett went on to win the 1961 and 1964 points championships. It was the second Grand National race in less than one week at the Southern States Fairgrounds.

Richard Petty won from the pole at the Nashville Speedway in 1964, the tenth of 61 times in his career. It was his 34th career victory.

Richard Petty won the 1970 Dixie 500 at Atlanta Motor Speedway, his second win in the annual event.

Ron Bouchard won the 1981 Talladega 500 for the only Winston Cup victory of his career. He was the 1981 Winston Cup Rookie of the Year.

Ricky Rudd won his only Brickyard 400 in 1997. It was the fourth annual event at the Indianapolis Motor Speedway. Ernie Irvan took the pole and Bobby Labonte finished second.

3

Danny Byrd was born in 1937. Byrd, who raced out of Taylor, MI, started four Grand National races in 1965 with one top–10 finish, the Fireball 200 at the Asheville-Weaverville Speedway (NC) in February.

Jim Paschal won the only top-level NASCAR race run in the state of Oklahoma, held on the half-mile dirt track of the Oklahoma State Fairgrounds in 1956. It was his 6th career win.

Jack Smith in 1958 won from the pole in the first of four Grand National races held at Bridgehampton Race Circuit, a 2.85-mile road course on Long Island Sound, between 1958 and 1966.

Joe Lee Johnson won his first of two career Grand National races in 1959 at Nashville.

In 1960, Ned Jarrett won the only NASCAR race ever held on the quarter-mile paved track of the Dixie Speedway in Birmingham, AL. Three Pettys finished in the top 10; Richard (2nd), Lee (3rd) and Maurice (8th).

In 1962 Joe Weatherly bagged his 21st Grand National victory in the Confederate 200 on the ⅓-mile paved track of the Boyd Speedway, aka Chattanooga International Raceway, in Chattanooga, TN. Richard Petty, who won his fifth pole, finished fourth in his #62 Plymouth. The track hosted two Grand National events, one each in 1962 and 1964.

James Sears died at the Starlite Speedway in 1973 at the age of 32. Sears ran six top-level Winston Cup events 1967–71 with two top–10s in 1970.

David Pearson won the second sanctioned Winston Cup event held at the Pocono International Raceway in the 1975 Purolator 500 at the Pennsylvania superspeedway for his 87th career victory. Bobby Allison won his 47th pole.

Neil Bonnett won the 12th Talladega 500 in 1980.

Dale Jarrett won the 1996 Brickyard 400 at Indianapolis Motor Speedway for his third win of the Winston Cup season. Jeff Gordon started on the pole for the second straight year, but crashed and finished 37th. Jarrett won four races that season.

Kevin Harvick became the second consecutive driver to win from the pole during the 2003 Winston Cup season when he captured the Brickyard 400 at the Indianapolis Motor Speedway. Ryan Newman had achieved the feat the prior week at Pocono.

4

Joe Leonard was born in 1934. Racing out of San Diego, CA, Leonard finished 31st in his only Grand National start in the 1969 Firecracker 400 at Daytona, FL.

Parnelli Jones won his first career NASCAR race in 1957 at the Kitsap County Airport in Bremerton, WA, with an average speed of nearly 39 MPH on a road course. Jones mostly drove Indy Cars in his racing career, but captured four career Grand National wins. It was the only Grand National or Winston Cup race held in the state of Washington.

The first Grand National event in Watkins Glen was won from the pole in 1957 by Buck Baker, the eventual champion. A historic racing town in upstate New York, Watkins Glen began hosting street-road races after World War II. As racing through town became hazardous, a new course was built in the outlying fields, Watkins Glen International. The original track hosted one race each in 1957, 1964 and 1965 before resuming a yearly Winston Cup visit in 1986.

At the Nashville Speedway in 1963, Jim Paschal captured his 17th of 24 career wins in the Nashville 400. Richard Petty won his 15th career pole and finished fourth.

LeeRoy Yarbrough won the 1968 Dixie 500 at Atlanta Motor Speedway, his seventh career checkered flag.

Jeff Gordon was born in 1971 in Vallejo, CA. Gordon debuted in the Winston Cup Series in 1992 and became the youngest point champion when he won the title in 1995 at the age of 24. He was the 1993 Winston Cup Rookie of the Year.

The inaugural Winston Cup race at Pocono International Speedway in Pennsylvania was won by Richard Petty in 1974. It was his 161st career NASCAR victory. Buddy Baker, who won his 17th career pole, finished second in the Purolator 500. The race was shortened to 480 miles due to rain.

Kurt Busch, born in 1978 in Las Vegas, NV, began his Winston Cup career in 2000 with seven starts. His first career win came in the 2002 Food City 500 at Bristol, TN. He started 114 races through 2003 with eight victories and two pole starts.

Gene Thoneson died in 1993 in a tractor accident at the age of 39. Thoneson managed one career Winston Cup start in 1981, finishing 22nd in the Winston Western 500 at Riverside, CA.

Bill Elliott won the 2002 Brickyard 400 at the Indianapolis Motor Speedway, his second straight win of the Winston Cup season. Elliott won only two races in 2002. The eventual points champion, Tony Stewart, started on the pole.

5

Gordon Johncock was born in 1936. A two-time Indy 500 winner, he recorded 21 NASCAR starts with four career top–10 finishes 1966–76.

Ronald Lee "Ronnie" Daniel, who raced out of Lynchburg, VA, was born in 1937. Daniel started eight career Winston Cup races 1971–73, including 16th place at Bristol, TN, in the 1973 Volunteer 500.

Dr. Richard Skillen was born in 1945. Skillen ran 17 Winston Cup races 1974–86, racing out of Claremont, NH. Skillen finished 31st in the 1976 Daytona 500, retiring his Singer Climate Control Chevrolet due to heating problems on lap 99.

Jim Paschal won in 1955 at the Southern States Fairgrounds in Charlotte, NC.

Jim Paschal's 12th career win was his second straight victory at the Nashville Speedway in the 1962

Nashville 500. Johnny Allen qualified on the pole, the third and final of his career.

In the final Grand National event held at the Cleveland County Fairgrounds in Shelby, NC, in 1965, Ned Jarrett captured his 46th career victory in the sixth top-level NASCAR race held at the half-mile dirt track.

Kenny Irwin Jr. was born in 1969 in Indianapolis, IN. He debuted in the Winston Cup Series in 1997 and ran 87 events through 2000, with 12 top–10s and three pole starts. He was the 1998 Winston Cup Rookie of the Year, driving for Robert Yates. He died in a 2000 practice crash at Loudon, NH.

Richard Woodland Jr. was born in 1970 and started one Winston Cup race apiece in 1993 and 1996. He was based in Templeton, CA.

Jerry Titus died in 1970 at the age of 41 of injuries suffered less than a month earlier in a race at Elkhart Lake, WI. Titus, who raced out of Tarzana, CA, started one Grand National race in 1968, finishing 39th and retiring after five laps at Riverside.

Darrell Waltrip won the 1979 Talladega 500.

Dale Earnhardt Sr. won the second Brickyard 400 in 1995. Jeff Gordon, last year's winner, won the pole. Earnhardt Sr. averaged over 155 mph in the win.

Bobby Labonte won the 7th annual Brickyard 400 in 2000. Labonte set a course record with an average speed of 155.912 mph. Ricky Rudd, who won the race in 1997, won the pole. Labonte won the Winston Cup Championship that season.

Jeff Gordon became the first driver to win three Brickyard 400 races with a victory in 2001. Gordon went on to win his third Winston Cup points championship with six wins on the season. Jimmy Spencer won his first of two pole position starts of the season.

6

Wilroy Clarence "Roy" Smith was born in 1944. Smith raced out of Victoria, British Columbia, Canada, to start 26 Winston Cup races between 1975 to 1989, never running more than three events in any one season. He led two races and finished in the top–10 four times in his career.

Jim Paschal began his three-year dominance at Nashville Speedway with a victory in the 1961 Nashville 500, the ninth of his Grand National career. Rex White won his 23rd career pole and went on to finish second in championship points that season.

Dick Hutcherson won the 1967 Dixie 500 at Atlanta Motor Speedway. It was Hutcherson's only win at the Hampton, GA, track and the first running of the event at the 500-mile distance. It was also the 14th and final win of his Grand National career.

Bobby Isaac continued his dominance at the Columbia Speedway with his fifth win in the past seven events at the South Carolina Track. Isaac's win was his 30th career checkered flag. Richard Petty's pole start was the 90th of his career.

Bobby Allison won the 1971 Myers Brothers Memorial at Bowman Gray Stadium. The win did not count in his career total of 84 official wins. Allison drove a Mustang to victory. It was the final NASCAR race at the Winston-Salem, NC, quarter-mile track that hosted a total of 29 Grand National events between 1958 and 1971.

James Hylton won the 1972 Talladega 500, his second and final career win. Hylton finished third in Winston Cup points that season, behind Richard Petty and Bobby Allison.

Lennie Pond captured the 10th Talladega 500 in 1978 for his only career top-level NASCAR win in 234 starts at both the Grand National and Winston Cup levels. He was the 1973 Winston Cup Rookie of the Year.

Harold "Frog" Fagan died in 1993 at the age of 53. Fagan ran three career Grand National races 1952–61, driving out of Willowdale, Ontario, Canada. Fagan finished a career-best eighth in the 1968 Fireball 300 at Asheville-Weaverville Speedway (NC).

The inaugural Brickyard 400 was run in 1994, marking the first time Winston Cup cars competed at the track made famous by the Indianapolis 500. Jeff Gordon was the first winner.

7

James "Jimmy" Helms, who raced out of Charlotte, NC, in the 1960s, was born in 1935. Helms ran 88 career Grand National races with seven top–10 finishes. He was 18th in championship points in 1965.

Bob Flock won his first career NASCAR race in the third race in circuit history in 1949. It was the longest race to date at 200 miles, held on a dirt track in Hillsboro, NC, at the Occoneechee Speedway, which hosted 32 top NASCAR races 1949–68. Jim Roper, who had won the first Strictly Stock race in NASCAR history, started his second race and finished 15th.

The final of two Grand National races, both won by Lee Petty in 1955, was held at the Forsyth County Fairgrounds in Winston-Salem, NC. Petty won the 100-mile dirt track race for his 24th career checkered flag.

Speedy Thompson won at the Columbia Speedway in 1958. It was the sixth of seven times Thompson captured the checkered flag from the pole.

Johnny Beauchamp's second of two career Grand National victories occurred in 1960 at Nashville, TN. Rex White captured his 16th career pole, his fourth straight at the Nashville Speedway.

David Pearson won from the pole for the third of 37 times in his career, capturing his ninth Grand National win and 13th top qualifying spot in 1964 at Myrtle Beach, SC.

Richard Petty won the 1966 Dixie 400 at Atlanta Motor Speedway, his first win at the Hampton, GA, track.

Donnie Allison won the 1977 Talladega 500. He was the 1967 Grand National Rookie of the Year.

Al Loquasto died in a private plane crash in 1991 at the age of 48. Loquasto ran six Winston Cup events 1981–82.

Dale Jarrett won his second Brickyard 400 in 1999. Jeff Gordon, who won the first event, captured the pole. It was the final of four wins that season for Jarrett, who went on to win the 1999 Winston Cup championship.

8

Woodrow "Woodie" Wilson was born in 1925. He competed in one Strictly Stock event in 1949, NASCAR's first year. He drove out of Mobile, AL, to record two career top–10 finishes out of nine Grand National races in his career. He was named the 1961 Grand National Rookie of the Year.

Bill Ward was born in 1930. He ran one Grand National and six Winston Cup events 1969–75. Racing out of Anniston, AL, Ward drove over 1000 miles at NASCAR's top level.

Thomas W. "Tommy" Ellis, who raced out of Richmond, VA, 1976–91, was born in 1947. Ellis ran 78 Winston Cup events with six top–10 finishes. He led six career races.

Richard Petty won the only NASCAR race ever staged at the quarter-mile paved Huntsville Speedway in Huntsville, AL, in 1962. It was the 39th event of the season.

Richard Petty captured his second straight Columbia Speedway event in the 1963 Sandlapper 200, winning from the pole for the fourth of six times that season.

Jack Sprague was born in 1964. Sprague, who raced out of Spring Lake, MI, ran 24 Winston Cup races 1996–2003, making his debut in the Pedigree Pontiac, finishing 23rd at the 1996 Dura Lube 500 at Phoenix.

Richard Petty won his 38th career event, the 1965 Western North Carolina 500 at Skyline Speedway.

David Pearson won at Columbia Speedway in South Carolina in 1968, his 41st career Grand National victory. Buddy Baker qualified first for the fifth time in his career.

The final of four top-level NASCAR events was held at the West Virginia International speedway in Huntington in 1971, won by Richard Petty for his 135th career victory. Bobby Allison qualified first for the 20th time in his career. It was the second consecutive time that Petty won and Allison captured the pole at the track.

Dave Marcis won at Talladega in 1976 with a late-race pass of Buddy Baker. Marcis's win was assured when his fuel strategy allowed him to remain on the track while Baker had to pit.

Mark Martin's first victory of the 1993 season started a string of four straight wins. Martin won from the pole at the 1993 Bud at the Glen at Watkins Glen, NY.

9

Len Sutton was born in 1925. Sutton ran five career Grand National races, one in 1956 and the rest in 1963, running out of Portland, OR.

Lloyd Dane, who raced out of

Eldon, MO in the 1950s and '60s, was born in 1925. Dane started 53 Grand National races with one pole and four wins 1951–64. Dane won two west coast races in 1956 with his first career checkered flag in Sacramento in July.

Joseph F. Eubanks, who raced out of Spartanburg, SC, in the 1950s and '60s, was born in 1925. Eubanks ran 159 career Grand National races with three poles and a single checkered flag in September 1958 at Hillsboro, NC. He finished 5th overall in points in 1954.

Billy Scott was born in 1935. Scott raced out of Union, SC, to two Winston Cup starts at Charlotte, NC, one each 1973–74. He finished 22nd in his debut in the 1973 World 600, a career-best.

After three straight races in new states, NASCAR returned home for a 100-mile event on the one-mile dirt track at Occoneechee Speedway in Hillsboro, NC. Curtis Turner captured the pole and won the race in his Oldsmobile, his ninth career win and first victory in over two years of Grand National competition. It was his sixth career pole.

Rex White won his third straight race at Bowman-Gray Stadium in 1961. White won the April 1962 race to capture four wins in a row at the Winston-Salem track. Nine consecutive races were won by White or Glen Wood at the track from June 1959 to April 1962.

Ned Jarrett won his 32nd Grand National race, taking the checkered flag at the 1964 Western North Carolina 500 at Weaverville, NC, in a Ford.

Kyle Petty's 5th career win came in 1992 at the Budweiser at the Glen, the road course at Watkins Glen, NY.

Jeff Gordon won from the pole on the road course of Watkins Glen International (NY) in 1998. Gordon achieved the feat of starting and finishing first for the third time in 1998 with his victory in the Bud at the Glen en route to his third Winston Cup championship.

10

Marvin Panch, who won the pole in the spring race at the Lincoln Speedway, came back to win the August event for his 7th career Grand National win. Tiny Lund won his third pole at the half-mile dirt track in New Oxford, PA.

Joe Weatherly's first career Grand National win came in Nashville, TN, in 1958. The Nashville Speedway hosted 42 Grand National and Winston Cup races between 1958 and 1984. He won 25 career events and won the points championship 1962–63.

The Bridgehampton Race Circuit on Long Island, NY, hosted four Grand National events between 1958 and 1966. The final race was won from the pole by David Pearson, his 24th career win.

David Pearson won the 1968 Myers Brothers Memorial at Winton-Salem's Bowman-Gray Stadium for his 42nd career victory.

LeeRoy Yarbrough won the 1969 Dixie 500 at Atlanta Motor Speedway, his second straight win in the annual event.

In the return of Winston Cup cars to historic Watkins Glen, NY, Tim Richmond won the inaugural Bud at the Glen in 1986 in upstate New York.

Rusty Wallace won his first race of 1987 with a first-place finish in the Bud at the Glen in Watkins Glen, NY.

At the 1997 Bud at the Glen, Jeff Gordon defeated Geoff Bodine for his first victory on the road course at Watkins Glen, NY.

A couple of Gordons dominated the 2003 Sirius at the Glen at Watkins Glen, NY. Jeff started on the pole, but spun out early in the race. Robby Gordon led most of the way for his second victory of the season, both on road courses.

11

Scotty Cain, who raced out of Venice, CA, was born in 1920. Cain made 36 Grand National and Winston Cup starts 1956–71 with 21 top–10 finishes. He led 19 laps and finished second in a 1960 race at the California State Fairgrounds, his only time in front.

Frankie Schneider was born in 1926. Schneider ran out of Lambertville, NJ, to enter 27 Strictly Stock and Grand National races 1949–58 with one win (4/58 in Manassas, VA), one pole (7/57 Raleigh, NC) and 15 other top–10 finishes.

Darrell Dake raced out of Cedar Rapids, IA, to make two Grand National starts each in 1960 and 1961, with one top 10 his rookie season.

Earl Brooks was born in 1929 and raced out of Lynchburg, VA. Brooks made 262 Grand National and Winston Cup starts 1962–79, leading one career race and finishing in the top 10 37 times.

George Robert "Bobby" Brewer was born in 1929. Brewer started on Grand National race in 1969, racing out of Winston-Salem, NC.

Lennie Pond was born in 1940. Pond raced out of Ettrick, VA, to start 234 Grand National and Winston Cup races 1969–89. He finished 5th overall in the 1976 points standings. Lennie's only series win came in the 1978 Talladega 500, although he finished in the top–10 87 other times in his career. He was the 1973 Winston Cup Rookie of the Year.

Stanley Monroe Starr Jr. was born in 1943. Racing out of Madison, TN, Starr managed one career Grand National start, finishing 22nd in the 1969 Talladega 500.

Glenn Jarrett was born in 1950. The son of Ned and older brother of Dale, Glenn started ten Winston Cup races between 1978 and 1983 and later went into broadcasting.

Steve Gray, who raced out of Rome, GA, in the 1970s and '80s, was born in 1956. Gray ran eight Winston Cup races 1979–85 and a 26th-place finish in the 1985 Van Scoy Diamond Mine 500 at Pocono, PA.

Fred Lorenzen won the 1963 Western North Carolina 500 at Weaverville, NC. It was his ninth career checkered flag.

The West Virginia International Speedway hosted four top-level NASCAR events, one each 1963–64 and 1970–71. Richard Petty won on this date in 1970 for his 112th career checkered flag (and would repeat in 1971). Bobby Allison won his 13th career pole.

Richard Petty won the 1974 Talladega 500. Petty began a string of five years when he was named the most popular Winston Cup driver. Petty won his fifth of seven driving championships in 1974 with 10 wins.

Bill Elliott captured his second straight win at Michigan with a first-place finish in the 1980 Champion Spark Plug 400.

J. D. McDuffie died in a one-car accident early in the 1991 Bud at the Glen race at Watkins Glen, NY. His car lost the brakes and crashed into a retaining wall at high speed, flipped and landed upside down. McDuffie's lone pole position start came at Dover in 1978.

Ernie Irvan, who won the Daytona 500 to start the season, won the 1991 Bud at the Glen on the road course at Watkins Glen, NY. It was his second and final win of the year.

A native of Chemung County, Geoff Bodine cruised to victory on his home track, the road course at Watkins Glen International, with a first-place finish in the 1996 Bud at the Glen. It was Bodine's 18th and final career Winston Cup win.

2002 Winston Cup champion Tony Stewart won his third race of the season at Watkins Glen International on the road course. Ricky Rudd qualified first. It was the reverse in the other road course of the season, in June at Sonoma, where Stewart qualified first and Rudd captured his only win of the season.

12

Richard "Dick" Brown was born in 1928. Brown made 21 Grand National and Winston Cup starts between 1961 and 1975 with one top–10 finish in 1970.

Edward A. Flemke, who raced out of New Britain, CT, was born in 1930. Flemke ran one Grand National race in 1961, earning $175 at NASCAR's top level.

Pete Stewart was born in 1931. Racing out of Statesville, NC, Stewart started 17 career Grand National races 1953–65. His best finish was 11th in a 1956 event at Concord (NC) Speedway and he finished 37th, managing two laps in the 1965 Daytona 500.

Parnelli Jones was born in 1933. He raced out of Torrance, CA. Known primarily for his Indy car racing, Jones ran 34 races at NASCAR's highest level over 14 years. His first win came in 1957 at Bremerton, WA, and his last in the 1967 Motor Trend 500 at Riverside, CA.

Ronald Gene "Pee Wee" Ellwanger, who raced out of Roanoke, VA, in the 1960s, was born in 1935. Pee Wee started five Grand National races 1965–66.

Jerry Jolly was born in 1941. Racing out of Denver, CO, Jolly started three races in 1978 and one each in 1979 and 1984. He finished 20th in the 1978 Daytona 500 in his debut.

Mark Stahl was born in 1951. Racing out of San Diego, CA, Stahl ran 30 Winston Cup races between 1981 and 1991, entering nine in 1987 for his career high. He finished 38th in the 1987 Daytona 500.

Tommy Thompson won his first NASCAR race in 1951 in the first sanctioned Grand National event held in Detroit, MI, at the Michigan State Fairgrounds. The checkered-flag finish in the in the inaugural Motor City 250 dirt track contest was the first manufacturer's win for Chrysler. Marshall Teague, with five wins in his career, captured his first-ever pole position. The race was part of the city's 250th Anniversary celebration.

Tim Flock won his 39th and final Grand National race in 1956, his fourth win of the season, with a checkered flag finish in Elkhart Lake, WI.

Scott Gaylord, who raced out of Lakewood, CO, was born in 1958. Gaylord started his Winston Cup career in 1991 and added one start each in 1992, 1993 and 1996.

Jim Paschal won the 1962 Western North Carolina 500 for his 13th career victory.

Richard Petty won the Myers Brothers Memorial at Bowman-Gary Stadium in 1967, his 66th career checkered flag. It was the 18th of 27 wins on the season for Petty, who would go on to win his second of seven career points championships in 1967.

Richard Brooks won the 1973 Talladega 500 at Alabama International Speedway with an average speed of 145.454 mph over runner-up Buddy Baker. It was the only Winston Cup victory of Brooks' career. He was the

1969 Grand National Rookie of the Year. Larry Smith died as the result of a crash in the race. Smith, who started 38 Grand National and Winston Cup races 1971–73, was 31 years old.

Darrell Waltrip won the 1984 Champion Spark Plug 400 at the Michigan International Speedway, his second win in the annual event. Bill Elliott started at the pole.

Ricky Rudd won the Bud at the Glen at Watkins Glen International for his only win of the 1990 Winston Cup season.

At the 2001 Global Crossing @ the Glen, Jeff Gordon won his second consecutive race and fifth of the season. Gordon remained in first place the remainder of the season to claim the Winston Cup points championship. Dale Jarrett, who finished second, earned his fourth pole start of the year. Gordon won his fourth Winston Cup Championship that year.

13

Jim Roper was born in 1916 and gained fame as the winner of the first official NASCAR race in 1949. He ran just one other race in his career, a second-place finish later that season in Hillsboro, NC.

Fireball Roberts won his first race in only his third start at NASCAR's top division with a first-place finish in 1950 at Hillsboro, NC.

Fireball Roberts, driving an Oldsmobile, won a 100-mile race on a one-mile dirt track in Hillsboro,

NC, in 1950 for his first career Grand National victory in only his third career start.

Terry Link was born in 1952. Racing out of Daytona Beach, FL, he started three Winston Cup events at Talladega, AL, 1974–75. His best finish was 37th in the 1974 Talladega 500.

In the first sanctioned event at the Southern States (Charlotte) Fairgrounds, Lee Petty captured the checkered flag in 1954. The half-mile dirt track hosted 17 Grand National events between 1954 and 1960.

Junior Johnson drove his Pontiac to victory at the Asheville-Weaverville Speedway in 1961 for his 24th career win. The race was marked by a fan riot when the event was shortened by 242 laps. Drivers and crew were held hostage for nearly four hours with no major injuries before the crowds were dispersed.

Ned Jarrett won the inaugural Moyock 300 at the Dog Track Speedway in Moyock, NC, in 1964, the 33rd win of his career.

Dick Hutcherson won the first Grand National event hosted by the Smoky Mountain Raceway in Maryville, TN, in 1965, his fifth career win. The track, a ½-mile paved oval, hosted 12 top-level NASCAR races 1965–71. Ned Jarrett started on the pole for the 32nd time in his Grand National career.

Tim Richmond died of complications of AIDS in 1989 at the age of 34. Richmond was the race rookie in the 1980 Indianapolis 500 and successfully made the transition to Winston Cup with 13 wins and 14 poles 1980–87. His first win came at Riverside, CA, in June 1982 and his final victory was at the same track in June 1987.

Rusty Wallace won the 1989 Bud at the Glen on the road course at Watkins Glen International. It was the fourth of six wins that season for Wallace, who won the Winston Cup Championship.

Clifford Allison died in a crash during practice for the 1992 Champion 400 at Michigan International Speedway. Clifford was the son of Bobby and the younger brother of Davey Allison.

Mark Martin captured his third consecutive Bud at the Glen at Watkins Glen, NY, in 1995. Martin also captured his third straight pole.

The #1 car of Steve Park traveled to the Winners Circle in the 2000 Global Crossing @ the Glen at Watkins Glen International. Bobby Labonte started from the pole. It was Park's first career win.

14

Salvatore "Sal" Tovella was born in 1928. He ran a total of 14 Grand National races between 1956 and 1964. Racing out of Chicago, IL, he qualified in one race in 1981, 17 years after his most recent start.

Jackie Oliver, who raced out of Walton-on-Thames, England, was born in 1943. Oliver ran eight races on the Winston Cup circuit 1971–72, with a career-best fourth place finish in 1972.

Driving a Chrysler, Fonty Flock

won the second of five races held between 1954 and 1957 at the 1.5 mile dirt track in LeHi, AR.

Russell William "Rusty" Wallace was born in 1956 in Fenton, MO, the older brother of Kenny Wallace. He was the 1984 Rookie of the Year and the 1989 Winston Cup points leader. He won the first NASCAR race run in Japan in 1996.

Mark Gibson, who raced out of Daytona Beach, FL, was born in 1957. Gibson made one Winston Cup start each in 1987 and 1989, finishing 33rd after a crash in the 1989 Pepsi 400 at Daytona, FL.

Rex White won at the Asheville-Weaverville Speedway in 1960. He was the most popular Grand National driver that year.

Ned Jarrett captured career win #20 at Spartanburg, SC, in 1963. Joe Weatherly qualified first, his 16th career pole.

Ned Jarrett won his 47th career race at Spartanburg, SC, in 1965. It was the fourth time in five races at the track that Jarrett won. Dick Hutcherson earned his eighth career pole start.

Richard "Dick" Carter was killed in a super modified race in Grand Rapids, MI, in 1965 at the age of 30. Carter ran seven career Grand National races 1954–61.

Bobby Isaac died of a heart attack after a short-track race in Hickory, NC, in 1977. Isaac won the 1970 Winston Cup championship in the #71 Dodge.

Ricky Rudd won his only race of the Winston Cup season on the road course at Watkins Glen in the 1988 Bud at the Glen.

In 1994, Mark Martin won for the second straight year on the road course in the annual Bud at the Glen at Watkins Glen, NY.

15

James V. "Jim" Cook, who raced out of High Point, NC, was born in 1922. He started one Grand National event in 1950, a 23rd-place finish in the Wilkes 200 at North Wilkesboro, NC.

Tim Flock won his second straight race, his fourth in five tries, finishing first at Rochester, NY, in the shortest race of the 1952 Grand National season, 88 miles on a .5-mile dirt track. There were no time trials. Flock won his first of two points championship that season.

Crew chief Robin Pemberton was born in 1956. Pemberton took over the Rusty Wallace team's position in 1995 and later assumed a role with Ford Racing in 2003.

Andy Petree was born in 1958. Petree became a mechanic and a crew chief in 1982 at the age of 24. He later worked with Dale Earnhardt during two championship seasons. He later went on to become an owner.

Richard Petty won at the Starkey Speedway in Roanoke, VA, in 1962, a paved ¼-mile track that hosted its third of four career Grand National races. Petty guided his #42 Plymouth to victory lane for his 10th career win. Jack Smith qualified first for the 20th time in his career but finished fifth.

Dick Hutcherson won in 1965 at the Augusta International Speedway, a half-mile dirt track in Augusta, GA.

Bobby Allison won his 25th career NASCAR race in 1971 in the Yankee 400 at the Michigan International Speedway driving a Mercury.

Mark Martin won his second straight race with a trip to victory lane in the 1993 Champion 400 at Michigan. It was the tenth career Winston Cup win for Martin.

Jeff Gordon won on the road course of Watkins Glen International in upstate New York, taking the checkered flag in the 1999 Frontier at the Glen. Rusty Wallace finished third, but started in the pole position. Ron Fellows, a road racing ringer, finished second in the #87 Bully Hill car.

16

John Alton Haddock, who raced out of Greenville, SC, in the 1950s, was born in 1915. Haddock started two races each in 1950 and 1951, with a lone top 10 Grand National finish in his final season.

Egnatius "Iggy" Katona was born in 1916. Katona started 13 Grand National/Winston Cup races in his career, five each in 1951 and 1952 and one each in 1965, 1966 and 1974, with three top–10 finishes.

Fonty Flock won the 100-mile race in Weaverville, NC, in 1953. Driving a Hudson, Flock averaged 62.434 mph on the half-mile dirt track. Curtis Turner won his second straight pole position. It was Flock's third win of the season and 14th of his career.

Lee Petty won his 28th career race at Old Bridge, NJ, in 1957, edging pole-sitter Rex White who finished second.

Bob Welborn's final of nine career Grand National wins came in 1959 at Weaverville, NC, in the Western North Carolina 500 at Skyline Speedway.

Cotton Owens won from the pole for the second of three times in his career in 1960 at Spartanburg, SC. It was the fourth win and eighth pole for Owens.

Junior Johnson captured the checkered flag at Bowman-Gray stadium in the 1963 International 200 in Winston-Salem, NC.

At the West Virginia International Speedway in Huntington, Richard Petty captured his 35th career victory. Billy Wade captured his fourth career pole. Alphabetically, of all the tracks that have hosted Grand National and Winston Cup events, this one is last.

Charlie Glotzbach won the 1970 Yankee 400 at the Michigan International Speedway.

Richard Petty won the 1981 Champion Spark Plug 400 at the Michigan International Speedway, his third win in the annual event held between 1975 and 1993.

Bill Elliott won his third race of 1987, his second in two weeks, with a win in the Champion Spark Plug 400 at Michigan.

Tim Richmond competed in his final Winston Cup race at Michigan in 1987.

Rick Newsom died at the age of 38 in a private plane crash in 1988. Newsom ran out of Ft. Mill, SC, to race intermittently at NASCAR's highest level 1975–86, starting 82 events. He finished 31st, yielding to engine trouble, in lap seven of the 1975 Daytona 500.

Harry Gant captured his final of 18 Winston Cup Series wins in 1992 at Michigan International Speedway in the Champion Spark Plug 400. At the age of 52, he became the oldest driver to win a NASCAR race at the highest level.

Jeff Gordon won his third consecutive race with a victory in the 1999 Pepsi 400 Presented by DeVilbiss at Michigan Speedway in the #24 DuPont Chevrolet. Ernie Irvan won the pole and finished sixth.

17

L.D. Austin was born in 1918. Austin raced out of Greenville, SC, and finished 6th in Grand National points in 58, 7th in 1959 and 8th in 1957. He ran 169 races with 54 top–10 finishes.

Rex Allen White was born in 1929. Racing out of Spartanburg, SC, White started 233 career Grand National events, winning the championship in 1960, when he won six times and finished in the top-five 25 times. In his career he captured the checkered flag 28 times and earned 36 pole starts. His first victory came in November 1957 at Fayetteville, NC. He was voted the most popular Grand National driver in 1960.

Bob Flock won for the first time in 1952 in the 100-mile race at Weaverville, NC. Flock, driving a dominant Hudson, averaged 57.288 mph on the .5-mile dirt track. Herb Thomas took the pole, his third straight, driving a Hudson. It was the second sanctioned NASCAR race in three days, both won by a Flock. It was the final of four career wins for Bob.

Ralph Moody won his second career Grand National race at the inaugural NASCAR race at Old Bridge Stadium, a half-mile paved oval in New Jersey. The track hosted six top-level NASCAR events between 1956 and 1965.

Fireball Roberts won the inaugural Western North Carolina 500 in 1958 at Skyline Speedway in Weaverville, NC, for his 17th career win.

Ken Miles was killed in a test crash at Riverside, CA, in 1966. Miles started one Grand National race in 1963, an 11th-place finish at Riverside, CA, in the Golden State 400. Richard Petty won from the pole for the 30th time in his career at Columbia Speedway in 1967. It was the 11th time in the 1967 Grand National season he achieved the feat.

David Pearson won the 1969 Yankee 600 at the Michigan International Speedway. It was his 10th of 11 wins in 1969, when he won his third Grand National Championship.

Buddy Baker won his second straight race at Talladega in the 1975 Talladega 500. Tiny Lund, age 39, died in a crash. A veteran of 20 Winston

Cup seasons, Lund won five career races including the 1963 Daytona 500.

Cale Yarborough won the 1980 Champion Spark Plug 400 at the Michigan International Speedway.

Bill Elliott won the 1986 Champion Spark Plug 400 for his second win of the season, both at Michigan International Speedway. It was his fourth straight win at the track.

Ernie Irvan's right-front tire blew during a training run sending him into the wall at the Michigan International Speedway in 1994. He was critically injured but was able to rehabilitate and returned to racing over a year later. In 1997, he returned to the raceway to win the Miller 400.

Mark Martin won the 1997 Devilbiss 400 at the Michigan International Speedway. Martin fell behind by two laps early, but recovered to win over Jeff Gordon.

Ryan Newman won his fifth Winston Cup race of the 2003 season at Michigan International Speedway in the GFS Marketplace 400. Bobby Labonte won his fourth pole of the season.

18

Wayne Andrews was born in 1938. Racing out of Siler City, NC, Andrews started six Winston Cup races, 1971 and 1973, with three top–10 finishes his rookie season.

Rex White won for the second consecutive event held at the Columbia Speedway, winning both 1960 races. Tommy Irwin captured his second, and final, career pole in 99 career races 1958–63.

Junior Johnson won from the pole for the fourth of 12 times in his career, capturing win #25 and pole #16 in 1961 at the Southside Speedway in Richmond. Johnson won seven races that season and finished sixth in championship points. The Southside Speedway hosted four Grand National races 1961–64 on a ¼-mile paved track.

Gene Blair was killed in a midget race at Cattaraugus Fairgrounds in upstate New York in 1962. He started one Grand National race in 1957.

Richard Petty captured the first of his four wins at Bowman-Gray Stadium in Winston-Salem, NC, in the inaugural 50-mile International 200 in 1962, his 11th career win.

In 1963 at the West Virginia International Speedway in Huntington, Fred Lorenzen won from the pole in the first sanctioned race held in the state of West Virginia, his 10th career victory and 13th career pole. It was the third of 11 times in his career that Lorenzen both qualified and finished first. The track hosted three Grand National races, one each in August 1963, 1964 and 1970, with one Winston Cup race in 1971.

For the third straight Columbia, SC, race, David Pearson captured the checkered flag in 1966. It was his 25th career Grand National win. Pearson went on to become the 1966 points champion. Bobby Allison won his third of 59 career poles.

David Pearson won the 1968 Western North Carolina 500 at Skyline

1971 and one in 1979, when he led the one and only lap of his NASCAR career.

Dick Linder won his first of three career NASCAR races in 1950 at Dayton, OH. The 97.5-mile event on a .5-mile dirt track marked the first time a car maker, Oldsmobile, claimed four straight wins. Linder also became the first driver to win the pole the previous race and claim the checkered flag the following event.

Popular trackside announcer Dr. Jerry Punch was born in 1953. Trained as a trauma physician, Punch works as a doctor during the week but became known as the pit doctor for his sideline reporting at NASCAR events.

Herb Thomas won for the second straight time at the Raleigh Speedway in 1955.

Junior Johnson's 20th career victory came in the first of 10 Grand National events hosted by the South Boston Speedway in Virginia, a ¼-mile paved oval. Johnson drove his #27 Chevrolet to victory while Ned Jarrett earned his fourth career pole start and Possum Jones finished second. Jarrett went on to capture the Grand National championship the following year, 1961. The track hosted annual events 1960–62, two events in 1963, and single races in 1964 and 1968–71.

David Pearson won the 1972 Yankee 400 at the Michigan International Speedway.

David Pearson won the 1978 Champion Spark Plug 400 at the Michigan International Speedway.

Herbert "Tootle" Estes, who raced out of Knoxville, TN, died in 1982, shortly after winning a late model race in Bulls Gap, TN. Estes ran 12 Grand National events, one in 1956 and 11 in 1958, with four career top 10s in his final season.

Rusty Wallace won the 1989 Champion Spark Plug 400 at the Michigan International Speedway. It was his second straight victory.

Bobby Labonte won his second straight race at Michigan with a victory in the 1995 GM Goodwrench Dealers 400.

Rusty Wallace's #2 Ford won the 2000 Pepsi 400 at Michigan International Speedway for his third win of the season. Dale Earnhardt Jr. captured the pole.

21

William "Walson" Gardner, who raced out of Laurinburg, NC, in the 1960s, was born in 1932. Gardner ran 24 Grand National events 1965–69 with two top-10s in 1968, when he started a career-high 14 races.

Clifford "Cliff" Hucul, who raced out of Prince George, British Columbia, Canada, in the 1980s, was born in 1948. Hucul made two Winston Cup starts in 1986.

Rex White won his second straight race at Bowman-Gray Stadium. White won the June 1959 race and went on to capture the August event, his 6th career win.

Richard Petty won from the pole at Spartanburg, SC, in 1962. Petty, who achieved the feat for the fourth time, did it 61 times in his career. It was his

12th career win and seventh career pole.

David Pearson won the 1964 Sandlapper 200 at Columbia Speedway for his tenth career Grand National victory.

Darel Dieringer won the 1966 Western North Carolina 500 at Skyline Speedway in Weaverville, NC. It was the fifth career Grand National victory for Dieringer, the Grand National's most popular driver that season.

Bobby Isaac won from the pole for the seventh of 11 times in the 1969 South Boston 100 in Virginia. It was his 14th career win. Isaac finished sixth in Grand National points in 1969 and went on to win the 1970 championship.

Cale Yarborough won the 1983 Champion Spark Plug 400 at the Michigan International Speedway.

Davey Allison won his first race of 1988 with a first-place finish in the Champion Spark Plug 400 at Michigan.

Geoff Bodine won the GM Goodwrench Dealers 400 in 1994, his first win at the Michigan International Speedway.

22

Jimmie Lewallen was born in North Carolina in 1919. Lewallen started 142 events 1949–60, capturing the pole once and finishing in the top 10 57 times in his career.

Elmo Langley was born in 1929. He was a popular NASCAR pace car driver in the 1990s. Langley ran 536 career races between 1954 and 1981. Langley won two career races, both in 1966. He was 5th overall in points in 1969 and 1971.

Larry Miller was born in 1934. Running out of Taylors, SC, he made 15 starts in 1967, his only Grand National experience, with a career-best seventh-place in the Pickens 200 at Greenville, SC.

Bob Burcham was born in 1935. Racing out of Rossville, GA, he ran 36 Grand National and Winston Cup events 1968–79 with six top–10 finishes.

Hershel McGriff won his first career NASCAR race in 1954 at San Mateo, CA. It was the first sanctioned event at the Bay Meadows Race Track, a one-mile dirt raceway. McGriff won three more times the remainder of the season, his only four wins at the top level, although he raced periodically until 1993.

Billy Myers' final of two career Grand National wins came in 1956 at Norfolk Speedway (VA), the first of two events hosted 1956–57 on the .4-mile dirt track. Ralph Moody captured his second career pole.

Lee Petty won at Bowman-Gray Stadium in a 50-mile short-track event in 1958. Petty won eight races in 1958, his second as the Grand National Champion.

Buck Baker captured his 40th career Grand National win in 1959 at Greenville, SC. Lee Petty qualified for his 14th pole start.

Junior Johnson won the 1964 Myers Brothers Memorial at Bowman-Gray Stadium. It was his 37th career Grand National win.

Bill Massey died at the age of 36 of injuries suffered in a bar fight in 1965. Massey recorded four starts at NASCAR's highest level between 1956 and 1960.

Richard Petty won from the pole at Bowman-Gray Stadium in Winston-Salem, NC, to capture the 1969 Myers Brothers Stock Car Spectacle for his 100th career Grand National win.

Bobby Allison posted his 26th career NASCAR win in 1971 at the Alabama International Motor Speedway. It was his second straight win of the season.

David Pearson won the 1976 Champion Spark Plug 400 at the Michigan International Speedway.

Darrell Waltrip won the 1977 Champion Spark Plug 400 at the Michigan International Speedway.

The 1981 Busch 500 was won from the pole by Darrell Waltrip, his second straight win from the pole at Bristol. It was the tenth time in his career that he won from the pole for his 35th career Winston Cup win.

Bobby Allison won his 71st career NASCAR race in 1982 at Michigan International Speedway. His win in the Champion Spark Plug 400 was his sixth of the season and his second win in the last three races.

Dale Earnhardt Sr. rode to his ninth win of 1987 in the Busch 500 at Bristol.

Mark Martin won the 1998 Goody's Headache Powder 500 at Bristol for his fifth win of the season in the #6 Valvoline Ford. Martin finished runner-up to Jeff Gordon in the Winston Cup points championship that season. Rusty Wallace won the pole and finished third.

Bobby Labonte won the 1999 Pepsi 400 Presented by Meijer at the Michigan Speedway in Brooklyn. Ward Burton won the pole but finished last when an accident ended his day early.

23

Herb Thomas became the first Grand National driver with 25 career victories when he won for the 11th time in 1953. Thomas took the 100-mile feature event at the Princess Anne Speedway in Norfolk, VA, averaging 51.040 mph on the half-mile dirt track in his Hudson. Curtis Turner won his third straight pole position, the eighth top start of his career. Thomas won the driving championship in 1953.

Ralph Moody's third career win came eight days after his second, with a victory at the Piedmont Interstate Fairgrounds (SC) in 1956. Larry Mann captured the only pole qualifying position of his career.

Scott Miller was born in 1957. Racing out of Garden Grove, CA, Miller ran six Winston Cup races at Riverside, CA, in the 1980s with a career-best 13th in the 1982 Budweiser 400.

Bob Welborn won at Myrtle Beach, SC, in 1958, his sixth Grand National checkered flag. Speedy Thompson qualified first for the 17th time in his career.

Glen Wood's third career Grand National victory was also his third straight win at Bowman-Gray Stadium in Winston-Salem, NC, to sweep all three races held there that season.

Kenny Wallace was born in 1963 in St. Louis, MO. He is the younger brother of Rusty Wallace and began in the Winston Cup Series in 1990. His first career Winston Cup win came in 2000 at the Food City 500. He went on to record a series of commercials for Stacker.

Floyd Powell was killed by his brother-in-law on this date in 1963. Needless to say, it ended his season. Powell had made five Grand National starts with two top–10 finishes in the 1963 season. He debuted with one series race the prior year.

The final of four sanctioned Grand National races at the Starkey Speedway was won in 1964 by Junior Johnson in his #27 Ford. It was his second win at the Roanoke, VA, track, the 38th of his career. Glen Wood qualified first for the 14th and final time of his career.

Steve Park was born in 1967 in Islip, NY. Park debuted in the Featherlite Division in 1995 and began racing at the Winston Cup level in 1997.

After a three year hiatus, the South Boston Speedway (VA) again hosted Grand National driving with Richard Petty winning from the pole for his 86th career victory in his #43 Plymouth.

Pete Hamilton won his second straight Talladega race with a win in the 1970 Talladega 500. Hamilton also won the Daytona 500 that year.

The 1980 Busch Volunteer 500 was won by Cale Yarborough for his 67th career win. Yarborough won from the pole for the 14th of 17 times in his career.

Darrell Waltrip won the 1986 Busch 500 at Bristol International Speedway.

Dale Jarrett won the 1997 Goody's 500 at the Bristol Motor Speedway. A number of crashes marred this race. Mark Martin finished second.

Kurt Busch's fourth victory of the 2003 Winston Cup season came at Bristol in the Sharpie 500. Jeff Gordon qualified first for his third pole of the season and the second time in three races he started from the top spot.

24

Roger McCluskey was born in 1930. Racing out of Tucson, AZ, he started one race each in 1969, 1970, 1972 and 1977. His best event was a runner-up finish in the 1970 Motor Trend 500 at Riverside, CA.

Joseph Charleton "Joe" Hines Jr., who raced out of Statesboro, GA, in the 1960s and '70s, was born in 1937. Hines ran one race each at NASCAR's top level 1969–71.

Walter Sprague died in 1951, the result of a crash in a race at the Monroe County Fairgrounds in Rochester, NY. Sprague, who raced out of Wellsville, NY, ran seven Grand National events that season with two top–10 finishes, his only year at NASCAR's top level.

Tim Flock won his fourth race of 1951 with a first place finish in the 100-mile contest at Morristown, NJ.

It was the first NASCAR race in the state of New Jersey and the first of five races held at the half-mile dirt track, also called Saranno Park, between 1951 and 1955. Flock also won the pole in his Oldsmobile.

Ray Clark, who raced out of Tucson, AZ, was killed in a race at the Ferndale, CA, fairgrounds in 1958. He ran two Grand National races in 1955.

Dick Hutcherson won the second and final Moyock 300 at the Dog Track Speedway in Moyock, NC, in 1965.

Bobby Allison won his third NASCAR race at the Beltsville Speedway in the 40th race of the 1966 season.

David Pearson won from the pole for the 12th time in his career in the 1968 Crabber 250. It was his 44th career win on his way to the Grand National championship that season.

Bobby Isaac won the final Western North Carolina 500 in 1969 at Asheville-Weaverville Speedway (NC). It was his 15th career win and second in four days. It was the final Grand National race held at the track, which hosted 34 events between 1951 and 1969.

Richard Petty won the 1975 Champion Spark Plug 400 at the Michigan International Speedway.

Dale Earnhardt Sr. won his second straight Bristol race in the 1985 Busch 500, winning from the pole for the first time in his career.

Alan Kulwicki won the 1991 Bud 500 at Bristol. It was Kulwicki's only Winston Cup win of the season, the third of his career. Bill Elliott won his 40th career pole.

Rusty Wallace captured the 1996 Goody's Headache Powder 500 at Bristol for his fifth win of the Winston Cup season. Mark Martin won his 31st career pole, his fourth consecutive top start at Bristol.

2001 Winston Cup champion Jeff Gordon, who qualified on the pole, won his first race of 2002 in the 24th event of the season in the Sharpie 500 at Bristol.

25

David "Legs" Whitcomb, born in 1931, ran one career Grand National race. He raced out of Valparaiso, IN, to a 21st-place finish at Santa Fe Speedway in Willow Springs, IL, in July 1954.

Ivan Randall "Randy" Hutchinson, who raced out of Newport News, VA, in the 1970s, was born in 1948. Hutchinson ran seven Winston Cup events in his career, six in 1971 with his lone top 10, and one final race in 1974.

In the second sanctioned NASCAR 100-mile race in two days, Bob Flock won his third career event on a .5-mile dirt track in Greenville, SC. It was the first of 29 top-level Grand National and Winston Cup events held at the Greenville-Pickens Speedway 1951-71.

Fireball Roberts won the first race at Rambi Race Track, also known as the Myrtle Beach Speedway, in Myrtle Beach, SC, in 1956. It was his fourth career victory. Ralph Moody won his third of four career pole positions. The track hosted 11 Grand National events 1956-65.

Dean Layfield died at age 42 of injuries suffered five days earlier in a Super Modified race in Perry, NY. Layfield ran one NASCAR race in 1957 and seven in 1958 with one 4th-place finish.

Don Johns was killed in a race at the Minnesota Fairgrounds in St. Paul, MN, in 1962 at the age of 28. Johns had started two Grand National races in 1957 with one top–10 finish.

In 1962, Ned Jarrett won the first NASCAR-sanctioned race at the Valdosta Speedway in Georgia, a half-mile dirt track.

The Beltsville Speedway in Maryland hosted ten Grand National races 1965–70. Ned Jarrett won the first one in 1965, when he won 13 events and retired as the Grand National Champion.

Richard Petty won in 1967 at the Savannah Speedway in Georgia, the 31st time in his career he both qualified and finished first.

Shane Hall was born in 1969. Racing out of Simpsonville, SC, he made his Winston Cup debut in 1995.

Buddy Baker captured the checkered flag in the 1973 Nashville 420. Cale Yarborough qualified first, his 24th career pole.

David Pearson won the 1974 Yankee 400 at the Michigan International Speedway.

Darrell Waltrip won the 1979 Volunteer 500 at Bristol, TN, for his 22nd career victory. Richard Petty claimed the top starting position for the 126th time in his career.

Terry Labonte broke Darrell Waltrip's string of seven straight wins at Bristol with his fourth career win in the 1984 Busch 500. Geoff Bodine won his fourth career pole and finished fourth. Labonte won his first of two Winston Cup Championships that season.

Ernie Irvan won his first NASCAR race in the 1990 Busch 500 at Bristol with a 21-second margin of victory.

Ernie Irvan captured his only win of 1990 with a trip to victory lane in the 1990 Busch 500 at Bristol, his first career win.

Tony Stewart captured his third win of the 2001 season by edging Kevin Harvick at Bristol in the Sharpie 500. Jeff Green qualified first for the only time in the Winston Cup season.

26

Wayne Woodward was born in 1934. He started seven races in 1956, his only season of Grand National competition. He raced out of Ringgold, GA.

James Hylton was born in 1935 in Inman, SC. Hylton appeared on the Grand National and Winston Cup circuit 1964–95 with two career wins in 601 races. He was the 1966 Rookie of the Year, when he finished second in points. He also finished second in 1967 and 1971. Between 1966 and 1977, Hylton finished in the top 10 in championship points all but two years. His first win came in March 1970 at Richmond.

Ivan Baldwin was born in 1946. He raced out of Modesto, CA to make six Winston Cup starts, all at Ontario or

Riverside, CA, in the 1970s. His best event was a 16th-place finish in the 1971 Winston Golden State 400 at Riverside.

David Earle "Swede" Savage Jr. was born in 1946. Racing out of Santa Ana, CA, and known mostly for Indy Car racing, Savage ran nine career Grand National events in the 1960s, finishing in the top 10 five times. He died of injuries suffered in the 1973 Indianapolis 500.

Royce Haggerty won his only career Grand National race in 1956 in Portland, OR. John Kieper maintained his strong performance at the speedway with his second pole in three starts at the race track with a win in June 1956. For the final time in his career, Herb Thomas led a Grand National race.

Gwyn Staley won his first of three career Grand National races in 1957 at Myrtle Beach, SC. Johnny Allen qualified on the pole, the first of three of his career.

Ray Evernham was born in 1957. Evernham gained fame as Jeff Gordon's crew chief in the mid–1990s when Gordon won several Winston Cup titles.

Cale Yarborough won his 55th career Grand National/Winston Cup race in the 1978 Volunteer 500 at Bristol. Lennie Pond won the fourth of his five career poles.

Darrell Waltrip won his fifth race of 1989 with a trip to victory lane in the Busch 500 at Bristol.

Terry Labonte won his 16th career Winston Cup race in the 1995 Goody's 500 at Bristol. Mark Martin finished fifth, but started first for the 28th time in his career.

Rusty Wallace captured the pole and cruised to victory in his #2 Ford in the 2000 GoRacing.com at Bristol Motor Speedway.

27

Henry "Junior" Spencer was born in 1937. Spencer raced out of Hamlin, WV, to 25 Grand National starts 1964–71, finishing with seven top–10 finishes.

Alton Jones was born in 1941 in Alabama. He managed 13 starts between 1970 and 1975 with four career top–10 finishes, his best a fifth-place in the 1974 Nashville 420.

Dick Linder won his second straight NASCAR race in 1950 on a .5-mile dirt track in Hamburg, NY. Linder, who also won the pole, captured the 100-mile event with an average speed of 50.747 mph.

Junior Johnson won his 26th career Grand National race in 1961 at the South Boston Speedway (VA). Cotton Owens qualified first for the 10th of 11 times in his Grand National career.

David Pearson won his second straight event at Bowman-Gray Stadium, the 1966 Myers Brothers Memorial. It was his 26th Grand National win.

Richard Petty closed the Columbia Speedway to NASCAR racing in 1971 with a win from the pole. It was the 54th time Petty achieved the feat for his 135th career victory. The Columbia Speedway hosted 44 races between 1951 and 1971, seven won by Richard and two more won by his father Lee.

Bobby Allison won his seventh race of 1972 at the Fairgrounds Speedway in the Nashville 420. It was Allison's 36th career victory.

Darrell Waltrip's sixth straight win at Bristol, TN, came in the 1983 Busch 500. Joe Ruttman captured his second of three career poles.

Dale Earnhardt Sr. won his third race of the 1988 season with a victory in the Busch 500 at Bristol.

Rusty Wallace captured his 37th career checkered flag in the 1994 Goody's 500 at Bristol. Harry Gant won the final pole of his career, the 17th.

28

Randy LaJoie was born in 1961. LaJoie started 38 Winston Cup races 1985–99 with three top–10 finishes, racing out of Norwalk, CT. His best was fifth at Martinsville in 1998. He has won 15 Busch Series races 1986–2003. He has also driven in the IROC and Craftsman Truck Series.

Junior Johnson captured his second straight Myers Brothers Memorial in 1965 at Bowman-Gray Stadium in Winston-Salem, NC. It was his 49th career Grand National win.

Richard Petty's 113th career victory came in the 1970 Myers Brothers Memorial on the short track of Bowman-Gray Stadium in Winston-Salem, NC.

In the final Grand National event held at the Hickory Speedway (NC), Tiny Lund won the 1971 Buddy Shuman Memorial in a Camaro.

Cale Yarborough won his fourth straight Bristol race in the 1977 Volunteer 500. It was the tenth time in his career he started and finished first.

Darrell Waltrip won his fourth straight race at Bristol with a checkered flag finish in the 1982 Busch 500. It was the 47th career victory for Waltrip while Tim Richmond captured the first of his 14 career top starts.

Mark Martin's third consecutive win in 1993 came at Bristol in the Bud 500. It was the second time in three races that he won from the pole.

Dale Earnhardt Sr. won the 1999 Goody's Headache Powder 500 at Bristol, TN. Tony Stewart, who won the pole, finished fifth. Jimmy Spencer was the runner-up.

29

Wendell Scott was born in Danville, VA, in 1921. The first successful African-American driver in NASCAR, his life was portrayed by Richard Pryor in the movie "Greased Lightning." Scott ran 495 Winston Cup races with one win (December 1963 in Jacksonville, FL) and one pole. He finished sixth overall in points in 1966.

John "Butch" Hirst, who raced out of Orange City, FL, in the 1970's, was born in 1940. Hirst ran five Grand National races in 1970 and made one Winston Cup start the following year to conclude his top-level driving career.

Tim Flock won the pole, but brother Fonty won the race for his 15th career Grand National win in 1953 at Hickory, NC. Flock, driving a Hudson, took the checkered flag on the half-mile dirt track. It was the 13th consecutive 100-mile race of the season series.

The only sanctioned NASCAR race run in the state of Kentucky was held at the Corbin Speedway in 1954. Lee Petty won the event on the half-mile dirt track.

Lee Petty won for the second consecutive event at the Columbia Speedway (SC) in 1959. Petty won ten races that season in capturing his final of three Grand National Driving Championships.

Brad Noffsinger was born in 1960. Noffsinger started 17 races in 1988, his only Winston Cup season, racing out of Huntington Beach, CA. Driving the Sunoco Buick, he led a lap in the 1988 Coca-Cola 600 at Charlotte, but crashed on lap 191 and finished 33rd.

Richard Petty won from the pole in the 1970 Halifax County 100 at South Boston Speedway in Virginia. It was the 47th of 61 times in his career that he qualified first and finished first. It was his 114th career victory and fifth win in the past six races at the ¼-mile paved oval.

Cale Yarborough won the 1976 Volunteer 500 at Bristol, for his second straight win at the Tennessee track, his 36th overall. Darrell Waltrip won his fourth career pole.

Darrell Waltrip's 82nd career win came at Bristol in the 1992 Bud 500.

Ernie Irvan captured his sixth career pole.

Veteran driver Roger McClusky died in 1993 of cancer at the age of 63. McClusky ran 17 Indianapolis 500 races but also ran sprint and stock cars in the 1960s and 1970s. He started four top-level NASCAR races between 1969 and 1977.

30

Art Lamey died in 1983. Lamey started four races in 1950 with three top–10 finishes. He was 19th overall in points in his only NASCAR season, finishing a career-best fifth-place in both events at Dayton, OH.

Jeff Gordon won from the pole for the fourth time in 1998 to win the Farm Aid on CMT 300 at Loudon, NH, on his way to a third Winston Cup championship in four years.

31

Pete Arnold was born in 1943. Racing out of Bellaire, TX, he made one Winston Cup start. He finished 14th in the Space City 300 in June 1971 in Houston, TX.

Tim Richmond won his fifth race of 1986 with a trip to victory lane in the Southern 500 at Darlington.

At the 1997 Mountain Dew Southern 500, Jeff Gordon defeated Jeff Burton at Darlington Raceway. Dale Earnhardt Sr. was taken to the hospital for observation after appearing woozy at the beginning of the race. With his victory Jeff Gordon won the Winston Million in 1997, becoming the second driver to win the prize. Bill Elliott did it first in 1985.

Terry Labonte's only win of 2003 came in the Mountain Dew Southern 500 at Darlington, SC. Ryan Newman qualified first.

SEPTEMBER

1

Herb Shannon was born in 1931. He raced out of Peoria, IL, to three Grand National starts; 1960 (1) and 1965 (2). His career highlight was a 24th-place finish in the 1965 Daytona 500, his final top-level NASCAR start.

For the third straight race in 1952 a different Flock won. Following in the footsteps of Tim and Bob, Fonty Flock won the Southern 500 on the 1.25-mile paved track at Darlington in 1952 with an average speed of 74.512 mph. Flock also took the pole with his Oldsmobile. It was the first race of the season where a Hudson failed to take the pole or finish first and was the second win for Olds.

Fireball Roberts won at Darlington in the 1958 Southern 500. Eddie Pagan won the final of his six career pole positions.

For the second straight Darlington race, the 1969 Southern 500, Cale Yarborough captured the pole while LeeRoy Yarbrough earned the victory.

Bobby Allison won for the second time in 1975 at Darlington Raceway, capturing the Southern 500. The victory was his 46th career win.

Terry Labonte won the 1980 Southern 500 at Darlington under caution for his first career NASCAR win. Darrell Waltrip started first.

Bill Elliott became the first person to win the Winston Million by winning the Southern 500 in Darlington. That week he also became the first Winston Cup driver on the cover of *Sports Illustrated*. Elliott held off Cale Yarborough for the win.

Harry Gant began a string of four consecutive wins in 1991, taking the checkered flag at Darlington in the Heinz Southern 500.

Jeff Gordon won the 1996 Mountain Dew Southern 500 at Darlington, his seventh win of the Winston Cup season.

Jeff Gordon's second consecutive win of 2002 came in the Mountain Dew Southern 500 at Darlington Raceway. Sterling Marlin qualified for his second of two top qualifying starts on the Winston Cup season.

2

William J. "Bill" Harrison, who raced out of Topeka, KS, in the 1940s and '50s, was born in 1910. Harrison made one Strictly Stock start in NASCAR's inaugural season of 1949 and ran nine Grand National races 1950–55 with four career top–10 finishes.

Don Hall, who raced out of Puyallup, WA, in the 1970s, was born in 1943. Hall ran one race each in 1974 and 1975 at Ontario, CA, finishing 11th in the 1975 Los Angeles Times 500.

Blair Aiken was born in 1956. Aiken raced out of Lakeport, CA, to make two Winston Cup starts in 1985, both at Riverside. He finished 29th in the 1985 Winston Western, the final event of his top-level NASCAR career.

Bobby Myers died in 1957 in a crash at Darlington. He was 30 years old. Myers ran 15 events 1951–57 with three top–10 finishes. Ironically, he led briefly for the only time in his career in the race that claimed his life.

Speedy Thompson won at Darlington for the only time in his career with a 1957 victory in the Southern 500, his 14th Grand National checkered flag. It was the first Grand National race in the 31-year career of then 18-year-old Cale Yarborough.

Fireball Roberts' 32nd career win came in the 1963 Southern 500 at Darlington, SC. Fred Lorenzen cap-

tured his fourth pole in the past six races at the South Carolina track.

Cale Yarborough won the 1968 Southern 500 at Darlington for his eighth career checkered flag finish. Charlie Glotzbach qualified on the pole for the second time of his career.

Cale Yarborough won the 1974 Southern 500 for his 27th career victory. Richard Petty qualified first for the 111th time.

Harry Gant captured the 1984 Southern 500 at Darlington, winning from the pole for the second and final time of his career.

Richie Panch was killed in a private plane crash in 1985 at the age of 31. Panch ran 28 of his 47 career Winston Cup races in 1974, finishing a respectable 14th in points and finishing in the top 10 seven times.

Dale Earnhardt Sr. captured the 1990 Heinz Southern 500 at Darlington. It was his seventh win of the Winston Cup season, the 46th of his career and the third time in his career he won from the pole.

Ward Burton garnered his only 2001 win with a first-place finish at Darlington in the 25th race of the Winston Cup season, the Mountain Dew Southern 500. Kurt Busch captured his only pole position start of the season. Burton went on to win the 2002 Daytona 500, the most prestigious win of his career.

3

Joseph R. Frasson, who raced out of Golden Valley, MN, in the 1960s and '70s, was born in 1935. Frasson ran 107 Grand National and Winston Cup events 1969–78 with 19 career top–10 finishes. He ranked 22nd in Grand National points in 1970, his best overall season.

Bill Butts was born in 1937. He raced out of El Cajon, CA, to make two Winston Cup starts on the west coast in 1972. His best finish was 15th in the Miller High Life 500 at Ontario, CA.

Herb Thomas won the second annual 500-mile race at Darlington in 1951. The Southern 500, run on the newly paved 1.25 mile track, saw Thomas average 76.906 mph in his Hudson for his third career win. Thomas went on to become the 1951 Grand National champion.

Curtis Turner's 11th career victory came in the 1956 Southern 500 at Darlington, driving a Ford. He was chosen as the Grand National Division's most popular driver that year, the first season the award was presented.

Larry Frank won his only career race in the 1962 Southern 500 in South Carolina. Fireball Roberts captured his 30th career pole position.

Cale Yarborough drove his Chevrolet to victory in the 1973 Southern 500 at Darlington, his 17th career victory. David Pearson, who won 11 races on the season, qualified on the pole for the 67th time in his career, but finished second in this race. Pearson was the season's leading money winner while Benny Parsons won the series championship.

David Pearson's 104th, and next to last, top-level NASCAR win came in the 1979 Southern 500. It was his ninth career win at Darlington.

Doug Cooper died in 1987 six days before his 49th birthday. The 1964 Grand National Rookie of the Year, Cooper started 114 Grand National races 1963–68, posted 11 top–10 finishes in 1964 and was 19th in series points in 1965.

Dale Earnhardt Sr. won his third race of 1989 with a first-place finish in the Heinz Southern 500 at Darlington. It was the first time the Southern 500 featured a corporate sponsor.

Jeff Gordon captured the 1995 Mountain Dew Southern 500 at Darlington for his eighth career Winston Cup victory. John Andretti captured his first (and only through 2003) career pole position start.

Bobby Labonte's #18 Pontiac won the 2000 Southern 500 at Darlington. Jeremy Mayfield started from the pole. Labonte won the Winston Cup Championship that season.

4

Charles Griffith, who raced out of Chattanooga, TN, in the 1950s and '60s, was born in 1929. Griffith managed three top–10 finishes in 17 career Grand National races.

Robert "Bobby" Wawak, born in 1939, ran 141 total races at NASCAR's top level between 1965 and 1987. Driving out of Villa Park, IL, Wawak led one race in 1982 and recorded 14 career top–10 finishes.

Earl Ross was born in Alsa Craig, Ontario, Canada, in 1941. With a Carling sponsored Chevrolet and an all–Canadian pit crew, Ross gained his only Winston Cup victory in the 1974 Old Dominion 500 at Martinsville, VA. He was the Rookie of Year and finished eighth in points that season, his one year as a regular at NASCAR's highest level. He managed nine other top–10 finishes that year. Ross raced on Canadian short-tracks for five years in the late 1970's.

Johnny Mantz won the first NASCAR race run on a paved surface when he took the checkered flag in the initial race at the 1.25-mile Darlington track in 1950, the Southern 500. The debut marked the first of the great superspeedways on the NASCAR circuit. Mantz averaged 75.250 mph in his Plymouth in the first 500-mile event in series competition. It was the only race of the season on a paved track, but marked the beginning of the end for the dirt-track era. It was the only career win for Mantz. Seventy-five cars began the race with Mantz winning in his Plymouth.

Nelson Stacy won his first of four career races in the 1961 Southern 500 at Darlington. Fireball Roberts sat on the pole for the fourth time in five races at the track.

Richard Petty won the 1967 Southern 500 for his 69th career Grand National victory, winning from the pole for the 32nd time in his career, the 13th time he achieved the feat this season.

Bobby Allison won his eighth race of 1972 in the Southern 500 at Darlington Raceway. It was his second straight win, the 37th of his career.

He was voted the most popular Winston Cup driver that season.

Cale Yarborough won his 56th career event in the 1978 Southern 500. David Pearson started first for the 106th time in his career.

Bill Elliott won his fifth race of 1988 in the Southern 500 at Darlington.

Bill Elliott won the 1994 Mountain Dew Southern 500 at Darlington. Geoff Bodine qualified first for the 34th time in his career.

5

Herb Thomas won at Darlington, SC, for the second straight year in 1955, notching his 43rd career checkered flag in the Southern 500.

Gwyn Staley won his second of three career Grand National races, all in 1957, closing the New York State Fairground in Syracuse to Grand National racing. The one-mile dirt track hosted yearly events 1955–57 with three separate winners, each from the pole.

Buck Baker won in 1958 at the Southern States Fairgrounds in Charlotte, NC.

Buck Baker won his 42nd career Grand National event in the 1960 Southern 500 at Darlington. Fireball Roberts captured his third consecutive pole at the track, the 16th of his career.

Darel Dieringer won the 1966 Southern 500 in South Carolina. It was his sixth career Grand National win and his third of the season. He was voted the most popular Grand National driver that year.

Bobby Isaac won the Buddy Shuman Memorial at the Hickory Speedway in 1969. It was his 16th career win and 19th career pole. Isaac was voted the Grand National division's most popular driver that year.

David Pearson won his 99th career Grand National/Winston Cup stock car race with a victory in the 1977 Southern 500. It was the ninth career pole for Darrell Waltrip, who won the spring race at the South Carolina track that year.

Bobby Allison won his fourth Southern 500 in 1983 with a victory at Darlington Raceway. It was his 77th career first place finish. Neil Bonnett qualified first.

Mark Martin's only four wins of the 1993 Winston Cup season came in consecutive races in August and September. The last in his string came in the Southern 500 at Darlington. Ken Schrader captured his 17th career pole.

Jeff Burton won the 1999 Pepsi Southern 500 at Darlington, SC. Kenny Irwin Jr. won the pole but finished a disappointing 31st. Jeff's brother Ward was the runner-up.

6

Norman McGriff was born in 1933. He raced out of Portland, OR, and started three west coast Grand National races in 1957 with two top–10 finishes. His best was a ninth-place in July at Portland.

William Mack "Bill" Hollar, who raced out of Burlington, NC, in the 1970s and '80s, was born in 1938.

Hollar ran 29 career Grand National and Winston Cup races with two top 10s, one each his first to years on the circuit, 1970–71.

Herb Thomas' 39th career win came in 1954 at Darlington, SC. Buck Baker captured his 14th pole.

Jeff Green was born in 1962 in Owensboro, KY. Green started in the Winston Cup Series in 1996. His older brothers David and Mark also raced in NASCAR top division. Jeff has yet to post a Winston Cup win.

Junior Johnson won the Buddy Shuman Memorial at the Hickory Speedway in 1963, his second straight win on the half-mile dirt track.

Ned Jarrett won the 1965 Southern 500 at Darlington, his 49th career Grand National win. Jarrett won the Grand National Championship for the second time and retired on top.

David Pearson won the Buddy Shuman Memorial at the Hickory Speedway in 1968. It was his 15th of 16 wins that season, his second of three as the Grand National Champion.

Bobby Allison won his eighth official NASCAR race of the season in 1971 at Darlington International Speedway in the Southern 500. It was Allison's 27th career victory and his 21st pole.

For the fourth time in his career, David Pearson won from the pole at Darlington to capture the 1976 Southern 500. It was his 96th top-level NASCAR win.

Cale Yarborough recorded his 74th top-circuit NASCAR win in the 1982 Southern 500 at Darlington, SC. David Pearson captured the final pole position of his career, #113.

Dale Earnhardt Sr. won his 10th race of 1987, his second straight, with a victory in the Southern 500 at Darlington.

Bobby Courtwright died in 1988 at the age of 54. Courtwright started six Grand National races in the 1950's with a career-best fifth place in a 1952 event.

Darrel Waltrip captured the 1992 Mountain Dew Southern 500 at Darlington for his 83rd and final career Winston Cup victory. Sterling Marlin captured his eighth career pole.

Dale Jarrett passed Jeff Burton with 40 laps remaining to win the 1997 Exide NASCAR Select Batteries 400 at Richmond, VA. Kenny Irwin made his first career start and became the first driver to start on the front row and finish in the top 10 (eighth-place finish) in a race debut.

Jeff Gordon won his ninth race of 1998 in the Pepsi Southern 500 at Darlington, SC. Dale Jarrett qualified first in the #88 Quality Care Ford and finished third. Gordon earned his third Winston Cup Championship in 1998.

Ryan Newman's sixth victory of the 2003 Winston Cup campaign came in Richmond, VA, in the Chevy Monte Carlo 400. Mike Skinner qualified first for the only time that season.

7

Donnie Allison was born in Hueytown, AL, in 1939. He started his NASCAR racing career in 1966 and was Rookie of the Year the following season. He finished fourth in the 1970 Indianapolis 500 but was critically injured in a 1981 crash at Charlotte that eventually ended his career.

Tim Flock won his fifth race of the 1951 NASCAR season with a checkered-flag finish on the .5-mile dirt track in Columbia, SC. Flock also took the pole. It was the first time that three consecutive Grand National races were held in the same state, South Carolina.

Lee Petty won his second race of 1952 with a trip to victory lane on the .5-mile dirt track in Macon, GA. Petty, registering the second win of the season for Plymouth, averaging 48.404 mph, just over 1 mph slower than the qualifying time of pole-sitter Fonty Flock for the 150-mile race.

Fonty Flock became the first driver to qualify over 100 mph outside of Daytona Beach, but Buck Baker won the 1953 Southern 500 at Darlington. The race, actually measured 500.5 miles on the paved 1.375-mile track. It was the third win of the season and fourth of Baker's career.

Fireball Roberts won the first NASCAR race held at the Fairgrounds Raceway in 1958. Eight races were staged at the Alabama track between 1959 and 1968, also known as Birmingham International Raceway/Speedway and Birmingham Super Speedway/Raceway.

Parnelli Jones won at Sacramento, CA, in 1958, the second of three career Grand National wins.

Jim Reed won his final of seven career Grand National races in 1959 with a victory in the Southern 500.

Rex White won the Buddy Shuman

Memorial race at the Hickory Speedway in 1962, his second straight win at the North Carolina track.

Buck Baker won the 1964 Southern 500 for his 46th and final career win and second victory in the fall race. Richard Petty won the 24th pole of his career.

Bobby Allison won his 15th career NASCAR race in the 1969 Capitol City 250 at the Richmond Fairgrounds Raceway.

Buddy Baker cruised to victory in the 1970 Southern 500 for his third career Grand National win. David Pearson started on the pole for the 54th time in his career.

Bobby Allison won his 56th career race with a first place finish at the Richmond Fairgrounds Raceway in the 1980 Capital City 400. It was his third win of the season. Cale Yarborough won his 56th career pole.

Neil Bonnett won the 1981 Southern 500 at Darlington for his 8th career victory. It was the third career pole position start for Harry Gant.

Tim Richmond won his second straight race, and his sixth race of the season, with a victory in the 1986 Wrangler Jeans Indigo 400 at Richmond International Raceway in his #25 Chevrolet. Harry Gant won his 13th career pole. Richmond had won the Southern 500 the previous week.

Harry Gant won his second consecutive race, and third of the 1991 Winston Cup series, with a victory in the Miller Genuine Draft 400 at Richmond. Rusty Wallace earned his 11th career pole.

Ernie Irvan won the 1996 Miller Genuine Draft 400 at Richmond International Speedway for his final of two wins on the season. Mark Martin qualified on the pole for the 32nd time in his career.

Matt Kenseth's fourth of five 2002 Winston Cup victories came in the Chevy Monte Carlo 400 at Richmond International Raceway. Jimmie Johnson captured his fourth of five top qualifying positions of the season.

8

Buddy Shuman was born in 1915. Shuman ran 29 Grand National races in the early 1950s, capturing his only NASCAR win at Niagara Falls, Ontario, in July 1952.

Aubrey Johnson "A.J." Cox was born in 1927. Cox raced out of Wilmington, DE, to start one Winston Cup race each in 1971 and 1972.

Frank Warren was born in 1937. He competed actively at NASCAR's top level between 1963 and 1980. Warren started 396 races with 29 top–10 finishes. He raced out of Augusta, GA. He finished a career-high eighth in points in 1971, Winston Cup's first season.

Larry Dickson, who raced out of Marietta, OH, in the early 1970s, was born in 1938. Dickson made one Winston Cup start in 1972.

David Ray Boggs was born in 1943 and raced out of Morrisville, NC. Boggs started 32 Winston Cup races 1971–73 with two top 10s his rookie season.

NASCAR ran a points race on a second consecutive day in 1951, this time a 100-mile contest on a .5-mile dirt track at the Central City Speedway. Herb Thomas captured his third win of the season in the first sanctioned race held in Macon, GA.

Lee Petty won his second race in three tries at Skyline Speedway in Weaverville, NC, in 1957. It was Petty's 29th career win, third on the season.

Danny Graves won the 1957 Grand National race on the one-mile dirt track at the California State Fairgrounds in Sacramento for his only career checkered flag.

Rex White won the Buddy Shuman Memorial at the Hickory Speedway in 1961. White won the 1960 Grand National Championship.

Ned Jarrett's win in the 1963 Capital City 300 was the 21st of his career. Joe Weatherly earned his 17th career pole. Jarrett won eight races to Weatherly's three, but finished fourth in the championship race, won by Weatherly.

Richard Petty won the Buddy Shuman Memorial at the Hickory Speedway in 1967. It was the first race on a paved surface at the speedway, which hosted Grand National cars for 14 years on a half-mile dirt track.

Richard Petty rode the pole to victory in the 1968 Capital City 300 at Richmond International Raceway (VA). It was the 38th time he both started and finished first. He won 16 races in 1968 but finished third in the championship race, won by David Pearson.

Richard Petty won the 1974 Capital City 500 at Richmond International Raceway, winning from the pole for his 163rd career win. It was the 56th of 61 times he qualified first and finished first. Petty won 10 races in 1974 to claim his fifth career Winston Cup championship.

Darrell Waltrip won the 1985 Wrangler Sanfor-Set 400 at Richmond in 1985. It was his 66th career win on his way to his third Winston Cup championship that season. Geoff Bodine captured his seventh career pole.

9

Johnny Thompson was born in 1922. Racing out of Jacksonville, FL, Thompson ran five Grand National events 1951–52 and earned $100 in his career at NASCAR's top level.

Phil Barkdoll was born in 1937. Barkdoll made 23 Winston Cup starts 1984–92, racing out of Phoenix, AZ. He debuted in the Winston 500 at Talladega and finished 17th in the 1992 Daytona 500 by STP.

Ben Douglas "Doug" Cooper, who raced out of Gastonia, NC, was born in 1938. Cooper made 114 Grand National starts 1963–68 with 30 top-10s. He was the 1964 Grand National Rookie of the Year.

Cuban native Felix Sabates was born in 1942. An immigrant who arrived in the United States in 1959, Sabates worked his way up through the toy industry and eventually purchased a racing team. He has also been part of an NBA ownership group and fielded an entry in the 1997 Indianapolis 500.

Born in 1946 and racing out of Newport Beach, CA, Sumner Mc-Knight ran six Winston Cup races at Riverside, CA between 1977 and 1985. His best finish was 14th in his final race, the 1985 Budweiser 400.

Buck Baker won the only Grand National race ever run at the Chisholm Speedway in Montgomery, AL, a half-mile dirt track. Baker won the 45th race of 1956 over Ralph Moody while Tim Flock won the pole. It was Baker's tenth win of the season, when he earned his first of two consecutive Grand National Championships.

Popular NASCAR announcer Jeff Hammond was born in 1956. He debuted as a crew chief for Darrell Waltrip in 1982, when they won the Winston Cup championship. Hammond and Chris Myers have teamed to become a mainstay of FOX television racing coverage since 2000.

Junior Johnson won the Buddy Shuman Memorial at Hickory Speedway in 1960.

Joe Weatherly won at Richmond International Raceway in the 1962 Capital City 300. It was his ninth and final win of the season, when he cruised to his first of two consecutive Grand National Championships.

David Pearson won the Buddy Shuman Memorial at the Hickory Speedway in 1966. It was his 14th of 15 wins on the season, his first of three as Grand National Champion.

Jerry Nadeau was born in 1969 in Danbury, CT. Nadeau began his Winston Cup experience in 1997 and ran 177 events through 2003. His lone win came in the 2000 Napa 500 at Atlanta Motor Speedway.

Richard Petty won the 1973 Capital City 500 in his #43 Dodge at the Virginia State Fairgrounds. It was his 153rd career checkered flag. Bobby Allison won his 40th career pole and finished third. It was the seventh straight win for Petty at Richmond.

Bobby Allison won his 56th career NASCAR race at the Richmond Fairgrounds Raceway in the 1979 Capital City 400. It was his fifth win of the season. Dale Earnhardt Sr. won his second career pole and finished fourth.

Darrell Waltrip won the 1984 Wrangler Sanfor-Set 400 at Richmond. He started first and finished first for the 22nd of 24 times in his career, his 62nd series win and 49th pole start.

Dale Earnhardt Sr. won his eighth race of 1990 with a first-place finish in the Miller Genuine Draft 400 at Richmond International Speedway. It was the third time in the 1990 Winston Cup season that he won two consecutive races. Ernie Irvan won his third pole position. Earnhardt went on to capture his third Winston Cup points championship.

Rusty Wallace captured the checkered flag in the 1995 Miller Genuine Draft 400 at Richmond. It was his 41st career Winston Cup victory. Dale Earnhardt Sr. captured his 20th career pole and finished third.

The #24 Chevrolet of Jeff Gordon won the 2000 Monte Carlo 400 at Richmond. It was Gordon's third win of the season. Jeff Burton captured the pole.

10

Ralph Moody was born in Taunton, MA, in 1917. Moody finished eighth in points his rookie season of 1956 when he won four races and captured five poles. He ran a limited schedule 1957–62, finishing his career with 47 starts and 27 top–10 finishes. Moody became a successful owner and engine builder.

Thomas J. Gale, who raced out of McKeesport, PA, 1968–86, was born in 1934. Gale ran 245 Grand National and Winston Cup races with four career top–10 finishes. He finished 15th in Winston Cup points in 1981, a career-best.

Eddie Gray won the final NASCAR race held at the California State Fairgrounds in Sacramento in 1961. He was the only driver to win twice on the track. It was the final of four career wins for Gray, all in the state of California.

Joe Weatherly's ninth career win came in 1961 at Richmond. Junior Johnson, who won his 17th pole, finished second. Weatherly won eight races in 1961 and finished fourth in points.

Richard Petty won the Buddy Shuman Memorial at the Hickory Speedway in 1965.

Richard Petty swept both 1967 events at the Richmond International Speedway, winning the Capital City 300 for his 71st career win. Petty cruised to 27 victories in 1967 alone, easily winning his second Grand National driving championship.

The 1972 Capital City 500 was won by Richard Petty, his fifth straight win at Richmond. It was the 146th career win for Petty. Bobby Allison qualified first and finished second. Petty won the points championship for the fourth time in 1972 while Allison finished second.

Darrel Waltrip won from the pole to take the 1978 Capital City 400 at Richmond. It was his 15th career win and 10th career pole, the second time in his career he both started and finished first.

Rusty Wallace won the 1989 Miller High Life 400 at Richmond for his sixth and final win of the season. Bill Elliott won his 36th career pole. Wallace went on to capture the Winston Cup points championship.

Terry Labonte won the 1994 Miller Genuine Draft 400 at Richmond International Raceway. It was the 12th career win for Labonte. Ted Musgrave qualified first for his second career pole start.

11

Robert "Bob" Harris, who raced out of Greensboro, NC, in the 1950s, was born in 1926. Harris ran one career Grand National event, in 1953.

Joe Lee Johnson was born in Chattanooga, TN, in 1929. Johnson ran 55 Grand National events 1956–62 with two career victories and 18 other top–10 finishes. His first win came at the Nashville Speedway in 1959, driving a Chevrolet. He also won at Charlotte in 1960.

Joy Fair was born in 1930. Racing out of Pontiac Springs, MI, in the 1950s, Fair made two Grand National starts in 1956 with one top 10 in his brief experience at NASCAR's top level.

Bill Whittington, born in 1949, ran two Winston Cup races in 1980. Driving out of Ft. Lauderdale, FL, Whittington managed one career top–10 finish.

Curtis Turner won his first career NASCAR race in the fourth official race in history, on a one-mile dirt track in Langhorne, PA, in 1949. Sara Christian finished 6th, the first woman to compete in a Grand National race. Turner became the fourth different winner in four races. Red Byron, the series' first winner, won his first pole.

Tim Flock won the second sanctioned NASCAR race held at Montgomery Motor Speedway in Alabama in 1955. Flock won his second of two Grand National Championships that year.

Lee Petty won at the Hickory Speedway in 1959. Petty won his third and final Grand National Championship, taking the checkered flag in ten events that season.

Jim Cook won at the California State Fairgrounds in 1960 for his only career Grand National victory. Cook raced out of Norwalk, CA, to start 39 Grand National races 1954–70 with six other top 10s.

The quarter-mile dirt oval of the Dog Track Speedway hosted its first Grand National event in 1962, won by Ned Jarrett. The Moyock, NC, raceway hosted seven top-level NASCAR races 1962–66.

David Pearson won the 1964 Buddy Shuman Memorial at the Hickory Speedway.

David Pearson swept the 1966 Richmond races with a win in the Capital City 300. Pearson won from the pole for the 8th of 37 times in his career for his 28th Grand National victory. It was his final of 15 victories in 1966, when he was the Grand National driving champion.

Bobby Isaac won his second straight Buddy Shuman Memorial race at the Hickory Speedway in 1970. It was his fourth straight win at the North Carolina track.

Neil Bonnett's first career win came in his #5 Dodge at Richmond, VA, in the 1977 Capital City 400. Benny Parsons earned his ninth career pole start and finished third. Bonnett died in February 1994, practicing for the Daytona 500.

Bobby Allison won his second consecutive NASCAR race, his fifth win of the season, at Richmond Fairgrounds Raceway in the 1983 Wrangler Sanfor-Set 400. The win was the 78th of his career. Allison went on to win the Winston Cup Championship in 1983. Darrell Waltrip, the winner of the previous two championships, earned his 43rd career pole and finished third.

Davey Allison won his second race of 1988 with a first-place finish in the Miller High Life 400 at Richmond. Allison won from the pole for the first of two times in his career. It was his fourth Winston Cup win and eighth top qualifying start.

Rusty Wallace captured his sixth victory of the 1993 Winston Cup season in the Miller Genuine Draft 400 at Richmond. Bobby Labonte started on the pole for the first time in his career. Wallace won ten times in 1993 and finished second to Dale Earnhardt for the Winston Cup championship.

Tony Stewart won the 1999 Exide NASCAR Select Batteries 400 at Richmond International Raceway in Virginia. Mike Skinner won the pole and finished 11th, his second top start of the season. It was the first career victory for Stewart, who would later become the 2002 Winston Cup champion.

12

Bob Reuther was born in 1927. Reuther recorded three career Grand National starts, one each in 1951, 1959 and 1960, managing a career-best ninth-place finish in the 1959 Nashville 300. He raced out of Nashville, TN.

Ron Keselowski was born in 1946. Keselowski started 68 Grand National/Winston Cup races between 1970 and 1974 with 11 top–10 finishes.

Kenneth Ragan was born in 1950. Racing out of Unadilla, GA, he started 50 Winston Cup races 1983–90. His career-best was an 11th-place finish in the 1984 Talladega 500. He was 21st in the 1985 Daytona 500.

Hershel McGriff won the final NASCAR race held at the Central City Speedway in Macon, GA, in 1954. The half-mile dirt track hosted seven Grand National events 1951–54.

Ralph Moody won in 1956 at the Southern States Fairgrounds in Charlotte, NC.

Ricky Rudd was born in 1956 in Chesapeake, VA. His Winston Cup career began in 1975 and he began winning races in 1983, winning at least one race per season through 1998, amassing 23 career wins through 2003. He was the Winton Cup Rookie of the Year in 1977 and finished second in championship points in 1991.

In the only Grand National race ever held at the Gastonia Fairgrounds in Gastonia, NC, Buck Baker captured the 1958 checkered flag.

Cale Yarborough won the 1976 Capital City 400 at Richmond International Raceway for his 37th career win. Benny Parsons qualified first for the sixth time. Yarborough went on to win nine races in 1976 on his way to his first Winston Cup championship, over second place Richard Petty who had won the previous three years.

Bobby Allison won his seventh race of 1982 with a victory at the Richmond Fairgrounds Raceway in the second Wrangler Sanfor-Set 400. Allison, with eight wins, finished second to Darrell Waltrip for the Winston Cup championship.

Rusty Wallace's only win in 1992 came in the Miller Genuine Draft 400 at Richmond. It was his 21st career checkered flag. Ernie Irvan won his 7th pole.

Jeff Burton won his second race of 1998 in the Exide NASCAR Select Batteries 400 at Richmond, VA. Rusty Wallace captured the pole and finished seventh. Jeff Gordon finished second.

13

Bill Kimmel was born in 1928. Racing out of Clarksville, IN, he ran three career top-level NASCAR races, two in 1969 and one in 1971, all at Daytona. His career highlight was a 46th place finish in the 1969 Daytona 500.

Terry Bivins was born in 1943. Bivins, who raced out of Shawnee Mission, KS, made 28 Winston Cup starts 1975–77 with eight top–10 finishes.

On the half-mile dirt track in Macon, GA, in 1953, Joe Eubanks captured his first pole and Speedy Thompson won the 100-mile event. Thompson averaged 55.172 mph in his Oldsmobile for his first Grand National win.

Eddie Gray won the 1959 Grand National Race at the California State Fairgrounds.

Cotton Owens both qualified first and finished first, driving the #6 Ford, for the first of three times in his career in 1959 at Richmond. It was his third career win and fifth pole. Owens finished second to Lee Petty for the 1959 Grand National driving championship.

Fred Lorenzen won at the Augusta International Speedway in 1962, his only win at the half-mile dirt track in Georgia.

Burn Skeen died in 1965 at the age of 28 as a result of injuries suffered at Darlington, SC, one week earlier. Skeen, in his rookie NASCAR sea-

son, started eight races that year with three top–10 finishes. He raced out of Denton, NC.

Bobby Isaac won the 1968 Maryland 300 at the Beltsville Speedway.

Richard Petty won the 1970 Capital City 500 at Richmond for his 115th career victory. Petty won 18 races that season but finished fourth in championship points, won by Bobby Isaac. It was the 48th time in his career that he qualified first and won.

Benny Parsons won the 1981 Wrangler Sanfor-Set 400 at Richmond International Speedway. Mark Martin qualified first for the second time in his career. It was the 20th career victory for Parsons, the 1973 Winston Cup Champion.

Dale Earnhardt Sr. won his third straight race with a victory in the 1987 Wrangler Jeans Indigo 400 at Richmond. It was Earnhardt's 11th and final win of the season, his third Winston Cup Championship campaign. Alan Kulwicki won his second career pole start.

14

Ken Rush was born in 1931. Rush ran 56 Grand National events 1957–72, winning two poles his first two seasons and finishing with 16 top–10 finishes.

Dr. Lee Reitzel was born in 1932. Reitzel ran 29 events at the Grand National level 1961–63, racing out of Charlotte, NC. His best finish was eighth place in a 1962 race at Concord Speedway (NC).

Larry Mann died of injuries

suffered on this date in 1952 at Langhorne, PA. He had entered six races.

Lee Petty won his second straight race, the first "win streak" of his career, with a first-place finish in the 250-mile event at Langhorne, PA, in 1952. Petty, who averaged 72.463 mph on the one-mile dirt track, gave Plymouth their first set of consecutive wins. Herb Thomas' Hudson qualified on the pole. Larry Mann entered six races in 1952, but died of injuries suffered at Langhorne in his final event.

Speedy Thompson won from the pole at Richmond in 1958, the final of seven times he both qualified and finished first. Thompson won two more races and one more pole in his career. He finished third in points for the 1958 Grand National championship, won by Lee Petty.

Cotton Owens won his final of nine career races with a first-place finish in the 1964 Capital City 300 at Richmond, VA. Ned Jarrett earned his 24th career pole position and finished fifth. Jarrett was the runner-up to Richard Petty in the points championship that season. Owens ran one more race, finishing second at Hillsboro, NC, less than a week later to end his driving career with 160 starts.

Dick Hutcherson won his 8th career Grand National race in the 1965 Pennsylvania 200 Classic at the Lincoln Speedway in New Oxford, PA. Richard Petty captured his 30th career pole. It was the final of seven top-level NASCAR races held at the half-mile dirt track between 1955 and 1965.

In 1969, the inaugural event at Alabama International Motor Speedway (Talladega) was boycotted by many of the NASCAR regulars, including star Richard Petty, due to safety concerns. Richard Brickhouse won the controversial event, his only career win, which was somewhat tainted by the absence of the "regular competition."

Richard Petty won for the fifth time in his career at Dover with a 1975 win in the Delaware 500. It was Petty's tenth of 13 wins that season, the sixth time he captured the points championship.

Darrell Waltrip won the 1980 CRC Chemicals 500 at Dover Downs International Speedway.

Ricky Rudd won the 1986 Delaware 500 at Dover Downs for his second win of the season.

Axel Anderson died in 1994 at the age of 73. Anderson started five Grand National races in the 1950s. His best finish was a 14th-place effort in April 1958 at Old Bridge, NJ.

Jeff Gordon won his 10th race of 1997 with a win in the CMT 300 at New Hampshire International Speedway. It was his second consecutive season with at least ten wins and he captured the Winston Cup Championship for the second time. Ernie Irvan finished second.

Jimmy Johnson's second win of 2003 came at the New Hampshire International Speedway in the Sylvania 300. The previous week's winner, Ryan Newman, captured the top qualifying spot.

15

George Green, who raced out of Johnson City, TN, in the 1950s and '60s, was born in 1927. Green started 116 career Grand National races with 29 top-10 finishes. He finished 16th in championship points in 1962.

Herb Thomas won his third race in 12 days in 1951 on the one-mile dirt track at Langhorne, PA. Thomas, who won the previous week in an Oldsmobile, won this 150-mile contest in a Hudson for his fourth win of the Grand National season. Fonty Flock, who won the pole, finished second.

In the only NASCAR race ever run at the Santa Clara Fairgrounds in San Jose, CA, Marvin Porter earned $800 with a 1957 win on the half-mile dirt track, the first of two in his career. Porter raced out of Lakewood, CA, and made 34 career Grand National starts 1957–67. He won a 250-mile race in Hanford, CA, in 1960 for his other career victory.

Gwyn Staley won his final of three career Grand National races, all within a month in 1957, at Langhorne, PA. It was the final top-level NASCAR race at the track, which hosted 17 races between 1949 and 1957.

The lone Grand National race run at the Gamecock Speedway, a ¼-mile dirt track in Sumter, SC, was a 1960 win by Ned Jarrett, the seventh of his career. David Pearson, who captured 112 career poles, qualified in the top spot for the first time in his career but finished second.

Richard Petty won the 1967 Maryland 300 at the Beltsville Speedway, the 33rd time in his career he both started and finished first. Petty went on to capture his second Grand National driving championship with 27 wins during the 1967 season.

Richard Petty won the final Grand National event held at the Occoneechee Speedway in Hillsboro, NC, in 1968. The one-mile dirt track hosted 32 Grand National races, beginning in NASCAR's inaugural year of 1949.

Richard Petty won his fourth career Dover Downs race with a checkered flag finish in the 1974 Delaware 500. It was the final of ten wins on the season for Petty, who won his fifth of seven driving championships.

Harry Gant won his second straight Delaware 500 in 1985 at Dover Downs.

Harry Gant won his third straight race, his fourth win of the 1991 season, with a first-place finish in the Peak Antifreeze 500 at the Monster Mile in Dover.

Jeff Gordon won his first of three consecutive races, his eighth win of the 1996 season. Gordon cruised to victory lane in the MBNA 500 at Dover Downs.

Ryan Newman's only win of 2002 came at Loudon, NH, in the Sylvania 300. Newman also started first, his third of six pole position starts on the season.

16

Gary Balough was born in 1947. Balough raced out of Ft. Lauderdale,

FL, to make 22 Winston Cup starts 1979–92 with two top–10 finishes in his career.

Dick Meyer was killed in a highway crash in 1953. Meyer started eight Grand National races 1951–53. He was traveling from Detroit to be with his pregnant wife at the time of his death.

Darin Brassfield was born in 1960. Brassfield raced out of Los Gatos, CA, to start three races in 1989. Driving for Dale Earnhardt Sr., he finished 12th at the 1989 Budweiser at the Glen.

David Pearson won the 1973 Delaware 500 at Dover Downs for his third straight win on the Monster Mile.

Richard Petty won his sixth race at the Monster Mile in Dover with a victory in the 1979 CRC Chemicals 500.

Harry Gant won the 1984 Delaware 500 at Dover Downs.

Bill Elliott won his only race of 1990 at Dover Downs' Monster Mile with a victory in the Peak Antifreeze 500.

17

Johnny Allen was born in 1934. Allen raced out of Greenville, SC, to start 173 career Grand National races 1955–67. He won his only race in June 1962 at the Myers Brothers Memorial at Winston Salem, NC. Allen won three poles and finished in the top 10 in 60 other events.

Lonnie LeeRoy Yarbrough was born in Jacksonville, FL, in 1938. He ran 198 Grand National and Winston Cup events with 14 career victories. He finished a career-high 15th in points in 1964. In 1969 he won seven major races, including Daytona.

Cecil Franklin "Sam" Sommers was born in 1939. Sommers started 30 Winston Cup races 1976–78 with nine top–10 finishes. He qualified on the pole for the November 1977 race at Atlanta Motor Speedway.

Fonty became the third Flock brother to win a NASCAR event with a first-place finish in the 200-mile race at Langhorne, PA, in 1950. Flock averaged 72.801 mph in his Oldsmobile on the one-mile dirt track to capture his first victory. Wally Campbell captured the only pole position of his career in 11 Grand National starts.

David Pearson won the first Dixie 400 at Atlanta Motor Speedway in 1961. The race was increased by 100 miles over the previous running in 1960. It was Pearson's third career win.

Richard Petty's 40th career win came in 1965 at the Old Dominion Speedway in Manassas, VA. Ned Jarrett, the 1965 Grand National champion, qualified first for the 35th time in his Winston Cup career and finished second.

Richard Petty won at the Occoneechee Speedway in Hillsboro, NC, in 1967, his second straight win from the pole and the 73rd trip to victory lane in his Grand National career.

David Pearson won at Dover Downs in 1972 in the Delaware 500.

Bobby Allison won his third race

of 1978 with a victory at Dover Downs International Speedway in the Delaware 500. It was Allison's 49th career NASCAR win.

Dale Earnhardt Sr. won the 1989 Peak Performance 500 at Dover Downs for his fourth win of the season and second win in three weeks.

Jeff Gordon won the 1995 MBNA 500 at Dover Downs International Raceway on his way to his first Winston Cup Championship.

After capturing the pole the previous week, Jeff Burton won the 2000 New Hampshire 300. Bobby Labonte won the pole for this race.

18

Johnny Mantz was born in 1918 in California. Racing out of Long Beach, Mantz ran 12 events 1950–56 and won his only race at the inaugural 500-mile race at Darlington his rookie season.

Dick Joslin was born in 1926. He started 10 races between 1955 and 1960 with two top–10 finishes. He raced out of Orlando, FL, to a seventh-place finish in his debut on the Beach & Road Course in Daytona Beach, FL.

Billy Foster, who raced out of Victoria, British Columbia, Canada, in the 1960s, died in 1967 at the age of 29. He ran one Grand National race in 1966 with a top–10 finish. He qualified ninth for the January 1967 Riverside event, but was killed in a practice mishap before the race.

Gerald Eugene "Jerry" Churchill, who raced out of Dearborne, MI, was born in 1938. Churchill made six Winston Cup starts in 1971 and one in 1984.

Jack White became the fifth different winner in NASCAR's first five official races in 1949. He drove his Lincoln to victory in a 100 mile race on a .5 mile dirt track in Hamburg, NY. It was the only win of his NASCAR career and the first sanctioned race in the state of New York.

For the second straight Langhorne Speedway event, Tim Flock started from the pole and captured the checkered flag on the one-mile dirt track. It was the 33rd pole and 32nd win of his Grand National career.

Richard took the third straight Petty checkered flag at the Occoneechee Speedway in 1960. His father Lee had won the previous two races at the one-mile dirt track in Hillsboro, NC.

Road racing specialist Boris Said was born in Carlsbad, CA, in 1962. He started two Winston Cup races in 1992 and returned in 2000, running one race. He won the pole for the 2003 road race at Sears Point and finished sixth. Said regularly ran at that track and Watkins Glen in the early 2000's.

Ned Jarrett won both 1964 races at Manassas, Virginia's Old Dominion Speedway. Jarrett cruised to his 34th career win in the September 1964 race while David Pearson qualified first for the 15th time of his career, and finished second.

Robert "Sonny" Black was killed in practice at 5-Flags Speedway in Pensacola, FL, in 1964. A native of

Forrest Park, GA, Black ran six career Grand National races with a career-best ninth-place finish in April 1951 at Lakeview (AL) Speedway.

In the 1965 Capital City 300, David Pearson won his 13th career race and Dick Hutcherson won his 10th pole. Hutcherson finished second to Ned Jarrett in championship points while Pearson won two races that season, but finished 40th.

Dick Hutcherson won at the Occoneechee Speedway in 1966 for the second straight checkered flag at the Hillsboro, NC, track.

Bobby Isaac's 13th win of 1969 came at Columbia Speedway (SC). It was his 17th career win.

Benny Parsons won the 1977 Delaware 500 at Dover Downs International Speedway.

Bobby Allison captured his third straight win of 1983 en route to the Winston Cup Championship. The win came at Dover Downs International Speedway and was his 79th career victory.

Bill Elliott won his sixth Winston Cup race of the 1988 season with a victory in the Delaware 500 at Dover Downs. Elliott won his only Winston Cup Championship that year.

Rusty Wallace won his third consecutive race at Dover Downs, taking his second straight Splitfire Spark Plug 500 in 1994.

19

Ken Wagner, born in 1917, ran three races each in 1949, 1950 and 1956. Racing out of Pennington, NJ, Wagner captured the pole in North Wilkesboro, NC, in 1949, the final race of the first Strictly Stock season.

Buck Baker won from the pole for the 11th time in his career, his 34th career Grand National checkered flag in 1957 at the Columbia (SC) Speedway.

Cale Yarborough won the 1976 Delaware 500 at Dover Downs International Speedway, his sixth of nine wins on the season. Yarborough went on to capture his first of three straight Winston Cup championships.

Darrell Waltrip won the 1982 CRC Chemicals 500 at Dover Downs International Speedway.

Rusty Wallace won his second straight Winston Cup race in 1993, taking the checkered flag at the Monster Mile in Dover in the Splitfire 500. Wallace, who started from the pole, won his seventh race of the season.

Joe Nemechek won his first career Winston Cup race in the 1999 Dura Lube/K Mart 300 at the New Hampshire International Speedway. Rusty Wallace won the pole and finished sixth.

20

Leslie "Les" Snow Jr. was born in 1925. Racing out of Bloomington, IL, Snow ran two Grand National races in 1951 and one race in 1969.

Raymond "Ray" Hill, who raced out of Concord, NC, in the 1960s, was born in 1931. Hill ran eight career Grand National events with three top–10s in six races in his rookie year of 1966, including a career-best seventh at Islip (NY) Speedway in July.

Dick Rathmann won the only 250-mile event of the 1953 Grand National season with a first-place finish at Langhorne, PA, on the one-mile dirt track. It was win #10 of Rathmann's career, his fifth of this season. Herb Thomas captured his 24th pole to lead all NASCAR drivers.

Lee Petty won at the Occoneechee Speedway in Hillsboro, NC, in 1959, his eighth of ten on the season when he went on to win his final of three Grand National Championships.

Ned Jarrett won at the Occoneechee Speedway in Hillsboro, NC, in 1964, his 35th career checkered flag.

Richard Petty won the second race staged at the Monster Mile at Dover, DE, with a win in the Mason-Dixon 300 in 1970. Petty had also won the first NASCAR race at the track in 1969.

Neil Bonnett won the 1981 CRC Chemicals 500 at Dover Downs.

Ricky Rudd won the 1987 Delaware 500 at the Monster Mile at Dover Downs.

Ricky Rudd won the 1992 Peak Antifreeze 500 at Dover Downs.

Mark Martin started first and won the 1998 MBNA Gold 400 at Dover, DE, his sixth win of the season.

21

Richard Raymond "Dick" Simon was born in 1933. Simon ran three Winston Cup races 1973–74, racing out of Seattle, WA. His best finish came in his debut, seventh-place in the 1973 Winston 500 at Talladega, AL.

Richard Childress was born on this date in 1945. Childress has done it all in his racing career from driver to team owner. Although he never won a Winston Cup race as a driver in 285 starts between 1969 and 1981, he finished in the top–10 76 times. He won six points championships as an owner with Dale Earnhardt Sr. as his driver between 1986 and 1994.

Frank Luptow died at the age of 38 in 1952 in a crash during a race at Lakewood Speedway in Atlanta, GA. Luptow started one race in 1950 and four in 1951 (with one fifth-place finish).

Dick Rathmann drove his Hudson to victory lane in 1952 at Dayton, OH. Rathmann, who won four times previously on the season, averaged 61.643 mph on the .5-mile paved track in the 150-mile event. Fonty Flock captured his 21st career pole position.

Buck Baker won his second consecutive fall race at the Cleveland County Fairgrounds. The Shelby, NC, track hosted two Grand National races each in 1956, 1957 and 1965.

Curtis Markham was born in 1959 in Virginia. Markham started five Winston Cup races, four in 1987 and one in 1994. He was involved in a crash and finished next-to-last in his debut in the 1987 Budweiser 500 at Dover, DE.

Richard Petty won the 1975 Wilkes 400. It was his 13th career win at the

.625-mile track in North Wilkes-boro, NC.

Bobby Allison won his 60th career NASCAR race with a victory in the Holly Farms 400 at the North Wilkesboro Speedway in 1980. It was his fourth win of the season.

Rusty Wallace won the 1986 Goody's 500 at Martinsville for his second and final win of the Winston Cup season. It was also the second career win for Wallace, who finished sixth in championship points that season. Geoff Bodine won his 17th career pole start.

Mark Martin won the 1997 MBNA 400 at Dover Downs International Speedway. It was his 22nd career Winston Cup win and his fourth of the season. Dale Earnhardt finished second.

Ryan Newman won for the seventh time in 2003 with a checkered flag finish in the MBNA America 400 at the monster mile of Dover, DE. Matt Kenseth, the season's eventual points champion, won his second pole of the season.

22

Steve Christman, who raced out of Ft. Wayne, IN, was born in 1947. Christman started 20 Winston Cup events in 1987, his only season at NASCAR's top level.

Fred Lorenzen won his 11th career Grand National race in the 1963 Old Dominion 500 at Martinsville. Junior Johnson started first for the 29th of 49 times in his career.

Jimmy Pardue died at the age of 33

in a crash during tire testing at Charlotte in 1964. Pardue was fifth in Grand National points and had 24 top–10 finishes in 50 races during his final NASCAR season.

Richard Petty won 16 races in 1968 including the Old Dominion 500 at Martinsville. Petty was voted the circuit's most popular driver for the third time in 1968. Cale Yarborough, 1967's most popular driver, qualified first for the eighth time in his career and finished as the runner-up.

Cale Yarborough drove to victory in the 1974 Wilkes 400 at North Wilkesboro, NC.

Dale Earnhardt Sr. won the 1985 Goody's 500 at Martinsville for his 15th career Winston Cup victory. Geoff Bodine won his eighth pole.

Harry Gant won his fourth straight race, his fifth victory of 1991, with a first-place finish in the Goody's 500 at Martinsville. Mark Martin earned his third straight pole at the Virginia track, the 16th of his career, and finished fifth.

Jeff Gordon won for the ninth time in 1996 with a first-place finish in the Hanes 500 at Martinsville. Bobby Hamilton won his second career pole and finished third. Gordon won ten 1996 races but finished second in the Winston Cup points championship to Terry Labonte.

Jimmie Johnson won for the final of three times on the 2002 Winston Cup season with a checkered flag finish in the MBNA America 400 at Dover Downs. Rusty Wallace won his only pole position of the year.

23

Oda Greene, who raced out of Toledo, OH, in the 1950s, was born in 1928. Green managed six Grand National starts in 1951 with three top–10 finishes. He ran one final race the following season at NASCAR's top level.

Eugene Black was born in 1943. He started 37 Grand National races 1965–68. Racing out of Arden, NC, Black managed six top–10 career finishes.

Fonty Flock won one of two sanctioned races held on this day in 1951 with a checkered-flag finish on the .5-mile paved track in Dayton, OH. Flock also won the pole for the 100-mile event for his sixth win of the season.

Herb Thomas won his third straight race on the .75-mile dirt track in Charlotte, NC, in 1951, one of two races on this day. Thomas, driving a Hudson, captured his fifth win of the season, but his fourth of the month of September.

Paul Goldsmith's first of nine Grand National wins came in 1956 at Langhorne, PA. Buck Baker started first for the 25th time of his career. Goldsmith also won the pole for his next two starts at the track.

Dane Lloyd won his second career Grand National race in 1956 at Portland Speedway in Portland, OR. It was his second win of 1956.

Nelson Stacy won his final of four career races in the 1962 Old Dominion 500 at Martinsville. Fireball Roberts won his 31st of 35 career top

qualifying positions.

Bobby Allison won the Wilkes 400 in 1973 at the North Wilkesboro Speedway. It was his 41st career win. He was voted the most popular Winston Cup driver for the fourth consecutive time that season.

Buddy Baker won the 1979 Old Dominion 500 at Martinsville, his 16th career win. He finished 15th in points that season and won three races. Darrell Waltrip won his 16th career pole but finished second to Richard Petty for the Winston Cup championship.

Darrell Waltrip won his 63rd career Winston Cup race in the 1984 Goody's 500 at Martinsville, VA. Geoff Bodine won his fifth pole position start.

Geoff Bodine won his third and final race of the 1990 season with a trip to victory lane in the Goody's 500 at Martinsville. It was his second straight win at the Virginia track. Mark Martin earned his 12th career pole start and finished third.

Earl Moss died in 1994 at the age of 69. Moss ran 11 races in the 1950s with two top–10 finishes.

Dale Earnhardt Jr. won his second of three Winston Cup races in 2001 with a victory at Dover Downs in the MBNA.com 400. Dale Jarrett qualified for his fifth pole start of the season.

24

Bobby Marshman was born in 1936 in Pottstown, PA. He started two races in the 1964 Grand National season but was killed in November that year while testing at Phoenix, AZ.

Leon Sales won the 125-mile race at North Wilkesboro, NC, in 1950 for his first NASCAR win. Sales drove his Plymouth to the checkered flag on the .625-mile dirt track.

Hershel McGriff won in 1954 at the Southern States Fairgrounds in Charlotte, NC.

Charlie Miller died as the result of a crash in a sprint car race in Shelby, NC, in 1955. Miller ran one Grand National race in 1953, earning $100.

Joe Weatherly's 10th career win came in the 1961 Old Dominion 500 at Martinsville. Fred Lorenzen won the pole for the fourth time in his career.

Ned Jarrett won at the Dog Track Speedway in 1963. Jarrett won four of the seven Grand National races run at the quarter-mile dirt track in Moyock, NC.

Dr. Lee Reitzel died in 1965 at the age of 32. Reitzel had run 29 top NASCAR events 1961–63, finishing in the top ten four times in his brief career.

Richard Petty won both Martinsville races in 1967, winning the Old Dominion 500 for his 74th career victory. Cale Yarborough won his third career pole.

Richard Petty won and Bobby Allison captured the pole and finished second in both 1972 Martinsville races. Petty earned his 147th win in the Old Dominion 500 while Bobby Allison's pole was the 35th of his career.

Cale Yarborough won the 1978 Old Dominion 500 at Martinsville, VA. It was his 57th of 83 career victories. Lennie Pond finished fifth but earned his fifth pole qualifying position. Yarborough went on to win the 1978 Winston Cup championship, his third consecutive, winning ten races on the season.

Darrell Waltrip won the 1989 Goody's 500 at Martinsville Speedway for his sixth win of the year and 79th of his career. Jimmy Hensley, the 1992 Winston Cup Rookie of the Year, won his only career pole. Waltrip was voted the most popular driver 1989–90, winning six races in 1989 but none the following season.

Dale Earnhardt Sr. won the 1995 Goody's 500 at Martinsville for his 67th career Winston Cup victory. Earnhardt Sr. won five races in 1995 and was the runner-up in the points race to Jeff Gordon.

At the 2000 MBNA Gold 400 at Dover Downs, Tony Stewart's #20 Pontiac won for the fourth time on the season. Jeremy Mayfield started from the pole.

25

Jimmy Florian, who ran out of Cleveland, OH, in the 1950s, was born in 1923. Florian ran 26 events 1950–54, capturing his lone pole in May 1950 at Canton, OH, and winning his lone race in Dayton, OH, that June.

Red Byron became the first NASCAR driver with two wins when he drove his Olds to victory at Martinsville, VA, in 1949 on a .5 mile dirt track. The 100-mile race was the sixth event in series history and the first sanctioned race run in the state of Virginia. Byron was the first Strictly Stock points champion.

Rex White's 12th career win came in the 1960 Old Dominion 500 at Martinsville. Glen Wood won his 10th career pole.

Fred Lorenzen's 24th career Grand National win came at Martinsville in the 1966 Old Dominion 500. Junior Johnson won the 46th pole of his career.

Cale Yarborough won for the third straight Martinsville race in the 1977 Old Dominion 500. It was his 49th career victory. Neil Bonnett again won the pole, his seventh. It was his final of nine wins in 1977, his second straight as Winston Cup Champion.

Ricky Rudd's second career victory came at Martinsville, VA, in the 1983 Goody's 500. Rudd won the pole for the previous two races at the track. Darrell Waltrip earned his 44th career pole start and finished third.

Darrell Waltrip captured his second win of the 1988 Winston Cup season in the Goody's 500 at Martinsville. It was his 73rd career Winston Cup victory. Rusty Wallace earned his second career top qualifying start.

The 1994 Goody's 500 at Martinsville was won by Rusty Wallace, his second straight win at the Virginia track. Ted Musgrave won his third career pole.

26

Marty Robbins was born Martin

David Robinson in Glendale, AZ, in 1925. Robbins served in the Navy in WWII and learned to play guitar. The country singer ran a total of 35 Grand National and Winston Cup races 1966–82 with six top-10 finishes. In his singing career, he placed 94 songs on the *Billboard* magazine country charts.

Herb Thomas started from the pole for the 33rd time and cruised to his 40th Grand National victory in 1954 at Langhorne Speedway in Pennsylvania.

Joe Nemechek was born in 1963 in Naples, FL. Nemechek began Winston Cup racing in 1993. In 1997 his younger brother John was killed in Las Vegas in a NASCAR Craftsman Truck race.

Jimmy Thompson died in 1964 at the age of 40. Thompson ran 46 NASCAR events 1949–62. In the inaugural Strictly Stock season, he ran two races, placing in the top 10 both times.

Junior Johnson's 50th career Grand National win came at Martinsville, VA, in the 1965 Old Dominion 500. Richard Petty won the pole, the 31st of his career, and finished second in the race.

Bobby Isaac won the 1971 Old Dominion 500 in his #71 Dodge. Isaac qualified first and won from the pole for the final of 20 times in his career. It was his 36th, and next to last, career win at NASCAR's top level. Isaac won four races and five poles in 1971 but finished 23rd in series points.

Ralph Earnhardt died in 1973 of a heart attack in North Carolina at the age of 45. Ralph, the father of Dale

Earnhardt Sr., raced out of Kannapolis, NC, to start 51 career Grand National events 1956–64. In his first race in Hickory, NC, in 1956, Earnhardt captured the pole and finished second. He was a renowned builder of race cars.

In the Old Dominion 500 at Martinsville, VA, Cale Yarborough captured his 39th career win. Darrell Waltrip won his fifth career pole and finished second.

Ernie Irvan won the 1993 Goody's 500 at Martinsville. Irvan, who started from the pole, won his second race of the season and eighth of his career. Irvin finished sixth in Winston Cup points in 1993.

Mark Martin won the 1999 MBNA Gold 400 at Dover Downs International Speedway in Delaware. Rusty Wallace qualified on the pole but finished 32nd. Tony Stewart was the runner-up for the second straight week.

27

Larry Shurter was born in 1917. Racing out of West Shokan, NY, Shurter ran five Grand National events in the 1950s with his debut in the February 1950 Beach & Road Course at Daytona Beach, FL, finishing 25th.

Johnny Mackison was born in Pennsylvania in 1935. He ran five Grand National races in 1957 and 11 in 1958 with five career top–10 finishes.

Dan Obrist was born in 1946. He raced out of Portland, OR. Obrist ran one Winston Cup race, a total of

seven laps in the 1995 Save Mart Supermarkets 300 at Sonoma, CA. He finished last, retiring after seven laps due to ignition problems.

Rex White won the 1959 Virginia Sweepstakes 500 at Martinsville for his seventh career victory on the Grand National circuit. Glen Wood qualified first and finished the race second.

In the 1964 Old Dominion 500 at Martinsville, Fred Lorenzen both started and finished first for the eighth time in his career. It was his 18th career victory.

Darrell Waltrip's 36th career win came from the pole in the 1981 Old Dominion 500 at Martinsville. It was the 11th of 24 times in his career that he both started and finished first. Waltrip recorded 12 wins in 1981 on his way to his first Winston Cup championship.

Darrell Waltrip won the 1987 Goody's 500 with a trip to victory lane at Martinsville. It was the only win of the season for DW. Geoff Bodine captured his 18th career pole.

Ricky Rudd won the 1998 NAPA AutoCare 500 at Martinsville Speedway (VA). Ernie Irvan won the pole and finished eighth while eventual season champion Jeff Gordon was the runner-up.

28

Larry Odo, born in 1922 and racing out of Chicago, IL, ran one race each in 1956 and 1959, winning a total of $250 as a Grand National driver. He debuted with a 19th-place finish in the 1956 Old Dominion 400 at Martinsville (VA) driving a Chevrolet.

Fred Bince was born in 1923. Bince raced out of Los Angeles to start nine career Grand National races. He raced as Fred Lee in 1951 and Sam Lamm in 1954 and 1956. He recorded two career top–10 finishes.

Paul Lewis was born in 1932. He started 114 career races between 1960 and 1968. He captured one pole (1965) and one win (1966) while finishing in the top 10 45 times in his career.

Announcer Jack Arute was born in 1950. Arute has worked on college football broadcasts, the Iditarod Sled Dog Race, and as a pit reporter for NASCAR and IROC.

Herb Thomas won his 13th career race in the 29th event of the 1952 Grand National season, driving his Hudson to victory in a 100-mile event at Wilson, NC, NASCAR's first appearance at this venue. Thomas also won the pole, the 12th of his career.

Ron Fellows was born in Mississauga, Ontario, Canada, in 1959. He first appeared on the Winston Cup scene in 1998 and ran mostly road courses through 2003, qualifying third and finishing seventh at Sears Point in 2003.

NASCAR's 1990 Rookie of the Year, Rob Moroso, was born in 1968. Racing out of Connecticut, Moroso was killed in a private vehicle highway crash in September 1990.

Richard Petty won his third straight Martinsville race in the 1969 Old Dominion 500. David Pearson, who won his 51st pole, finished second. It was Petty's 101st career win but he finished second to Pearson in the season points championship.

Dave Marcis won the 1975 Old Dominion 500 at Martinsville for his first NASCAR victory. Cale Yarborough captured his 30th career pole.

Dale Earnhardt Sr., who earned his first Winston Cup championship in 1980, won the Old Dominion 500 at Martinsville. Buddy Baker qualified for his 36th career pole and finished second.

Darrell Waltrip won the 1986 Holly Farms 400 at North Wilkesboro, his fifth win in six years in the fall event at the .625-mile track.

Ray Hendrick died in 1990 at the age of 61. Hendrick ran 17 career Winston Cup and Grand National races between 1956 and 1974. In 1968, he ran a career-high four events and finished in the top 10 in each race.

June "Glen" Cleveland, who raced out of McBean, GA, died in 1991. Cleveland ran nine Grand National races 1950–53 with two top–10 finishes. His best race was a fourth-place finish at the Hayloft Speedway in Augusta, GA, in 1952 in a race shortened due to rain.

Geoff Bodine's 12th career victory came at Martinsville in the 1992 Goody's 500. Kyle Petty earned his fifth career pole start and finished fourth.

Michael Waltrip's second and final win of the 2003 Winston Cup season came at Talladega in the EA Sports 500. Waltrip had won the Daytona 500 to start the season. Elliott Sadler won his second pole of the season.

29

Buck Baker won in Columbia, SC, on this date in 1956, his 23rd career Grand National victory.

Joe Eubanks won the only Grand National race of his career in 1958 in a 99-mile event at Hillsboro, NC.

Marvin Panch won the 1963 Wilkes 250 at North Wilkesboro, the only 250-mile length for the annual event which was later held as the Wilkes 400 until 1978.

Richard Petty won his second consecutive Wilkes 400 in 1968 at North Wilkesboro, NC.

Earl Ross' only career Winston Cup win came in the 1974 Old Dominion 500 at Martinsville, VA. Ross, who raced out of Alsa Craig, Ontario, Canada, started 26 career Winston Cup races, 21 in 1974 when he finished eighth overall in championship points. Richard Petty, who won his 114th pole, won the 1974 Winston Cup championship.

Harry Gant won the 1985 Holly Farms 400 in 1985, breaking Darrell Waltrip's string of four straight wins in the fall event at North Wilkesboro.

Dale Earnhardt Sr. won the Tyson Holly Farms 400 at North Wilkesboro for his fourth and final win of the 1991 Winston Cup campaign. Earnhardt Sr. earned his fifth of seven points championships that year.

Nathan "Smokey" Boutwell died in 1993. Racing out of Pelham, NH, Boutwell made two Grand National starts at Daytona, FL, in 1964, finishing 20th in the Daytona 500.

Ivan Baldwin died in 1996 at the age of 50. Baldwin raced out of Modesto, CA, to start six Winston Cup races between 1971 and 1975. He ran five races at Riverside and one at Ontario, CA, finishing 16th in the 1971 Winston Golden State 400 at Riverside.

Jeff Gordon won his third consecutive race, his tenth and final win of 1996. Gordon finished first in the Tyson Holly Farms 400 at North Wilkesboro. It was the final Winston Cup event at the .625-mile track, which hosted NASCAR racing since 1949.

Jeff Burton won the 1997 Hanes 500 at Martinsville Speedway. His brother Ward won the pole. Dale Earnhardt finished second for the second consecutive race.

Jeff Gordon's third and final win of the 2002 campaign came at the Kansas Speedway in the Banquet 400. Dale Earnhardt Jr. captured his second and final pole start of the year. Gordon won the 2001 Winston Cup championship while Tony Stewart led in points in 2002.

30

Fonty Flock won for the second straight week, his seventh victory of 1951, at Wilson, NC. Flock won the 100-mile event on a .5-mile dirt track in his Oldsmobile. It was the first sanctioned Grand National race of 12 run at the Wilson Fairgrounds in Wilson, NC.

Fonty Flock won for the second straight time at the Raleigh Speedway in 1955.

Fireball Roberts won at the Occoneechee Speedway in Hillsboro, NC, in 1956.

Richard Petty won his second consecutive North Wilkesboro race with a 1962 victory in the Wilkes 320.

Richard Petty won the 1970 Home State 200 at the North Carolina State Fairgrounds. It was the final of three Grand National races held at the half-mile dirt track in Raleigh between 1955 and 1970.

Richard Petty won the 1973 Old Dominion 500 at Martinsville for his 154th career victory. Cale Yarborough won the pole, his 25th, and finished second.

Al Holbert died at age 42 in a private plane crash. Racing out of Warrington, PA, Holbert had 19 Winston Cup starts 1976–79, with four career top–10 finishes. His best was 8th in the 1979 World 600 at Charlotte, NC.

Mark Martin won his third and final race of 1990 with a first-place finish in the Tyson Holly Farms 400 at North Wilkesboro.

Rob Moroso was killed in 1990 when his private vehicle collided with another car on his way home from dinner with his girlfriend. The other driver was also killed. His girlfriend survived. Moroso had just raced at North Wilkesboro and was posthumously named NASCAR Rookie of the Year.

In the inaugural race at the Kansas Speedway, Jeff Gordon won his sixth and final Winston Cup race of 2001 in the Protection One 400. Jason Leffler captured the pole. Ryan Newman finished second. Gordon went on to hold off Dale Jarrett for his fourth Winston Cup points championship.

OCTOBER

1

Clarence DeZalia, who raced out of Aberdeen, MD, in the late 1950s, was born in 1919. DeZalia started 58 Grand National races 1955–59, finishing 15th overall in points in 1958. He finished in the top–10 12 times.

Mel Larson, born in 1929, ran 47 top-level NASCAR races between 1955 and 1978. He earned two poles and finished in the top–10 14 times.

Henry Neil "Soapy" Castles, who raced out of Charlotte, NC, was born in 1934. Castles started 497 Grand National and Winston Cup races 1957–76. He was fourth in championship points in 1969 and fifth the following year. He recorded 178 top–10 finishes and led four career top-level NASCAR races.

John Krebs was born in 1950. Racing out of Roseville, CA, he ran 19 races at the Winston Cup level between 1982 and 1994. He led two laps in his career, both on the road course at Sonoma, CA, where he finished 38th in 1991's Banquet Frozen Foods 300.

Dick Linder captured his fourth pole, and won his third and final Grand National race of the 1950 NASCAR season in the 100-mile event at Vernon, NY. It was the second and final top-level NASCAR race at the track.

Rex White won his third straight North Wilkesboro race in the second annual Wilkes 200 in 1961. Lee Petty had won the previous three races at the North Carolina track.

Richard Petty won the 1967 Wilkes 400 at North Wilkesboro, NC, his eighth straight Grand National victory. It was the final of 27 wins on the season for Petty, who won his second of seven career points championships in 1967.

Richard Petty won the 1972 Wilkes 400 at North Wilkesboro, NC. It was the eighth and final win of the season for Petty, who captured his fourth of seven career Grand National/Winston Cup Championships.

Cale Yarborough won his third

Wilkes 400 in six years in 1978. It was the final Wilkes 400, replaced in 1979 by Holly Farms as a corporate sponsor. The race began in 1960 as the Wilkes 200.

Ernie Irvan finished sixth at North Wilkesboro in 1995, his first race since a near-fatal practice crash in August 1994 in Michigan. Mark Martin won the event, his 18th career checkered flag.

Tony Stewart captured the pole and rode to victory lane in the NAPA Autocare 500 at Martinsville Speedway. It was his second straight, and fifth overall, Winston Cup victory in 2000.

2

Paul Goldsmith was born in 1927. From 1956 to 1969 Goldsmith won nine competitions while running in 127 Grand National/Winston Cup races. He won four races in 1957 and holds the distinction of winning the final beach/road course race at the old Daytona track in 1958. He finished fifth overall in points in 1966.

Jack Bowsher was born in 1930. Bowsher made four Grand National starts, two each in 1966 and 1967. He raced out of Springfield, OH.

Roy Musten Trantham was born in 1941. He made five Grand National starts in 1968. Trantham raced out of Asheville, NC, to record one top–10 finish in his only season at NASCAR's top level.

Glen Ward was born in 1946. He ran one career Winston Cup event, racing out of Ashland, OR, to a 35th-place finish in the 1980 Los Angeles Times 500 at Ontario, CA.

Patriarch Lee Petty won his first of 54 career NASCAR races in 1949 at Heidelberg Speedway in Pittsburgh, PA, with an average speed of nearly 57.458 MPH. He won $1,500 for his effort. Al Bonnell qualified first. It was the first of four top-level NASCAR races held at the track between 1949 and 1960, the first sanctioned race in the state of Pennsylvania and the seventh official race of NASCAR's first season.

Randy Becker was born in 1952. Becker made two Winston Cup starts each at Riverside in 1982 and 1983. Racing out of Highland, CA, his best finish was 15th in his final event, the 1983 Winston Western 500.

Lee Raymond was born in 1954. Racing out of Dayton, OH, Raymond made his only Winston Cup start in 1989.

Rex White won the inaugural Wilkes 200 at North Wilkesboro in 1960, the first of three straight Grand National wins over two seasons for White at the North Carolina track. It was his sixth and final win of 1960, when he was the Grand National Champion and Most Popular Driver.

Dick Hutcherson captured the 1966 Wilkes 400 at North Wilkesboro, NC.

Darrell Waltrip won the 1977 Wilkes 400 at North Wilkesboro, NC.

Darrell Waltrip won his third straight Holly Farms 400 in 1983. It was his fifth straight win at North Wilkesboro.

Geoff Bodine won the 1994 Tyson/Holly Farms 400, his second

win in three years in the fall event at North Wilkesboro.

Banjo Matthews died in 1996 at the age of 64. Matthews, a native of Asheville, NC, ran 51 races 1952–63 with 13 top–10s and three poles. He finished fifth in his debut in the 1952 Southern 500 at Darlington, SC.

After qualifying to race in the previous 716 Winston Cup races, Darrell Waltrip was the 48th-fastest of 50 cars and failed to gain a provisional start in the 1997 GM/UAW Teamwork 500.

3

David Mote was born in 1940. Racing out of Siler City, NC, he started seven Grand National races in 1968. His best finish was in the 1968 Fonda 200 at Fonda, NY, where he came in 14th.

Herb Thomas captured his series-leading 27th career win in the only sanctioned race ever held in Bloomsburg, PA, in 1953 at the Columbia County Fairgrounds. Thomas, in his trademark Hudson, won the 100-mile event on the half-mile dirt track. Jim Paschal won his first career pole in a Dodge.

The 1965 Wilkes 400 at North Wilkesboro, NC, was the 21st and final win in the career of Junior Johnson.

Cale Yarborough won the Wilkes 400 in 1976, his second win in three years in the annual fall event at North Wilkesboro Speedway. It was his final of nine wins on the season, when he won his first of three straight Winston Cup season championships.

Darrell Waltrip won his second straight Holly Farms 400 in 1982 at North Wilkesboro.

Dale Earnhardt Sr. won his fourth race of 1986 with a victory in the Oakwood Homes 500 at Charlotte.

Rusty Wallace won the 1993 Holly Farms 400 at North Wilkesboro International for his eighth win of the Winston Cup season.

Jeff Gordon won the 1999 NAPA AutoCare 500 at Martinsville, VA. Joe Nemechek won the pole for the second time in 1999, but finished a disappointing 38th. It was Gordon's sixth win of the season. Earl Ross attended the race to commemorate the 25th anniversary of his only career Winston Cup victory in the Old Dominion 500. Ross was the Winston Cup Rookie of Year and finished eighth in points in 1974.

4

Leon Sales was born in 1923. Racing out of Winston Salem, NC, Sales started eight Grand National races 1950–52, with his only win at North Wilkesboro, NC, in September 1950, his rookie season.

Robert "Bob" Scott was born in 1928. Scott drove various cars in his career, racing out of Los Angeles, CA. He ran one Grand National race in 1950. He died in an Indy Car race at Darlington in July 1954.

Steve Pfeifer was born in 1938. He raced out of San Francisco, CA, making eight career NASCAR Winston Cup starts 1978–81.

Larry Manning was born in 1952

and raced out of Salisbury, NC. Manning started 71 races 1963–74 with 14 top–10 finishes, including an eighth-place in his debut in 1963 at Hillsboro, NC.

Herb Thomas won a sanctioned 100-mile NASCAR race for the second consecutive day in 1953 with a win on the half-mile dirt track in Wilson, NC. Thomas, who also took the pole, claimed his 27th career checkered flag and his 25th career pole.

Bobby Isaac took the checkered flag in the 1970 Wilkes 400 at North Wilkesboro, NC. It was his final of 11 wins of the season, when he won his only Grand National Championship.

Curtis Turner, the first president of the Charlotte Motor Speedway, died in a private plane crash in Pennsylvania in 1970. On Halloween 1965, he won the first 500 mile race at the North Carolina Motor Speedway. He ran 184 career Grand National races with 17 career wins.

Darrell Waltrip won the 1981 Holly Farms 400 at North Wilkesboro.

Terry Labonte won his only race of 1987 with a first-place finish in the Holly Farms 400 at North Wilkesboro.

Mark Martin won the 1998 UAW-GM Quality 500 at Charlotte Motor Speedway, his seventh win of the season. Derrike Cope, who finished 14th, earned his first career pole position start.

5

Julian Taylor "J.T." Putney was born in 1928. Putney ran out of Arden, NC, and started 125 Grand National races 1964–67, finishing 7th in points in 1965. He finished in the top–10 49 times in his career.

Donald Graham, who raced out of Rio Linda, CA, in the 1970s, was born in 1943. Graham started one race each 1977–79, ending with a 22nd-place finish in the 1979 Winston Western 500 at Riverside.

Lee Petty won in 1954 at the Southern States Fairgrounds in Charlotte, NC, the third sanctioned Grand National race held that season at the track.

Only one Grand National race was ever run at the Salisbury Super speedway in Salisbury, NC. Lee Petty captured the checkered flag in an Oldsmobile for the 1958 dirt-track event. Gober Sosebee qualified for the pole.

Richard Petty won the final of three sanctioned races held between 1962 and 1963 at the Tar Heel Speedway in Randleman, NC. The track was also referred to as the Kings Kountry Motor Speedway.

David Pearson won the 1968 Augusta 200 at the Augusta International Speedway in Georgia. It was his final of 16 wins in 1968, when Pearson won his second of three Grand National Championships.

David Pearson was victorious in the 1969 Wilkes 400 at North Wilkesboro, NC. It was his 11th and final win of the season, when he earned his third Grand National Championship.

Richard Petty won the 1975 National 500 at Charlotte Motor Speedway. He was named the Winston

Cup's most popular driver for the sixth of eighth times in his career that season.

Dale Earnhardt Sr. won the 1980 National 500 at Charlotte Motor Speedway, his first win at the North Carolina superspeedway. It was the fifth and final win of the season for Earnhardt Sr., who earned his first of seven Winston Cup Championships that year.

Geoff Bodine won the 1992 Tyson/Holly Farms 400 at North Wilkesboro.

Dale Jarrett won his sixth race of the 1997 Winston Cup season in the GM/UAW Teamwork 500 at the Charlotte Motor Speedway. Bobby Labonte finished second.

Ryan Newman's 8th win of 2003 came at the Kansas Speedway in the Banquet 400. Jimmie Johnson captured his second pole of the season.

6

Darrell Bryant was born in 1940. He started 18 top-level NASCAR events, ten Grand National races 1964–66 and eight Winston Cup races in 1976. He raced out of Thomasville, NC.

Tim Flock's 33rd career Grand National win came in Greenville, SC, at the Greenville-Pickens Speedway in 1955. Bob Welborn won his first of seven career pole positions.

Racing out of Waterloo, NY, Mike McLaughlin was born in 1956. McLaughlin's only Winston Cup starts were two races in 1994, at Loudon, NH, and Watkins Glen, NY.

McLaughlin ran over 300 Busch Series races through 2003, with six victories.

Bob Welborn's first of nine career Grand National wins came in the 1957 Sweepstakes 500 at Martinsville. In 183 career events, he managed 102 top–10 finishes.

David Pearson won the 1974 National 500 at Charlotte Motor Speedway, his second straight win at the track.

Cale Yarborough won the 1985 Miller High Life 500 at Charlotte.

Geoff Bodine won his only race of 1991 with a first-place finish in the Mello Yello 500 at Charlotte.

Terry Labonte won for the second time in 1996 with a trip to victory lane in the UAW-GM Quality 500 at Charlotte. Labonte earned his second Winston Cup Championship in 1996, 12 years after his first championship in 1984.

Dale Earnhardt Jr.'s second and final victory of 2002 came in the EA Sports 500 at Talladega, his second straight win at the superspeedway in Alabama. Jimmie Johnson captured his second straight pole at the track, his fifth and final top start of the year.

7

Duane Michael "Red" Duvall, who raced out of Hammond, IN, in the 1950s, was born in 1923. Duvall ran eight career Grand National events 1951–54 with four top–10 finishes.

Curtis Wade "Crawfish" Crider was born in 1930. Racing out of

Abbeyville, SC, Crawfish started 232 career Grand National races 1959–65, finishing fourth overall in Grand National points in 1964. He finished in the top–10 70 times in his career, 30 in 1964.

Harold Dunnaway, who raced out of Gastonia, NC, in the 1960s, was born in 1933. Dunnaway ran his lone Grand National event in 1966.

For the third consecutive week in 1951, the pole sitter won the race. This time, Herb Thomas claimed his sixth victory of the season in the 150-mile event at Hillsboro, NC, on a one-mile dirt track. It was the first career pole for the 1951 Grand National champion.

The Tennessee-Carolina Speedway in Newport, TN, a ½-mile dirt track, hosted its first of two Grand National events on this date in 1956. Fireball Roberts captured his sixth career win and Joe Eubanks started from his third and final career pole.

Mike Laws was born in 1957. Racing out of Orlando, FL, Laws started two Winston Cup races in 1986, his only experience at NASCAR's top level, finishing 24th in the Atlanta Journal 500.

Cale Yarborough drove his Chevrolet to victory in 1973 at Charlotte Motor Speedway in the National 500. It was the first Winston Cup event for Harry Gant, who finished 11th. He ran 473 more races in his 22-year career.

Cale Yarborough won the 1979 National 500 at Charlotte Motor Speedway.

Bill Elliott won the 1984 Miller High Life 500 at the Charlotte Motor Speedway.

Davey Allison won his second race of 1990, taking the checkered flag in the Mello Yello 500 at Charlotte.

Sterling Marlin won his second race of 2001 in the 28th event of the Winston Cup schedule with a victory at the Lowe's Motor Speedway in the UAW-GM Quality 500.

Jimmy Spencer qualified on the pole for the second of two times that season.

8

Worth McMillion was born in 1926. He ran 62 Grand National races in the 1960s with one top-five and a total of 18 top 10's in his career.

Ferrel Harris, who raced out of Pikeville, KY, in the 1970s and '80s, was born in 1940. Harris ran 41 career Winston Cup events 1975–82, with all five career top–10 finishes coming in 1978.

Bill Elliott was born in Cumming, GA, in 1955. Elliott began his Winston Cup career in 1976. In 1985 he won 11 races and claimed the first Winston Million. He was the 1988 Winston Cup Champion and Driver of the Year. His first win came at Riverside in November 1983. He was voted the most popular Winston Cup driver 1984–88, 1991–2000 and 2002.

Bobby Allison won his 38th career race, the ninth win of 1972, at the Charlotte Motor Speedway in the National 500.

William "Whitey" Gerkin died at

the age of 43 in 1973, one day after suffering critical injuries in a crash at the Illiana Speedway. Gerkin started five Grand National races 1960–67, leading two laps his final season.

Bobby Allison won his fourth race of 1978, the National 500, with a victory at Charlotte Motor Speedway for his 50th career NASCAR first place finish.

Ken Schrader won his only race of 1989 with a first-place finish in the All-Pro Auto Parts 500 at Charlotte Motor Speedway.

Mark Martin won the UAW-GM Quality 500 at Charlotte in 1995.

Bobby Labonte's #18 Pontiac rode to victory in the 2000 UAW-GM Quality 500 at the Lowe's Motor Speedway for his fourth win of the season. Jeff Gordon captured the pole. Labonte won the Winston Cup Championship that season.

mid–1950s with 26 top–10 finishes. He was eighth overall in points in 1952.

Speedy Thompson won the second 1955 race held at the Memphis-Arkansas Speedway in LeHi, AR.

Ned Jarrett won the fall race of 1964 at the Savannah Speedway in Georgia. Jarrett was the 1961 and 1965 Grand National Champion.

Benny Parsons won the 1977 National 500 at Charlotte Motor Speedway.

Richard Petty won the 1983 Miller High Life 500, ending the reign of the former National 500 which ran from 1961 to 1982 at the Charlotte Motor Speedway (it was run as the National 400 prior to 1966).

Rusty Wallace won his third race of the Winston Cup season with a victory in the 1988 Oakwood Homes 500 at Charlotte.

Dale Jarrett won the 1994 Mello Yello 500 at Charlotte.

9

Ernest Anthony "Ernie" Shaw was born in 1942. Shaw raced out of Winston-Salem, NC, to nine Grand National and Winston Cup starts 1969–79 with one top–10 finish.

Ron Esau, who raced out of Lakeside, CA, 1975–90, was born in 1954. Esau ran 17 career Winston Cup races and currently works as a salesman and fund raiser in Southern California.

Ray Duhigg, who raced out of Toledo, OH, died in a race at Salem, IN, in 1955 at the age of 26. Duhigg ran 54 Grand National races in the

10

Ralph Liguori was born in 1926. Liguori started 76 races 1951–56, finished in the top–10 30 times and was 10th overall in Grand National points in 1954.

Clyde Dagit was born in 1941. He raced out of Pekin, IL, to start one Winston Cup race each in 1974 and 1975. His career best was 15th in the 1975 Carolina 500 at Rockingham, NC.

Bill Scott was born in 1948. He raced out of San Bernardino, CA, to one Grand National start in the 1970 Falstaff 400 at Riverside, CA.

Buck Baker won the first NASCAR sanctioned race held in the state of Arkansas, at the Memphis-Arkansas Speedway in LeHi in 1954. It was the first of five races held at the track in the 1950s.

Bobby Allison won his ninth race of the 1971 NASCAR season at the Charlotte Motor Speedway in the National 500 for his 28th career victory.

Dale Earnhardt Jr. was born in Kannapolis, NC, in 1974. He was a 2000 NASCAR rookie. A third generation NASCAR driver, he is the son of Dale Sr. and grandson of Ralph. He debuted at the Winston Cup level in 1999 and won the 2004 Daytona 500, the location of his father's tragic death in 2001. Earnhardt Jr. notched nine wins and six pole starts through 2003.

Donnie Allison won the 1976 National 500 at Charlotte Motor Speedway.

Harry Gant won the 1982 National 500 at Charlotte Motor Speedway.

Neil Bonnett won the 1986 Nationwise 500 at Rockingham. It was his only win of the season, the 16th of his career.

Ernie Irvan won the 1993 Mello Yellow 500 at Charlotte Motor Speedway. His 154.537 mph average, in his third win of the season, set a track record.

11

Cyrus "Cy" Fairchild, who raced out of Saginaw, MI, in the 1960s, was born in 1936. Fairchild started one

Grand National race, logging a total of 45 miles in a Daytona 500 Qualifier in 1966 before being flagged.

James "Jimmy" Hensley Jr., who raced out of Ridgeway, VA, 1975–95, was born in 1945. Hensley ran 98 career Winston Cup races with a career highlight of capturing the pole for the 1989 Goody's 500 at Martinsville. He was the 1992 Winston Cup Rookie of the Year.

Speedy Thompson captured his second career win in 1953, less than a month after his first Grand National triumph. Thompson drove his Oldsmobile to victory on the .625-mile dirt track at North Wilkesboro, NC. Buck Baker started from the pole, the seventh of his career.

Lee Petty won his third career race at the Asheville-Weaverville Speedway in 1959. It was his 47th career victory.

Marvin Panch won the Wilkes 400 in 1964, the first 400-mile running of the annual event. Panch won the Wilkes 250 the previous year.

LeeRoy Yarbrough won the 1970 National 500 at Charlotte Motor Speedway. It was the final of 14 Grand National wins in Yarbrough's career.

Darrell Waltrip won the 1981 National 500 at Charlotte Motor Speedway. It was his 11th of 12 wins on the season, his first of three as Winston Cup Champion.

Bill Elliott won the 1987 Oakwood Homes 500 at Charlotte for his fourth win of the season.

Mark Martin won the 1992 Mello Yellow 500 at Charlotte.

Dale Jarrett won the 1998 Winston

500 at Talladega Superspeedway. Ken Schrader won the pole but finished 24th in his #33 Skoal Bandit Chevrolet. It was the third win of the season for Jarrett.

Jeff Gordon won for the second straight week, his seventh win of the season, with a first-place finish in the 1999 UAW-GM Quality 500 at Lowe's Motor Speedway in North Carolina. Bobby Labonte, who started on the pole, was the runner-up.

Tony Stewart's second win of the 2003 came at the Lowe's Motor Speedway at Charlotte in the UAW-GM Quality 500. Ryan Newman won his sixth pole of the season.

12

Lou Figaro, who raced out of Inglewood, CA, was born in 1917. Figaro ran 13 Grand National races in 1951 and won from the pole in June at Gardena, CA. He ran three races in 1954 and died after a crash at North Wilkesboro in October.

Ernest E. Gahan, who raced out of Dover, NH, in the 1960s, was born in 1926. Gahan started 11 Grand National races 1960–66, with one top–10 each in 1961 and 1962.

Ned Jarrett was born in Newton, NC, in 1932. Jarrett, the father of 2000 Winston Cup champion Dale Jarrett, went on to a successful broadcasting career after his racing days. Ned won the Grand National series twice, 1961 and 1965. He posted 14 race wins in 1964.

Neil Cole became the fourth straight person to win from the pole when he captured the first sanctioned NASCAR race held in the state of Connecticut. Cole drove his Oldsmobile to victory in the 100-mile event held at the .5-mile paved Thompson International Speedway for his first career Grand National victory.

Fonty Flock won his 11th career race in 1952 with a checkered-flag finish at the 150-mile contest at Hillsboro, NC. Flock, driving an Oldsmobile, averaged 73.489 mph, just over 2 mph slower than Bill Blair's qualifying speed. It was the first time in the NASCAR season that Olds captured both the pole and the event.

The Newberry Speedway, a ½-mile dirt track in Newberry, SC, hosted its lone Grand National event in 1957, won by Fireball Roberts for his 13th career checkered flag. Jack Smith won his second career pole.

Fireball Roberts won the 1958 Old Dominion 500 at Martinsville, his 20th career Grand National victory. Glen Wood captured his first of 14 career poles.

Donnie Allison won the 1969 National 500 at Charlotte Motor Speedway.

Darrell Waltrip's second career victory came in Richmond, VA, in the 1975 Capital City 500. Benny Parsons, the 1973 Winston Cup champion, won his fourth career pole.

Terry Labonte passed his brother Bobby in the final laps of the 1997 Diehard 500 at Talladega for his first victory of the season. Terry won the Winston Cup points championship in 1996.

13

Jack Lawrence, born in 1931 and racing out of Grand Rapids, MI, ran three Grand National races in the 1950s with a top–10 finish in his final event at Wilson, NC, in March 1958.

Fireball Roberts won at the Concord Speedway (NC) in 1957 for his 14th career Grand National victory. It was the only sanctioned top-level NASCAR event hosted by the track.

Junior Johnson won his second straight National 400 at Charlotte in 1963 for his 35th career victory.

Tony Roper died of injuries suffered in a crash on the 32nd lap of the Craftsman Truck Series 2000 O'Reilly 400 at Texas Motor Speedway the previous day.

Jamie McMurray's only win of 2002 came in the UAW-GM Quality 500 at the Lowe's Motor Speedway at Charlotte. The eventual points champion of the year, Tony Stewart, captured his third of four poles.

14

Johnny "Jack" Wynn was born in 1931. He started 21 races, all during the 1966 Grand National season. Racing out of Grand Rapids, MI, Wynn recorded five top–10 finishes.

Just two days after the 100-mile race in Thompson, CT, NASCAR sanctioned three official races on the same day in 1951. Tim Flock won the 100-mile event at Shippenville, PA, in his Oldsmobile. It was his 7th career victory and the only Grand Na-

tional race ever run at the Pine Grove Speedway.

Frank Mundy claimed his second win of the Grand National season at Martinsville, VA, in a 100-mile contest on a .5-mile dirt track. It was one of three official NASCAR events scheduled that day.

Marvin Burke captured the third NASCAR race scheduled for this date in 1951, this one held on a .625-mile dirt track at Oakland Stadium in Oakland, CA, the first Grand National race at that venue. Burke cruised his Mercury to victory lane in the 250-mile event. It was Burke's only career Grand National win.

Buck Baker won the final of 12 sanctioned NASCAR events held between 1949 and 1956 at the Charlotte Speedway. The track hosted the first-ever Strictly Stock event in 1949.

Junior Johnson won the 1962 National 400 at Charlotte.

Benny Parsons captured the 1979 Holly Farms 400 at North Wilkesboro, NC, the fall event previously known as the Wilkes 400.

Darrell Waltrip won his fourth straight Holly Farms 400 in 1984 at North Wilkesboro.

15

Gober Sosebee was born in 1915. Sosebee, who raced out of Atlanta, GA, ran 71 Strictly Stock and Grand National races 1949–59. He won two times, both in the state of Georgia, in June 1952 in Atlanta and April 1954 in Macon.

Chuck Stevenson was born in 1919. Racing out of Sidney, MT, Stevenson ran two Grand National races. His final race, in November 1955, was a victory in the inaugural 2.5-mile oiled dirt road race at Lancaster, CA, in November 1955, the third race of the 1956 season.

Announcer Chris Economaki was born in 1920 in Brooklyn, NY. Economaki was inducted into the Motorsports Hall of Fame in 1994 and is recognized as the "Dean of Motorsports Journalists."

Clyde Minter was born in 1921. Racing out of Martinsville, VA, he ran 42 Grand National races 1949–55 with 19 top–10 finishes. He ran two events in 1949, the first Strictly Stock season, with a fourth-place finish at Martinsville in his debut.

Johnny Lain Halford, who raced out of Spartanburg, SC, was born in 1930. Halford ran 41 Grand National and Winston Cup races 1969–78, with 25 starts in 1970 and a lone top–10 finish in 1972.

Charles "Red" Farmer, who raced out of Hialeah, FL, 1953–75, was born in 1932. Farmer made a total of 36 starts at the Grand National and Winston Cup level with three career top–10 finishes. He ran seven races in 1968, a career-high, leading one race for a lap.

Roland Wlodyka, born in 1938, ran 11 career Winston Cup events 1977–78. He raced out of Boston, MA, to finish 19th in the 1978 Daytona 500.

Herb Thomas captured his first NASCAR series checkered flag with a win at Martinsville, VA, in 1950, in one of two sanctioned races run on this date. Thomas won the 100-mile event in a Plymouth on a .5-mile dirt track. Fonty Flock was the top qualifier, the first of 32 poles of his career.

In one of two NASCAR races at the top level run on this day in 1950, Lloyd Moore won at Winchester, IN. It was the first circuit win for Moore and the second win for automaker Mercury. It was the only race run on the oiled dirt track.

Tim Flock's 34th career Grand National victory came in 1955 at the Columbia (SC) Speedway. Flock won his second of two points titles that season, ahead of Buck Baker.

Joe Weatherly won in 1961 at the Charlotte Motor Speedway in the second annual National 400.

In 1967 at Charlotte, NC, Buddy Baker notched his first career NASCAR Grand National victory in the National 500 at Charlotte.

Geoff Bodine won the 1989 Holly Farms 400 at North Wilkesboro for his only victory of the season.

The #3 Chevrolet of Dale Earnhardt Sr. rode to victory at the Winston 500 at Talladega in 2000 in the 30th Winston Cup race of the season. Joe Nemechek started from the pole. It was the final victory of Earnhardt's career.

Ricky Craven captured his first career NASCAR win in the 2001 Old Dominion 500 at Martinsville, his only win of the season. Todd Bodine won his third and final pole start of the year. Craven was the 1995 Rookie of the Year.

16

Bill Champion was born in 1921. He raced out of Norfolk, VA, to record 289 Grand National and Winston Cup starts 1951–76. He finished seventh in championship points in the Winston Cup's first official season of 1971. He finished in the top–10 in 39 races.

Budd Olsen was born in 1924 in Paulsboro, NJ. Olsen ran one race in 1949 and one in 1961 at the top level of NASCAR. He finished 12th in the fourth race of the inaugural Strictly Stock season, at Langhorne (PA) Speedway.

Lionel Johnson was born in 1928. He raced out of Unionville, VA, and started 15 races 1965–66 with two top–10 finishes his rookie season in eight starts, his best a ninth-place in the Capital City 300 at Atlantic Rural Fairgrounds in Richmond, VA.

Clem Proctor was born in 1928. Proctor ran nine Grand National races 1960–73, finishing with one top–10 (1961). He raced out of Compton, CA.

Bob Flock won his second race of 1949 with a victory in a 100-mile, .5 mile dirt-track event in North Wilkesboro, NC. It was the final event of the inaugural NASCAR season, known as Strictly Stock at the time.

Speedy Thompson's fourth career win came in 1955 at Martinsville, his second win of the season.

Norman Nelson's only career Grand National win came in 1955 at Las Vegas, NV at the one-mile dirt track of the Las Vegas Park Speedway, the only sanctioned event held at the track.

Speedy Thompson won the 1960 National 400 at the Charlotte Motor Speedway, the second Grand National race staged at the 1.5-mile paved oval.

LeeRoy Yarbrough won the 1966 National 500 at Charlotte, the first year the race was lengthened from its previous 400-mile format.

Rusty Wallace won his second straight race, his fourth of the 1988 Winston Cup season, with a win at North Wilkesboro in the Holly Farms 400.

Jimmie Lewallen died in 1995 at the age of 76. Lewallen started 142 events in NASCAR's first 12 seasons. He finished 8th overall in points in 1954 and 9th in 1953 and 1955, when he captured his only career pole at Columbia, SC.

17

Ed Livingston, of Folly Beach, SC, was born in 1935. Livingston started 47 races at NASCAR's highest level 1961–64 with two top–10 finishes. His career-best was a fourth-place finish in December 1963 at Jacksonville, FL.

Eugene "Gene" Hobby, who raced out of Henderson, NC, in the 1960s, was born in 1937. Hobby ran 35 Grand National events 1964–66 with five top–10 finishes.

Lee Petty won from the pole in 1954 at Martinsville, VA, the second of six times in his Grand National career that he both started and finished first. It was his 18th career win and third pole.

Harold Kite died at the age of 43 due to injuries suffered in a crash at the NASCAR race in Charlotte, NC, in 1961. Kite had won one career race in 1950.

Fred Lorenzen won his second straight National 400, and third straight race at Charlotte, with a 1965 checkered-flag finish.

Tommy Kendall was born in 1966 in LaCanada, CA. Kendall ran 14 Winston Cup races, no more than three in any season, 1987–98, with one top 10. He also drove in the IROC and Busch Series in the 1990s.

Bobby Isaac won at the Savannah Speedway in Georgia in 1969, his 18th career victory. Isaac was voted the Grand National circuit's most popular driver that season.

Richard Petty won for the third time in four races at Dover Downs, DE, with a win in the 1971 Delaware 500.

Darrell Waltrip won the 1982 Old Dominion 500 at Martinsville for his 50th career victory. Ricky Rudd qualified first for the fifth time in his career and finished second. For the second straight season, Waltrip won the Winston Cup championship for the second straight season, winning 12 races in both 1981 and 1982.

Jeff Gordon won the 1998 Pepsi 400 at Daytona International Speedway. Bobby Labonte won the pole in his #18 Interstate Batteries Pontiac and finished second. Gordon went on to close the season with his third Winston Cup Championship.

Dale Earnhardt Sr. won the 1999 Winston 500 at Talladega, AL. Joe Nemechek won the pole for the third time on the season, but finished 30th. It was Earnhardt Sr.'s third win of 1999.

18

Jim Paschal won his first career NASCAR race with a win in the 100-mile contest at the half-mile dirt track in Martinsville, VA. Driving a Dodge, Paschal broke a string of 15 races that had been won by either Hudson (11) or Oldsmobile (4). Fonty Flock claimed the pole position, the 24th of his career.

Lee Petty won at North Wilkesboro for the second straight time in 1959. Petty, the Grand National Champion for the second straight year, captured his tenth and final checkered flag of the season.

Fred Lorenzen won the 1964 National 400 at Charlotte, his 19th career checkered flag.

Richard Petty won the 1970 Old Dominion 500 at Martinsville, his 118th career triumph. Bobby Allison captured his 14th pole and finished second.

Hershel White died in 1996 at the age of 79. White raced out of Speedway City, IN, to start one Grand National race, finishing tenth in 1952 at Dayton (OH) Speedway.

19

Billy Myers was born in 1924. Myers ran 84 Grand National races 1951–58. He won twice, finished second six times and captured one pole in 1956, when he finished sixth in championship points.

Dave Mader was born in Alabama in 1930. Mader started six Grand National races in 1961, his only appearances at NASCAR's highest level.

Paul Dorrity, who raced out of Modesto, CA, in the 1960s and 1970s, was born in 1943. Dorrity started seven career top-level NASCAR races 1968–72.

Harold Miller was born in 1950. Racing out of Emerson, GA, Miller ran 14 Winston Cup races in the 1970s. He finished 34th in his debut, the 1975 Winston 500 at Talladega.

Junior Johnson won at North Wilkesboro in 1958, his second straight checkered flag at the .625-mile North Carolina track.

Bobby Isaac won the final NASCAR-sanctioned event at the Augusta International Speedway in 1969.

Cale Yarborough won the 1975 American 500 at Rockingham, NC. It was his second American 500 win (1970) and his second straight win at the North Carolina Motor Speedway.

Cale Yarborough won the 1980 American 500 at Rockingham, NC, his fourth win in the annual fall race at the North Carolina Motor Speedway.

Marshall Sargent died in 1990. Sargent, who raced out of Salinas, CA, ran 12 Grand National races 1957–64 with three top–10 finishes. His best was seventh place in his second race at Eureka, CA, in May 1957.

Jeff Gordon dominated the 2003 Subway 500 at Martinsville, VA, winning from the pole for his second victory of the Winston Cup season.

20

Bob Burdick was born in 1936. Burdick, who raced out of Omaha, NE, started 15 Grand National races 1959–62. He won two poles in 1959 and won his only top-level event in the 1961 Atlanta 500.

Jack Smith won at North Wilkesboro in the 1957 Wilkes 160, his fifth of 21 career checkered flag finishes.

Richard Petty swept both races during the only season the South Boston Speedway hosted two events, winning the second South Boston 400 of the season for his 27th career win. Jack Smith qualified on the pole for the 23rd of 24 times in his career, capturing one more top start before the end of 1963. Petty finished second in Grand National points for the second straight year and went on to his first championship in 1964.

Charlie Glotzbach's first of four wins at NASCAR's top level came in 1968 at Charlotte in the National 500.

David Pearson won his second consecutive American 500 in 1974 at Rockingham, NC.

Davey Allison won his fourth race of the 1991 Winston Cup season with a trip to victory lane in the AC Delco 400 at Rockingham. Allison won yet again the following week at Phoenix.

Ricky Rudd won his only race of 1996 in the 1996 AC Delco 400 at Rockingham.

Kurt Busch won his second of four 2002 Winston Cup events with a trip to victory lane in the Subway 500 at Martinsville. Ryan Newman won his fourth of six poles of the season.

21

Elar "Tubby" Gonzales, who raced out of Houston, TX, in the 1960s, was born in 1919. Gonzales started nine Grand National races 1961–62 with a career-best fourth-place finish in a race his rookie season.

Morgan Shepherd was born in 1941 in Ferguson, NC. Shepherd started his Winston Cup career in 1980 and notched four career wins and over 150 top–10 finishes. He won three of his four career races at Atlanta Motor Speedway, including his first victory in March 1986 and his last in March 1993. He raced out of Conover, NC.

Fonty Flock won a 125-mile race at North Wilkesboro, NC, in 1951. Flock averaged 67.791 mph on the .625-mile dirt track for his eighth victory of the Grand National season. Herb Thomas started at the pole but suffered radiator trouble.

David Pearson drove to victory lane in his Mercury at North Carolina Motor Speedway in the 1973 American 500.

Richard Petty won the 1979 American 500 at the North Carolina Motor Speedway in Rockingham, NC.

Bill Elliott captured the checkered flag at the 1984 Warner W. Hodgdon American 500 at Rockingham, NC. It was his third victory of the season and the fifth of his career. Geoff Bodine started at the pole.

Alan Kulwicki won his only race of the 1990 Winston Cup season with a first-place finish in the AC Delco 400 at Rockingham.

Dale Earnhardt Jr. won another restrictor plate race at Talladega in 2001. It was his third and final win of the season for Junior in the 30th event of the season. His father had died in the first race of the season at Daytona. Stacy Compton qualified first for the second time in his career.

22

Wayne Watercutter, born in 1944, ran five Winston Cup races 1979–80. He raced out of Sydney, OH, to a 12th-place finish in his debut in the 1979 Busch Nashville 420 at Nashville, TN.

Joe Weatherly's 12th career Grand National win came in the 1961 Southeastern 500 at Bristol, TN. Bobby Johns qualified first, his second and final career pole.

Bobby Allison captured his tenth win of 1972 with a victory at the North Carolina Motor Speedway in the American 500. It was his 39th career first place finish.

Cale Yarborough won the 1978 American 500 at Rockingham, NC. It was his second win in the annual fall race at the North Carolina Motor Speedway. It was his 10th and final win of 1978, his third straight season as Winston Cup Champion.

Mark Martin won his first career race, his only victory of 1989, with a first-place finish in the AC Delco 400 at Rockingham.

Mark Martin won the AC Delco 500 at Rockingham for his first career NASCAR win in 1989.

Ward Burton captured his first

career NASCAR win with a victory in the AC Delco 400 at Rockingham in 1995.

Dale Jarrett rode his #88 Ford to victory in the Pop Secret 400 at North Carolina Motor Speedway in 2000. It was his third win of the season. Jeremy Mayfield started from the pole.

23

Nofri Samuel "Nick" Fornoro was born in 1920. He raced out of Danbury, CT, to start one 1953 Grand National race with a top–10 finish and a $200 pay-off in his only top-level NASCAR appearance.

Buck Baker completed a sweep at North Wilkesboro in 1955 with a win in the second race of the season at the .625-mile track.

In 1956, in the second race held at the Cleveland County Fairgrounds in Shelby, NC, Buck Baker captured his 13th win of the season. In the race, Grand National pioneer Herb Thomas was seriously injured, suffering partial paralysis, in a crash that limited his career to only three more starts.

Speedy Thompson won his 20th career Grand National race at Richmond in 1960. Ned Jarrett won his second straight pole at the track and again finished third.

Donnie Allison won the 1977 American 500 at Rockingham, NC.

Rusty Wallace captured his third straight victory with a first-place finish in the AC Delco 500 at Rockingham. It was his fifth win of the 1988 season.

Innes Ireland died at age 63. Ireland, a native of Prestiegne Rads, Great Britain, finished in the top 10 in a qualifying race at Daytona and finished 27th in the 1967 Daytona 500.

Dale Earnhardt Sr. won the 1994 AC Delco 500 at Rockingham, NC, his second victory ever at the North Carolina Motor Speedway and his 63rd career Winston Cup win. Darrell Waltrip finished a Winston Cup race for the 40th consecutive event, ending his career best longevity streak. Earnhardt Sr. won for the final time in 1994, his seventh and final season as the Winston Cup Champion.

24

Jerry Titus was born in 1928. He started one Grand National event in 1968. Titus, who raced out of Tarzana, CA, managed just five laps and 14 miles in his debut.

Clayborne Bettie "C.B." Gwynn, who raced out of Marion, VA, was born in 1935. Gwynn ran one 1969 Grand National race, logging 194 miles as a top-level NASCAR driver.

Hershel McGriff's fourth and final NASCAR win came in 1954 at North Wilkesboro. McGriff won all four of his career races that year.

Tracy Leslie was born in 1957. Racing out of Mt. Clemens, MI, Leslie ran five Winston Cup events 1989–90. He debuted in the 1989 Coca-Cola 600 at Charlotte, NC.

Dave Blaney was born in 1962 in Hartford, OH. He was a 2000

NASCAR rookie, although he started one race in 1992 and five in 1999. Blaney, in this writer's home county of Mercer, PA, purchased and operated the Sharon Speedway, the site of one Grand National race in 1954. In seven Winston Cup seasons, Blaney has started 149 events with 17 top 10s and one pole start.

Dick Hutcherson won at the Occoneechee Speedway in Hillsboro, NC, in 1965.

Richard Petty won the 1971 American 500 at Rockingham, his 19th Winston Cup victory of the season. Petty won 21 races in 1971 on his way to his third Winston Cup championship.

Richard Petty won the 1976 American 500 at Rockingham, NC, his second of three straight wins at the North Carolina Motor Speedway.

Rusty Wallace won the 1993 AC Delco 500 at North Carolina Motor Speedway in Rockingham. It was his second win in the last three Winston Cup events and ninth victory of the season.

Jeff Burton won his sixth race of the season with a checkered flag finish in the 1999 Pop-Secret Microwave Popcorn 400 at Rockingham, NC. Mark Martin won the pole and finished sixth.

25

Lou Figaro died at the age of 37, one day after a serious crash at North Wilkesboro, NC. Figaro ran 16 career Grand National races with a win from the pole at Gardena, CA, in June 1951.

Jack Smith won at the Concord Speedway in 1959, his second win at the North Carolina track.

Ward Burton was born in 1961 in Danville, VA. He began his NASCAR career in 1994. His younger brother Jeff also raced in the Winston Cup Series.

In the first of two Grand National races held at the Harris Speedway in North Carolina, Richard Petty captured the 1964 checkered flag and the $1000 first-prize. It was his final of eight wins in 1964, when he earned his first of seven Grand National/Winston Cup Championships.

Eddie Gray died of a heart attack in 1969. Gray, who had suffered a heart ailment in a Sportsman race at Riverside in January, was 49. Gray started 22 Grand National races 1957–66 with four wins. His first victory occurred in the 1958 Crown America 500 at Riverside. Gray, who raced out of Gardena, won all four of his top-level victories in California.

Johnny Mantz died at the age of 54 in an automobile crash. Mantz won the first Southern 500 in Darlington in 1950, his only Grand National victory in 12 starts in the 1950s.

Darrell Waltrip won the 1985 Nationwise 500 at North Carolina Motor Speedway. The race was a "corporate replacement" for the old Carolina 500 that had been run annually in the fall since 1967. It was his third and final win of the season, when he won his third and final Winston Cup Championship.

Bill Elliott won his second straight race and his fifth of the season at the 1987 AC Delco 500 at Rockingham.

Kyle Petty won the 1992 AC Delco 500 at Rockingham, NC, for his 6th career Winston Cup win, his second victory of the season.

Rusty Wallace won the 1998 Dura Lube/K Mart 500 at Phoenix International Raceway. Ken Schrader won the pole and finished 22nd, his third career top start.

26

Jimmy Pardue was born in 1930 in North Carolina. Pardue ran 217 races 1955–64, before he was killed in a crash during a tire test at Charlotte. Pardue won two career Grand National races and finished in the top–10 88 other times. He finished fifth in championship points in his final season.

Rick O'Dell was born in 1948 in Canada. He raced out of Victoria, British Columbia. O'Dell started one Winston Cup race, finishing 16th in the 1981 Warner W. Hodgdon 400 at Riverside, CA.

Herb Thomas won his second straight race in 1952 with a first-place finish in the 125-mile event held at North Wilkesboro, NC. Thomas, driving a Hudson, took the pole on the .625-mile dirt track. He won his seventh race of the Grand National season with an average speed of 67.044 mph. It was the 100th official NASCAR event.

Sammy Swindell was born in 1955. Swindell started one Winston Cup race each in 1985 and 1991, running out of Bartlett, TN. He finished a career-best 30th in his debut, the 1985 Atlanta Journal 500.

Junior Johnson won in 1958 at Lakewood Speedway in Atlanta, GA. Johnson won six races in 1958 and finished eighth in Grand National points.

LeeRoy Yarbrough won the 1969 American 500 at Rockingham, NC.

Jeff Gordon won for the second straight race in 2003 with a victory in the Bass Pro Shops MBNA 500 at the Atlanta Motor Speedway. Ryan Newman started on the pole for the seventh time of the season.

27

Richard Brickhouse was born in 1939. Racing out of Rocky Point, NC, Brickhouse ran 39 career Grand National and Winston Cup races with his only win coming in 1969 at the inaugural race at Talladega, a race boycotted by many drivers due to safety concerns. He managed 12 additional top–10 finishes.

Richard "Dick" Trickle was born in 1941 in Wisconsin Rapids, WI. Trickle began in the Winston Cup Series in 1970, but raced only 16 races at that level until 1989, when he became a regular and was voted Rookie of the Year at the age of 48. His lone pole position came in the 1990 Budweiser 500 at Dover.

Kevin Terris was born in 1944. He ran 11 career Grand National and Winston Cup races 1970–84. Running out of Hermosa Beach, CA, Terris notched three top–10 finishes.

Buck Baker won at the Greensboro Agricultural Fairgrounds in 1957. It was his final of ten wins that season, when he earned his second consecutive Grand National Championship.

Joe Weatherly won his 25th and final career Grand Nation event in 1963, his second win at the Occoneechee Speedway in Hillsboro, NC. Weatherly was the Grand National Champion 1962–63, but died in January 1964 at Riverside, CA.

Richard Petty won the 1968 American 500 at Rockingham. Petty was voted the circuit's most popular driver for the third time in 1968.

Bobby Hamilton won the next to last race of the 1996 Winston Cup season with a trip to victory lane in the Dura Lube 500 at Phoenix, edging Terry Labonte. It marked the only win of the season by a Pontiac and the first of Hamilton's career. He was the 1991 Winston Cup Rookie of the Year.

Bobby Hamilton won his second career Winston Cup race in 1997 at Rockingham with a first-place finish in the AC Delco 400. Dale Jarrett finished second in the race, held on Monday due to a rainout on Sunday.

Winston Cup champion Tony Stewart qualified on the pole for the final of three times on the 2002 season, but Kurt Busch captured the checkered flag for his third win in the Bass Pro Shops MBNA 500 at the Atlanta Motor Speedway.

28

Walter Hansgen, who raced out of Westfield, NJ, in the 1960s, was born in 1919. Hansgen started two Grand National races in 1964, finishing third in each event. He ran one race the following season and finished in the top 10. He died in 1966 of injuries suffered practicing for the 24-hour Le Mans race.

Charlie Roberts was born in 1940. Roberts started 75 races 1970–74, driving out of Anniston, AL. Roberts finished 16th overall in Winston Cup points in 1972.

Joe Ruttman was born in 1944. Ruttman, who raced out of Upland, CA, ran 218 career Grand National and Winston Cup races 1963–96, finishing with 60 top–10 finishes. He never won a top-level NASCAR race, but won three poles, his first in Dover, DE, in May 1983.

Danny Weinberg captured his only career Grand National win in 1951 in a 100-mile event on the .5-mile dirt track at Marchbanks Speedway in Hanford, CA. The win was the second career victory for manufacturer Studebaker. It was the first race run at the California track.

Jack Smith won his first career NASCAR race in the 1956 Mixed 400 at Martinsville Speedway. Smith won 21 races in 264 starts in his Grand National career.

Junior Johnson won his 27th career race in 1961 at the Greenville-Pickens Speedway in South Carolina.

Rex White won the 1962 Dixie 400 at Atlanta Motor Speedway, his 28th and final career win. White won the 1960 Grand National Championship.

Darel Dieringer died in 1989 at the age of 63. Dieringer raced 12 Winston Cup seasons between 1957 and 1975. His final win came in 1967 at North Wilkesboro.

Jeff Burton won for the second Phoenix International Raceway event in 2001 in the 31st race of the Winston Cup schedule, the Dura-Lube 500. The wins were the only two on the season for Burton. Casey Atwood earned his only pole start of the season.

29

Lee Petty won the final event of the 1950 NASCAR season with a first-place finish in the 200-mile event at Hillsboro, NC. It was Petty's second career win, with one victory in each of NASCAR's first two campaigns. Fonty Flock won the pole, the first driver to qualify in excess of 80 mph on the dirt track at the Occoneechee Speedway.

Herb Thomas won at Martinsville, VA, in his Hudson in 1952, averaging 47.556 mph. It was the 14th career win for Thomas. Perk Brown recorded the only pole position start of his 28-race career, also driving a Hudson, for the 100-mile event on a .5-mile dirt track.

Joe Weatherly won at the Occoneechee Speedway in 1961. It was his first of two career wins at the Hillsboro, NC, track, which eventually hosted a memorial race in his honor in 1965 and 1966.

Bobby Allison won his 8th career NASCAR race in the 1967 American 500 at North Carolina Motor Speedway in 1967. It was his first win in a Ford and his fifth victory of the season.

Ricky Rudd won the 1995 Dura-Lube 500 at Phoenix.

30

In the last race of the 1955 season, Tim Flock won at the Occoneechee Speedway in Hillsboro, NC. Flock, who finished 35th in points in 1954, captured his second Grand National championship in 1955, over 1500 points ahead of runner-up Buck Baker.

Bobby Johns won the inaugural Atlanta 500 in the second sanctioned Grand National race held at the Atlanta Motor Speedway in 1960. It was his first of two career Grand National wins.

Fred Lorenzen won the 1966 American 500 at Rockingham, NC, for his 25th career Grand National win.

Terry Labonte won the 1983 Warner W. Hodgdon American 500 at Rockingham, NC. It was his second career victory.

Terry Labonte won the 1994 Slick 50 500 at Phoenix.

31

Tom Bigelow was born in 1939. Bigelow raced out of Winchester, IN, to make one Winston Cup start, in the 1986 Atlanta Journal 500.

Elliott Forbes-Robinson, who drove out of La Crescenta, CA, in the 1970s and '80s, was born in 1943. Forbes-Robinson started 22 Winston Cup races 1977–84 with his best season coming in 1981 when he ran 11 events and captured his only three top-10s.

Tony Bettenhausen Jr. was born in

1950. Bettenhausen made 33 Winston Cup starts between 1973 and 1982 but was better known as an Indy car driver.

In the first race at the North Carolina Motor Speedway in Rockingham, NC, in 1965, Curtis Turner captured the American 500, an annual event hosted until 1981, replaced in 1985 by the Nationwise 500. It was Turner's final career win.

Darrell Waltrip won his second straight fall race at Rockingham with a victory in the 1982 Warner W. Hodgdon American 500. It was the first time the fall race ran with a corporate sponsor.

Mark Martin won the 1993 Slick 50 500 at Phoenix International Raceway.

NOVEMBER

1

Ken Miles was born in 1963. Racing out of Hollywood, CA, he ran one Grand National race in 1963. He finished 11th in the Golden State 400 at Riverside, CA. He died testing a Ford at Riverside, CA, in 1966.

Buck Baker won the final sanctioned Grand National race of 1953 with a 100-mile win at the one-mile dirt track in Atlanta, GA. Baker, in his Oldsmobile, won for the fifth time of his career. Tim Flock won his 14th career pole position.

Darel Dieringer won the 1964 Jaycee 300 at the Augusta International Speedway in Georgia, the 61st points race of the season.

Gene "Stick" Elliott died in 1980 at the age of 46. Elliott started 93 Grand National and Winston Cup races 1962–71 with a career-best second place finish in a 1965 event at Greenville-Pickens Speedway (SC).

Darrell Waltrip won the 1981 American 500, his second straight win at the Rockingham, NC, track. It was the 12th and final win of the season for Waltrip, who won his first Winston Cup Championship.

Davey Allison won the 1992 Pyroil 500 at Phoenix over Mark Martin in the next-to-last event of the Winston Cup season. Allison maintained his points lead over Alan Kulwicki.

Clyde Lynn died in 1996 at the age of 60. Lynn was 4th in overall points in 1968, when he started 49 of his 165 career races 1965–76. He finished in the top–10 73 times.

Jeff Gordon won his 12th race of the season with a victory at Rockingham in the 1998 AC Delco 400. Gordon went on to win the final race of the season and capture the Winston Cup championship for the third time in four years. Mark Martin won the pole and finished fourth. Gordon earned his third Winston Cup Championship in 1998.

2

Peter Frazee, who raced out of Rahway, NJ, in the 1950s, was born in 1926. He started two 1958 Grand National races and won a total of $310 at NASCAR's top level.

Donald "Dutch" Hoag, who raced out of Penn Yan, NY, in the 1950s, was born in 1926. Hoag started four career Grand National races with a lone top–10 in two events entered in 1955.

Harry Jefferson was born in 1946. Jefferson started 12 Winston Cup races 1973–77 with three career top–10 finishes. His best was a seventh-place finish in the 1974 National 500 at Charlotte (NC) Motor Speedway.

Larry Pearson was born in 1953. Racing out of Spartanburg, SC, Pearson ran 57 career Winston Cup races 1986–91 with three top–10 finishes. He tied a career-best with a sixth-place finish in the 1987 Oakwood Homes 500 at Charlotte.

At the Peach State Speedway, aka Jeffco Speedway, in Jefferson GA, Bobby Isaac won the 1969 Jeffco 200. It was the final of two annual Grand National events run at the track.

Richard Petty swept the Bristol events in 1975, winning the fall race, the Volunteer 500. It was his 177th career win. Cale Yarborough qualified for his 31st pole start. It was the final of 13 races Petty won in 1975 on his way to his sixth of seven points championships.

Cale Yarborough won the 1980 Atlanta Journal 500 at Atlanta Motor Speedway.

Dale Earnhardt Sr. won his fifth and final race of 1986 with a victory in the Atlanta Journal 500. Earnhardt Sr. earned his second of seven Winston Cup Championships that season.

Bill Blair died in 1995 at the age of 84. Blair was a NASCAR pioneer, finishing fourth in points during the first Strictly Stock season of 1949. He won three career races in 123 starts and qualified on the pole once, in 1952 in Hillsboro, NC.

Dale Jarrett won his seventh race of 1997 with a victory in the Dura-Lube 500 at Phoenix International Raceway. It marked a career-high for wins in a season for Jarrett. Rusty Wallace finished second.

Dale Earnhardt Jr. won his second and final race of the 2003 season with a checkered flag finish in the Checker Auto Parts 500 at Phoenix. Ryan Newman won his second consecutive pole, his eighth of the year.

3

Dexter L. Gainey, who raced out of Taylors, SC, in the 1960s, was born in 1930. Gainey made two Grand National starts in 1968 for his only appearances at NASCAR's top level.

Greg Sacks was born in 1952. Racing out of Mattituck, NY, Sacks was a NASCAR regular in the 1980s and 1990s with one career win, in the 1985 Firecracker 400 at Daytona. He was a driver and consultant for the movie *Days of Thunder*.

Rex White's first Grand National win came in 1957 in Fayetteville, NC, in the first sanctioned event at the Champion Speedway, a .333-mile paved track that hosted a total of four races 1957–58. This was the first race of the 1958 points season. White won the 1960 Grand National Championship.

Trevor Boys was born in 1957. Racing out of Alsa Craig, Ontario, Canada, Boys made 102 Winston Cup starts 1982–94 and finished 17th in Winston Cup points in 1984. He led 11 races in his career and had one top–10 finish each in 1983 and 1984.

Derrike Cope was born in 1958 in San Diego, CA. Cope began his Winston Cup career in 1982 and won the 1990 Daytona 500. He also won in 1990 at Dover Downs.

Darel Dieringer won the Golden State 400 at Riverside International Raceway in 1963 in the fourth NASCAR event held at the track. It was the first of seven career wins for Dieringer, 1966's most popular Grand National driver.

In the first of two NASCAR races held at the Jeffco Speedway, a half-mile paved track in Jefferson, GA, Cale Yarborough won the 1968 Peach State 200 over Richard Petty.

Bill Elliott won the 1985 Atlanta Journal 500 at Atlanta Motor Speedway, his second straight win at the Hampton, GA track.

Davey Allison won the 1991 Pyroil Chemicals 500 at Phoenix for his second consecutive victory and fifth of the Winston Cup season.

Johnny Benson's first career victory, and only win of 2002, came at the North Carolina Motor Speedway in the Pop Secret Microwave Popcorn 400. Ryan Newman won his fifth of six pole position starts of the Winston Cup season. Benson was the 1996 Winston Cup Rookie of the Year.

4

Banks Simpson was born in 1916. Simpson raced out of Concord, NC, to start seven Grand National races in 1955, his only season at NASCAR's top level.

Mike James, racing out of Medford, OR, was born in 1941. He started five top-level NASCAR races in the early 1970s, all at Riverside, CA, or Ontario, CA. He finished 18th in his last race, the 1974 Tuborg 400 at Riverside.

Brian Ross was born in 1944. Ross, racing out of Ballston Spa, NY, ran one Winston Cup race each in 1990 and 1991. He finished 27th in his debut in the 1990 AC Spark Plug 500 at Pocono, PA.

John McFadden was born in 1951. Racing out of Forrest City, NC, McFadden ran 11 Winston Cup races between 1982 and 1992 and finished 24th in his debut at Bristol, TN, in the 1982 Valleydale 500.

Herb Thomas won his seventh race of 1951, and also took the pole, in the first sanctioned race held in Jacksonville, FL. Thomas drove his Hudson to an average speed of 53.412 mph in the 100-mile dirt track event at Jacksonville Speedway Park on his way to the Grand National championship that season.

Jim Pascal won the opening race of the 1963 NASCAR Grand National season in 1962 at Birmingham International Raceway, Alabama.

Neil Bonnett won the 1979 Dixie 500 at Atlanta International Raceway. It was the final running of the annual race. The fall race was renamed the Atlanta Journal 500 the following year.

Dale Earnhardt Sr. won his ninth and final race of 1990 in the Checker 500 at Phoenix. Earnhardt Sr. won his fourth Winston Cup Championship that season.

Joe Nemechek won his first career Winston Cup race on this date in 2001 at Rockingham in the Pop Secret 400 at North Carolina Speedway. Kenny Wallace captured the pole, his only top start of the season.

5

Harold Paul Wensink was born in 1929. He ran one Grand National race in 1952, racing out of Deshler, OH, to a 12th-place finish at Playland Park Speedway in South Bend, IN, in his only event.

Jim Reich was born in 1942. Racing out of Turlock, CA, Reich started two Winston Cup races in 1982, his only career appearances at NASCAR's highest level.

Everett Elton Sawyer was born in 1959. Sawyer, racing out of Chesapeake, VA, began his Winston Cup career in 1995 when he started 20 events followed by nine the following season to conclude his top-level NASCAR experience. He finished 27th in the 1996 Daytona 500.

Douglas George, who raced out of Atwater, CA, was born in 1960. George started two Winston Cup races in 1995, finishing 31st in the Save Mart Supermarkets 300 at Sonoma, CA.

Jack Smith won at the Concord Speedway (NC) in 1961, his third win at the half-mile dirt North Carolina track and 17th career NASCAR victory.

Bobby Allison won his 9th career NASCAR race at Asheville-Weaverville Speedway in the 1967 Western North Carolina 500. It was his 6th victory of the season and his second in a row.

Donnie Allison won the 1978 Dixie 500 at Atlanta Motor Speedway, his second straight win at the track.

Bill Elliott won his third and final race of 1989 with a first-place finish in the Autoworks 500 at Phoenix.

Dick Goode died in 1992 at the age of 65. Goode started two Grand National races, finishing tenth in a Daytona qualifying race then finishing 37th in the 1963 Daytona 500.

Jeff Burton's #99 Ford won the Dura Lube 500 at Phoenix International Raceway in 2000. It was the fourth win of the season for Burton. Rusty Wallace captured the pole.

6

Bobby Courtwright was born in 1923. He started six Grand National races 1950–54. Racing out of Butler, NJ, Courtwright managed two top–10 finishes.

Steve Moore was born in 1958. Racing out of Carrollton, GA, Moore ran 18 Winston Cup races 1977–88. He finished 19th in his debut in the 1977 Talladega 500.

Joe Weatherly won the first race of the 1961 Grand National season with a 1960 win at the Southern States Fairgrounds. It was the final NASCAR-sanctioned race at the half-mile dirt track, which hosted 17 Grand National events between 1954 and 1960. It was replaced by the Charlotte Motor Speedway, a paved superspeedway that opened in June 1960.

Darrell Waltrip won the 1977 Dixie 500 at Atlanta Motor Speedway, his first win at the Hampton, GA, track.

Neil Bonnett won the 1983 Atlanta Journal 500 at Atlanta Motor Speedway, his second win in the annual event that began in 1980 and was previously known as the Dixie 500.

Alan Kulwicki captured his first career win in 1988 with a first-place finish in the Checker 500 at the Phoenix International Raceway. It was the next to last race of the Winston Cup season and the first NASCAR race in Arizona in 28 years, inaugurating the Phoenix raceway. Kulwicki celebrated his first Winston Cup victory with a backwards "Polish Victory Lap." He was the 1986 Rookie of the Year.

Bill Cheesbourg, who raced out of Tucson, AZ, died in 1995 at the age of 68. Cheesbourg finished 13th in his only Grand National race, the 1951 Poor Man's 500 at Canfield, OH.

7

Dick May was born in New York State in 1930. May started 185 races 1970–85 with eight top–10 finishes. He was 15th in Winston Cup points in 1978.

David Watson was born in 1945. Watson ran one Winston Cup race in 1978 and four in 1979, when he finished with one top 10 and seven laps led. He raced out of Milton, WI.

In the first race of the 1955 season points series, held in 1954, Lee Petty won the final of two Grand National races held at the Tri-City Speedway in High Point, NC.

Ned Jarrett won his final of 50 NASCAR races in 1965 at the Dog Track Speedway in the one and only Tidewater 300 at Moyock, NC. Jarrett won the from the pole and retired after winning his second Grand National points championship.

Bobby Allison won his tenth race of 1971 at the Middle Georgia Raceway. It was his 29th career victory and the final NASCAR event at the Macon, GA, track, which hosted nine Grand National events 1966–71.

Dave Marcis won the 1976 Dixie 500 at Atlanta Motor Speedway. Bobby Allison won his 73rd career NASCAR race in 1982 at Atlanta International Raceway in the Atlanta Journal 500. It was his eighth win of the season.

Tony Stewart won his second career race in 1999 at Phoenix International Raceway in the Checker Auto Parts/Dura Lube 500. John Andretti captured the pole and finished eighth. Mark Martin was the runner-up.

8

Erick Erickson, who raced out of Lancaster, CA, in the 1950s, was born in 1916. Erickson ran 25 career Grand National events with ten career top–10 finishes.

Joe Mihalic was born in Pittsburgh, PA, in 1926. He started 38 Winston Cup races in the 1970s with two top–10 finishes. He debuted in the 1974 Daytona 500 with a 37th-place finish. His best finish was a seventh-place in the 1974 Southeastern 500 at Bristol (TN).

Jack Smith won in 1959 at the Southern States Fairgrounds in Charlotte, NC.

Ned Jarrett won the final of two sanctioned races held at the Onslow (Jacksonville) Speedway in 1964. The half-mile dirt track also hosted an event in 1957. It was his final of 14 wins that year. The race was the 62nd sanctioned Grand National event of the season, the longest in NASCAR history.

Richard Petty won the 1970 Georgia 500 at Middle Georgia Raceway in Macon, GA.

Neil Bonnett won the 1981 Atlanta Journal 500 at Atlanta Motor Speedway.

Rusty Wallace won his second race of 1987 in the Winston Western 500 at California Speedway.

Jim Fitzgerald died in 1987 at the age of 65 in a road race in Florida. Fitzgerald raced out of Pittsburgh, PA, to start one Winston Cup race each 1986–87.

Norm Nelson died in 1988 at the age of 65. Nelson won one (Las Vegas) of two races he ran in his rookie season of 1955. He started five career races, two in 1955 and one each 1966–68.

Jeff Gordon went out in style in 1998, winning his 13th race of the season at Atlanta in the NAPA 500, clinching his third career Winston Cup point championship. Kenny Irwin Jr. finished 16th after winning the pole.

9

Al Straub was born in 1940. Straub raced out of Louisville, KY, to make one Grand National (1969) and one Winston Cup (1971) start. He finished 30th in his finale, the 1971 West Virginia 500 at Ona, WV.

Don Satterfield was born in 1953. Satterfield, who raced out of Spartanburg, SC, ran one Winston Cup event in 1981 and three in 1983.

Rick Carelli was born in 1955. Carelli raced out of Arvada, CO, to make nine Winston Cup starts 1992–94. He finished a career-best 21st in both the Slick 50 500 and the Save Mart Supermarkets 300K in 1993.

William France, after finalizing an agreement to lease land in Daytona Beach, FL, in 1957, announced plans for a "500-mile national championship" race on a new paved speedway to be constructed to replace the Beach & Road Course.

Bob Welborn won in 1958 at the Champion Speedway in Fayetteville, NC, the final of four Grand National races held at the .333-mile paved track. It was his second straight win at that venue.

Bobby Allison won his 16th career NASCAR race in 1969 at the Middle Georgia Raceway in a Dodge.

Buddy Baker won the 1975 Dixie 500 at Atlanta Motor Speedway.

Bill Elliott's only win of the 2003 Winston Cup season came on this date at Rockingham in the Pop Secret Microwave Popcorn 400. Ryan Newman qualified first for the third straight week, the ninth time of the season.

10

Ralph Sheeler was born in 1910. Sheeler raced out of Paterson, NJ, to start three Grand National races in 1953. He debuted in July at the Monroe County Fairgrounds in Rochester, NY, with a career-best 12th-place finish.

Charles Dyer, who raced out of North Bergen, NJ, in the 1950s, was born in 1917. Dyer made three Grand National starts in 1955 with two top–10 finishes.

Frank Brantley was born in 1932 and raced out of Savannah, GA. Brantley made three Grand National starts, two in 1962 and one in 1964.

Ned Jarrett's 23rd career win came at the Concord Speedway in North Carolina in 1963.

Bobby Labonte won the final race of 1996 at Atlanta.

Matt Kenseth captured his fifth and final checkered flag of the 2002

Winston Cup season in the Checker Auto Parts 500 at Phoenix International Raceway. Ryan Newman won his second straight pole start, his third in four weeks and sixth of the season.

11

Buck Peralta was born in 1934. Peralta finished 11th in the 1974 Tuborg 400 at Riverside, CA, his only Winston Cup exposure. He raced out of Lake Oswego, OR.

Sam McQuagg, born in 1937, ran 62 races between 1962 and 1974 with one win, a 1966 victory in the Firecracker 400 at Daytona. He was the 1965 Grand National Rookie of the Year.

James Sears was born in 1940. Sears, who raced out of Rockingham, NC, ran six Grand National and Winston Cup Events 1967–71 with two top–10 finishes. His career-best was seventh in the 1970 Columbia 200 at Columbia, SC. He was killed in a race at the Starlite Speedway in 1973.

Alvah R. "Al" Holbert, who raced out of Warrington, PA, in the 1970s, was born in 1946. Holbert ran 19 Winston Cup races 1976–79 with four top–10 finishes. He led five laps in a race his final year on the circuit.

In one of two races held on this date in 1951, Bill Norton drove his Mercury to victory in a 100-mile contest held on the .5-mile dirt track of the Carrell Speedway in Gardena, CA. Fonty Flock, whose brother Tim won the other race on the east coast, took the pole in California. It was the only career win for Norton.

Tim Flock won his eighth race of 1951 in the 100-mile event at Lakewood Speedway in Atlanta, GA, one of two races on this day. He drove his Hudson at an average speed of 59.960 mph on the one-mile dirt track in the first NASCAR race ever held in Atlanta. Flock went on to capture the 1951 Grand National championship.

Speedy Thompson won his second straight race at the Hickory Speedway with a 1956 win in the Buddy Shuman Memorial.

Jack Harrison died in 1956 at the age of 26 due to stomach ulcers. Harrison ran one Grand National race each in 1952 and 1954, winning a total of $75 as a top-level NASCAR driver.

In the first official race of the 1957 NASCAR season, held in 1956, Marvin Panch won the final of two races held at Willow Springs International Raceway in Lancaster, CA.

NASCAR's first champion, Red Byron, died in 1960 at the age of 45. Byron won the Strictly Stock Division in 1949, edging Lee Petty. He ran only 15 career top-level NASCAR events with two wins and seven other top–10s.

In the only NASCAR-sanctioned Grand National race at the Golden Gate Speedway in Tampa, FL, a .333-mile dirt track, Richard Petty won the second race of the 1963 season, held in 1962.

Terry Schoonover, who raced out of Royal Palm Beach, FL, died as a result of a crash at the 1984 Atlanta

500. It was only his second career Winston Cup start.

Dale Earnhardt Sr. won the 1984 Atlanta Journal 500 at Atlanta Motor Speedway.

Jim Bennett died in 1990. Bennett ran seven career Grand National events 1961–62, racing out of Jonesboro, GA, with two career top–10 finishes.

Gober Sosebee died in 1996 at the age of 81 as a result of a farming accident. Sosebee was a NASCAR pioneer, running three races the inaugural season and winning the pole in the second sanctioned event on the beach-road course at Daytona Beach, FL. He ran 71 career races with two wins, four poles and 31 other top–10 finishes.

At Homestead-Miami Speedway, Bill Elliott won for the only time in 2001, also capturing the pole (his second of the year), in the Winston Cup's 33rd event of the season, the Pennzoil Freedom 400.

12

Harold Kite was born in 1921. He ran nine career Grand National races with one win (1950). He was killed in a 1965 NASCAR race at Charlotte, NC.

John Rostek was born in 1925. Rostek, who raced out of Ft. Collins, CO, ran six career Grand National races with a win in Phoenix, AZ, in 1960 and two other top 10s.

Eddie Bond was born in 1930. Bond raced out of Bedford, IN, to start six Winston Cup races in 1973, his only top-level NASCAR starts. His best finish was 12th in the Winston 500 at Talladega.

Rex White won at the Skyline Speedway in Weaverville, NC, in 1961, the second official race of the 1962 Grand National season.

Bobby Allison won his 10th career race with a victory in the Middle Georgia 500 at the Middle Georgia Raceway in 1967.

Buddy Baker won the 1972 Texas 500 at the Texas World Speedway in College Station. It was the sixth career victory for Baker. A.J. Foyt qualified first for the eighth of ten times in his career and finished second.

Dale Earnhardt Sr. won the 1995 NAPA 500 at Atlanta Motor Speedway.

The #20 Pontiac of Tony Stewart won the 2000 Pennzoil 400 at Homestead-Miami Raceway in Florida. It was Stewart's sixth Winston Cup win of the season. Steve Park captured the pole.

13

Joseph Maurice "Rene" Charland was born in 1928. Racing out of Agawam, MA, Charland ran nine top-level events 1964–71 with a career-best third place finish in a 1966 Grand National race.

Pete Keller, born in 1929 in Columbia, SC, started one career Grand National race, but failed to earn any prize money. He finished 58th out of 75 cars, driving a Studebaker, in the 1950 Southern 500 at Darlington.

Bob Cooper, who raced out of Gastonia, NC, was born in 1935. Cooper ran 63 Grand National events 1962–69 with eight top–10 finishes.

In the first race of the 1956 points race, held at the Hickory (NC) Speedway in 1955, Tim Flock captured the checkered flag in a Chrysler.

Lewis Grier "Buddy" Shuman died in 1955 in a hotel fire in Hickory, NC, at the age of 40. Shuman ran 29 Grand National races 1951–55 with a win in the first sanctioned NASCAR race held in Canada, at Niagara Falls, Ontario, in July 1952. Shuman raced out of Charlotte, NC.

Richard Petty won his second consecutive race at the Augusta International Speedway in 1966 with a first place finish in the Augusta 300, the first race of the 1967 points competition. It was the first of 27 wins on the season for Petty, who won his second of seven career points championships in 1967.

Mark Martin won the 1994 Hooters 500 at Atlanta Motor Speedway for his 15th career Winston Cup win, his second of the 1994 season.

14

Richard Petty won the 1965 Georgia Cracker 300 at the Augusta International Speedway. It was the first race of the 1966 NASCAR points competition.

Richard Petty won the 1971 Capital City 500, completing a sweep of the Richmond races. Bill Dennis won his only career pole in 83 races 1962–81. It was Petty's 20th victory of the season as he cruised to his third career Winston Cup points championship.

In the final event of the 1993 Winston Cup season, Rusty Wallace captured the Hooters 500 at Atlanta Motor Speedway.

Tony Stewart won for the second straight week, gaining his third career win in the 1999 Pennzoil 400 Presented by K Mart at the Homestead-Miami Speedway. David Green won the pole but finished 22nd.

15

Herring Burl (H.B.) Bailey was born in 1936. Bailey raced out of Houston, TX, to make 85 top level NASCAR starts 1962–93, never running more than seven events in any one season. He finished in the top 10 five times with a fifth-place finish in the 1972 Southern 500.

Cale Yarborough won the 1970 American 500 at Rockingham.

In the final NASCAR-sanctioned event held at the Ontario Motor Speedway, Benny Parsons captured the win in the 1980 Los Angeles Times 500. It was his third victory of 1980 and his 17th career Winston Cup win.

Bill Elliott won the 1992 Hooters 500 at Atlanta Motor Speedway, his second straight win at the track. It was the final NASCAR race in the career of Richard Petty, who finished 35th in the STP Pontiac in his 1184th start.

16

Bill Amick was born in 1925. Amick raced out of Portland, OR, to start 48 Grand National events between 1954 and 1965. His only series win came in 1957 in Sacramento, CA. He finished in the top 10 26 other times and claimed five career poles.

Donald Thomas won his first pole and earned his first Grand National win in 1952 under odd circumstances. At the age of 20, he remains the youngest driver to capture a top-level NASCAR race. The next-to-last race of the 1952 season came at Atlanta, GA, on a one-mile dirt track. During the race, his brother Herb suffered mechanical difficulties, flagged Donald down, and replaced him behind the wheel. He subsequently caught up and captured the win. This tactic was protested by the other drivers, but by prevailing rules, the driver that started the race was awarded the win.

Terry Labonte was born in 1956 in Corpus Christi, TX. He was the Winston Cup Champion in 1984 and 1996, the longest span between championship seasons for a driver. His younger brother Bobby won the 2000 championship. Labonte ran 781 events 1978–2003 with 22 wins and over $34 million in earnings.

Tim Richmond won the final race of the 1986 Winston Cup season, the Winston Western at Riverside, CA. It was his seventh win of the season.

Jeff Gordon battled qualifying difficulties and the use of a backup car to finish 17th in the final race of the 1997 season the NAPA 500 at Atlanta Motor Speedway, to capture the Winston Cup points title for the second time in his career. Gordon won by only 14 points over Dale Jarrett and 29 over Mark Martin for the closest finish in NASCAR history. Bobby Labonte won with Jarrett finishing second. Gordon had won the Winston Million in 1997, the second driver to win the prize. Bill Elliott did it first in 1985.

Bobby Labonte won the 2003 Ford 400 on this date at Homestead-Miami Speedway in Homestead, FL, his second win of the season in the final Winston Cup race in history. Jamie McMurray captured his only pole of the season. Beginning with the 2004 Daytona 500, the top NASCAR division began sponsorship with Nextel.

17

Mario Rossi was born in 1932. Racing out of Trenton, NJ, Rossi started four Grand National events 1955–58, managing a top–10 finish in his debut at Langhorne Speedway in September 1955.

In 1963, Fireball Roberts drove to victory on a road course in Augusta, GA. It was the final of 33 victories of his NASCAR career and the only race ever run on the three-mile paved road course. The race was the second race staged in the official 1964 points race.

Richard Petty won his third race in five starts at the Middle Georgia Raceway in 1968.

Ricky Rudd won the 1985 Winston Western 500 at Riverside, CA. He was the 1977 Winston Cup Rookie of the Year.

Mark Martin won the final race of the 1991 Winston Cup season with a first-place finish in the Hardee's 500 at Atlanta. It was his only win of the season.

In the final points race of the 2002 season, Kurt Busch won his fourth race of the year in the Ford 400 at Homestead-Miami Speedway (FL). Busch started first for the only time of the campaign. Tony Stewart finished with the Winston Cup points championship.

18

Gary Bettenhausen was born in 1941. Better known as an Indy Car driver, Bettenhausen made eight Grand National and Winston Cup starts, three in 1967 and five in 1974. He raced out of Monrovia, IN.

Buck Baker won the 100-mile dirt-track event at Wilson County Speedway in Wilson, NC, in 1956 for his 27th career victory and 14th of the season. Baker won his first Grand National Championship that year.

Benny Parsons won the 1979 Los Angeles Times 500 at Ontario Motor Speedway.

Geoff Bodine captured the 1984 Winston Western 500 at Riverside, CA.

Morgan Shepherd won his only race of 1990 in the 29th and final event of the Winston Cup season, the Atlanta Journal 500 at Atlanta Motor Speedway.

Bobby Labonte won for the second time in 2001 with a late victory in Atlanta. Jerry Nadeau ran out of gas on the last lap to help the 2000 Winston Cup points leader to the checkered flag. Dale Earnhardt Jr. won his second and final pole start of the year.

19

Rod Osterlund was born in 1934. A California businessman and car owner, Osterlund is credited with giving Dale Earnhardt Sr. his opportunity to drive at NASCAR's highest level, replacing driver Dave Marcis. The rest is history.

Racing out of Cologne, Germany, Lothar Motschenbacher was born in 1938. He started one NASCAR race in 1970, a 40th-place finish in the Motor Trend 500 at Riverside, CA.

Al Keller died in an Indy Car race at the Phoenix Fairgrounds in 1961 at the age of 41. Keller won two NASCAR races and one pole in 1954 and started 29 career races, including one in the inaugural season of Strictly Stock.

Bobby Allison posted his fifth win of the season in 1978 at the Ontario Motor Speedway. It was Allison's 51st career NASCAR win.

Dale Earnhardt Sr. won the final race of 1989 with a first place in the Atlanta Journal 500 at Atlanta Motor Speedway. It was his fifth win of the season. Grant Adcox died in a crash in the race.

20

John Zeke was born in 1920. Zeke ran four Grand National races in the mid–1950s. He ran out of Levittown, NY. He finished 43rd in his debut in the 1953 Raleigh 300, won by Fonty Flock.

Eugene Glover, who raced out of Kingsport, TN, in the 1950s, was born in 1934. Glover made one career Grand National start in 1957, earning $100 as a top-level NASCAR driver for his 18th place finish at Shelby, NC.

Charles "Leonard" Blanchard was born in 1936. Blanchard raced out of Jackson, KY, to start three career top-level NASCAR races. He finished 33rd in the 1970 Daytona 500 and ran two other qualifying races at Daytona.

In the first of two NASCAR-sanctioned races run at Willow Springs International Raceway in Lancaster, CA, Chuck Stevenson won the third race of the 1956 season, run on this date in 1955. It was Stevenson's only career Grand National win.

Fonty Flock won his 19th, and final, Grand National race in 1955 at Charlotte, NC. It was the second official race of the 1956 season.

Andy Belmont was born in 1957. Belmont, who raced out of Langhorne, PA, made ten Winston Cup starts 1989–92. His best finish was a 28th-place finish at Pocono in 1992 in the Miller Genuine Draft 500. Belmont returned in 2004 to race sparingly on the Nextel circuit.

The first race in over five years was held at the Jacksonville Speedway

Park in Florida in 1960. Lee Petty won, as he did in the previous race held in February 1955. This event, held in November 1960, was the second points race of the 1961 season and was the final of 54 career victories for Petty.

Neil Bonnett won the 1977 Los Angeles Times 500 at Ontario Motor Speedway for his second career win.

Bill Elliott won his first NASCAR race in 1983 at the Riverside International Raceway in California. He was voted the most popular Winston Cup driver 1984–88, 1991–2000 and 2002.

In the final race of the 1988 Winston Cup season, Rusty Wallace captured his fourth win in the past five races with a victory in the Atlanta Journal 500 in Atlanta. It was the sixth win of the season for Wallace. The race was the final Winston Cup appearance for legend Cale Yarborough, the points champion 1977–79, who started 560 career events.

Jerry Nadeau won the final race of the 2000 season at the Atlanta Motor Speedway in the NAPA 500, his first career win. Jeff Gordon started from the pole. Bobby Labonte finished fifth and captured the Winston Cup championship. Darrell Waltrip competed in his 809th and final career race, finishing 34th.

21

Travis Carter was born on this date in 1949. Carter has owned Winston Cup racing teams and has worked extensively as a crew chief in his career.

Tiny Lund drove to a first-place finish in the 1971 Wilkes 400 at North Wilkesboro, NC.

David Pearson won the 1976 Los Angeles Times 500 at Ontario Motor Speedway.

Tim Richmond won his second straight race at Riverside International Raceway in the 1982 Winston Western 500.

Elmo Langley died in 1996 at the age of 69. Langley ran 536 career Grand National and Winston Cup races 1954–81 with 193 top–10 finishes. He was also a long-time pace car driver.

Bobby Labonte won the final race of the 1999 season with a victory in the NAPA 500 at Atlanta Motor Speedway. Kevin Lepage won his first career pole and finished 17th. Dale Jarrett finished second to capture his first career Winston Cup championship. Labonte finished second in the points race.

22

Roscoe Morris "Pappy" Hough, who raced out of Paterson, NJ, in the 1950s, was born in 1902. Pappy started 21 early Grand National events 1950–55 with seven career top–10 finishes.

Wister "Wes" Morgan was born in 1922 in Alexandria, VA. He competed in five Grand National races 1960–61 with a lone top–10 finish in June 1961 at the Starkey Speedway in Roanoke, VA.

Bob Derrington, who raced out of Houston, TX, in the mid–1960s, was born in 1930. Derrington ran 80 races 1964–66 with 22 top–10 finishes. In 1965, he finished sixth overall in Grand National points.

Maynard Troyer was born in 1938. He ran 13 Winston Cup races in 1971 and one in 1973. Driving out of Spencerport, NY, Troyer recorded three top–10 finishes, all in his debut season.

David "Salt" Walther, born in 1947, ran four Winston Cup races in the mid–1970s. Walther raced out of Dayton, OH, and completed over 1200 miles at NASCAR's top level.

The Tar Heel Speedway in Randleman, NC, hosted three Grand National events 1962–63. Jim Paschal won the 1962 Turkey Day 200.

Bobby Allison captured his 19th career NASCAR victory in 1970 at Langley Field Speedway. Benny Parsons captured the first pole start, and would win 20 more in his career.

Bobby Allison won his fifth race of 1981 with a first place finish at the Riverside International Raceway. It was the 65th NASCAR victory of his career.

Bill Elliott won the first and last race of 1987, and four more in between. His sixth win came at the Atlanta Journal 500 at Atlanta Motor Speedway.

23

Niles Henry Gage Jr., who raced out of Milton, ME, in the 1960s, was born in 1934. Gage made one Grand National start in 1968, the final event held at the Oxford Plains Speedway, the 1968 Maine 300, earning a career paycheck of $155 at NASCAR's top level.

Ron Bouchard was born in 1948. Bouchard, the winner of the 1981 Talladega 500, raced out of Fitchburg, MA, to 160 career Winston Cup starts 1981–87. He also captured three poles, one a year 1981–83. He finished eighth in championship points in 1982. He was the 1981 Winston Cup Rookie of the Year.

Buddy Baker won the 1975 Los Angeles Times 500 at Ontario Motor Speedway.

Robby Gordon became the 19th winner of the 2001 season in the final race of the schedule, the New Hampshire 300 at Loudon, NH. It was his first career victory. The race had been rescheduled to the end of the season due to the 9/11 terrorist attacks. Jeff Gordon, who won his eighth pole start of the year, finished the season with his third Winston Cup points championship.

24

Buddy Parrott was born in 1939. Parrott is one of the most successful crew chiefs in Winston Cup history. He started in the pits in 1970 and later became a crew chief for Darrell Waltrip, Richard Petty and Derrike Cope.

Bill Osborne, who raced out of Rialto, CA, was born in 1946. Osborne ran 16 Winston Cup races 1971–86, all but one in California. He finished a career-best 16th in the 1975

Winston Western 500 at Riverside, CA.

Bobby Allison won his second race of 1974 at the Ontario Motor Speedway. It was Allison's 43rd career win and his first driving an AMC Matador as he won the Los Angeles Times 500.

25

Joe Gibbs was born in 1940. Gibbs initially gained notoriety as coach of the Washington Redskins and led them to three Super Bowl wins in 1982, 1987 and 1991. After his retirement as a coach, Gibbs plunged into NASCAR as a Winston Cup team operator with Dale Jarrett as his first driver. He signed a contract to return to coach the Redskins in 2004. In 1996, he was elected to the Pro Football Hall of Fame.

Bruce Blodgett was born in 1945. Blodgett raced out of Fresno, CA, to make one Winston Cup start. He started and finished 15th in the 1976 Virginia 500 at Martinsville.

Announcer Mike Joy was born in 1949. Joy was chosen by FOX to anchor NASCAR broadcasts in 2002.

Frank Mundy and Studebaker finished the 1951 Grand National circuit with a pole and a win in the season finale at Mobile, AL. Mundy won the 112.5-mile event on a .75-mile dirt track in the final of two NASCAR events staged at the Lakeview Speedway. It was the final of three career wins for Mundy, all in 1951.

26

Dick Kranzler was born in 1938 in California. Kranzler ran nine Grand National and Winston Cup races in the 1970s, all at either Riverside or Ontario, CA. He made his debut in the 1970 Motor Trend 500 at Riverside, CA.

David Simko was born in 1954. Racing out of Clarkston, MI, Simko ran 10 races 1982–88, starting a career-high four races in 1987. His career-best was a 16th-place finish at the 1987 Miller American 400 at Michigan.

Dale Jarrett was born in 1956 in Newton, NC. He began in the Winston Cup Series in 1984 in three races and returned for good in 1987. In 1996 he won both the Daytona 500 and Brickyard 400. In 1997, he won seven races and finished second in the points standing.

Ned Jarrett won at the Columbia Speedway in 1959 for his third career win. It was the sixth career pole position for Junior Johnson.

Richard Petty won at the Montgomery Motor Speedway in 1967, the second race of the 1968 points championship.

27

Melvin K. "Red" Foote, who raced out of Southington, CT, in the 1960s, was born in 1927. Foote started ten career Grand National races 1962–65.

Billy Standridge was born in 1953. Racing out of Shelby, NC, Standridge began his Winston Cup career in 1994, running 23 events through 1998. He crashed and finished 42nd in the 1994 Goodwrench 500 at Rockingham, NC.

28

Charles Barrett was born in 1944 and made four Winston Cup starts in 1973. Barrett raced out of Cleveland, GA, to record a career-best 10th-place finish in the Winston 500 at Talladega, won by David Pearson.

Maurice Randall was born in 1952. Racing out of Charlotte, MI, Randall ran four Winston Cup races 1984–85. He debuted in the Coors 420 at Nashville Speedway(TN) with a 30th-place finish.

29

Baxter Larry Price was born in 1938. Price raced out of Monroe, NC, to start 90 NASCAR races 1973–81. He started a career-high 24 races in both 1978 and 1979. His best finish was 11th in the 1978 Virginia 500 at Martinsville.

Vic Parsons, born in 1939, raced out of Willowdale, Ontario, Canada. Parsons started 19 races 1972–73 with seven top–10 finishes. His best finish was seventh in the 1973 Firecracker 400 at Daytona.

30

Andy Hampton, who raced out of Louisville, KY, was born in 1928.

Hampton made four Grand National starts, one in 1959, one (a top 10) in 1968 and two in 1969 (with one top 10).

Dick Hutcherson was born in 1931. He raced out of Keokuk, IA. Hutcherson won 14 career races at NASCAR's highest level in 103 events in the mid–1960s. His best year was 1965, when he won nine times and finished second in championship points to Ned Jarrett. A well-known short-track driver, in 1976, he was a member of the only Winston Cup team ever to enter the 24 Hours of LeMans. He went on to operate an automobile chassis business.

David F. Dion, who raced out of Hudson, NH, in the 1970s and '80s, was born in 1943. Dion started 12 career races with a lone top–10 finish in the 1980 Capital City 400.

Chauncey "Jocko" Maggiacomo, born in 1947 and running out of Poughkeepsie, NY, ran 23 Winston Cup events 1977–88. He finished 26th in his debut at Pocono in the 1977 Coca-Cola 500.

The 1952 NASCAR Grand National season concluded with the 34th race, at the same location as the first race of the campaign, West Palm Beach, FL. Herb Thomas won this 100-mile contest in his Hudson, averaging 58.008 mph on the .5-mile dirt track. It was the fourth time that season that Thomas won from the pole position.

DECEMBER

1

Jim Fitzgerald, who raced out of Pittsburgh, PA, in the 1980s, was born in 1921. Fitzgerald started one event each in 1986 and 1987 but died in a Florida road race in November 1987 at the age of 65. He debuted in the 1986 Winston Western at Riverside, CA.

Richard "Dick" Goode, who raced out of Mishawaka, IN, in the 1960s, was born in 1927. Goode ran two Grand National events in 1963, capturing a top–10 finish in a Daytona 500 qualifying race and earning $700 as a driver at NASCAR's top level.

James Massey was born in North Carolina in 1929. Massey started 51 races 1955–64 and qualified first for a race in Weaverville, NC, in 1958, his only pole.

Gene Thoneson, born in 1953, ran one Winston Cup event. He finished 22nd in the 1981 Winston Western 500 at Riverside, CA. Racing out of Reedley, CA, he was killed in a farming accident in 1993.

Wendell Scott, the trend-setting African American driver, won his only NASCAR race in 1963. He ran 495 career races between 1961 and 1973 and was the inspiration for the Richard Pryor character in *Greased Lightning*. It was the final sanctioned NASCAR race at the Jacksonville Speedway Park. Buck Baker was believed to be the winner until a scoring error was corrected, giving the win to Scott in an event that was actually extended by two laps due to the error.

Stanton Barrett was born in Bishop, CA, in 1972. Barrett ran two events during the 1999 season, debuting with a 30th place finish in the Las Vegas 400. His father, Stan Barrett, made 19 career Winston Cup starts 1980–90.

2

Louis Volk was born in 1910. Volk raced out of Paterson, NJ, to a top–10 finish in his only race of the inaugural

1949 Strictly Stock season. He also ran one Grand National race in 1950.

Allen "Rags" Carter, racing out of Miami Springs, FL, and born in 1928, started one Grand National race at West Palm Beach, FL, in 1952 and finished sixth.

Jack Rounds, born in 1930, raced out of Huntington, WV. Rounds made his lone Grand National start in 1958, finishing 12th at Riverside in the Crown America 500 won by Eddie Gray.

In the second race of the 1957 points race, Marvin Panch won at the Concord Speedway in 1956.

3

Bobby Allison was born in 1937 in Miami, FL. Allison was a three-time winner of the Daytona 500 and finished second twice. He was the most popular driver in NASCAR six times, 1971–73, 1981–83. In 1983 he won his only Winston Cup Series Championship. He finished second five times. He won 85 NASCAR races in his career and later became a car owner. His two sons followed their father into racing. Unfortunately, Clifford died in a practice crash in 1992 while Davey died in a helicopter crash en route to a race track in 1993. In 1998, Bobby was named one of NASCAR's 50 Greatest Drivers.

4

Pottstown, PA, native Bobby Marshman died at the age of 28 in a test-session crash at Phoenix International Raceway in 1964. Marshman recorded one top–10 in two starts during the 1964 Grand National season, his best an 8th place finish in a second qualifying race for the 1964 Daytona 500.

Doug Keller was born in St. Joseph, MO, in 1972. He ran 17 Craftsman Truck races 2001–03. His best finish was a 17th place at Darlington in 2003's Craftsman 200.

5

Jim Paschal was born in High Point, NC, in 1926. He won 25 races in the 1950s and 1960s, mostly on short tracks. In 422 career races, he won 12 poles and finished in the top 10 a total of 230 times. He finished 23rd in the first Strictly Stock race in 1949 at Charlotte and raced in at least one top-level NASCAR event every year through 1969.

James Ernest "Jim" Hurtubise, who raced out of North Tonawanda, NY, 1957–79, was born in 1932. Hurtubise ran 35 career Grand National and Winston Cup races with one win and nine other top–10 finishes. His only victory came in the 1966 Atlanta 500.

John Delphus (J.D.) McDuffie was born in 1938 in Sanford, NC. McDuffie, one of the last independent racers, ran 653 events with no wins and one pole (Dover — 1978). He finished in the top 10 106 times and was 9th in Winston Cup points in 1971. He died in a crash in the early stages of the 1991 Bud at the Glen at Watkins Glen, NY.

Earle Canavan, who raced out of Ft. Johnson, NY, was born in 1938. Canavan made 68 career Grand National and Winston Cup starts 1969–86 with a career high 12 starts in 1975.

Ronnie Sanders was born in 1945. Sanders made numerous qualifying attempts in the 1980s, running a total of three career races at the Winston Cup level. He raced out of Fayetteville, GA, to an 18th-place finish in his debut in the 1981 Daytona 500.

South African native Sarel van der Merwe was born in 1946. Racing out of Port Elizabeth, South Africa, van der Merwe started one career Winston Cup race, a 24th-place finish in the 1990 Budweiser at the Glen in Watkins Glen, NY.

6

William O. "Blackie" Watt was born in 1933. Watt raced out of New Alexandria, PA, to start 20 Grand National races in 1966 and four the following year. He managed nine top–10 finishes, all during his rookie season.

Christian Elder was born in Bloomington, MN, in 1968. Elder, hoping for a Nextel Cup ride, began his Busch Series career in 2001 and ran 24 events over two seasons.

7

John Utsman was born in 1939. He ran 14 Winston Cup races 1973–80. Driving out of Bluff City, TN, Utsman recorded a top–10 finish in his debut season at NASCAR's top level in the Southeastern 500 at Bristol, TN.

Paul "Little Bud" Moore, born in 1941, ran 41 races 1964–73 with 19 top–10 finishes and one pole in Greenville, SC, in April 1965. He finished second in the 1968 Smoky Mountain 500 at Maryville, TN, behind Richard Petty.

The Texas World Speedway in College Station was a two-mile paved track that hosted eight Grand National/Winston Cup events 1969–81. Bobby Isaac won the 1969 Texas 500, the first Grand National event staged at the track. It was his 21st career win and 17th and final of the season. Buddy Baker qualified first.

LeeRoy Yarbrough died in a nursing home in 1984 at the age of 56. Yarbrough had Rocky Mountain spotted fever in the 1970s, which severely impacted his health. Yarbrough finished in the top-10 21 times in 30 races in 1969. He ran 198 races between 1960 and 1972. His first victory came in May 1964 in Savannah, GA.

8

John Meggers was born in 1928 in Washington, D.C. He finished in the top 10 in three of his five career Grand National races, all in 1953. His best finish was 7th place in his debut at the Monroe County Fairgrounds in Rochester, NY.

Budd Hagelin, who raced out of Camden, NJ, in the 1970s, was born in 1944. Hagelin made his Winston

Cup debut in the 1974 Winston Western 500 and ran the 1976 Mason-Dixon 500 at Dover.

Perry Smith died in a private plane crash in 1951. Smith ran only one Grand National race, finishing fourth in his debut at the Altamont-Schenectady Fairgrounds (NY). He raced out of W. Columbia, SC, and was killed trying to fly an 80-year-old woman to Chicago, IL, for medical treatment.

David Sosebee was born in Georgia in 1955. Racing out of Dawsonville, Sosebee started ten Winston Cup races 1979–88. He finished 28th in his debut in the 1979 Gabriel 400 at Michigan International Speedway.

Bobby Allison's 12th career NASCAR victory came in 1968 at the Montgomery Speedway. Of his 85 NASCAR race wins, 84 officially, this was his only career victory in a Plymouth. It was the final of six races held at the half-mile dirt track.

Kevin Harvick was born in 1975 in Bakersfield, CA. Harvick, the 2001 Winston Cup Rookie of the Year, won two races in his first season at NASCAR's top level. His first victory came in the 2001 Cracker Barrel Old Country Store 500 at Atlanta. Harvick was chosen to drive Dale Earnhardt's car after his death at Daytona. He remained active with 107 top-level starts through 2003 with 4 wins and two pole starts. He has also had wins in the Busch, Craftsman Truck and IROC series.

Ryan Newman was born in 1977 in South Bend, IN. Newman, the 2002 Winston Cup Rookie of the Year, started 80 races 2000–03 and remained active in 2004. He won eight races in September 2003 and captured his first career checkered flag in the 2003 New Hampshire 300 at Loudon, NH, winning from the pole.

Singer-driver Marty Robbins died in 1982 at the age of 57. Robbins ran 35 top-level NASCAR races 1966–82, never more than five races in any one season. He finished in the top 10 six times. He placed 94 songs on the *Billboard* charts, topping the charts with "A White Sport Coat (And a Pink Carnation)" in 1957 and "El Paso" in 1959.

9

Fred Johnson was born in 1929 in North Carolina. He started two races in NASCAR's first season, 1949, and ran five other races 1950–56, with two career top–10 finishes.

Bill Dennis, who raced out of Glen Allen, VA, 1962–81, was born in 1935. Dennis ran 83 career Grand National and Winston Cup races with 21 top–10 finishes. He won one career pole, in November 1971 at Richmond, VA. He was the 1970 Grand National Rookie of the Year.

Brad Teague, born in 1947, ran 44 Winston Cup events between 1982 and 1995. Racing out of Johnson City, TN, Teague led one race in his career, 17 laps in 1987.

10

Al Tasnady died in December 1988 at the age of 59. Research failed to yield the exact date. Tasnady ran three career Grand National races 1957–67, racing out of Vineland, NJ. He was a local favorite at the Reading Fairgrounds.

NASCAR announced in 2003 that when the Nextel Cup Series replaced Winston as a sponsor to begin the 2004 season, consideration would be given to modifying the points system and developing a playoff format for the upcoming year.

11

Herman Beam was born in 1929. Beam was 4th in Grand National points in 1959 and started 194 races 1957–63. He finished in the top 10 57 times, racing out of Johnson City, TN.

Jim Danielson, who raced out of Chico, CA, in the mid–1970s, was born in 1930. Danielson started five Winston Cup races 1972–76 with a top–10 finish in his only start of 1973 in the Tuborg 400 at Riverside, CA.

Herb Thomas, driving a Chevrolet, won his third straight race at the Palm Beach Speedway, a 1955 win over Al Keller.

Don Stumpf died in 1991 at the age of 64. Stumpf raced out of Ridgefield Park, NJ, to start one Grand National race in 1953, a 22nd-place finish at Morristown, NJ, to earn $75 at NASCAR's top level.

12

Wally Dallenbach Sr. was born in East Brunswick, NJ, in 1936. Dallenbach ran one Grand National race each in 1962 and 1964 with one Winston Cup start in 1974. In his debut at NASCAR's highest level, Dallenbach finished 6th in a qualifier at Daytona in February 1964. He was more renowned as an open wheel racer, running in 13 straight Indianapolis 500 races in the 1960s and 1970s. His son, Wally Jr., was a Winston Cup regular 1991–2001.

Mark Hurley was born in 1936 in Johnson City, TN. He ran 16 career Grand National races between 1961 and 1964 with two top–10 finishes in his career, one each in 1963 and 1964. His career best was a 4th place finish at the Dog Track Speedway in Moyock, NC, in July 1963.

Larry Hedrick was born in 1940. Hedrick debuted as a team owner in 1990. In 1995 his driver Ricky Craven was named Rookie of the Year on the Winston Cup circuit.

Bob Senneker was born in 1944. Racing out of Dorr, MI, Senneker ran six career top-level NASCAR races with one race each in 1968, 1970 and 1981. He ran five Winston Cup events in 1983. He debuted with a 13th-place finish in the 1968 Daytona 500, his only appearance at Daytona, FL.

Richard Petty's 140th career win came in the 1971 Texas 500 at the Texas World Speedway. Pete Hamilton captured his third and final career pole position while finishing fourth. In 1971, Petty won his third championship, the first under the sponsorship of the Winston Cup.

13

Earl Balmer was born in 1935. Balmer raced out of Floyds Knob, IN, to make 32 career Grand National starts. His lone win came in a 100-mile event at Daytona in February 1966.

Jim Vandiver was born in 1939. He started 85 career events at the Grand National and Winston Cup level 1968–83. Vandiver raced out of Huntersville, NC, to record 24 top–10 finishes and lead six career events. His career highlights were a second-place finish in the 1969 Talladega 500 and a third-place in the 1972 Daytona 500.

James "Jim" Hopkinson, who raced out of Carmichael, CA, in the 1970s and '80s, was born in 1942. Hopkinson ran one Winston Cup race, the 1980 Warner W. Hodgdon 400 at Riverside.

James Cox, who raced out of Radford, VA, was born in 1945. Cox started 22 career Grand National and Winston Cup races between 1969 and 1972.

Don Oldenberg died in 1983, five days before his 61st birthday. Oldenberg ran 20 career Grand National races in the 1950s with nine top–10 finishes.

14

Hershel McGriff was born in Oregon in 1927. He ran 86 races 1950–93.

His best year was 1954 when he captured all five of his career poles and four wins in 24 events to finish 6th in Grand National points. His first career victory came in August 1954 at the Bay Meadows Race Track in San Mateo, CA.

Bernard V. Alvarez was born in 1939. Racing out of Jacksonville, FL, he started nine career Grand National races 1964–65. He never finished a race, due to a variety of mechanical problems, and his career best was 15th place in the 1964 Moyock (NC) 300.

Denny Zimmerman was born in 1940. Zimmerman ran one Grand National race, a 15th-place finish at Old Dominion Speedway in Manassas, VA, in September 1964. Zimmerman raced out of Glastonburg, CT.

The beginning of the NASCAR series can be traced to this date in 1947 when Bill France began a series of meetings at the Streamline Hotel in Daytona Beach. Thirty-five participants debated the future of their sport and subsequently, a professional racing series was organized, first called Strictly Stock, and eventually evolving into the NASCAR Nextel Cup Series.

Alan Kulwicki was born in Greenfield, WI, in 1954. Kulwicki was the 1986 Rookie of the Year. He was the 1992 Winston Cup Champion when he led 20 races, won two and grabbed six pole positions. Kulwicki ran 207 Winston Cup races with 5 wins and 24 poles. He died in a plane crash en route to a race in 1993 at the age of 38.

Johnny Chapman, who raced out of Statesville, NC, was born in 1967. He started one Winston Cup race, the 1993 Goodwrench 500 at Martinsville, finishing 368 laps before retiring due to handling difficulties.

15

Eli Gold was born in 1953. A popular announcer on MRN and TNN NASCAR broadcasts for several decades, he was replaced when FOX and NBC took over television rights. In recent years he has been known as the voice of the Alabama Crimson Tide football and basketball games.

In 2003, NASCAR driver Mike Wallace joined NY Yankees first baseman Jason Giambi and professional wrestler Kurt Angle on a USO-sponsored trip to support military personnel overseas.

16

Dick Beaty was born in 1924. Beaty, who raced out of Charlotte, NC, made 38 Grand National starts 1955–58 with ten top–10 finishes.

Tom Raley was born in 1936. Racing out of North Beach, MD, Raley made his only nine Grand National starts in 1967. He debuted, and finished 21st, in a Daytona 500 qualifying race won by Fred Lorenzen.

Donald Thomas died in 1977 at the age of 45. Thomas, who raced out of Olivia, NC, ran 79 Grand National races 1950–56 with one win and 36 other top-10 finishes. His only pole start and victory came in November 1952 in a 100-mile dirt track race in Atlanta, GA. He was the youngest of the five Thomas Brothers, the most famous of whom was Herb, a two-time Grand National champion in the 1950s.

Peter Holden Gregg died as a result of suicide in 1980 at the age of 40. Gregg, who raced out of Jacksonville, FL, made one Winston Cup start in the 1973 World 600 at Charlotte but ended his top-level NASCAR career with a crash on the 34th lap.

17

Richard "Dick" Zimmerman, born in 1918, ran five early NASCAR events, one in 1949 and two each in 1954 and 1955. Zimmerman raced out of Milwaukee, WI.

Leon Fox, who raced out of Bremerton, WA, in the 1970s, was born in 1937. Fox made one start each in 1973 and 1974 at Riverside, CA, and finished 14th in his final event, the Tuborg 400.

Ken Meisenhelder was born in 1942 in Springfield, MA. He made 51 starts at NASCAR's top level 1968–71 with three top–10 finishes, including his final event, the 1971 Sandlapper 200 at Columbia, SC.

Richard White was born in 1946. Based in Escondido, CA, White started 12 Winston Cup races

1973–79 and finished in the top 10 in his first two events, both at Riverside, CA. He finished a career-best sixth in the 1973 Tuborg Gold 400.

Jerry Barnett, born in 1951, made two Winston Cup starts in 1971. He raced out of Bonita, CA. He debuted at the age of 19 in the 1971 Golden State 400 at Riverside, CA, finishing 30th.

18

William A. "Bill" Holland, who raced out of Bridgeport, CT, in the 1950s, was born in 1907. Holland ran eight Grand National races with two top–10 finishes 1951–52.

Don Oldenberg was born in 1922. Racing out of Highland, IN, Oldenberg made 20 starts in the 1950s with nine top–10 finishes. He finished fifth in two events, a November 1951 event at Lakeview Speedway in Mobile, AL, and the inaugural race of 1953 at the Palm Beach Speedway (FL).

Bob Cameron was born in 1927 and raced out of Kenmore, NY. Cameron started one Strictly Stock race in the inaugural season of 1949 (Hamburg, NY) and ran one additional event in 1953 (Rochester, NY).

Theodore "Ted" Hairfield, who raced out of Richmond, VA, in the 1960s, was born in 1931. Hairfield made two Grand National starts in 1963 and earned $675 in winnings at NASCAR's top level. He finished next-to-last in his final race, yield-ing to clutch problems in the 1963 Daytona 500.

Early Harry "Bub" Strickler was born in 1938 and raced out of Timberville, VA. Strickler made 20 Grand National and Winston Cup starts 1965–80 with two top–10 finishes in his rookie season. His best was an eighth-place in the 1965 Fireball 200 at Weaverville, NC, in his third career Grand National start.

Ted Musgrave was born in 1955 in Evanston, IL. He began Winston Cup racing in 1990 and was second in the 1991 Rookie of the Year standings. Through 2003, he ran 305 events with 55 top–10 finishes and five pole starts, his first coming in 1994's Pontiac Excitement 400 at Richmond.

Howard Rose was born in 1963. He started one career Winston Cup race, racing out of Ashland, KY, to a 30th place finish in the 1986 Delaware 500 at Dover.

Stan Fox, born Stanley Cole Fuchs in 1952, died in 2000 at the age of 48. Fox ran two events in 1992, finishing 37th after a crash in the Champion Spark Plug 400 at Michigan.

19

Arthur Binkley was born in 1920. Binkley made five Grand National starts 1954–57 racing out of New Albany, IN. His best finish was a 21st-place at Langhorne, PA, in September 1957.

Patty Moise was born in 1960. Racing out of Jacksonville, FL, she ran five Winston Cup races in the late 1980s. One of the few women to run in recent NASCAR seasons, she was a regular in the Busch Series with 133 starts 1986–98. She finished 33rd in her Winston Cup debut in the 1987 Budweiser at the Glen at Watkins Glen, NY.

20

Johnny Steele was born in 1934. Racing out of Carmichael, CA, Steele made 10 Grand National and one Winston Cup start 1965–71. He finished 13th in the 1966 Motor Trend 500 at Riverside, CA, his career-best.

Ludwig Everard "Rod" Eulenfeld, who raced out of Jacksonville, FL, 1964–72, was born in 1953. Eulenfeld ran five Grand National and one Winston Cup event in his career. He finished 21st in the 1968 Daytona 500.

Chuck Wahl was born in 1950. He made 13 Winston Cup starts between 1973 and 1980. Racing out of Burbank, CA, Wahl managed two top–10 finishes and led three laps in a 1976 race. His best finish was 6th place in the 1975 Tuborg 400 at Riverside, CA.

Benjamin "Ben" Hess, who raced out of Dayton, OH, in the 1980s and '90s, was born in 1964. Hess ran 12 Winston Cup races 1988–95, starting a career-high nine in 1989. He finished 28th in the 1995 Daytona 500, his final top-level NASCAR race.

21

Clyde Minter died at the age of 50 in 1971. One of NASCAR's pioneers, Minter ran two races in 1949, the inaugural season, finishing fourth in both events. He ran 40 other contests in the 1950s with 17 additional top–10 finishes.

22

David Pearson was born in Spartanburg, SC, in 1934. Pearson was the 1960 Rookie of the Year and raced until 1986. He ran 574 races with 105 wins (second only to Richard Petty) and 113 pole starts. He won the points championship three times, 1966 and 1968–69.

William "Freddy" Smith was born in 1946. Smith ran two Winston Cup races in 1979, racing out of Kings Mountain, NC. He is one of at least 35 Smiths to start a top-level NASCAR race.

Larry "Butch" Hartman died in 1994 at the age of 54. Hartman, who raced out of Zanesville, OH, ran 20 career Grand National and Winston Cup races between 1966 and 1979 with one top-5 and four other top-10 finishes. His career-best was a fifth-place finish in the 1972 National 500 at Charlotte, NC.

23

Greg Biffle, born in Vancouver, WA, in 1969, began his Winston Cup career in 2002 and has raced in the

Busch, Craftsman Truck and IROC series. His first win came at Daytona in the 2003 Pepsi 400 and he went on to win the pole for the 2004 Daytona 500.

Wendell Scott died in 1990 at the age of 69. Scott ran 13 Winston Cup seasons and is regarded as breaking the color barrier in NASCAR. His only win came at Jacksonville in December 1963. He retired after a serious crash at Talladega in 1973.

24

Paul "Wimpy" Ervin, who raced out of Bloomfield, NJ, in the 1950s, was born in 1917. Wimpy ran 10 career Grand National races with two top–10 finishes, his best an 8th place in the inaugural race at the Altamont-Schenectady Fairgrounds (NY) in 1951.

Slick Gardner, who raced out of Buellton, CA, in the 1970s, was born in 1946. Gardner ran one Winston Cup race in 1973, logging nine laps and 24 miles at Talladega in the Winton 500 won by David Pearson.

Robin Schildnecht was born in 1953. Racing out of Louisville, KY, Schildnecht ran two Winston Cup events in 1977, finishing 21st in the Richmond 400 in his debut.

Aaron "Shorty" York died of suicide in 1970 at the age of 46. York ran 12 Grand National events 1950–60 with one top–10 finish. He raced out of Mocksville, NC, to a career-best second-place finish at the Charlotte Speedway in September 1951.

25

Arnold Gardner, who raced out of Batavia, IL, was born on Christmas day in 1926. Gardner started four Grand National races in 1960 and earned a total of $575 at NASCAR's top level.

Roy Lee Hendrick, who raced out of Richmond, VA, in the 1980s, was born on Christmas day 1953. Hendrick ran one career Winston Cup event in 1986, lasting 91 miles at NASCAR's top level.

26

Tex Keene, born in 1917, raced out of Marietta, GA, to enter two races in 1950, but failed to earn any prize money. He crashed at Darlington and finished 18th at North Wilkesboro in the Wilkes 200.

Dean Roper was born in 1938. Racing out of Fair Grove, MO, Roper ran five Winston Cup races 1983–84. His debut was a 15th-place finish in the 1983 Daytona 500.

Edward Cooper, who raced out of Clark Lake, MI, was born in 1946. Cooper started three Winston Cup events, one in 1985 and two in 1990, completing 101 career laps at NASCAR's top level.

Robert Sprague was born in 1959 in North Bend, OR. He started, and led a lap, in one Winston Cup event in his career, the 1991 Banquet Frozen Foods 300 at Sears Point International Raceway.

Budd Olsen died in 1991 at the age of 67. Olsen ran two top-level

NASCAR races, one in 1949 and one in 1961. He earned $250 in his career at the Strictly Stock and Grand National level. He finished 13th in the 1961 Yankee 500 at the Norwood (MA) Arena in his final event.

27

Thomas D. "Tommie" Elliott, who raced out of Bloomfield, NJ, in the 1950s, was born in 1935. Elliott started seven Grand National races 1951–58 with four top–10s. In 1954 he ran three of the first five races and finished in the top 10 each event.

Ron McGee was born in 1947. Racing out of Sunnyvale, CA, he started one race and earned $950 for his Winston Cup experience in the 1977 Los Angeles Times 500 at Ontario, CA.

28

William "Nelson" Stacy was born in 1921. Stacy raced out of Cincinnati, OH, to 45 Grand National starts between 1952 and 1965. He won four career races, his first in the September 1961 Southern 500. He finished 14th overall in Grand National points in 1963.

Jack Ingram, who raced out of Asheville, NC, was born in 1936. Ingram ran 19 races at NASCAR's highest level between 1965 and 1981. He placed second in the 1967 Buddy Shuman 250 at Hickory, NC, and

managed three other top–10 finishes in his career.

29

Tony Bonadies was born in 1916. Bonadies raced out of Bronx, NY, to start two Grand National races in 1952. He died in a Midget race in Williams Grove, PA, in 1964.

Russell Bennett was born in 1920 and raced out of Milford, DE, to two Grand National starts in 1950, running both events at Langhorne, PA.

Ernie Stierly was born in 1930. He raced out of Vancouver, British Columbia, Canada, to start five Winston Cup races 1976–78, four at Riverside, CA, and one at Ontario, CA. His best finish was 19th in the 1978 Winston Western 500 at Riverside driving the Allied Plating Chevrolet.

Charlie Blanton was born in 1935. Blanton, who raced out of Gaffney, SC, made three Winston Cup starts 1973–78, debuting in the 1973 World 600 at Charlotte.

Ray Kelly was born in 1946. Racing out of West Covina, CA, he started one Winston Cup race, the 1986 Budweiser 400, finishing 36th.

Richard Petty won the Sunshine 200 at Savannah Speedway (GA) in 1963, the fourth race of the 1964 Grand National season, his 28th career checkered flag.

Rina Andretti, the matriarch of the Andretti family, died in 2003 at the age of 90 in a personal care home in Bethlehem, PA. The mother of Mario, she was born in Italy in

1913 and immigrated with her family to Nazareth, PA, in the 1950s, raising twin sons and a daughter.

30

Fred Lorenzen was born in 1934 in Elmhurst, IL. He ran 158 races between 1956 and 1972, winning 26 and starting from the pole in 33. He won eight races in 1964. His final win came in 1967 at Daytona. He was 3rd in points in 1963 and led the Grand National series in "laps led" while being named the circuit's most popular driver. He was also the most popular driver in 1965.

Lloyd Dolph (L.D.) Ottinger was born in 1938 in Newport, TN. Ottinger ran 10 Grand National/Winston Cup races 1966–84. He finished a career-best second-place finish in the 1973 Volunteer 500 at Bristol, one of two top–10 finishes in three races that season.

In the only Grand National race ever held at the Titusville-Cocoa Speedway in Titusville, FL, Fireball Roberts claimed a win in 1956 in the third race of the 1957 season.

31

Bill Miller died in 1952. A native of Evansville, IN, Miller ran ten NASCAR races 1951–52 with two top 10s in 1951, the first a 7th place finish at Weaverville.

BIBLIOGRAPHY

American Racing Classics. Concord, NC: Griggs Publishing Company, Inc., 1992.

Bud at the Glen. Program Guide. Daytona Beach, FL: NASCAR. August 11, 1996.

Fleischman, Bill and Pearce, Al. *The Unauthorized NASCAR Fan Guide.* Farmington Hills, MI: Visible Ink Press. 1999.

Frontier @ The Glen. Program Guide. Daytona Beach, FL: NASCAR. August 15, 1999.

Global Crossing @ The Glen. Program Guide. Daytona Beach, FL: NASCAR. August 9, 2001.

Golenbock, Peter, and Fielden, Greg. *The Stock Car Racing Encyclopedia.* New York: MacMillan, 1997.

Gregoire, Francois-Michel. *Who Works in NASCAR.* Dover, Kent, UK: Starting Blocks International Limited, 1998.

Latford, Robert. *A Celebration of 50 Years of NASCAR.* London, England: Carlton Books Limited, 1998.

McCullough, Robert. *My Greatest Day in NASCAR.* New York: St. Martin's Press, 2000.

Moriarty, Frank. *The Encyclopedia of Stock Car Racing.* New York: Michael Friedman Publishing Group, Inc. 1998

Neely, William. *Daytona U.S.A.* Tucson, AZ: AZTEK Corporation, 1979.

Pennsylvania 500. Program Guide. Daytona Beach, FL: NASCAR. July 21, 1997.

The Official Directory for the NASCAR Winston Cup Series. Charlotte, NC: Bell South Advertising. 1995.

The Official NASCAR 2002 Preview and Press Guide. Daytona Beach, FL: NASCAR. 2002.

The Official NASCAR 2003 Preview and Press Guide. Daytona Beach, FL: NASCAR. 2003.

Watson, Dick. *The Glory Road.* New York: Stadia Sports Publishing, Inc. 1973.

Websites:

www.nascar.com
www.mphmotorsports.com/birthdays.htm
jayski.thatsracin.com/pages/birthdays.htm
users.commkey.net/fussichen/otdauto.htm
www.wheelsofspeed.com/driver-T.html
dbserver.iscmotorsports.com
www.motorsportshalloffame.com
www.motorsportsone.net
www.racing-reference.com
www.daytonausa.com

INDEX

Aaron's 499 4/6/2003, 4/21/2002
Abel, Bobby 1/31/1995, 4/20/1930
AC Delco 400 10/20/1991, 10/20/1996,
    10/21/1990, 10/22/1989, 10/22/1995,
    10/27/1997, 11/1/1998
AC Delco 500 1/25/1955, 4/11/1998,
    7/26/1962, 10/22/1989, 10/23/1988,
    10/23/1994, 10/24/1993, 10/25/1987,
    10/25/1992
AC Spark Plug 500 6/5/1952, 7/22/1990,
    7/23/1989, 7/24/1988, 11/4/1944
Acton, Marv 2/3/1944
Adams, Carl 4/24/1942
Adams, Weldon 5/9/1995
Adcox, Grant 1/2/1950, 11/19/1989
Adkins, Allen 3/29/1929
Advance Auto Parts 500 4/13/2003,
    4/14/2002
AIDS 6/7/1955, 8/13/1989
Aiken, Blair 9/2/1956
Airborne Speedway (NY) 6/19/1955
Alabama: Anniston 3/12/1915, 8/8/1930,
    10/28/1940; Bessemer 7/30/1946; Birm-
    ingham 6/4/1961, 6/9/1963, 6/21/1964,
    6/24/1961, 7/21/1934, 8/3/1960,
    9/7/1958; Birmingport 1/24/1958; Calera
    6/24/1961; Chelsea 1/27/1961; Eastaboga
    3/25/1937; Fairfield 7/30/1936; Fort
    Payne 3/21/1921, 5/11/1924; Gadsden
    6/26/1963; Gardendale 4/2/1917; Glen-
    coe 3/15/1958; Hueytown 2/25/1961,
    9/7/1939; Huntsville 2/20/1940,
    3/15/1936, 4/23/1934, 5/29/1950,
    8/8/1962; Maylene 6/30/1955; Mobile
    4/8/1951, 8/8/1925, 11/25/1951,

12/18/1922; Montgomery 9/9/1956; Tal-
    ladega 1/25/1941, 1/29/1945, 2/1/1939,
    2/15/1936, 2/15/1957, 7/11/1993,
    9/14/1969
Alabama Crimson Tide 12/15/1953
Alabama 500 2/15/1936, 4/12/1970
Alamo 500 2/1/1944
Albany-Saratoga Speedway (NY)
    7/7/1970, 7/14/1971
Albany-Saratoga 250 7/7/1970, 7/14/1971
Alexander, John 5/22/1954
Alexander, Mike 7/31/1957
All-Pro Auto Parts 500 10/8/1989
All-Star Open 5/17/2003
Allen, Johnny 6/16/1962, 8/5/1962,
    8/26/1957, 9/17/1934
Allen, Loy 2/20/1994
Allen, Loy, Jr. 4/7/1966
Allied Plating 12/29/1930
Allison, Bobby 1/11/1981, 1/19/1975,
    2/14/1982, 2/14/1988, 2/15/1981,
    2/19/1978, 2/24/1961, 2/24/1974,
    2/25/1961, 2/25/1973, 2/27/1972,
    2/27/1983, 3/1/1968, 3/4/1979, 3/4/1984,
    3/7/1976, 3/19/1978, 3/23/1969,
    3/25/1979, 3/26/1972, 3/27/1967,
    3/29/1970, 4/9/1972, 4/9/1978,
    4/13/1975, 4/20/1969, 4/25/1971,
    4/27/1969, 4/28/1967, 4/30/1972,
    5/3/1981, 5/4/1986, 5/6/1973, 5/6/1979,
    5/11/1974, 5/15/1983, 5/16/1971,
    5/16/1982, 5/17/1981, 5/18/1980,
    5/24/1981, 5/27/1984, 5/28/1970,
    5/30/1971, 5/31/1970, 6/4/1972, 6/6/1971,
    6/6/1982, 6/10/1967, 6/10/1979,

4/12/1992, 4/14/1996, 4/16/1989,
4/17/1988, 4/17/1994, 4/18/1993,
4/20/1986, 4/21/1985, 4/21/1991,
4/22/1990
Fisher, Terry 5/24/1962
Fittipaldi, Christian 1/18/1971
Fitzgerald, Jim 11/8/1987, 12/1/1921
Flaherty, Pat 1/6/1926
Fleming, Bobby 3/20/1941
Flemke, Eddie 3/30/1984, 8/12/1930
Flock, Bob 4/16/1918, 5/11/1924,
5/16/1964, 8/7/1949, 8/17/1952,
8/25/1951, 9/1/1952, 10/16/1949
Flock, Fonty 3/21/1921, 3/26/1955,
4/15/1951, 4/22/1951, 4/29/1951,
5/11/1924, 5/30/1953, 6/1/1952, 6/8/1952,
6/15/1952, 6/28/1953, 7/8/1951,
7/15/1951, 7/15/1972, 7/16/1926,
7/29/1951, 7/31/1951, 8/1/1951,
8/14/1955, 8/16/1953, 8/19/1951,
8/29/1953, 9/1/1952, 9/7/1952, 9/15/1951,
9/17/1950, 9/21/1952, 9/23/1951,
9/30/1951, 9/30/1955, 10/12/1952,
10/15/1950, 10/18/1953, 10/21/1951,
10/29/1950, 11/11/1951, 11/20/1920,
11/20/1955
Flock, Julius "Tim" 1/20/1952, 1/20/1999,
2/11/1951, 2/26/1956, 2/27/1955,
3/26/1955, 3/31/1998, 4/3/1950,
4/5/1953, 4/8/1951, 4/8/1956, 4/17/1955,
4/20/1952, 4/24/1955, 5/8/1955,
5/9/1953, 5/11/1924, 5/15/1955,
5/22/1955, 6/1/1952, 6/8/1952, 6/10/1951,
6/17/1955, 6/24/1955, 6/29/1952,
7/1/1951, 7/4/1952, 7/6/1952, 7/6/1955,
7/10/1955, 7/15/1955, 7/20/1952,
7/30/1955, 7/31/1955, 8/12/1956,
8/15/1952, 8/19/1951, 8/24/1951,
8/29/1953, 9/1/1952, 9/7/1951, 9/9/1956,
9/11/1955, 9/18/1955, 10/6/1955,
10/14/1951, 10/15/1955, 10/30/1955,
11/1/1953, 11/11/1951, 11/13/1955
Florian, Jimmy 6/25/1950, 9/25/1923
Florida: Bartow 1/31/1953; Bradenton
1/13/1921, 6/6/1990; Clearwater
1/26/1952; Daytona 12/13/1935; Daytona
Beach 1/3/1930, 1/5/1965, 1/8/1958,
1/20/1929, 1/22/1922, 1/23/1972,
1/26/1952, 2/11/1951, 2/11/1959,
2/15/1948, 2/17/1922, 5/9/2001,
5/25/1933, 5/28/1917, 7/10/1949,
7/29/1989, 8/13/1952, 8/14/1957,
9/7/1953, 11/9/1957, 12/14/1947; Ft.

Lauderdale 9/11/1949, 9/16/1947;
Hialeah 10/15/1932; Hollywood
3/30/1944, 5/12/1926; Homestead
1/8/1977, 1/11/1997; Jacksonville
3/12/1938, 4/24/1916, 5/4/1940,
5/24/1922, 6/19/1928, 7/9/1951,
8/29/1921, 9/9/1922, 9/17/1938,
10/17/1935, 11/4/1951, 12/14/1939,
12/16/1980, 12/19/1960, 12/20/1935;
Lighthouse Point 3/21/1925; Long Boat
Key 1/11/1934; Lutz 6/3/1936; Merritt Island 4/20/1950; Miami 1/8/1929,
5/5/1992, 8/20/1938, 12/3/1937; Miami
Beach 5/4/1929; Miami Springs
12/2/1928; Naples 9/26/1963; North
Miami 2/23/1948; Orange City
8/29/1940; Orlando 5/31/1949,
9/18/1926, 10/7/1957; Pensacola
4/8/1931, 9/18/1964; Port Charlotte
4/24/1942; Royal Palm Beach 11/11/1984;
St. Augustine 2/8/1913, 2/20/1959,
5/6/1910; St. Petersburg 5/15/1906;
Tampa 11/11/1962; Titusville 12/30/1956;
West Palm Beach 5/23/1993, 11/30/1952,
12/2/1928
Florida Dash 200 2/12/1993
Follmer, George 1/27/1934
Fonda Speedway (NY) 4/21/1956,
6/18/1955, 7/11/1968, 7/13/1967,
7/14/1966, 10/3/1940
Fonda 200 10/3/1940
Food City 500 1/10/1940, 3/23/2003,
3/24/2002, 3/25/2001, 3/26/2000,
3/27/1957, 3/29/1998, 3/31/1996,
4/2/1995, 4/4/1993, 4/5/1992, 4/10/1994,
4/11/1999, 4/13/1997, 4/30/1975,
8/4/1978, 8/23/1963
Foote, Melvin 11/27/1927
Forbes-Robinson, Elliott 10/31/1943
Ford 2/20/2000, 3/5/2000, 3/26/2000,
4/9/2000, 4/17/1960, 4/28/1957,
4/30/2000, 5/2/1976, 5/15/1958,
5/16/1964, 5/18/1958, 5/18/1996,
5/20/2000, 5/28/2000, 6/1/2000,
6/18/2000, 6/19/1949, 6/21/1959,
6/25/1950, 7/3/1942, 7/4/1957,
8/15/1956, 8/20/2000, 8/22/1998,
8/26/2000, 9/3/1956, 9/6/1998,
9/13/1959, 10/11/1992, 10/22/2000,
10/29/1967, 11/5/2000
Fornoro, Nofri "Nick" 10/23/1920
Forsyth County Fairgrounds (NC)
5/14/1933, 5/29/1955, 8/7/1955

Grand River Speedrome (MI) 7/1/1951,
  7/11/1954
Grant, Jerry 1/23/1935
Graves, Danny 9/8/1957
Gray, Eddie 1/18/1969, 5/27/1961,
  6/1/1958, 9/10/1961, 9/13/1959,
  10/25/1969, 12/2/1930
Gray, Henley 1/3/1933
Gray, Steve 8/11/1956
Greased Lightning 1/3/1956, 8/29/1921,
  12/1/1963
Green, David 1/28/1958, 9/6/1962,
  11/14/1999
Green, George 9/15/1927
Green, Jeff 2/13/2003, 2/16/2003,
  8/25/2001, 9/6/1962
Green, Mark 9/6/1962
Greene, Bobby 6/12/1925
Greene, Oda 9/23/1928
Greensboro 5/1/1955
Greensboro Agricultural Fairgrounds
  (NC) 4/28/1957, 5/1/1955, 5/11/1958,
  10/27/1957
Greenville 200 4/8/1969, 4/10/1971,
  6/27/1970
Greenville-Pickens Speedway (SC)
  3/28/1964, 4/8/1969, 4/9/1966,
  4/10/1971, 4/19/1962, 4/23/1960,
  5/3/1958, 5/10/1956, 6/13/1959,
  6/19/1965, 6/21/1969, 6/22/1968,
  6/26/1971, 6/27/1970, 7/14/1962,
  7/30/1963, 8/25/1951, 10/6/1955,
  10/28/1961, 11/1/1980
Gregg, Peter 5/4/1940, 12/16/1980
Griffith, Charles 9/4/1929
Grissom, Steve 6/26/1963
Grubb, Johnny 4/23/1914
Gurney, Dan 1/17/1965, 1/19/1964,
  1/20/1963, 1/21/1968, 1/23/1966,
  4/13/1931
Guthrie, Janet 3/7/1938
Gwyn Staley 400 2/22/1941, 3/27/1977,
  4/4/1976, 4/6/1975, 4/8/1973, 4/15/1962,
  4/16/1967, 4/16/1978, 4/17/1966,
  4/18/1965, 4/18/1970, 4/18/1971,
  4/19/1964, 4/20/1969, 4/21/1968,
  4/21/1974, 4/23/1972, 4/28/1963
Gwynn, C.B. 10/24/1935

Haas-Carter Motorsports 3/27/2002
Habering, Harold 2/21/1964
Haddock, Alton 8/16/1915
Hagan, Billy 3/22/1932

Hagelin, Budd 12/8/1944
Haggerty, Royce 8/26/1956
Hairfield, Ted 12/18/1931
Halford, Johnny 10/15/1930
Halifax County 100 5/9/1971, 8/29/1970
Hall, Don 9/2/1943
Hall, Roy 3/14/1991
Hall, Shane 8/25/1969
Hamby, Roger 7/2/1943
Hamilton, Bobby 1/8/1977, 4/20/1998,
  4/22/2001, 5/29/1957, 9/22/1996,
  10/27/1996, 10/27/1997, 12/12/1971
Hamilton, Pete 2/11/1971, 2/22/1970,
  4/12/1970, 7/20/1942, 8/23/1970
Hammersley, Bill "Red" 5/30/1908
Hammond, Jeff 9/9/1956
Hampton, Andy 11/30/1928
Hanes Activewear 500 4/29/1990
Hanes 500 2/28/1955, 4/23/1995,
  4/24/1994, 4/25/1993, 4/26/1992,
  4/28/1991, 6/30/1955, 9/22/1996,
  9/29/1997
Hansgen, Walt 4/2/1966, 4/7/1966,
  10/28/1919
Harb, Fred 4/15/1963, 6/14/1930
Hardee's 500 11/17/1991
Harden, Jack 4/23/1934
Harless, Pearley "Bud" 1/21/1924
Harmon, Mike 1/24/1958
Harn, Otis "Rock" 7/29/1924
Harris, Bob 9/11/1926
Harris, Ferrel 10/8/1940
Harris, Gayther "Runt" 6/4/1927,
  6/30/1990
Harris Speedway (NC) 5/30/1965,
  10/25/1964
Harrison, Bill 9/2/1910
Harrison, Jack 11/11/1956
Hartman, Larry "Butch" 5/11/1940,
  12/22/1994
Hartsville Speedway (SC) 6/23/1961
Harvick, Kevin 2/14/2002, 3/11/2001,
  6/24/2001, 7/6/2002, 7/14/2002,
  7/15/2001, 8/3/2003, 8/25/2001, 12/8/1975
Hassler, Raymond "Friday" 2/17/1972,
  4/15/1971, 6/29/1935
Hayloft Speedway (GA) 6/1/1952,
  9/28/1991
Hedgecock, Jay 2/28/1955
Hedrick, Larry 12/12/1940
Heidelberg (Speedway) Raceway (PA)
  1/12/1980, 7/10/1960, 7/15/1951,
  7/21/1959, 10/2/1949

10/2/1946, 11/15/1980, 11/18/1979,
  11/19/1978, 11/20/1977, 11/21/1976,
  11/23/1975, 11/24/1974, 12/27/1947
Opperman, Jan 2/9/1939
Orange Speedway (NC) 1/25/1930
Oregon: Ashland 10/2/1946; Lake Oswego
  11/11/1934; Medford 11/4/1941; Mil-
  waukie 4/5/1965; North Bend
  12/26/1959; Portland 2/12/1932,
  2/22/1954, 4/28/1957, 6/24/1956,
  6/24/1960, 7/13/1958, 7/14/1957,
  8/9/1925, 8/26/1956, 9/6/1933,
  9/27/1946, 11/16/1925; Sandy 5/24/1962
O'Reilly 400 10/13/2000
Orr, Rodney 2/14/1994
Osborne, Bill 11/24/1946
Osterlund, Rod 11/19/1934
Ottinger, L.D. 12/30/1938
Owens, Cotton 2/14/1960, 2/17/1957,
  3/4/1961, 4/2/1961, 4/20/1961, 5/19/1962,
  5/21/1924, 6/5/1959, 7/20/1961,
  7/25/1958, 8/16/1960, 8/27/1961,
  9/13/1959, 9/14/1964
Owens, Trent 1/4/1975
Oxford Plains Speedway (ME) 7/9/1968,
  7/11/1967, 7/12/1966, 11/23/1934

Pagan, Eddie 4/25/1958, 5/26/1957,
  6/8/1957, 7/14/1957, 8/1/1918, 8/19/1956,
  9/1/1958
Palm Beach Speedway (FL) 1/20/1952,
  2/6/1955, 3/4/1956, 12/11/1955,
  12/18/1922
Palmer, Norm 5/30/1940
Panch, Marvin 2/26/1961, 3/3/1936,
  3/22/1964, 3/30/1964, 4/11/1964,
  4/11/1965, 4/27/1957, 5/2/1965,
  5/17/1964, 5/22/1966, 5/28/1926,
  5/28/1954, 5/30/1957, 5/30/1964,
  6/13/1965, 7/12/1957, 7/14/1957,
  7/14/1965, 7/18/1965, 7/29/1956,
  8/1/1954, 8/10/1957, 9/29/1963,
  10/11/1964, 11/11/1956, 12/2/1956
Panch, Richard 5/28/1954, 9/2/1985
Pannill Sweatshirts 500 4/23/1989,
  4/24/1988
Pardue, Jimmy 4/13/1963, 4/15/1963,
  5/4/1962, 7/11/1963, 9/22/1964,
  10/26/1930
Park, Steve 2/26/2001, 3/26/2000,
  4/27/2003, 5/17/2003, 7/5/2003,
  8/13/2000, 8/23/1967, 11/12/2000
Parrott, Buddy 2/9/1964, 11/24/1939

Parrott, Todd 2/9/1964
Parsons, Benny 2/14/1982, 2/16/1975,
  2/26/1978, 3/18/1984, 4/9/1978,
  4/13/1980, 4/15/1973, 4/15/1984,
  4/27/1975, 5/7/1977, 5/8/1976, 5/9/1971,
  5/9/1981, 5/16/1976, 5/25/1980, 6/7/1981,
  6/10/1984, 6/11/1978, 6/15/1980,
  7/8/1973, 7/12/1941, 7/16/1976,
  7/16/1977, 7/20/1975, 7/30/1978,
  7/31/1977, 9/3/1973, 9/11/1977,
  9/12/1976, 9/13/1981, 9/18/1977,
  10/9/1977, 10/12/1975, 10/14/1979,
  11/15/1980, 11/18/1979, 11/22/1970
Parsons, Phil 5/1/1988, 6/21/1957
Parsons, Vic 11/29/1939
Paschal, Jim 3/27/1955, 4/17/1966,
  4/24/1966, 5/5/1963, 5/9/1954,
  5/15/1955, 5/16/1954, 5/19/1967,
  5/24/1964, 5/28/1967, 6/2/1961,
  6/2/1967, 6/22/1962, 6/27/1967,
  7/9/1955, 7/12/1958, 7/29/1962,
  8/3/1956, 8/4/1963, 8/5/1955, 8/5/1962,
  8/6/1961, 8/12/1962, 10/3/1953,
  10/18/1953, 11/4/1962, 11/22/1962,
  12/5/1926
Passwater, Dick 4/5/1953
Patterson, John 7/5/1969
Paul, Donny 1/2/1961
Paul, John, Jr. 2/19/1960
Peach Blossom 500 3/13/1966
Peach State Speedway (GA) 4/11/1998,
  11/2/1969
Peak Antifreeze 500 9/15/1991, 9/16/1990,
  9/20/1992
Peak Performance 500 9/17/1989
Pearson, David 1/16/1977, 1/18/1976,
  2/11/1971, 2/15/1976, 2/20/1969,
  3/5/1978, 3/9/1969, 3/10/1964,
  3/16/1969, 3/17/1968, 3/18/1973,
  3/19/1967, 3/20/1966, 3/21/1976,
  3/24/1968, 3/25/1967, 3/28/1964,
  3/28/1971, 4/1/1973, 4/3/1966, 4/5/1970,
  4/7/1966, 4/7/1974, 4/8/1969, 4/9/1966,
  4/10/1971, 4/11/1966, 4/11/1976,
  4/13/1980, 4/15/1973, 4/16/1964,
  4/16/1972, 4/21/1968, 4/28/1968,
  4/29/1973, 5/5/1968, 5/5/1974, 5/6/1973,
  5/7/1972, 5/9/1970, 5/11/1968, 5/15/1966,
  5/17/1968, 5/17/1969, 5/18/1968,
  5/19/1975, 5/21/1924, 5/21/1978,
  5/26/1974, 5/27/1973, 5/28/1961,
  5/29/1966, 5/30/1976, 6/2/1961,